Ethnocracy

Ethnocracy

Land and Identity Politics in Israel/Palestine

OREN YIFTACHEL

PENN

University of Pennsylvania Press

Philadelphia

10   9   8   7   6   5   4   3   2   1

Published by
University of Pennsylvania Press
Philadelphia, Pennsylvania 19104-4112

Library of Congress Cataloging-in-Publication Data

Yiftachel, Oren, 1956–
   Ethnocracy : land and identity politics in Israel/Palestine / Oren Yiftachel.
      p. cm.
   Includes bibliographical references (p.) and index.
   ISBN-13: 978-0-8122-3927-0 (alk. paper)
   ISBN-10: 0-8122-3927-X (alk. paper)
1. National characteristics, Israeli.   2. Israel—Ethnic relations.   3. Ethnicity—Israel.
4. Multiculturalism—Israel.   5. Nationalism—Israel.   6. Power (Social sciences)—Israel.
7. Jews, Oriental—Israel.   8. Palestinian Arabs—Israel.   I. Title.
DS113.3.Y54 2006
305.80095694—dc22   2005056359

In memory of my beloved father, Arye

Contents

Preface

This book is a culmination of nearly a decade of work on ethnocratic societies. Equally, it is a product of living in the midst of such a society, and being thickly involved in its volatile turns and tribulations. The book is a result of much research, reading, listening, and reflection, but it is also a fruit of love—love of theory, critique, scholarship, and teamwork—and, most importantly, profound empathy for the people of Israel/Palestine, who have had to struggle against enormous odds in very trying circumstances.

Writing a full-length book is always a daunting task. This is particularly so on a topic like ethnic relations in Israel/Palestine—a hotbed of tensions, conflicts, and violence. It's particularly hard when one writes from within and at the same time takes a critical stance, as attempted in this book. The space for local critical scholarship is always narrow in ethnocratic nationalistic societies, and Israel is no different.

The timing of the writing of this book (summer 2004) has added to the difficulties. The fast series of events so typical to Israel/Palestine always threatens to make one's work outdated before it is even printed. Furthermore, the hostile nature of events in Israel/Palestine during the last five years—known as the al-Aqsa *intifada*—has made both societies even less attentive to and often openly intimidating toward critical voices. This book has thus been written within an atmosphere of adversity and suspicion, against the grain of a general move of academic, political, and cultural forces into the cozy ethnonational center.

However, several key factors made the writing of this book an experience to cherish. First and foremost, I have had the privilege to work with a set of young, dynamic, and innovative scholars, who have given me much energy and inspiration. Their contribution to the development of the concepts outlined in the book and to the gathering of evidence has been crucial, through debate, critique, and fieldwork. These are the scholars who participated in the various research projects I have conducted on Israel's land regime, urban planning, and ethnic relations. This group includes Batya Roded, Erez Tzfadia, Haim Yacobi, Asad Ghanem, and Sandy Kedar, whose specific contributions are highlighted on the pages of the various chapters. Other researchers who have participated in the projects have also made important contributions, namely Yosef Jabareen, Nurit Alfasi, Yizhak Aharonowitz, Jeremy Forman, Ella Bauer, and Chaia Noach. I am very grateful for their contributions, although the final text remains my sole responsibility.

I have been greatly assisted in the writing of this text by the editorial skills of Tamar Almog, who chastised me ceaselessly and rightfully for inconsistencies, duplication, or general sloppiness. Na'ama Razon, Elana Boteach, Benjamin Okyere, and Roni Livnon-Bluestein have also assisted greatly with their copyediting and cartographic skills. Last but by no means least, Amanda Yiftachel—a best friend, critic, and editor—has not only read, corrected, and debated most of the book's chapters, but has also tirelessly held our family and home together during the writing period—a difficult and most appreciated task.

Moreover, a wider circle of scholars has also been part of the making of this book, unknowingly. These are the many people kind enough to read my work, engage with my ideas, comment, debate, and criticize. They have been my valuable partners in many scholarly conversations over the years, often sharpening—and at times also destroying—my concepts and observations. While the entire list is too long to mention here, I would like to highlight my special appreciation of a group of excellent colleagues and friends at Ben-Gurion University in Beer-Sheva, particularly those associated with the Humphrey Institute and the journal *Hagar*, which I edited for five years. Our frequent gatherings at the seminars of the Humphrey Institute and other settings have produced some of the best intellectual debates to which one can aspire, where academic frankness and critical scholarship have remained vibrant, even during hard political and financial times.

Finally, despite the difficulties, and despite the recent period of hostility and violence gripping Israel/Palestine, let me express the cautious hope that some of the insights outlined on the pages of this book will help open people's eyes to the ominous processes currently unfolding in our homeland and to the few remaining rays of hope. Perhaps one or two lessons drawn from the historical and comparative analyses presented here will transform some of the intransigent attitudes so prevalent in Israel/Palestine, particularly Israel's futile and brutal attempt to continue to occupy the Palestinian territories and the equally futile and brutal faith of many among both Jews and Palestinians in the effectiveness and desirability of violent action. Of course, the road between theory, research, evidence, and corrective action is long and arduous, but it is hopefully worth taking.

Much of the data in the book was generated in four related projects financed by the Israeli Science Foundation ("The Israeli Land Regime"), the Ministry of Science ("Absorption Policy and Ethnic Relations in the Development Towns"), the Israeli Lottery ("Multicultural Planning in Local

Councils"), and the Social Science Research Council ("Ethnic and Religious Movements in the Middle East"). I am grateful for the generous support granted by these foundations, without which this research would have not been possible.

I would like to thank the ACUM (Israeli Association of Writers), Mrs. Naila Ziyyad, and Sobhi al-Zobaidi for granting permission to use the lyrics cited in the book. I am also grateful for the permission given by my colleagues and co-authors, as well as the academic publishers Lexington, Frank-Cass, Littlefield, and Taylor and Francis, to use previously published material in some sections of the book, drawn from the following articles:

Tzfadia, E., and O. Yiftachel. 2001. Political Mobilization in the Development Towns: The Mizrahi Struggle over Place (Hebrew). *Politika* (Israeli Journal of Political Science) 7: 79–96.

Yiftachel, O. 1999. Between Nation and State: "Fractured" Regionalism among Palestinian-Arabs in Israel. *Political Geography* 18(2): 285–307.

———. 2002. Territory as the Kernel of the Nation: Space, Time, and Nationalism in Israel/Palestine. *Geopolitics* 7(3): 215–48.

Yiftachel, O., A. Ghanem, and N. Rouhana. 2000. Is Ethnic Democracy Possible? (Hebrew). *Jama'a* (Journal of Middle East Studies) 6: 58–80.

Yiftachel, O., and S. Kedar. 2000. Landed Power: The Emergence of an Ethnocratic Land Regime in Israel (Hebrew). *Teorya Uvikkoret (Theory and Critique)* 19(1): 9–23.

Yiftachel, O., and E. Tzfadia. 2000. Trapped Children: Local Identity in Development Towns (Hebrew). *Panim* 13 (spring): 44–54.

Yiftachel, O., and H. Yacobi. 2002. "Planning a Bi-National Capital: Should Jerusalem Remain United?" *Geoforum* 33:137–45.

———. 2003. Control, Resistance, and Informality: Jews and Bedouin-Arabs in the Beer-Sheva Region. In N. Al Sayyad and A. Roy, *Urban Informality in the Era of Globalization: A Transnational Perspective.* Boulder, Colo.: Lexington, 118–36.

Part I
Settings

Chapter 1
Introduction

The book in your hand offers the concept of *ethnocracy* as a most appropriate account for the development of Zionist society and regime in Israel/Palestine. Ethnocratic regimes promote the expansion of the dominant group in contested territory and its domination of power structures while maintaining a democratic facade.[1] Ethnocracy manifests in the Israeli case with the long-term Zionist strategy of Judaizing the homeland—constructed during the last century as the Land of Israel, between the Jordan River and the Mediterranean Sea. The very same territory is also perceived by most Palestinians as their rightful historical homeland, invaded and seized by Jews. The development of ethnic relations in Israel/Palestine has been fundamentally shaped by the material, territorial, political, and cultural aspects of the Judaization dynamic and by the various forms of resistance to that project.

Let us begin the long journey taken by this book with a telling incident. In February of 2002, several light planes were sent, for the first time ever, by the Israeli government to spray twelve thousand dunams of crops with poisonous chemicals. This act repeated itself in October of 2002, April of 2003, and April of 2004. The destroyed fields had been cultivated for years by Bedouin Arabs in the Negev (Naqab) region near the city of Beer-Sheva on land they claim as their own. The minister responsible for land management, Avigdor Lieberman, claimed on that day: "We must stop their illegal invasion into state land by all means possible; the Bedouins have no regard for our laws; in the process we are losing the last resources of state lands; one of my main missions is to return power to the Land Authority in dealing with the non-Jewish threat to our lands. At the same time, we must settle the land by building new communal settlements and family farms. If we don't do this, we shall lose the Negev forever."[2]

With expressions such as "our" land, "our" law, and "their" invasion, Lieberman's words expose a forceful separation of Arab and Jewish citizens used to demarcate the limits of identity and the rights of Arabs in the Jewish state. This was echoed in May of 2003 by Ehud Olmert, the new minister responsible for planning who was trying to promote a new plan to concentrate rural Bedouins into seven urban centers. Olmert responded to charges of ignoring the wishes of the local community by stating: "We plan to talk to the Bedouins, but I assume they will object to our plan from the outset. Still, we shall not be afraid to implement our decisions. . . . If we depend on Bedouin consent, it will never come. . . . The government will implement the plan, either peacefully or by force."[3]

The two ministers failed to explain why the state used such violence and never attempted to resolve the issue by negotiation, cooperation, or legal means. Further, they overlooked the ramifications of this unprecedented brutal attack: a growing sense of alienation among Bedouin Arabs, once a community keen to integrate into Israeli society.

As a response, and in an open challenge to the ministers and the state, the chief holders of the disputed land, the al-Touri tribe, built a small village on the site, with some forty shacks, tents, herds of cattle, and communal facilities. During 2002 and 2003, the site was demolished and forcibly evacuated by the Israeli police three times, resulting in clashes with the locals and scores of arrests.

This brutal incident is but the last in a long string of ethnocratic planning measures aimed against Palestinian Arabs in general, and the Negev Bedouin Arabs in particular, as detailed on these pages. In the late 1940s the Bedouins were concentrated in a small and barren area of southern Israel and were placed under military rule. During the 1960s, military rule was replaced by a plan to urbanize the (previously seminomadic) Bedouins. The state planned to move them into seven towns and clear the rest of the land for Jewish settlement and military purposes. However, a large number of Bedouins refused to be forcibly urbanized, as such a move would force them to relinquish their land claims and seriously jeopardize their traditions and culture. They remained on the land, in what is termed "spontaneous settlement" or "dispersal." The Bedouins were subsequently declared by the state to be "invaders"—"illegally" occupying their ancestors' land—and their villages (or the shanty towns) classified as "unrecognized." For the last three decades the state has attempted to coerce their migration into the towns using a range of pressure tactics, including widespread demolition of housing, denial of most social services, and refusal to build physical infrastructure or initiate plans for the village. Given this, the bitter words of Hassan Abu-Quider, a Bedouin activist who addressed in 1998 a meeting with the then chairperson of the Jewish Agency, Avraham Burg, echo loudly: "Only in one instance shall we, the Bedouin Arabs, get our full and equal rights in the Jewish State: only if miraculously we'll stop occupying, needing, or using any land. Then we shall receive what we truly deserve—full air rights. . . ."[4]

The recent spraying of Bedouin fields with poison, however, marks a new stage in the state's attempts to control the Bedouins' land use. It sent shockwaves among southern Bedouin Arabs, who began a campaign to convince public opinion of their rightful claims to the land in question and the persistent discrimination against their community. Yet the active public debate, in talk shows, public demonstrations, and political speeches, never addressed the following key points:

- Bedouin Arabs in the Beer-Sheva region are formally full citizens of the state of Israel; why should their use of state land be considered an invasion, while their fellow Jewish citizens are encouraged to come and use the same land?
- Lieberman is an immigrant who arrived from the former Soviet Union; how acceptable is a situation in which an immigrant evicts indigenous groups who have lived on the land for generations?
- Lieberman is a West Bank settler; that is, he embodies Israel's breach of a series of international conventions and norms that prohibit the transfer of populations into occupied areas and the confiscation of occupied lands; indeed, Lieberman, according to international law, is an invader himself.

These observations, made from a critical southern perspective, are rarely discussed in Israeli public discourse. They illustrate the contradictions and tensions embedded in the regime ruling over Israel/Palestine, termed in this book "a settling ethnocracy". This is a regime premised on a main project of ethnonational *expansion* and control and on a parallel self-representation of the system as democratic. However, the three observations challenge the very basic tenets of a modern democratic regime. They exhibit the structural elevation of Jewish over Arab citizens; the privileging of Jewish diasporas (and hence immigrants) over local Arab citizens; and the blurring of state borders, which allows West Bank Jewish settlements to continue to form a (de facto) part of Israel, while their immediate Palestinian neighbors remain disenfranchised.

Indeed, issues of land, borders, immigration, settlement, development, and political conflict make up the main materials of this book. The struggles over these elements have created the tensions, confrontations, dramas, tragedies, and constant oscillation between hope and despair so prevalent in Israel/Palestine. The book will attempt to shed further light on the Zionist-Palestinian conflict by providing a new framework for analysis— the ethnocratic regime—and by presenting one of the only accounts of the conflicts that focuses on the nexus of space, ethnicity, and power.

The need for the new approach is twofold. First, on a general conceptual level, past accounts, models, and interpretations of the making of Israeli society and the Zionist-Palestinian conflict have generally fallen short. By and large, past works did not provide sufficiently rigorous accounts and hence failed to delineate the main forces at work or to predict the course of evolving events. Second, there has been a conspicuous lack of conceptual and critical work by geographers on the shaping of Israel/Palestine, although the geographical perspective offers illuminating insights. This critique is elaborated throughout the chapters that follow.

The analysis presented in this book is guided by a critical, materialist perspective, which emphasizes the interdependence of geographical, economic, cultural, and political processes. The emphasis is on political geography and political economy as key pillars of shaping ethnic relations and politics. The approach draws inspiration from neo-Gramscian perspectives (see Laclau and Mouffe 1985; Hall 1992; Lustick 1993), from related critical approaches (see Lefebvre 1991; Said 1992; I.M. Young 2002), and from critical analysts in the social sciences, mainly in geography, political science, and urban studies (see Friedmann 2002; Harvey 2001; Marcuse and Van Kempen 2000; Samaddar 2000; Sibley 1995).

My own approach stresses the reciprocity of material, cultural, and political forces, and it attempts to deconstruct dominant categories, discourses, and historical accounts. On this basis, it attempts to propose new conceptualizations, aimed at both offering more revealing and accurate accounts of societal processes and laying the foundation for new consciousness and praxis. In this way, the analysis I offer is not merely aimed at outlining a destructive critique. It rather derives from my empathy for both Jewish and Palestinian peoples and personal participation in many attempts to rebuild a just and sustainable polity in Israel/Palestine.

The topics discussed in the book are relevant to a wide spectrum of scholarly fields. Indeed, this is the intention of the interdisciplinary approach adopted here. Beyond geography and urban studies already mentioned, the book also converses with and seeks to contribute to several ongoing debates in the literature, most notably dealing with

- nationalism and ethnic relations;
- political regimes, political stability, and the nature of democracy;
- settler societies and (post)colonial studies; and, of course
- Israel, Palestine, and Arab-Jewish relations in the Middle East.

The Argument and Its Contribution

The main theoretical contribution of this book combines two dimensions: the development of a critical ethnocratic theory and the integration of geography as a key factor in the analysis of social, economic, and political relations. This approach posits that ethnicization constitutes the main force shaping ethnocratic regimes, putting in train a set of typical societal processes. These typically manifest in the territorial, political, economic, legal, and cultural spheres of society.

Consequently, the book's main empirical claim is that the process of *Judaizing Israel/Palestine*, with its associated dislocations, struggles, and contradictions, forms a major spine around which ethnic relations have evolved in that land. This applies first and foremost to relations between Jews and Palestinians but also to the location and changing position of groups such as Ashkenazi and Mizrahi Jews, orthodox and "secular" Jews, recent "Russian" and Ethiopian immigrants, Bedouin Arabs, Druze Arabs, and immigrant workers. As elaborated in the book's chapters, the Judaization project has advanced in many spheres, most notably in the territorial pursuits of Zionism, as well as in the grip of the Jewish religion on Israeli public life. But Judaization has also profoundly affected the role of armed forces, the ethnic logic in the flow of capital and the location of development, the establishment of a legal system, the shaping of public culture and gender relations, and the conduct of politics. The argument continues by tracing the various consequences of the ethnicization-Judaization project and by delineating the process of "creeping apartheid" that is increasingly evident in the governance of Israel/Palestine and has recently turned further into concrete reality with the unilateral construction of a massive separation barrier (wall or fence) in the West Bank.[5]

Importantly, the book does not attempt to advance a single, reductionist explanation. Rather it seeks to highlight the power of ethnicization (that is, Judaization) among other powerful forces at work in the shaping of Israel/Palestine. These include, but are not limited to, the impact of foreign powers, especially the United States; the role of religion in the Middle East; changing Arab political orientations; the fluctuation of Palestinian violence; and the gradual transformation of the Israeli economy, first toward a state-controlled mixed market and later toward globalizing neoliberalism. However, while avoiding unidimensional reductionism, it is still possible to claim that the Judaization project has, and continues to be, a most powerful and dynamic factor in shaping the space, wealth, and political power in Israel/Palestine.

The book was researched and written from the mid-1990s to the early 2000s. During the former period some of the concepts presented here were published, offering critical interpretations of the forces shaping Israel/Palestine. These often ran against the grain of mainstream scholarship, resulting in some fierce debates on topics such as the nature of the Israeli regime (see Ghanem et al. 1998; Gavison 1998; Shafir and Peled 1998, 2002; Smooha 1998, 2002), the linkages between the Zionist project and the marginalized position of the Mizrahim in Israel (Yiftachel 1998b), the association between territorial and socioeconomic process (Sharkansky 1997), and the inherent problems of the Oslo peace process (Yiftachel 2001b, 2004).

The dramatic events of the 2000–3 period brought many of these processes into sharp relief. These included the failed peace process between Israel and the Palestinians, the eruption of the al-Aqsa *intifada* (uprising) in the Palestinian occupied territories, the October Events of 2000 in Israel, the continuing liberalization of the Israeli economy, and subsequent transformations of ethnic and social relations. This set of new circumstances presented a unique opportunity to revisit the scholarly debates of the 1990s against the unfolding reality.

While portions of these debates are sprinkled on the pages of this book (especially in Chapters 5, 6, 7, and 9), it is worth highlighting here that—by and large—the recent events have validated the ethnocratic approach. At the same time, they undermined many of the opposing arguments held by mainstream scholars, on several grounds. First, the unstable nature of the Israeli ethnocratic regime became highly conspicuous. The area under Israeli control became characterized once again by cycles of violent oppression, countermobilization, and widespread terror against Israeli civilians, repeated economic crises, and growing socioeconomic gaps. Within the Green Line, the conflict between the Palestinian Arab minority and the Jewish state entered a new stage of renewed state repression and deepening mutual mistrust.

Israel also suffered governmental instability, with five prime ministers serving in office and four election campaigns taking place during the last eight years (since the assassination of Yitzhak Rabin). These events and processes, in one way or another, are linked to key ethnocratic dynamics, namely, Israeli attempts to continue the Judaization of Israel/Palestine, and the continuing manipulation of public policy and resources by the dominant ethnoclasses, with the effect of deepening ethnic disparities and conflict.

It also became clear during the 2000–3 period that the entire area under Israeli control—that is, Israel/Palestine between river and sea—should be analyzed as one political-geographic unit. Moreover, the Palestinian and Jewish diasporas—both with concrete claims on this land—must also be taken into account in the analysis of the forces shaping Israel/Palestine. The common scholarly and political attempts to portray the existence of Israel proper within the Green Line, which is "Jewish and democratic," are hence both analytically flawed and politically deceiving.

Accordingly, events and processes taking place in most parts of Israel/ Palestine are interlinked, resembling what Portugali termed a decade ago "implicate relations" (Portugali 1993), whereby neighboring entities develop and change in constant interaction, becoming "enveloped" through a process of mutually dependent development. Today, the interdependence of processes across Israel/Palestine persists, despite the historically significant attempts by the Rabin, Barak, and Sharon governments to recarve an exclusive Israeli political territory, leading to a repartition of Palestine.

On the ground, however, Israel has deepened its occupation of Palestinian territories, more than doubling the size of Jewish settlements since the signing of the Oslo agreement, while placing severe restrictions on Palestinian development and mobility. This has made more conspicuous the preferential treatment of Jews and the coerced geographical mixture of privileged Jews and the disenfranchised. Indeed, as mentioned above,

Israel created—with its own hands—a system of creeping apartheid, most obvious and brutal in the West Bank and Gaza, but—as with the earlier Bedouin example—now diffusing into other parts of Israel.

The recent "disengagement" from the Gaza Strip may appear as a dramatic change of policy, in which Israel has willingly evacuated, for the first time, Jewish settlements from the "holy" Jewish homeland (the Land of Israel). However, during the same period, Israel continued to settle Jews in the West Bank by expanding most settlements, and accelerated the construction of the separation barrier which effectively annexes to Israel nearly 10 percent of the West Bank and large parts of East Jerusalem.

As argued in Chapter 3, Zionism has entered a new phase, by restraining its expansionist pulse from external or peripheral frontiers. Instead, Israel prefers to consolidate territorial gains by further Judaizing areas with a substantial Jewish presence, while ridding itself of the responsibility for densely populated Palestinian areas and isolated Jewish settlements. Despite the important precedent of evacuating the Gaza settlements, the emerging political geography, at least in the foreseeable future, is characterized by violent Jewish domination, strict separation, and ethnic inequality—all in line with the concept of creeping apartheid.

This is a logical, though not inevitable, extension of an expansive ethnocratic regime. As predicted by the ethnocratic interpretation, the evolving political geography of Israel/Palestine has continued to constitute a major factor in shaping and reshaping politics and social relations.

The Book

The book will substantiate the above claims by developing the ethnocratic argument in three main directions. In Part I, it will elaborate on the conceptual architecture and language (Chapter 1); on theoretical foundations of ethnocratic regimes (Chapter 2); and on their ability to construct and maintain the myth of the ethnonational homeland as a fundamental mobilizing force (Chapter 3). In Part II, the book will outline in some detail the history, geography, and politics of the ethnocratic regime in Israel/Palestine, focusing on the development and territorialization of Zionist and Palestinian nationalisms (Chapter 4); the debate over Israeli democracy (Chapter 5); the making of the Israeli ethnocratic regime (Chapter 6); the land system (Chapter 7); and the cultural construction of the Zionist homeland (Chapter 8).

In Part III, the book will provide more focused empirical accounts of particular communities and places, beginning with the development of fractured regionalism among Palestinian Arabs in Israel (Chapter 9); the making of an ethnocratic metropolitan area around the city of Beer-Sheva (Chapter 10); and the emergence of a peripheral Mizrahi ethnoclass in Jewish development towns (Chapters 11 and 12). In the fourth and final part, the book will provide a look into the future, outlining an alternative plan for a binational and multicultural Jerusalem/al-Quds capital region (Chapter 13) and ending with a discussion about the need to create a demos as a foundation for a stable and prosperous political community in Israel/Palestine.

Finally, it should be stressed that the analysis of this book, while presenting a broad spatial-political perspective, does not claim to be comprehensive. Several central aspects of ethnocratic societies are underanalyzed in the proceeding chapters, including gender relations, the link between ethnocracy and militarism, the repercussions of globalization, liberalization, and the interrelations between cities, urbanization, and ethnocratic regimes. In addition, the analysis of Israeli society does not accord due space to several large and influential communities such as Haredi Jews and immigrants from the former Soviet Union and Ethiopia. These aspects are vital to the development of the ethnocratic model and to the understanding of Israel/Palestine. Hence, they present future research directions for the author of this book and hopefully for others.

Chapter 2
The Ethnocratic Regime: The Politics
of Seizing Contested Territory

This chapter offers a theoretical framework to account for the making and character of ethnocratic regimes. It seeks to examine the impact of such regimes on ethnic relations and political stability, thereby setting an analytical agenda for the analyses and discussions of the entire book, although short theoretical discussions also take place in some of the following chapters.

Three central theoretical arguments are advanced here: (a) the existence of an ethnocratic regime as a distinct identifiable type; (b) the existence of a set of mechanisms that shape the ethnocratic regime and explain both persistent patterns of ethnic dominance and regime instability; and (c) the fact that while ethnocratic regimes draw their legitimacy from a world order of nation-states, their structure and practices undermine this very order. The emphasis of this chapter is theoretical, and hence readers interested in the details of Israel/Palestine may move directly to Chapter 4.

One of the main assertions of this chapter is that the structure, features, and trajectories of the ethnocratic regime can be articulated and generalized, and that the model proposed below can frame a new understanding of politics and geography in many states embroiled in protracted ethnic conflicts. Such understanding forms a necessary step in managing the typically volatile intergroup relations of ethnocratic societies. The chapter also attempts to illustrate its main points by briefly comparing the relevant cases of Sri Lanka, Australia, and Estonia. Apart from the discussion of these three cases, the chapter is rather abstract, presenting several concepts and theories in relative brevity. However, the following chapters often integrate theoretical discussions, which elaborate and substantiate the concepts presented here.

I define ethnocracy as a particular regime type, frequently found on the world political map but rarely studied by social scientists and geographers. This regime facilitates the *expansion, ethnicization, and control* of a dominant ethnic nation (often termed the charter or titular group) over contested territory and polity. Regimes are defined as legal, political, and moral frameworks determining the distribution of power and resources. They reflect the identity, goals, and practical priorities of a political community.

The state is the main vehicle of the regime, providing institutions, mechanisms, laws, and legitimized forms of violence to implement the projects articulated by the regime.

Ethnocratic regimes may emerge in a variety of forms, including cases of ethnic dictatorships or regimes implementing violent strategies of ethnic cleansing, as occurred in Rwanda and Serbia, and those whose strategies consist of control and exclusion, as happened in Sudan and pre-1994 South Africa (Mann 1999). In this chapter, however, I am interested in ethnocratic regimes that represent themselves as democratic and uphold several formal democratic mechanisms, such as elections, civil rights such as freedom of movement, a parliamentary system, and a relatively open system of media and communication. But despite their democratic representation, these regimes still facilitate an undemocratic expansion of the dominant ethnonation. They can thus be described as open ethnocracies. Examples of such ethnocratic regimes at present include Sri Lanka, Malaysia, Estonia, Latvia, Serbia, and Israel, as well as past cases such as nineteenth-century Australia.

Ethnocracy: Historical Constellation

The theorization of ethnocracy begins with identifying the main political and historical forces that have shaped the politics and territory of this regime. It focuses on the time-space intersection of three major political-historical engines: (a) the formation of a (colonial) settler society; (b) the mobilizing power of ethnonationalism; and (c) the ethnic logic of capital. As shown in the proceeding chapter, the fusion of these three key forces in Israel/Palestine has resulted in the establishment of the Israeli ethnocracy and determined its specific features. But the formation of ethnocracy is not unique to Israel. It is found in other settings where one ethnonation attempts to extend or preserve its disproportionate control over contested territories and rival groups. This political system also typically results—as part and parcel of the same geographical and historical processes—in the stratification of ethnoclasses and in patterns of long-term segregation and ethnic polarization.

A SETTLER SOCIETY

Settler societies, such as the Jewish community in Israel/Palestine, pursue a deliberate strategy of immigration and settlement that aims to alter the country's ethnic structure. Colonial settler societies have traditionally facilitated European migration into other continents and legitimized the exploitation of indigenous land, labor, and natural resources. Other settler societies, mainly non-European, have migrated internally and resettled in order to change the demographic balance of specific regions. In all types of settler societies a frontier culture develops, glorifying and augmenting the settlement and expanding the control of the dominant group into neighboring regions (see McGarry 1998; Murphy 2002).

One common type of colonial settler society has been described as the "pure settlement colony," which has been shown to be most appropriate to the Israeli-Zionist case (Fredrickson 1988; Shafir 1989). Studies have also shown that "pure" settler societies are generally marked by a broad stratification into three main ethnoclasses: (a) a founding charter group, such as the Protestant-Anglos in North America and Australia; (b) a group of later immigrants from different cultural backgrounds, such as southern Europeans in North America and Australia; and (c) dispossessed indigenous groups, such as the Aborigines in Australia, Maoris in New Zealand, North American Indians in Canada and the United States, and Palestinians in Israel/Palestine (Stasiulis and Yuval-Davis 1995). In recent times, a fourth stratum has emerged in most settler societies—"alien" or foreign workers. This group is incorporated economically, but largely remains excluded from society's main political and social arenas (Sassen 1999).

The charter group establishes the state in its own vision, institutionalizes its dominance, and creates a system that both assimilates later immigrants into the dominant culture and incorporates them unevenly into politics and the economy (Soysal 1994). At the same time, residential and economic segregation is maintained vis-à-vis marginalized immigrant and local groups. Such a system generally reproduces the dominance of the charter group for several generations.

The establishment of "pure" settler societies highlights the political and economic importance of extraterritorial ethnic links, which are crucial for the success of most colonial projects. The links typically connect the settler society to a co-ethnic metropolitan state or to supportive ethnic diasporas. As elaborated below, extraterritorial ethnic links are a defining characteristic of ethnocracies. These regimes rely heavily on support and immigration from external ethnic sources as a key mechanism in maintaining their dominance over minority groups.

ETHNONATIONALISM

Ethnonationalism, as a set of ideas and practices, constitutes one of the most powerful forces to have shaped the world's political geography in general, and that of Israel/Palestine in particular. Ethnonationalism is a political movement that struggles to achieve or preserve ethnic statehood. It fuses two principles of political order: the post-Westphalian division of the world into sovereign states, and the principle of ethnic self-determination (Murphy 1996). The combined application of these two political principles created the nation-state as the main pillar of today's world political order. Although the nation-state concept is rarely matched by political reality (as nations and states rarely overlap), it has become a dominant global model owing to a dual moral base of popular sovereignty (after centuries of despotic and/or religious regimes) and ethnic self-determination (see Connor 1994, 2002).

The principle of self-determination is central for our purposes here. It appears in its simplest form enshrined in the 1945 United Nations Charter—"every people has the right of self-determination." This principle has formed the political and moral foundation for the establishment of popular sovereignty and democratic government. Yet most international declarations, including the United Nations Charter, leave vague the definition of a "people" and the meaning of self-determination, although in contemporary political culture it is commonly accepted as independence in the group's "own" homeland state. Once such a state is created, the principle is reified and issues such as territory and national survival become inseparable from ethnonational history and culture. This has powerful implications for other facets of social life, most notably male dominance, militarism, and the strategic role of ethnoreligions, although a full discussion of these important topics must wait for another opportunity.

As fully elaborated in the next chapter, the dominance of the ethnonational concept generates forms of ethnic territoriality that perceive control over "homeland" territory and its defense as central to the survival of the group in question, often basing the perceptions on selective and manipulative historical, cultural, or religious interpretations. As I argue below, the application of this principle has been a major bone of contention in the struggle between Jews and Palestinians and in the formation of the Israeli ethnocracy, which has ceaselessly attempted to Judaize the land in the name of national self-determination in a Jewish homeland.

The global dominance of ethnonationalism and the nation-state order has prompted Billig (1995) to consider national identities as "banal." But despite its dominance, the political geography of nation-states is far from stable, as a pervasive nation-building discourse and material reality are continually remolding the collective identity of homeland ethnic minorities. Such minorities often develop a national consciousness of their own that destabilizes political structures with campaigns for autonomy, regionalism, or sovereignty, intensifying, in Anderson's words, "the impending crisis of the hyphen between nation and state" (Anderson 1996, 8).

THE (ETHNIC) LOGIC OF CAPITAL

The third structural force that shapes the political geography of Israel/Palestine and the nature of its regime has been associated with the onset of capitalism and its ethnic and social consequences. Here the settings of a settler society and ethnonationalism combine to create a specific logic of capital flow, development, and class formation on two main levels.

First, labor markets and development are ethnically segmented, thereby creating an ethnoclass structure that tends to accord with the charter-immigrant-indigenous hierarchy noted above. Typically, the founding charter group occupies privileged niches within the labor market, while immigrants are marginalized, at least initially, from the centers of economic power and thus occupy the working and petit bourgeois classes. Indigenous people are typically excluded from access to capital or mobility within the labor market and thus virtually trapped as an underclass (see Stasiulis and Yuval-Davis 1995).

Second, the accelerating globalization of markets and capital movement has weakened the state's economic power. This phenomenon has been typically accompanied by the adoption of neoliberal policies, the subsequent deregulation of economic activities, and the privatization of state functions. Generally, these forces have widened the socioeconomic gaps between the charter, immigrant, and indigenous ethno classes. Yet in the setting of militant ethnonationalism, as in Israel/Palestine, the globalization of capital and the associated establishment of supranational trade organizations may also subdue ethnonationalism and expansionism previously fueled by territorial ethnic rivalries.

Particularly significant in this process is the globalization of the leading classes among the dominant ethnonation, which increasingly search for opportunities and mobility within a more open and accessible regional and global economy. A conspicuous tension between the global and the local thus surfaces, with a potential to intensify intranational tensions but at the same time also to ease international conflicts, as has recently been illustrated in South Africa, Spain, and Northern Ireland (see Agnew 1999; Murphy 2002). Yet, owing to the same process of globalization, new ethnoclass chasms have developed in most developed societies between citizens and new, disenfranchised migrant laborers. The emergence of this growing group illustrates the persisting tensions between the logic of capital, which encourages globalization and new waves of immigration, and the logic of ethnic control, which seeks to preserve existing patterns of territorial control in the name of "the nation." At times, the two processes—economic growth and ethnic control—may reinforce one another, giving rise, for example, to pervasive exploitation of "foreign" workers. However, the tensions in such unequal societies are likely to cause long-term instability and economic decline, thereby forcing structural change.

Regime Principles

The intersection and fusion of the three forces—colonialism, nationalism, and capitalism—create a regime type defined here as ethnocracy. Such a regime's main goal is to maximize ethnic control over a contested multiethnic territory and its governing apparatus. Ethnocracy develops when control over territory is challenged and when a dominant group is powerful enough to determine the character of the state. An ethnocratic regime is characterized by several key principles:

- Despite declaring the regime as democratic, ethnicity (and not territorial citizenship) is the main determinant of the allocation of rights, powers, and resources, and politics is characterized by constant democratic-ethnocratic tension.
- State borders and political boundaries are fuzzy: there is no clear demos, mainly owing to the active role of ethnic diasporas and the bounded, unequal citizenship of ethnic minorities.
- A dominant, "charter" ethnoclass appropriates the state apparatus and determines the outcome of most public policies.
- Segregation and stratification occur on two main levels: ethnonations and ethnoclasses.
- The socioeconomic sphere is marked by long-term ethnoclass stratification.
- The logic of ethnic segregation is diffused into the social and political system, enhancing multidirectional processes of essentializing political ethnicization.
- Significant (though partial) civil and political rights are extended to members of the minority ethnonation, distinguishing ethnocracies from *Herrenvolk* (apartheid) or authoritarian regimes.

A central point is that in ethnocratic regimes the notion of *the demos is severely ruptured*. That is, the community of equal resident citizens (the demos) does not feature high in the country's policies, agenda, imagination, symbols, or resource distribution and is therefore not nurtured or facilitated. But while recognizing that even in the most advanced democracies full equality can never be achieved, the demos forms a necessary basis for the establishment of democracy (demos-cracy). It forms a foundation for the most stable and legitimate form of governance known to human society. Its diminution highlights the structural tensions between ethnocracy and democracy and tends to generate long-term political instability, relating, inter alia, to three notable factors: the central role of religion, the various levels of ethnic affiliation, and the structural obstacles to state legitimacy. Let us elaborate briefly on these points.

RELIGION

While the main force behind ethnocratic politics is ethnonationalism, in most cases the "national" question is intimately involved with an institutionalized and politicized religion, as the religion held by the dominant majority is often an ethnic religion. This creates reciprocal relations, where the religion is influenced by contemporary ethnic and national struggles, while the nature of the ethnonational struggle is in turn shaped by religious narratives. The expansive type of ethnonationalism typical to ethnocracies is thus able to develop resilient forms of internal legitimations based on the mutual reinforcement of nationalism and religion.

Hence, and despite the putatively secular historical foundation of nationalism (Anderson 1991), the histories, identities, and boundaries of the dominant nation in ethnocratic societies are never very far from its religious affiliation. Religious logic is instrumental for most ethnocratic regimes because it generates a discourse of rigid political and social boundaries. The existence of such boundaries is commonly justified in public opinion, in politics, and in the media as stemming from divine or ancient roots and is thus portrayed as ascriptive and insurmountable (see A.D. Smith 1995).

The reinforcement of boundaries by nationalism and religion thus assists the dominant and expanding ethnic nation to *segregate and marginalize* peripheral minorities. Moreover, because ethnonationalism is enmeshed in the definition of the state, and because it often has clear religious undertones, the entry of marginalized minorities to a common good defined by the state is extremely difficult. The regime can also use religion to create formal and informal differentiations between citizens, where "objective" or "God-given" religious criteria function as a basis for essentializing minorities and maintaining discriminatory policies in the allocation of resources, power, and prestige (see also Akenson 1992).

Examples of the intimate connection between religion and ethnonational segregation are rife in ethnocratic states and are evident in the cases of Sri Lanka (with a major Buddhist-Hindu division), Israel/Palestine (Jewish-Muslim), Serbia (Eastern Orthodox-Catholic), Northern Ireland (Protestant-Catholic), Estonia (Lutheran-Russian Orthodox), and Malaysia (Muslim-confutes). Yet, my analysis of the ethnocratic model still points to the general subordination of religion vis-à-vis ethnonationalism. This is the reason the terminology and explanation stress the ethnic and national engines of mobilization, through which religion assumes its contemporary political and cultural potency.

The power of ethnonationalism and religion also tends to overshadow class politics in ethnocratic societies, although socioeconomic considerations are still central in the shaping of the political struggle over resources. Typically, such considerations are expressed indirectly by the politics of religion and ethnicity, with a general association between poverty, religion, and nationalism. As noted above, the ethnic logic of capital operates constantly in ethnocratic societies and generates mechanisms that generally result in persisting ethnic stratification.

LEVELS OF ETHNICITY

Politics in ethnocratic states appears to operate on two distinguishable levels: ethnonations and ethnoclasses (for a fuller discussion, see Yiftachel 1998a, b). As depicted in Figure 2.1, the ethnonational forces possess an assimilating-uniting trajectory. However, the ethnic logic of politics and the legitimacy of ethnically based stratification generated by the ethnonational struggle are often diffused into both majority and minority communities, causing the emergence of various forms of ethnoclass division. Hence ethnocratic regimes not only denote the dominance of a specific ethnonation but also the dominance of ethnicity as political and economic criteria. This gives legitimacy to the nondemocratic use of ethnic affiliation as a determinant of resource allocation in multiple societal arenas. It is often impossible to make a sharp distinction between ethnonational and ethnoclass stratification, but the ("ideal-typical") analytical distinction helps us trace the central role of ethnicity in both national and economic lines of demarcation.

Hence, the contours of political mobilization and organization within each ethnic nation often combine ethnic, religious, and class affiliations. The patterns of ethnoclass stratification typical to ethnocracies have been explained and elaborated elsewhere (see Stasiulis and Yuval-Davis 1995). Beyond presenting a more accurate account of the different levels of ethnicity,

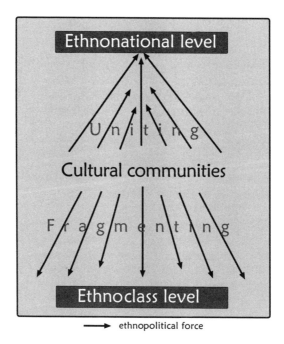

Figure 2.1. Two Levels of Political Ethnicity in (Settling) Ethnocratic Societies

the importance of the distinction between ethnonation and ethnoclass lies in two factors: (a) the attention it draws to the material aspects of ethnic struggle by highlighting the critical role of class, particularly in intranational arenas (this angle is frequently overlooked in recent scholarship on politics and identities), and (b) its illumination of the inherent tension between the parallel regime projects of (ethnically centered) nation building and (civil) state building. Ethnocratic nation building fully exposes the tension between the use of ethnic and civil categories because it entails an active exclusion of groups of citizens or residents represented as external by the prevailing discourse of the dominant nation. This status is reified by a combination of political practices, legal measures, public policies, and cultural norms. The excluded are usually indigenous peoples or peripheral minorities but also collectivities marked as enemies or foreigners. Yet at the same time these groups are incorporated (often coercively) into the project of state building. The crises emanating from the process of "incorporation without legitimation" (Mann 1999) are at the heart of the *chronic instability* experienced by ethnocratic regimes.

STRUCTURAL OBSTACLES TO LEGITIMACY

The chronic instability of ethnocratic regimes often takes some time to develop because ethnocratic regimes are usually supported by cultural and ideological apparatuses that legitimize and reinforce the skewed reality. This is achieved by constructing historical narratives about the dominant ethnonation as the rightful owner of the territory in question. Such narratives degrade all other contenders as historically or culturally unworthy to control the land or achieve political equality.

A further legitimizing apparatus is the maintenance of *selective openness*. The introduction of several democratic institutions is common in ethnocratic states. These institutions add legitimacy to the expansionist project, to the leadership of the charter ethnoclass, and to the incorporation of peripheral groups. But, as noted, these "democratic" institutions commonly exclude indigenous or "foreign" minorities. This is achieved either formally, as was the case in Australia until 1967, or more subtly by leaving such groups outside decision-making circles, as is the case in Sri Lanka. Here the concept of illiberal democracy articulated by Zakaria (1997) is helpful because it draws attention to a regime with a formal democratic appearance but with centralizing, coercive, and authoritarian characteristics. As noted by Zakaria, illiberal democracies use the democratic facade to enhance their internal and external legitimacy, although such legitimacy is rarely sustained owing to its illiberal foundation.

Externally, selective openness is established as a principle of foreign relations and membership in international organizations. This has become particularly important with the increasing opening of the world economy and the establishment of supranational organizations, such as the European Union and the North American Free Trade Agreement. Membership in such organizations often requires at least the appearance of open regimes, and most ethnocracies comply with this requirement.

Given these powerful legitimizing forces, ethnocratic projects usually enjoy in the short term a hegemonic status, which originates among the charter group and is successfully diffused among the populace. The hegemonic moment, as convincingly formulated by Gramsci (1971), is marked by a distorted but widely accepted diffusion of a given set of principles and practices. It is an order in which a certain social structure is dominant, with its own concept of reality determining most tastes, morals, customs, and political principles. Given the economic, political, and cultural power of the elites, a hegemonic order is likely to be reproduced until severe contradictions with "stubborn realities" generate counterhegemonic mobilizations (see Lustick 1993).

But, critically, the hegemonic reign of most ethnocratic regimes is diffused only among the expanding ethnonational group and hence faces great difficulties in prevailing for the long term. A set of intensifying contradictions often surfaces in the public arena through the mobilization of dispossessed and disgruntled minorities. These contradictions, which derive from the tensions between the democratic representation of the regime and its ethnocratic, exclusive practices, may threaten its very existence (see Lustick 1993).

Let me illustrate now the main arguments made above about the nature of ethnocratic regimes in general, and the *dynamic* project of ethnicization in particular. The next section will explore, in a somewhat broad-brush fashion, the three illustrative cases of Sri Lanka, Australia, and Estonia. These states display many characteristics comparable to the case of Israel/Palestine, but they also illuminate three different trajectories of ethnoterritorial and political developments. On the basis of these cases, I will then proceed to delineate the structural elements of ethnocratic states.

The Making of Ethnocratic Regimes: Learning from Sri Lanka, Australia, and Estonia

Why compare these three nations? First, the common political-geographical elements emerging from these three examples will assist the "extraction" of the structural forces at the basis of the ethnocratic regime. The comparative analysis below will then help to create a framework that will capture the main forces shaping ethnocratic regimes, thereby enabling a more refined analysis of the political-geography of Israel/Palestine.

Second, as in all comparative analyses, there are obvious differences between the three states, in history, economy, culture, and geography. However, the main commonality, which makes these cases comparable, is the institutionalization of the ethnicization project within a self-declared democratic setting. Hence, several important democratic characteristics, such as separation of powers and elections, exist alongside a state project of deepening ethnic territorial, political, and demographic controls, which entails the exclusion of "external" communities. This combination sets ethnocratic states, including the three cases compared here, apart from most other nation-states, and makes the comparative analysis an important step in generalizing the distinctness of ethnocratic regimes.

This point requires some elaboration. It is often claimed that most nation-states advance a project of ethnic domination (see Brubaker 1996), thereby diminishing the distinctiveness of the ethnocratic type (see Smooha 2002). However, I claim that there exists a qualitative difference between what Brubaker (1996) terms "nationalizing states," and ethnocratic regimes. This differences lies in the deliberate undermining of the political demos. As elaborated below, ethnocratic regimes work ceaselessly to prevent the making of an inclusive demos—a community of equal citizens within definable territory. Instead, they use the rhetoric of the nation-state but do not allow minorities any feasible path of inclusion. Indeed, the ethnocratic project is often constructed specifically *against* these minorities. There is no attempt to assimilate "external" communities of citizens; to the contrary, their identity is well demarcated and structurally marginalized.

Put differently, contrary to most nation-states, ethnocratic regimes actually work against the project of universal citizenship. While the universal project is of course never complete in most nation-states and often involves oppressive policies and practices, such as forced assimilation, discrimination, or state-led economic stratification, the state framework, de jure, still leaves minorities an option of integration (often bearing a high cost).

Ethnocracies, in contrast, annul this inclusionary option. The state is constructed so as *to prevent* the integration of minorities, typically through the rejection of citizenship, limiting personal laws, restriction on immigration and land rights, or denial of accessibility to decision-making powers. This is a significant structural difference, which sets ethnocratic regimes apart from most "normal" nation-states. Hence, one may point to the zone on a continuum between actively exclusionary and inclusionary regimes as the "tipping zone" between democracy with an ethnic bias and ethnocracy. It is analytically difficult to sharply define this zone, which may contain contradictory movements (concurrently toward democracy and ethnocracy), as evident by the Israeli case detailed in the following chapters. However, when the political demos has been fundamentally undermined by the state's ethnocratic laws, policies, and institutions, the regime can be said to have crossed the ethnocratic threshold, as evident in Sri Lanka. Estonia, in contrast, appears to be moving across the tipping zone in the other direction, from ethnocracy to democracy.

The three brief cases outlined in the following pages were selected to demonstrate the above processes. They were also chosen because they display different *trajectories* of the ethnocratic project—deterioration into an open ethnic war, and the possibility of peaceful democratization. In Sri Lanka, deepening oppression and intensifying minority resistance have led to a virtual collapse of the state into a protracted civil war. In Estonia, the opposite process of nonviolent democratization and gradual inclusion of the Russian minority has been gathering pace. In Australia, white expansionism in general and a clear domination of Anglo-Celtic culture in particular have given way to a more multicultural and democratic approach.

The different trajectories of political development are highlighted by the political and cultural freedom index data, compiled by the Freedom House project (www.freedomhouse.org). It uses a scale of 1 to 7, with 1 being the most free, to indicate the status of the nations it studies. Estonia scored low on political and cultural freedoms during the early 1990s (3 on both assessments). But it improved significantly in the last few years, scoring 1 and 2 respectively in 2003. Australia scored very high—1 on both counts, both in the 1990s and 2003. While data does not exist on the period of Australian ethnocracy, it is safe to assume that it has improved dramatically since the period of white expansion and Aboriginal exclusion and genocide. In contrast, Sri Lanka scored relatively well during the 1970s with 2 on political freedom and 3 on cultural freedom. The situation deteriorated during the 1990s, when Sri Lanka scored a very low 4 and 5, only to improve slightly during 2003, with scores of 2 and 3 respectively. Given these trajectories, the three cases provide a wide spectrum of development possibilities apparent under ethnocratic regimes.

Finally, while the following analyses emphasize regime activity, public policies, and state strategies vis-à-vis minorities, it should be emphasized that the development of both ethnic relations and regime structure are dialectical. That is, state actions and majority politics in ethnocratic states are informed and fueled by minority activity and mobilization. While the dialectics are commonly asymmetrical (with the state having far more power than marginalized minorities), the evolution of these regimes cannot be understood without acknowledging the role of minority mobilization, especially as regards the use of violence and terror and the articulation of dissenting, often threatening, collective narratives.

Sri Lanka: From Biethnic Democracy to Sinhalese Ethnocracy

The island state of Sri Lanka (previously Ceylon) is composed of two main ethnonational groups. Sinhalese, who are mainly Buddhist, make up 75 percent of the state's 19 million inhabitants. Tamils, who are mainly Hindu, make up 18 percent. Historical accounts of ethnic settlement are hotly contested, although there is evidence that both groups have existed on the island for more than two millennia (Perera 1990). Sri Lanka gained its independence from Britain in 1948 after an anticolonial struggle dominated by the Sinhalese groups but shared by Tamils, as well as other ethnic groups on the island. However, in the decade following independence the state gradually turned toward a Sinhalization strategy. This orientation intensified owing to Tamil resistance and an ensuing process of ethnic polarization.

Sri Lanka was formed as a democratic state, with formal institutions and governing procedures following, initially, the Westminster model (Little 1993). But in later years, the Sri Lankan state was gradually appropriated by the Sinhalese community, mainly owing to its demographic advantage and strong sense of ethnonationalism (De-Silva 1986; Uyangoda 1994). The Sinhalese used their dominance in the legislative, judiciary, and executive arms of government to advance an explicit Sinhalization process. As declared in 1983 by the Sri Lankan development minister, "Sri Lanka is inherently and rightfully a Sinhalese state. . . . This must be accepted as a fact and not a matter of opinion to be debated. By attempting to challenge this premise, Tamils have brought the wrath of the Sinhalese on their own heads; they have themselves to blame" (Nissan 1984, 176).

This approach found expression in several key policies and programs, beginning in the 1950s with the adoption of religious Buddhist state symbols, which denote, in the Sri Lankan context, a purely Sinhalese affiliation. Another major step was taken in 1956 when Sinhalese was declared the only official state language. The state's official culture was also developed around a series of Buddhist invented histories, symbols, and values, glorifying the link between the Buddha and the Sinhalese "guardians" of "his" island (Little 1993), and glorifying the images of the Sinhala nation as the indigenous "sons of the earth," and hence the only rightful owners and controllers of the state (Uyangoda 1994).

A further aspect of the Sinhalization strategy was evident in Sri Lanka's *demographic and citizenship policies.* More than one million long-term Tamil residents who migrated to the island during the period of British rule, mainly as plantation workers, have been denied citizenship as part of the Sinhalization approach by being officially classified as "Indian Tamils." This move forced large sections of this community to leave the island and settle in India during the 1950s and 1960s. The rest of the group has remained to date without full citizenship or voting rights. The Sinhalese majority has thus managed to contain the size of the Tamil community and reinforce geographical and political intra-Tamil cleavage between "Indian" and "Sri Lankan" Tamils. Geographically, Indian Tamils mainly reside in the island's central heights, while Sri Lankan Tamils inhabit the island's northern and eastern regions. Politically, the disenfranchised Indian Tamils became totally dependent on the Sinhalese regime for basic rights and services and hence remained politically immobilized. Consequently,

Indian Tamils have rarely participated or assisted in the militant resistance staged by Sri Lankan Tamils against the Sinhalizing state.

The island's ethnic geography has also been the main cause of another notable ethnocratic policy—the *Sinhalization of contested space.* The British rulers had already encouraged the Tamils to immigrate into Sinhalese areas, breaking a centuries-long tradition of (mainly voluntary) spatial separation. Likewise, the Sri Lankan government encouraged Sinhalese to settle in the island's central and eastern regions, which previously were dominated and claimed by Tamils as part of their "own" regions.

This has been most evident in the large-scale Mahaweli irrigation and settlement project carried out predominantly during the 1970s and 1980s (Roded 1999). The project opened up large tracts of agricultural land in the island's central and northeastern regions, which were offered mostly to landless or impoverished farmers. By 1993 1.1 million people (the vast majority of whom were Sinhalese) were resettled in these regions, creating a new Sinhalese regional lower-class collectivity and exacerbating the conflict with the Tamils, who considered the region part of their historical "Elam" homeland (Peiris 1996).

Subsequently, the regions in question became a destination for large-scale (and mainly unauthorized) Tamil countersettlement. As the two populations increasingly intermingled in competitive settings (largely as a result of settlement initiatives like the Mahaweli project), antagonism and discrimination against the minority deepened, intensifying the breakdown of social and political order since the early 1980s.

The civil (ethnic) war, which has dominated the Sri Lankan state since the early 1980s, has brought to the fore *the military* as a major agent in the Sinhalization of contested space and the reinforcement of Sinhalese dominance in Sri Lankan politics. The army gradually extended state (that is, Sinhalese) control north and eastward, confining the resisting Tamil groups to the Jaffna Peninsula at the state's northeastern end. It has also caused a major internal refugee problem, with some 550,000 residents losing their homes during the fighting, 78 percent of them Tamils (de Silva 1996). During the same time, a series of emergency and "security" legislation reduced the protection of Tamil citizens against arbitrary state oppression (Uyangoda 1998). A parallel constitutional change increased the powers of a popularly elected president at the expense of the previously powerful legislature. Earlier, in 1978, several Tamil parliamentarians were disqualified on the basis of "acting against the Sinhalese state," reducing the already limited Tamil political power (Little 1993).

The accumulating alienation of Tamils from the Sri Lankan state drove them to boycott the political process altogether. From 1978 until 2001, the majority of Tamils boycotted the Sri Lankan elections and only rarely participated in other state affairs. The state, on its part, did little to induce the Tamils back into the political arena until 1987, when further constitutional reforms attempted to ease ethnic tensions by decentralizing state authority and granting autonomy to regional authorities. However, the Tamils did not accept the plan that was prepared without their participation, claiming that: (a) it compromised their drive for self-determination, and (b) it legitimized the "unlawful" Sinhalese domination of the eastern regions (Nissan 1996). Further, the state maintained ultimate control by classifying "national projects" that could bypass the proposed decentralized forms of decision making (Gunasekara 1996).

The Sinhalization strategy generated widespread Tamil resistance. The Tamils initially struggled for territorial-political autonomy within the Sri Lankan state. Some autonomy was indeed offered to the Tamils in a (failed) Peace Plan, following a 1987 Indian invasion, seen by most Tamils as part of the government effort to control their regions. Following the state's ethnocratic policies and brutal opression a dialectical process of violent escalation began, leading to Tamil disengagement from the state and eventually the breakout of civil war. When it was offered then, autonomy did not suffice. The fighting reached a peak of massive interethnic violence and terror during the mid-1990s, exacting an immense toll estimated at 70,000–80,000 casualties, most of them civilians. In parallel the militant Liberation Tigers of Elam (LTTE) gained a position of sole Tamil leadership following a violent campaign against all other Tamil groups and leaders (Bloom 2003).

Only in 2002 was a ceasefire declared, when the Tamil leadership agreed to return to negotiations after the Sinhalese promised serious constitutional amendments and made a more genuine attempt to include the Tamils in devising a new, highly devolved state structure. But the road to reforming the Sri Lankan ethnocracy is still fraught with severe difficulties. In December of 2003, real advances in negotiations toward genuine Tamil autonomy in the northeast created a political crisis and a return to government of political forces objecting to Tamil self-rule (even if limited). In addition, the highly ethnicized nature of the conflict has caused the more than one million Sri Lankan Muslims to form collective political demands, thereby complicating the task of rebuilding Sri Lanka.

The case of Sri Lanka thus illustrates well the emergence of ethnocracy and the inherent tensions between formal democratic procedures and a parallel state project of ethnicizing contested spaces and political institutions, while marginalizing and radicalizing the minority. It demonstrates the inability of an ethnocracy to be sustained for the long term and its need to reform structurally in order to survive as a state.

Australia: From a Settling Ethnocracy to an Aspiring Multicultural Democracy

During the eighteenth and nineteenth centuries, Australia represented a classical settling ethnocracy. As part of global European colonialism, it was settled in 1788 by the British, who established six main colonies in what later became the Australian states of New South Wales, Victoria, Queensland, South Australia, Tasmania, and Western Australia. Within a few decades, white settlers (who were attracted by the country's natural resources and ample land) gained control over large tracts of habitable land by usurping the territorial control of the 400,000–600,000 indigenous Aboriginal inhabitants through ethnic cleansing, genocide, and exclusion (Head 2000; Pettman 1988; Reynolds 1987; Young 1995). White domination was reinforced by the imposition of a capitalist economy over a precapitalist seminomadic society with little resources, knowledge, or power to compete against the economic might of a European empire (Reynolds 1987).

Australia developed as a "pure" settler colony, with near total segregation between local Aborigines and white settlers, who initially established a polity and culture that closely resembled the British mother country. At the same time, white settlement continued to expand by imposing further violent controls over the Aborigines, which included classifying them as noncitizens and concentrating them into several large reserves (see Attwood et al. 1994; Bennett 1988). During the first 120 years of white settlement, 80 to 90 percent of native Australians perished, while in the twentieth century, their population slowly rose to reach more than 620,000 in the year 2000, constituting 2.5 percent of the population.

Until the mid-twentieth century, immigration was guided by a "white Australia policy" and was a central mechanism in shaping the *demography* of the settling nation and enhancing the process of white ethnicization. In 1901, upon federation of the six colonies into the Australian Commonwealth, the Immigration Restriction Law was enacted, which imposed a series of entry conditions that in effect maintained a predominantly white population. This law was accompanied by a policy designed to assimilate forcefully the remaining Aborigines into the white population. By the forced removal of Aboriginal children from their parents for the purpose of reeducation and planned mixed marriages, the Australian government strove to wipe out the black Australian race (Reynolds 1989).

The 1950s and 1960s saw a reduction in Anglo-Celtic immigration from the British Isles, and as a result Australian authorities began actively to recruit white immigrants from other cultural backgrounds, especially southern Europeans. These immigrants arrived in large numbers at Australia's main urban centers, creating a new ethnoclass of low-income, blue-collar workers. Since the 1970s, however, with the enactment of several antidiscrimination laws covering immigration and citizenship, the "white Australia" approach has been replaced with a more pluralistic immigration policy, moving Australia further into a multicultural structure, with particular emphasis on Asian immigrants. In the year 2000, 21 percent of Australia's citizens were born overseas, about half of them in non Anglo-Celtic countries

(Department of Immigration and Multicultural Affairs [DIMA] 2000). During the 1980s and 1990s, the Australian government also launched a range of multicultural programs in education, cultural production, communication, and community development, although these have also spawned an anti-immigration backlash and the rise of new racist movements (Anderson 2001).

With federation, the Australia Constitution created a two-tier democracy, with civil rights enshrined in the federal Constitution. Yet, racist laws and policies toward the Aborigines remained for some decades, especially at the state level, enabling the process of white expansion and dispossession of the Aborigines to continue unabated. Aborigines were finally enfranchised in 1949, and only in 1967, following a national referendum, were they permitted Australian citizenship. This referendum also canceled the discriminatory clauses in the Constitution and moved most Aboriginal affairs to the domain of the (federal) commonwealth government. Later, in 1988, the federal government established the Aboriginal and Torres Islanders Commission (ATSIC), which created sixty Aboriginal Regional Councils and devolved resources and decision-making powers to Aboriginal communities, particularly in rural areas.

During the 1980s and 1990s, Aboriginal-white relations experienced a gradual process of reform, moving simultaneously in the direction of equal citizenship and minority autonomy. While progress was achieved, none of these policies attained civil equality or genuine native self-government (Howitt 2001). The mood of reform also drew on the growing liberalization of Australian society, which was evident in several committees and initiatives for racial reconciliation and the appointment of a royal commission to investigate the alleged kidnapping of Aboriginal children. In 1999, Australia's prime minister expressed "regret" over past injustices against the Aborigines, although this fell short of the expected apology, offer of compensation, or recognition of a range of human rights abuses against the native people (Howitt 2001).

Land policies were central to the white ethnicization of Australia. As is typical in settler societies, legal authorities exploited the lack of written Aboriginal land titles to declare the land *terra nullius* (empty land). This enabled white settlers and mineral explorers to drive Aboriginal holders off most fertile or mineral-rich lands and created a new network of white settlement and primary industry in most rural regions (Mercer 1993; Reynolds 1987). Aborigines were concentrated into reserves or housed in the main cities, thereby removing any obstacles for further white land seizure, agriculture, and mineral exploitation.

However, the concentration of Aborigines into reserves or specific neighborhoods also assisted in the preservation of their identity and provided a platform for their mobilization against white control. Nowhere was this more evident than in the issue of land rights, which became the focus of the Aboriginal struggle after the 1960s. Land rights campaigns were staged on the federal level and in most states of the Australian Commonwealth (Gale 1990). On the federal level, a continuous challenge was mounting against the concept and convention of *terra nullius* (Howitt 2001).

In 1992, after a protracted ten-year legal battle in what is known as the *Mabo* case, the Australian High Court handed down a watershed decision that recognized native land ownership and retracted the *terra nullius* convention. This gave Aborigines their greatest land rights victory to date and paved the way for the enactment of the Native Title Act (1994, amended 1998), under which Aborigines can make title claims based on their collective and continuous occupation of land. Successful native title claims depended, however, on highly restrictive conditions, with the intention that little land would be returned to Aboriginal ownership. The *Mabo* ruling was reinforced in 1996 by what is known as the *Wik* case, in which the High Court ruled that a native title is not extinguished by long-term pastoral leases of the type common in Australia's rural areas.

In the meantime, land rights struggles have continued in each state with varying degrees of success. In related milestone decisions, mining was prohibited by the federal government in Coronation Hill, a (disputed) Aboriginal sacred site in the Northern Territory, and the Aborigines were given control over one of Australia's most famous landscapes, Ayers Rock (or Uluru, the official name), marking further notable achievements in the Aboriginal campaign for land rights (Jacobs 1993). Despite these important legal and political victories, the geography of Aboriginal-white relations in Australia is yet to change in any significant way. Powerful land interests, mainly held by mining and pastoral companies, and a political shift to the right during the late 1990s have dramatically slowed any progress in the allocation of land control to Aboriginal groups (Howitt 2001). Yet land rights struggles managed to halt further native dispossession and created a significant and far more united Aboriginal presence in Australian politics and society.

In overview, parallel processes of violent occupation, white only immigration policies, economic marginalization, and land seizure were the bases of a white ethnocratic settler society in Australia. During the second half of the twentieth century, however, the regime began to change with the advent of more liberal attitudes toward immigration of non-Europeans, the ensuing multiculturalism, and concerted Aboriginal campaigns for equality and autonomy. These, together with a neoliberal economic agenda, have brought about significant regime changes, during which Australia has been transformed to a liberal-democracy, characterized mainly by economic ethnoclass stratification. However, the structural marginalization of Aborigines has remained conspicuously evident.

ESTONIA: FROM A SOVIET COLONY TO A DEMOCRATIZING ETHNOCRACY

The independent Estonian state re-emerged during the collapse of the Soviet Union in the 1989–92 period. It is situated on the Baltic coast, and has a population of 1.5 million, of whom 65 percent are ethnic Estonians, 15 percent Russians with citizenship, and 20 percent noncitizen residents (mainly Russian speaking) (EHDR 2000).

The new polity was formed as a result of an anti-Soviet (and by implication anti-Russian) struggle and has since adopted an explicit program of Estonization (de-Russification), designed to reinstate the ethnic and national situation existing during a previous period of independence (1918–39). During that period, ethnic Estonians dominated the state—politically, demographically, economically, and culturally. The Soviet Union subsequently promoted a process of Russification and encouraged Russian immigration to Estonia, thereby threatening Estonian demographic and cultural dominance in the Estonian homeland. Since official independence was declared in 1992, state building has assumed ethnocratic characteristics. For example, in 1992 the Riigikogu, Estonia's Parliament decided not to grant citizenship to "nonethnic" Estonians. It classified them as "aliens," thus excluding them from the 1992 referendum on a new Constitution. Estonian state policies in the 1989–2000 period clearly aimed to ensure the political, territorial, and cultural dominance of ethnic Estonians by focusing on citizenship, land, culture, and language. It should be noted, however, that unlike nineteenth-century Australia or contemporary Sri Lanka, the process of ethnicizing the Estonian polity has largely been nonviolent—a factor assisting greatly its recent democratization moves.

In 1992, Estonia adopted a new Constitution, according to which the bearers of the supreme power are "the people" (that is, the citizens; Article 1). The constitutional preamble contains a clause obliging the state to ensure the preservation of the (ethnic) Estonian nation and culture. Courts have actively referred to this preamble in a variety of rulings on citizenship and property matters. The Citizenship Law of 1992 (amended 1995) granted citizenship to all pre-1940 citizens and their descedants and prohibited dual citizenship. Because in 1940 the state was 92 percent ethnic Estonian, this law actually granted superior citizenship rights to ethnic Estonians (in and outside the state) over the state's own Russian residents. In other words, the citizenship laws attempted fundamentally to control the state's demography in order to ensure a solid (ethnic) Estonian majority despite the residence of a large Russian minority.

Hence, the new Constitution includes special clauses concerning the priority of ethnic Estonians, Estonian culture, and Estonian language (Ruutsoo 1998, 176). Every Estonian is entitled to preserve his or her national identity, but no special minority rights are recognized by the Constitution.

Some state symbols are of purely ethnic character (for example, the flag, the national anthem, stamps, and official letterheads). State holidays include Protestant sacred days, but not Russian Orthodox sacred days. There is no state church in Estonia, but the majority of ethnic Estonians are (Protestant) Lutheran, and Estonian nationalism is widely associated with a Lutheran way of life as an antithesis to the Orthodox Russian influence. During the Communist years the population became largely secular, but since the return of Estonian nationalism as a legitimate ideology, the church has increased markedly its public profile (www.Estonica.org).

Estonian legislation set a difficult path for acquisition of citizenship by non-Estonians, including long-term state residents who previously had full (Soviet) citizenship rights and are now considered "aliens." Such "aliens" are required to reside in Estonia for at least five years, pass demanding language tests, prove command of the Estonian Constitution, have a steady income, establish permanent residency, and pledge allegiance to the state and its (ethnic) character (The Aliens Law 1989, 2000; Human Rights Watch 2000).

The ethnicization strategy is also evident in Estonia's *language and cultural policies*, which have reinforced the imposed dominance of the Estonian language in most spheres of life, including education, street signs, and government services. This dominance was deepened by a new language law, introduced in 1989 (and amended in 1995, 1999, and 2000), which demoted Russian to the status of a "foreign" language, similar to dozens of other languages used by immigrants and minorities. The new law severely restricts the public usage of any language except Estonian. For example, "foreign" languages are prohibited in all street and commercial signs, and all television broadcasts must have Estonian subtitles. Estonian is the compulsory language in Parliament and local councils, for state employees, and for government dealings in both public and private sectors. The only exception is minority language usage in territories where such a language forms a majority, but this is implemented in a very restrictive manner.

In 1993, the Riigikogu enacted the Law for Cultural Autonomy of National Minorities (RT 1993, 71,1000). But the law defined a minority as consisting of citizens only. Thus, the state did not recognize special rights of the vast majority of the non-Estonian population. Previously, the Soviet Law on National Rights allowed minorities full enjoyment of certain rights obtainable through special autonomous organs and under the supervision of the state.

In a different policy arena, the Estonian government attempted to reinforce *ethnic land control* by resurrecting the traditional "indigenous" Estonian system of family farms to replace the Kolchoz and Sobchov Soviet system of collective cultivation. This was aided by the Law for Land Reform (1992), the Law of Agrarian Reform (1994), and a complex system of financial incentives designed to assist the restitution and privatization of land, while at the same time restrict the benefits of this process chiefly to ethnic Estonians (Andersen 1999).

Ethnicization has also been prominent on the political level. After 1992, right-wing nationalist parties have dominated the Riigikogu. A process of *ethnic political polarization* has seen electoral competition revolving around the intensity of the Estonization (and de-Russification) process. Changes of government during the 1990s did not result in any significant change in Estonia's policies toward its Russian minority. Russians have suffered persistent political underrepresentation: in the 1992 Parliament there were no ethnic Russians, while in 1995 and in 1999 their numbers rose to only six members (out of one hundred). In the Riigikogu, Russians have always belonged to the opposition and have had no significant influence on the decision-making process.

Ethnic Estonian dominance is also expressed in the denial of state recognition of the local Orthodox Church under its prewar name, the Estonian Apostolic Orthodox Church (see Theile 1999). That means the deprivation of the church's prewar property in the process of property restitution, as noted below. In 1993, the government registered the EAOC an "exile" entity whose legitimacy is highly disputable.

As expected, and as planned by Estonian policymakers, the laws created considerable difficulties for nonethnic Estonians to acquire citizenship and have caused substantial emigration, mainly into Russia, with some 133,000 Russians leaving Estonia during the 1990s (Statistical Office of Estonia 2000). By 1999, only about 38 percent of this group had received Estonian citizenship, while 19 percent had retained foreign (mainly Russian) citizenship, and 43 percent had remained stateless. Noncitizens are excluded from many political and economic arenas in Estonian life and are prohibited from voting or being elected at a national level. The Russians have voting rights for local elections but cannot stand for mayorship (EHDR 1999; Hallik 1998).

The discrepancy between citizenry and the residential composition of Estonia is highlighted by the following figures: in 1999, ethnic Estonians constituted 81 percent of the citizenry but only 65 percent of the population. Russians were 28 percent of the residents, but only 14 percent of the citizenry. However, the norms of the European Union, which admitted Estonia as a member in 2004, as well as pressures from international human rights organizations and internal democratization forces, have forced Estonia to begin to ease its ethnocratic policies. At the beginning of the 2000s, it introduced in several measures naturalization for the Russians, associated mainly with language acquisition, military service, and contribution to the Estonian public (Berg 2002; Pettai and Hallik 2002).

In sum, like Sri Lanka and Australia, but within its own historical and geographical setting, Estonia demonstrates the deep logic of ethnicization behind its state structure and policies. Estonia adopted a structure of an "open" formal democracy, but at another level it has set into motion an ethnic transformation of the state from a Russified Communist republic into an ethnic Estonian state. The new state actively facilitates the Estonization of institutions, politics, culture, and territory. However, unlike Sri Lanka, the ethnicization process appears to be waning, mainly owing to the influence of the European Union and the globalization of ethnic politics. Estonia is being integrated into the European Union, which requires it to safeguard the rights of minorities and allow them a path of equal inclusion as citizens. Hence, Estonia appears to be an ethnocracy undergoing a gradual process of democratization, demonstrating a possible nonviolent path of democratizing ethnocracy.

To conclude the comparative exploration, Table 2.1 highlights the main landmarks in the process of ethnicization teased out of the three cases. This summary enables our exploration to move into a new level of generalization, as conducted in the next section.

Key Regime Dimensions

The foregoing accounts of Sri Lanka, Australia, and Estonia highlight the changing ethnic relations in states undergoing a planned process of ethnicization, as well as the possibility of changing the ethnocratic trajectory, as evident by the democratization of Australia (albeit after thorough destruction of Aboriginal communities) and to some extent of Estonia. The discussion will turn now to a theoretical level, identifying the relationships between ethnocracy and five key regime dimensions: democracy, regime structure and features, minority status, political instability, and the homeland.

ETHNOCRACY AND DEMOCRACY

The "open" ethnocratic regimes studied here combine partial elements of both authoritarian and democratic systems. But regardless of the formal political system, they enhance a rule by, and for, a specific ethnos. As such, they cannot be classified as democracies in a substantive sense because they structurally privilege one group of citizens over others and strive to maintain that privilege. Ethnocracies are, therefore, neither democratic nor authoritarian (or *Herrenvolk*) systems of government. The lack of democracy, as noted above, rests on *the rupture of the concept of the demos* unequal citizenship and laws and policies that enable the seizure of the state by one ethnonational group. At the same time, they are not authoritarian because they extend significant (though partial) political rights to ethnic minorities.

TABLE 2.1. Landmarks in the Ethnicization Process: A Comparative Summary

Australia	Estonia	Sri Lanka
• 1788: British conquest and colonization • practice and legal declaration of *Terra Nullius:* empty land • white frontierism and "free" land seizure • genocide and spatial concentration of Aborigines • Anglo-Celtic dominated "white Australia" immigration • post-WWII southern European immigration; onset of cultural diversity • 1949: citizenship granted to Aborigines • 1975: Racial Discrimination Act • 1970s–80s: Asian immigration and introduction of multicul- turalism policies • 1970s–90s: land rights struggle in states • 1992, 1995: High Court recognizes constitutional native title to land *(Mabo; Wick);* enactment of Native Title Act • 1999–2001: (limited) white apology to Aborigines; ongoing reconciliation process	• post-1990: Estonization (de-Russification) to reverse Soviet policies • 1992 Constitution to safeguard Estonian identity, language, and culture • restitution of land to ethnic Estonians • prevention of minority universal citizenship and rights to own land • encouragement of minority emigration • citizenship rights granted to "returning" Estonians • encouragement of Estonization of "Russian" regions • prevention of Russian land ownership • stressing of "traditional Estonian" rural values • mid to late 1990s: introduction of European democratic standards • recent moderation of ethnicization agendas—possibilities for minority naturalization • gradual liberalization and democratization; some collective minority rights	• joint Sinhalese-Tamil anticolonial struggle • 1948: democratic Constitution as unitary state • post–1948: Sinhalization of state • 1956: Sinhala declared official language • citizenship denied to "Indian" Tamils • Budhism de facto state religion and culture • arid zones irrigation projects—resettlement of Sinhalese in Tamil-populated regions • armed forces in total Sinhalese dominance • neglect of Tamil regions • discrimination in public resources against Tamils • 1980s–90s: Tamil secessionist mobilization; armed resistance and terror • 1983: civil war—massive violence and political instability • 1987: Indian invasion, constitutional amendments, proposed partial devolution • 1990s: economic liberalization • 2002: peace talks and ceasefire • 2003–4: political crisis stalls granting of genuine Tamil autonomy

This discussion of ethnocratic regimes aims to formulate a critique of their common, and deceptive, representation as democratic. On the one hand, such a regime claims to be a full (and often even liberal) democracy, while on the other, it routinely oppresses and marginalizes peripheral minorities and constantly changes the state structure in the majority's favor. The oppression of minorities is often exacerbated by the legitimacy granted to the state as "democratic" in the international arena.

This critique emerges from two main positions. First, I employ a Gramscian-informed perspective that seeks to discover the underlying logic of power relations within a system of hegemonic cultures (for elaboration, see Gramsci 1971; Hall 1997; Laclau 1994; Said 1994). This perspective is suspicious of official rhetoric and declarations, and it is constantly searching for the deeper political and historical forces, and for the hegemonic norms, often unseen or silent, that navigate these forces. Here the combined political-geographical and political-economic approach taken by this book assists in focusing on material (territorial and economic) changes, regardless of the deceptive rhetoric in which they are often wrapped. Second, the critique emerges after privileging a look at society from the periphery into the core, hence peeling off much of the self-legitimizing democratic narrative held by the society's mainstream. This angle often reveals the impregnable, stratifying, and nondemocratic nature of the ethnocratic regime.

Importantly, the term democracy is not used here uncritically. I recognized that it is a contested concept, hotly debated, rarely settled, and widely abused, particularly in multiethnic states (see Mann 1999). It is an institutional response to generations of civil struggles for political and economic inclusion, gradually incorporating and empowering the poor, women, and minorities into the once elitist polity (Held 1990; Tilly 1996). This is not the place to delve deeply into democratic theory. Suffice it to say that several key principles have emerged in the literature as consensual foundations for achieving the main tenets of democracy—equality and liberty. These include equal citizenship; protection of individuals and minorities against the tyranny of states, majorities, or churches; and a range of civil, political, and social rights (Held 1990). A stable constitution, periodic and universal elections, and a free media generally ensure these principles (Dahl 1995).

In multiethnic or multinational polities, as illustrated by the seminal works of Lijphart (1984), Kymlicka (1995), Rawls (1999), and I. M. Young (2002), a certain parity, recognition, and proportionality between enduring ethnic collectivities is a prerequisite for democratic legitimacy and political stability. While no state ever implements these principles fully, and thus none is a perfect and complete democracy, ethnocratic regimes are conspicuous in breaching the spirit, purpose, and major tenets of the democracy ideal.

REGIME STRUCTURE AND FEATURES

To fathom further the workings of "open" ethnocracies, I differentiate analytically between regime *features* and *structure*. As noted in Figure 2.2, some
ethnocracies possess visible democratic features, such as periodic elections,
a free media, relatively open gender relations, and an autonomous judiciary that protects and even promotes (some) human rights legislation. But
these features tend to work on a surface level, while the deeper structure of
such regimes is undemocratic, mainly because it facilitates and promotes
the seizure of territory, resources, and power by one expanding ethnos. It
thus contradicts, as noted, key democratic principles and most severely undermines the existence of the demos—the enjoyment of equal substantive
rights and capabilities by all residents under the auspices of the regime.

The analytical differentiation between features and structure highlights
the selective and manipulative use of the term democracy by the dominant
ethnic group. But the use of a democratic discourse, hollow as it is, has the
effect of legitimizing the regime, especially in the eyes of the majority
group, as evidenced by the cases of Sri Lanka, Australia, and Estonia. The
distinction between features and structure is, of course, not rigid or stable
because of a constant flow of mutual influences. For example, elections can
bring political change at the level of features, but this may lead to structural
change through the accumulation of small reforms in legislation, resource
allocation, and representation. However, during the intense process of state
building, the ethnocratic logic of the regime structure generally dictates

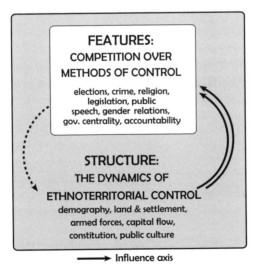

FEATURES:
COMPETITION OVER
METHODS OF CONTROL

elections, crime, religion,
legislation, public
speech, gender relations,
gov. centrality, accountability

STRUCTURE:
THE DYNAMICS OF
ETHNOTERRITORIAL CONTROL
demography, land & settlement,
armed forces, capital flow,
constitution, public culture

⟶ Influence axis

Figure 2.2. Structure and Features of the Ethnocratic Regime: A Conceptual
Framework

the terms of much of what transpires in the more visible arenas of political features.

Ethnocracies thus operate simultaneously in several levels and arenas and create a situation where political struggles are often waged around the state's features, while little is said and relatively few battles are fought over the deeper hegemony that makes its structure and dynamics appear natural and taken for granted. As well articulated by Sassoon (1987, 232), a "moment" of hegemony is marked by "the unquestioned dominance of a certain way of life . . . when a single concept of reality informs society's tastes, morality, customs, religious and political principles. . . ."

The hegemonic order reflects and thus reproduces the interests of the dominant ethnic nation and its leading ethnoclasses by representing the order of things in a distorted manner as legitimate, democratic, and moral and by concealing its oppressive or more questionable aspects. This public perception is maintained by preventing, deflecting, or ridiculing voices that challenge the regime structure, thereby containing public debate to the shallower bounds of regime features.

Given the analytical distinction between features and structure, and drawing on the cases of Sri Lanka, Australia, and Estonia, I have identified several structural bases that constitute the foundation of ethnocratic regimes. These bases form the most critical elements of power centers in the modern state, that is, the chief repositories of power in the existing global political system: demography, violence, territory, economy, law, and culture. The practices of the state and its associated elites in these arenas daily reproduce the dominant hegemony, while usually enjoying the protection offered by the hegemonic barriers imposed on public discourse and political discussion.

The main bases of the ethnocratic regime thus include the following.

- *Demography*: the state's ethnic composition is of utmost importance, achieved chiefly through controls over immigration and citizenship. Rights of entry and membership define political and social boundaries, and the all-important access to political power. In ethnocracies, immigration and citizenship are chiefly determined by affiliation with the dominant ethnic nation.
- *Land and settlement*: land and territory are absolutely central for ethnonational politics. As such, the ownership, use, and development of land, as well as planning and settlement policies, are shaped by the state's project of extending ethnonational control over its (multiethnic) territory.
- *Armed forces*: violent force is critical in assisting the state to maintain (oppressive) ethnonational control over contested regions and resisting groups. To that end, the armed forces (the military, the police), which bear the name of the entire state, are predominantly affiliated with the leading ethnic nation.

- *Capital flow*: while the flow of capital and development is deeply influenced by an "ethnic logic," privileging the dominant ethnoclasses, these market mechanisms are often represented as free or neutral and hence beyond challenge.
- *Constitutional law*: legalism often depoliticizes and legitimizes patterns of ethnic control. Such controls are often premised on redundant, absurd, nonexistent, or only partially functional constitutional settings. These are often presented as the law of the land, and subsequently placed outside the realm of legitimately contested issues.
- *Public culture*: the ethnocratic public space is formulated around a set of cultural and religious symbols, representations, traditions, and practices, which tend to reinforce the narratives of the dominant ethnonational group, while silencing, degrading, or ridiculing contesting cultures or perspectives.

These regime bases, each separately and in varying combinations, powerfully mold ethnic relations in contested territories but are rarely subject to day-to-day or electoral deliberation. When these issues are questioned by resisting groups (say, in Parliament, or through the media) they are usually silenced or ridiculed. But the dominance of the various "truths" behind these regime bases is of course not absolute and may be exposed and resisted as political entrepreneurs exploit the tensions and contradictions in the system, particularly between the declared "democracy" and its substantive discriminatory manifestations. When such topics enter the public arena and become subject to genuine public debate, cracks are likely to appear in the ethnocratic structure. The first to expose and mobilize around such openings are likely to be marginalized minorities.

ETHNOCRACY AND MINORITIES

A hallmark of the ethnocratic system is its ability to maintain the dominance of the leading ethnonational group, which is premised on the exclusion, marginalization, or assimilation of minority groups. But not all minorities are treated equally. Some are constructed as internal, whereas others are marked as external. A critical difference exists between those considered part of the historical, religious, or even genetic community, and others whose presence is portrayed as mere historical coincidence, or as a danger to the security and integrity of the dominant ethnos. These discourses strip external minorities of a means of inclusion into the meaningful collective spaces of institutions of the nation (Penrose 2000).

Ethnocracies are driven, first and foremost, by a sense of collective entitlement among the majority group to control "its" state, and "its" homeland, as part and parcel of what is conceived as a universal right of self-determination. Thus, belonging to the dominant ethnonation is the key to mobility and resources among peripheral groups and a strategy adopted by most immigrant minorities, who tend to distance themselves from indigenous or other external minorities. As such, ethnocratic societies continuously maintain an ethnic project, which, similarly to the racial project identified by Omi and Winant (1994) in American society, attempts to build an informal public image of separate and unequal groups. This image is diffused into most societal arenas (such as public culture, politics, universities, and the economy), causing a long-term reproduction of inequalities.

The leading ethnoclass (also termed the charter or titular group), which is composed of the group that led the drive for national independence, generally forms the state's elites and upper strata. This charter group can thus play a dual game: on the one hand, it articulates a discourse of belonging that incorporates immigrant and peripheral groups not associated with any external or "rival" nation and "invites" them to assimilate into the moral community of the dominant ethnonation, while on the other hand, it uses this very discourse of inclusion and belonging to conceal the uneven effects of its strategies, which often marginalize the immigrants and "deviant" groups economically, culturally, and geographically. It would be a mistake, however, to treat this as a conspiracy; it is rather an expression of broad social interests, generally unarticulated, that privilege social circles that are closest to the ethnonational core. This "natural" process tends to broadly reproduce, though never replicate, patterns of social stratification.

The strategy toward indigenous and/or national minorities, or fragments of rival nations, is generally more openly oppressive. These groups are represented and treated, at best, as external to the ethnonational project, or, at worst, as a subversive threat. As illustrated by the examples of Sri Lanka, Australia, and Estonia, the tenets of self-determination are used only selectively, pertaining to ethnicity and not to an inclusive geographical unit, as required by the basic principles of democratic statehood. Many of the expansionist projects typical to ethnocracies—namely, ethnic settlement, land seizure, cultural dominance, military expansion, or uni-ethnic economic development—encroach into the sphere of local minorities. These projects are often wrapped in a discourse of modernity, progress, and democracy, but the very material reality is unmistakable, entailing minority dispossession and exclusion.

Therefore, minorities are trapped by the ethnocratic regime, either inside the expansionist national project (as are assimilating immigrant groups), or outside the boundaries of the fledgling nation (as are often indigenous, national, or migrant-worker groups). But, as noted above, the two types of entrapment are clearly different, with immigrant minorities joining actively in the ethnocratic project, albeit at an inferior economic and cultural position, while local minorities remain excluded and marginalized. Yet, both types of minorities are trapped in positions that allow them little space to mobilize political or identity projects that threaten, challenge, or subvert the logic of the ethnocratic regime.

However, even this entrapment tends to run its course. The self-representation of most ethnocracies as democratic creates structural tensions, as it requires the state to go beyond lip service and empower minorities with some (though less the equal) formal political powers, economic capabilities, and cultural rights. It is in these cracks and crevices that minorities mobilize, which gives rise to the tensions and conflicts typical of ethnocratic regimes (see also Mann 1999; J. M. Young 2002).

ETHNOCRACY AND POLITICAL INSTABILITY

One of my main theoretical arguments relates to the inherent instability of ethnocratic regimes, which derives from a major contradiction: the ethnocratic state uses the rhetoric, language, institutions, and legal status of a nation-state, but its practices often undermine the foundations of this very political order. This phenomenon is most evident in the creation of structurally unequal citizenship, by the geographical and political rupturing of the demos, and by the ongoing state-sponsored project of expanding and reinforcing disproportionate ethnic control. The accumulating impact of ethnicizing policies tends to exacerbate intergroup tensions, with a potential to destabilize the entire regime.

My intention here is not to enter the diverse and rich discussion over the definition and measurement of political stability beyond noting that I accept the main parameters offered by Lane and Ersson (1991) or McGarry and O'Leary (1995). They see political instability as strongly related to the perception of regime illegitimacy among minorities, which results in a combination of social disorder and breakdown of regime functions. This is often followed by the bypassing of the regime by disgruntled minorities, by increasing forms of political polarization, and by intensifying waves of antigovernmental protest and violence.

In this sense, the ethnocratic model builds on, and critiques, the control model of political stability first offered by Lustick (1979, 1993), and later used by geographers such as Taylor (1994) and Rumley (1999). Lustick's argument pointed usefully to the ability of regimes to maintain stability through a range of control mechanisms, including the construction of hegemonic discourses and institutions and the cooptation and fragmentation of oppositional elements. But here I claim that in ethnocratic regimes such controls are only viable for the short term, leading in the long term to a destabilizing momentum.

The instability of "open" ethnocratic regimes stems from a combination of two of their main attributes: (a) the long-term impact of the spatial, political, and economic expansion of the dominant majority, and the associated control mechanisms exerted over ethnic and national minorities, and (b) the democratic self-representation of the regime. The first factor is quite clear: ethnocratic regimes often exacerbate ethnic tensions and conflicts because they structurally privilege one ethnic nation. As clearly shown in the cases of Sri Lanka, Australia, and Estonia, the dominant group then uses the state apparatus and the international legitimacy accorded to sovereign states to expand its power, resources, and prestige, often at the expense of minorities. In this sense, ethnocratic regimes tend to generate constant tensions between minorities and majorities.

However, minority resistance to control and discrimination is necessary, but not sufficient, to destabilize the regime. It is the semi-open nature of ethnocratic regimes, their partial democratization, and the limited rights extended to minorities that combine to develop, in a complex process, the situation of structural instability. In the short term, partial democratization, and especially the extension of mere procedural measures (such as representation without influence, commonly allowed to minorities in ethnic regimes), may actually prolong the control of the dominant group.

At the same time, the claim to democracy, despite its violation, does enable the development of minority consciousness and political mobilization. Such mobilization typically rallies around the contradictions and tensions embedded in the coterminous existence of limited democratic institutions and procedures and entrenched patterns of ethnic dominance. Such struggles are also likely to draw on the growing importance of human and minority rights in the international political discourse and on the growing institutionalization of democratic norms among the international community. Owing to the strengthening links between international politics and economy, these new arenas can, and do, influence majority-minority relations traditionally perceived as internal (Soysal 2000).

The effectiveness of minority mobilization, however, is generally limited, as it encounters nearly insurmountable cultural, political, economic, and geographical obstacles to full integration and/or equality within the state. Within such settings, "external" minorities have several options, which include assimilation (unlikely in ethnocracies), the intensification of their protest to escalating levels of violence, or the establishment of competing frameworks of governance and resource allocation accompanied by disengagement from the state. The last two courses of action tend to reinforce one another and undermine the political stability of divided states and regions. They have been evident in the cases of Sri Lanka and Australia, but not in Estonia as yet. The difference may lie in the short time period since the establishment of the ethnocratic Estonian state and the possibilities opened up by the European influence for the Russian minority to improve its situation by political means (Hallik 1998). This hope has been abandoned totally by Tamils in Sri Lanka (De Silva 1986).

The susceptibility of such regimes to the surfacing of open ethnic conflict and their chronic instability are powerful engines of political change. Yet, this change may take varying, and at times contrasting, directions. A number of ethnocratic states have responded to these pressures with a series of democratization steps, such as Canada, Belgium, Spain, Greece, Malaysia, and most recently South Africa and Northern Ireland. In most of these states, prospects for stability have been enhanced with the effective decline of ethnocracy. This is evident with the cessation of expansionist ethnic policies, a subsequent decline in the level of ethnic inequalities, and an ongoing process of procedural and substantive democratization.

At the same time, other ethnocracies have reacted to the grievances of marginalized minorities by tightening their control over minorities and by deepening the state's undemocratic ethnic structure. Several other states—such as Israel, Estonia, and Slovakia—have oscillated between the two options, attempting to keep their links with the western democratic world, with the democratization this entails, and concurrently preserve the control of the dominant ethnic group.

The dynamics of ethnocratic regimes should thus be understood as moving along a continuum between the *poles of democratization and ethnicization*. Quite often, no clear direction prevails for long periods, and the state policy agenda may be driven by crises rather than design. A thorough discussion of the possible transition of regimes from ethnocracy to democracy remains outside the scope of this chapter, but clearly it is one of the most urgent challenges facing such regimes.

ETHNOCRACY AND THE HOMELAND

At the heart of ethnocratic project lies the national "homeland," believed to be the birthplace of the nation and the territory on which it ought to establish its collective future. In the current international regime of nation-states—notwithstanding a certain waning in state power as a result of globalization—the connection between national collectivity and "its" homeland constitutes a critical factor in attaining collective power. Given the multilayered history of almost any territory, claims for collective ownership of a homeland often form the basis for the most protracted ethnic conflicts (see Gans 2003; Kaiser 2002; Murphy 2002).

A critical link in the emergence of national movements is the articulation of collective political claims for territorial self-determination. Such claims invariably follow the development of a homeland discourse—a multitude of messages, maps, signs, cultural icons, speeches, and official documents aimed at shaping a particular piece of territory as a national homeland. The territoriality associated with homeland groups shapes a useful analytical distinction between a relatively rigid homeland collective identity as compared to the more flexible and malleable immigrant identities evident among most diaspora communities (see Kymlicka 1995). The homeland then often becomes what Winichakul (1994) defines as a "geobody"—a spatial icon (designed by the shape of the state's map or aspired territory) ceaselessly used and "performed" to gain a sacred status in the national canon. As shown in the next chapters, the map of Israel/Palestine (ironically shaped more by the British and the French colonial powers then the geographical history of the two nations) has assumed the character of such a sacred geobody and has become a notable icon for the mobilization of both Zionists and Palestinians over the very same piece of land.

But the homeland, needless to say, is never a given, immutable, or permanent entity, despite the common rhetoric of popular discourse and national leaders. Its borders, features, and demography have been dynamic, responding to particular needs in specific historical periods. Due to this malleability, the concept of the homeland has also been forcefully utilized and manipulated by national elites to homogenize the population and counter threats of internal division and instability. Ethnic diasporas have also mobilized, thereby strengthening their own identities and often supporting the ethnocratic spatial policies of their brethren in the national homeland.

The prominence of the homeland concept can be traced to the phenomenon of human territoriality, defined as the mobilization of a collectivity for a particular piece of land, over which it attempts to maintain control and toward which it fosters a special bond (see Sack 1986). Territoriality is expressed by the division of "our" and "their" space and by the dynamics of territorial expansion and contraction. Ethnic territoriality has formed a central foundation for nation-building projects since the onset of modern nationalism in the eighteenth century, gaining particular force in ethnocratic societies, where politics and identities are often woven within critical questions of ethnic territorial control.

Nationalism and the Homeland: A Geographic Critique

During the last two decades one of the most important and lively debates in the social sciences and the humanities has dealt with the origins, making, and nature of nationalism. Several leading interpretations offered instrumental, cultural, material, and constructivist accounts for the immense power of nationalism to reshape human history during the last two centuries (see Hobsbawm 1990; Gellner 1983; Anderson 1991; A. D. Smith 2002; Brubaker 1996; Hechter 2000). Notwithstanding the conflicting interpretations, most schools of thought appear to concur on several key assumptions, including the existence of nationalism as one global phenomenon and the ultimate aim of nationalism to merge nation and state. As explained below, these assumptions are questionable when viewed from the perspective of critical political geography.[1]

Despite the breathtaking scope and valuable insights offered by most theories of nationalism, they display several deficiencies, which emanate from their global scope and all-encompassing explanatory ambition. I focus here on three such deficient aspects: the chronic confusion between nations and states, the overlooking of relevant geographic scholarship, and—subsequently—unduly privileging the dynamics of time over space. The critique draws inspiration from the seminal works of Gramsci (1971) and Lefebvre (1991), who perceived nation-building, intra alia, as a sophisticated and highly effective way of expanding the domination of upper strata through discourses and practices of spatial transformation, including conquest, settlement, boundary setting, and development.

First, many theories of nationalism too readily confuse or ignore the critical gap between nation and state. Hence, they tend erroneously to equate the processes of state building with nation building. This is clear from the various definitions of nationalism offered by leading theorists, which emphasize joint political institution, common economy, and shared territory (see, for representative examples, A. D. Smith 1996; Gellner 1996). Scholars such as Smith, Anderson, Hobsbawm, and Gellner are undoubtedly aware of the frequent dominance of one group within the new political community defined as the nation. But these scholars often interpret such a setting as a temporary gap between the historical nation (or "ethnie") and the state. This gap, it is predicted, will close gradually through inclusive political mobilization, growing institutional capacity, and cultural homogenization. As Billig (1995) notes, the legitimacy of the "hyphen" in the term nation-state is now taken as "banal" (for critical views on the relations between nation and state, see Chatterjee 1993; Connor 1994, 2002; Kaufman 2004).[2]

Given this dominant analytical perspective, most social science literature has assumed a priori the (contentious) existence of the nation-state. The research activity of an entire generation of scholars has been based on state statistics, textbooks, maps, and state-based images of society (Hakli 2001). As such, it has legitimized the nation-state construct, in an approach termed by Agnew (1999) "methodological nationalism." But clearly, the nation-state rarely exists as such (Iceland may be a rare exception), and it is always shaped by contested historical-geographical processes. The blurring of nation and state has made most theories of nationalism overlook the abuse of the nation-state model in ethnocratic regimes. These often exploit the international autonomy bestowed on the nation-state, as the principal and protected expression of national self-determination, to facilitate the expanding seizure of territorial, political, and material resources by the dominant ethnic group at the expense of minorities (see Yiftachel 1999a). Hence, ethnocratic regimes simultaneously draw on the legitimacy of the nation-state order but at the same time undermine its major tenets, especially regarding equal citizenship and the inclusion of all groups in the sovereign political community.

The state/nation mismatch leads to a second critique, focusing on the spatial blindness of leading accounts of nationalism. This is expressed by both a relative lack of analysis on the links between space and nationalism and a conspicuous paucity of reference in the main social science literature to a rich tradition of geography and geographers. Social science work on nationalism tends to "flatten" the state's human space, overlooking the dynamic geographical contours of ethnicities, classes, genders, borders, and development, so critical for shaping the nature of political community (Lefebvre 1991). These dynamic spatialities often run across, below, or above the putative, flat, and stable national territory (see Herb and Kaplan 1999; Newman and Paasi 1998; D. Newman 2004; Penrose 2000; Taylor 1994, 2001). Therefore, the analysis of national movements must hinge on the understanding of active space, which is not merely a backdrop or a container of social change but exerts itself as a vital influence on group identities and relations. The links between space, development, collective identities, and group relations are thus reciprocal (Jackson and Penrose 1993). That is, while political processes create spatial outcomes, these outcomes, in turn, create new political dynamics.

In particular, we must perceive space as a key factor in the generation and reproduction of collective identities. Group spatiality may include the degree of ethnic concentration or mix, the group territoriality, its proximity to interstate brethren, the degree of its peripherality, and the process of "territorial socialization" involved in its identity construction (Murphy 2002). These factors exert a decisive influence on group identity, shaping collective memories, cultural norms, accents, networks, accessibility to material and symbolic resources, socioeconomic status, and position vis-à-vis the Others. Hence the very materiality of the struggle over space ceaselessly shapes the social, ethnic, and national landscapes (Paasi 2000; Keith and Pile 1993).

Finally, I argue that leading theories of nationalism often privilege the dynamics of time over space. This is a common theme, illustrated by the dominance of historical work and the recent preoccupation with the question of national origins, memory, and temporal transformation in identity and ideology.[3] While most scholars do refer occasionally to territory and homeland, it is likened to a passive nest of the nation, not an active determinant of national trajectory and identity (see Anderson 1991, 11–12 or A. D. Smith 1995, 10).

National time, history, and memory are indeed central to the making of national movements (see Anderson 1991; Greenfeld 1992; Brubaker 1996; Hutchinson 2000; A. D. Smith 2002). Yet, national time, so prominent in these works, can never be divorced from the ongoing construction of a material-geographic national homeland. National history is made by a ceaseless interweaving of time and space, shaped by the "grids of power" ever present in the making of spaces and places (Massey 1993). Hence, there can be no credible account of historical development without fathoming the thick enmeshment of political processes within places, spaces, and territories, which combine to produce the national homeland. Homeland making is hence both a geographical and political process and a central axis in the daily reproduction of national consciousness.

In ethnocratic states this is even more pronounced, given the great emphasis placed by such regimes on the ethnicization of contested territory.

The link between geography and political power thus becomes a central grid of such a regime, empowering members of the in group to control space, thereby essentializing group identities and fueling the drive to exclude and marginalize minorities. Therefore, as noted above, the political project of such movements is rarely driven by a will to merge nation and state, as portrayed by leading theories of nationalism. Quite the opposite— they attempt to keep alive the tension between ethnonational belonging and formal citizenship as a form of legitimizing further ethnic expansion and segregation. In ethnocratic societies, space, then, is not only active but also dynamic. It constantly produces new ethnic geographies and thus new conditions for socialization and mobilization. In such societies space becomes a main kernel of national identity, as clearly shown in the case of Israel/Palestine.

In overview, then, we must regard the concept of the homeland as a most powerful mobilizer of the collective politics in most modern states and nation building. It may be useful here to draw an analytical distinction between three prototypes: (a) a civic homeland, which regards all citizens as fully belonging regardless of their ethnic background; (b) a cultural homeland, which conditions full membership on cultural assimilation; and (c) an ethnocratic homeland, which claims the state to be the homeland of one group only.[4] The first and second types have the potential to create an inclusive sense of collective territoriality, with the first tending to be more liberal, hence "privatized" substate identities, while the second attempts to build a common republican identity (see Habermas 2001). These two types, despite notable differences, especially on multiculturalism, tend to create a popular sense of patriotism, that is an inclusive attachment to the homeland (see Viroli 1995).[5] The third type—the ethnocratic homeland—is driven by an opposite force, a desired seizure of the entire territory by one ethnic group at the exclusion or inferior incorporation of minorities and immigrants.

Looking Ahead

This chapter presented a framework for an ethnocratic theory, showing that in certain geographical and historical circumstances, various forces combine to create such regimes. The chapter focused on "open" ethnocracies, where the state represents itself as democratic, while simultaneously facilitating the seizure of a contested territory (claimed as homeland) and polity by the dominant ethnic nation. It outlined the structure of such regimes; analyzed the mechanisms used to maintain ethnic dominance; discussed their relation with minorities, democracy, and political instability; and explored the tensions and contradictions that generate their decline and transformation. The various elements, flows, and transformations are summarized in Figure 2.3, which forms the framework for the analysis of the chapters that follow.

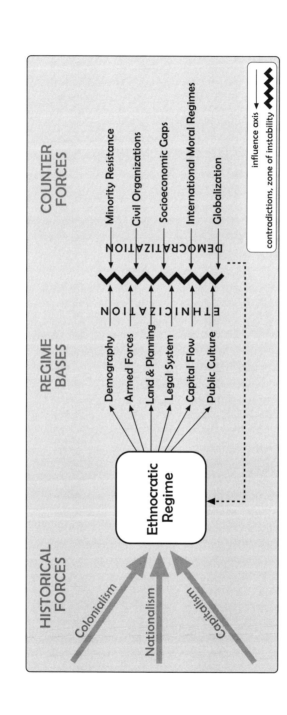

Figure 2.3. The Ethnocratic Regime: Forces, Bases, and Counterforces

The framework presented here is both broad and preliminary. Clearly, it needs to be tested, challenged, and expanded in order to gain depth, validity, and robustness. Such efforts can advance in various directions, including: (a) comparative research that would test, calibrate, and modify the assertions made above; (b) in-depth case studies, which would study the more detailed and subtle forms of ethnocratic expansion and hegemony, as well as the forms of resistance and challenge to the system; and (c) theoretical explorations and modifications, especially vis-à-vis new structural forces influencing the nation-state, such as the increasingly globalizing world economy, and/or the growing force and influence of the discourse of human rights and multiculturalism. The following chapters will attempt to advance all three goals, although the in-depth exploration of Israel/Palestine will form the book's main thrust. But first, I will focus on a most central element to the construction of an ethnocratic society—control of the homeland, to which I now turn.

Part II
Ethnocracy and Territory in Israel/Palestine

Chapter 3

Zionist and Palestinian Nationalism: The Making of Territorial Identities

> *The Land of Israel was the birthplace of the Jewish people. Here its spiritual, religious, and political identity was shaped. Here it first attained statehood, created cultural values of national and universal significance. . . . After being forcibly exiled from their land, the people kept faith with it throughout their diaspora and never ceased to pray and hope for their return. . . . By virtue of our natural and historic right . . . we hereby declare the establishment of a Jewish state in the Land of Israel.*
>
> —Israel's Declaration of Independence, May 15, 1948[1]

> *Palestine . . . is where the Palestinian Arab people was born, on which it grew, developed and exceled. . . . [Its] willed dispossession and expulsion . . . was achieved by organized terror. In Palestine and in exile, the Palestinian Arab people never faltered and never abandoned its conviction in its rights of return and independence . . . and the right of sovereignty over territory and homeland. . . . The Palestinian National Council . . . hereby declares the establishment of the State of Palestine on our Palestinian territory. . . .*
>
> —Palestinian Declaration of Independence, November 15, 1988[2]

This chapter opens the book's second part, devoted to the political geography of the Land of Israel/Palestine. This territory (*Eretz Yisrael* and *Filastin*—in Hebrew and Arabic, respectively) stretches over an area demarcated by the British as "Palestine" in 1922. Over the years, it has been subject to multiple national and religious claims, drawing on rivaling interpretations of historical origins (the "when") and place (the "where") of collective identities. During the last one hundred years, the land has become associated with a bitter struggle between Zionist Jews and Palestinian Arabs, both claiming the territory to be their own national homeland. The population of Israel/Palestine at the end of 2002 was 9.9 million, of whom 52 percent were ethnic Jews, 46 percent Palestinian Arabs, and 2 percent other groups (CBSa 2003).

The chapter has two main goals: (a) to account for the struggle between

Zionists and Palestinians over Israel/Palestine and thus provide a historical-geographical background for the proceeding chapters; and (b) to draw on the earlier theoretical discussion and examine the significance of territory to the identities and politics of both nations. The chapter shows that because of the inconclusive territorial struggle, territory has become the main—though by no means sole—shaper of Zionist and Palestinian identities. As noted earlier, this runs counter to the thrust of leading theories on nationalism, which generally privilege national time, culture, or economy over the dynamics and intricacies of collective space.

The territorial emphasis is well illustrated by the Israeli and Palestinian Declarations of Independence quoted above, both of which place great importance in grounding their national claims and identities in a specific location, thereby embodying their histories, memories, cultures, religions, and desired futures.

Beyond local details, the present chapter also offers a better understanding of the conditions giving rise to ethnocratic regimes. Contrary to most understandings of the modern nation (see A. D. Smith 1995, 2002; Anderson 1991), the ethnocratic national project, especially in settler societies, does not aspire to merge nation and state but attempts to essentialize and segregate group identities. In such conditions, the chapter shows, the ethnocratic nation and its opposing collectivities place increasing weight to the "where" rather than the "when" of its narratives and practices.

Conceptions of national time (that is, origins and history), and hence time/space interactions, remain highly important in Israel/Palestine, but over the course of the conflict these have tended to become mythical and homogenous. The "when" of the Zionist and Palestinian narratives provides both sides with rigid historical accounts geared to justify their claims to temporal priority (and hence legitimacy) in their current territorial aspirations. Consequently, many of the political, cultural, and practical emphases of Zionist and Palestinian nation building have been shaped by an acre-by-acre struggle for land control.

The territorial thrust has spawned another transformation: during the last three decades, the heart of the conflict has shifted from a previous preoccupation with history and the sufferings of Jewish *galut* (exile, diaspora) and Palestinian *manfah* or *ghourba* (dispersion, estrangement) to a focus on contemporary political spaces shaped by the people living in Israel/Palestine itself. Consequently, the main feature of the conflict during the last three decades has pitted expansive Jewish settlement *(hityashvut, hitnahalut)* against Palestinian resistance and steadfastness *(sumud)*. With these broad observations in mind, we move now to a more detailed account of the rise of nationalism in Israel/Palestine.

The Palestinian-Zionist Conflict: From Time to Space

HISTORICAL ROOTS: DIASPORAS, COLONIALISM, AND A CONTESTED HOMELAND

Both Zionists and Palestinians claim priority status, which—in their own narratives—grants them a higher moral claim for contemporary control over Israel/Palestine. The Jews draw on the divine promises contained in ancient Jewish texts, on the actual reign of biblical Hebrew kingdoms over the territory, on a myth of forced eviction, and on continuous spiritual connection to the land. The Palestinians concentrate on their unbroken residence on and cultivation of the land, on their recent (partial) expulsion and dispossession, and on their current status as a stateless nation.

The ancient biblical golden age of Hebrew kingdoms, as well as their defeat and dispersal, provide vivid images for constructing the historical narrative of contemporary Zionists. Yet historical sources show that following the last defeat of their kingdoms (associated with the destruction of the Second Temple in 70 A.D.), Hebrews remained on the Land of Israel in relatively large numbers for centuries (and were not forcefully evicted from the land, as the Zionist narrative claims). At the same time, other Hebrews emigrated and formed a chain of diaspora Jewish communities in Middle Eastern, North African, and European countries (Shor 1998, 158–67).

Over the ensuing centuries Jews maintained a spiritual and religious connection to the land, mainly through an intergenerational cultivation of collective memories, texts, and myths that often glorified the promised land. In recent years, Palestinians have also begun to construct ancient narratives of belonging to the land, focusing on their historical links with the Canaanite and Jebusite tribes believed to have resided on the land prior to the Hebrew biblical conquest (see al-Hout 1991; Segal at al. 2001).

In later periods, the Land of Israel/Palestine was conquered by the Greek, Assyrian, Roman, Persian, Arab, Crusader, Byzantine, and Ottoman empires. The name Palestine derives from the Roman title for the province, Palestina, which in turn was based on the supposed location of the biblical Philistine people. The people known today as Palestinians are probably a mixture of groups (Hebrew tribes and other communities) who remained on the land, converted to Christianity and Islam, and were later joined by migrants of Arab descent (Doumani 1995).

The Ottoman Empire conquered the land in 1516 and ruled for four hundred years. At the end of the nineteenth century, the population of the area was estimated to be half a million, of whom 6 percent were Jews. It was during this period that both Jewish and Palestinian movements began to emerge. Jews were profoundly affected by the ethnonational, often anti-Semitic, nationalism appearing in central and eastern Europe (where most of them lived), as well as by the assimilating emancipation promised in the more liberal West. Both anti-Semitism and assimilation posed serious threats to Jewish collective existence, either through exclusion and physical oppression or through the new openings into previously impregnable paths of societal integration and assimilation.

Zionism emerged in late nineteenth-century Europe as a direct response to these threats. It encouraged Jews to immigrate to the remembered Land of Israel as a form of *collective survival*. The nascent Zionist movement sought to compete with other (more popular) movements, such as the Bund, which called for Jewish autonomy in Europe, or with mass Jewish migration to the West. Its efforts, however, were largely unsuccessful, as the early Zionists remained a small minority among world Jewry. In 1914, for example, only sixty thousand Jews were living in Israel/Palestine, comprising less than 1 percent of the world's Jewry and about 8 percent of the local population (Khalidi 1997). In general, immigration of Jews to Palestine proceeded almost only when Jews faced pressing circumstances and were denied the option of immigrating to the West (Dellapergola 1992).

Time-space interactions became crucial for Zionism. It was embodied in the perception that resurrecting Jewish *history* is only possible in the *Land* of Israel. But given the very pressing, practical territorial and economic agendas of early Zionists, the historical origins of Jewish nationalism quickly became mythical and homogenous, rarely subject to open debate over the dynamic and diverse national past(s). For example, the study of Jewish antiquities and archaeologies was, in the main, a tool for validating present Jewish colonization rather than for prompting genuine interest in national histories and trajectories (Abu al-Haj 2001). National time became, in effect, ahistorical, providing a unified, linear, and repeatedly recited backdrop for contemporary practices of territorial expansion (Zerubavel 1995). The aims and energies of the Zionist movement became territorial par excellence: purchase land, attract immigrants, build cities, develop agriculture, establish industries, settle colonies, and launch an international struggle for Jewish political sovereignty (see Morris 1999). From an early period, then, space, place, and territory became the kernels of the Zionist project.

But as Shafir (1989) notes, Zionist space was to be "pure," attempting to maximize both Jewish control and exclusivity—territorial, economic, and social. A corollary move was to represent the country (Eretz Yisrael, the Jewish homeland) as *terra nullius*—an empty land awaiting its Jewish redemption after centuries of neglect. Zionists thus coined the now infamous idiom: "a people without land to a land without a people." The territorial double strategy (create a new Zionist nation while denying the legitimate existence of Palestinian nationalism) remained the main Zionist strategy until the early 1990s. It illustrated both the prevalence of spatial control as a major national goal and the effective use of nation-state imagery of ethnic self-determination

(Jewish state in Eretz Yisrael) to seize a contested territory and marginalize its indigenous population. This is starkly evident from the continuous Zionist effort to settle Jews in all parts of Israel/Palestine. This has formed one of the fundamental projects of contemporary Jewish nationalism, with a profound effect on the geography of the land (Figure 3.1).

In parallel, the Palestinian national movement was also surfacing. During the twilight of Ottoman rule, Palestinians lived as a typical Middle Eastern agrarian society, spread over 950 villages and a dozen urban centers and undergoing gradual modernization and urbanization (Doumani 1995). The Arabs of Palestine started to form a collective consciousness, mainly inspired by an Arab national "awakening" resonating throughout the region and by a common local culture shaped through centuries of settling and working the land (see Abu Manneh 1978; Khalidi 1997; Salih 1988).

In 1917 Britain conquered the land and issued the Balfour Declaration, which promised to facilitate a "Jewish national home" in Palestine, but remained careful not to mention a Jewish state or to sacrifice the rights of local populations. The land was renamed Palestine and its (still current) boundaries were demarcated for the first time (Brawer 1988). The new territory, which does not overlap any known space in either Jewish or Arab history, quickly became embedded in the collective imaginations of the two national movements. "Palestine" began to define the Palestinians (its Arab inhabitants), but the same unit also became "Eretz Yisrael"—no longer an abstract and vague icon present in Jewish myth and prayer but a concrete, bounded territory to be claimed and seized (see Kimmerling 1983; Naor 2001).

Following the demarcation of Palestine in 1921, and after a short attempt to join a Syrian-led national project, the Palestinians began to focus their consciousness on a collective claim to the land. This was facilitated by the 1916 Hussein-McMahon correspondence in which Britain also committed itself to assist the establishment of an Arab state in the region (Morris 1999). It is likely that, in the absence of Jewish immigration to the land, Palestinians would have formed a typical anticolonial national movement similar to the cases of Egypt or Syria. Palestinian nationalism was developing, then, with a strong territorial focus. However, it was markedly different from the Zionist engagement with territory. Whereas the Palestinians saw their collective territorial identity as inclusive (that is, all people residing in Palestine were considered Palestinians, including "pre-Zionist" Jews), Zionists only regarded Jewish newcomers as part of the nation. Palestinian nationalism was, then, on course to develop incrementally as a modernizing territorial-political organization typical to in situ collectivities.

However, this was not to be, with Jews increasing their immigration to Palestine during the third, fourth, and fifth decades of the twentieth century. Between the two world wars Zionism became an organized colonial settler society, supported by international Jewish organizations, which purchased Palestinian lands for the purpose of Jewish settlement, agriculture, and

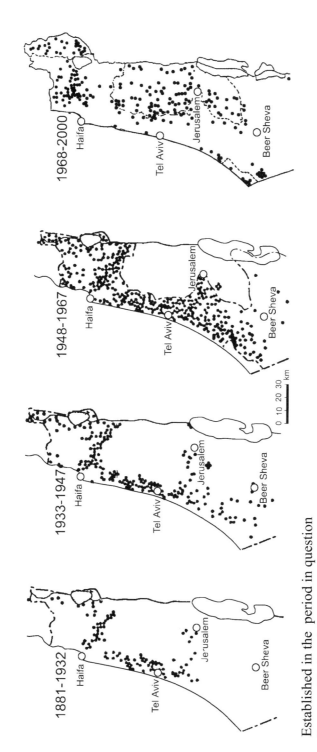

Established in the period in question
Source: Updated from Newman 1996.

Figure 3.1. The Progression of Jewish Settlement in Israel/Palestine, 1881–2000

industry. Still, aside from a small group of Zionist ideologues, most Jews arriving in Palestine were refugees or immigrants in search of a safe haven. This combination of an ideology of national revival/liberation in the ancient homeland and the need to shelter stateless Jews shaped the characteristics of the early Zionist endeavor as a colonialism of ethnic survival now with a specific claim to a Jewish state in Palestine.

During the 1920s and 1930s, the Land of Israel/Palestine was shaped as what was defined in the previous chapter as a geobody—a powerful symbolic spatial icon held by most national movements (see Hakli 2001; Paasi 2000; Winichakul 1994). To date, the identical map of the Land of Israel/Palestine functions as the clearest collective code and mobilizing image, used commonly by Jews and Palestinians in official and unofficial maps, on shirts, murals, and pamphlets, and in political publications. Since the British Mandate period, then, the Zionist-Palestinian struggle became an all-consuming race for territorial control. The spatial practices and ideologies of each movement profoundly influenced the other, in what Portugali (1993) termed "implicate relations." The goals of land control also became a major axis to guide the nation-building efforts of the two communities, culturally, economically, and politically. Around that time, territory aspired to become the kernel of the two national movements.

The collective memory of centuries of Jewish persecution and the immediate dangers emanating from Arab political and violent opposition also shaped Zionism as a particularly intransigent colonial movement. Its major goal was to "Judaize" the land and "indigenize" its Jewish inhabitants. But this was represented as a form of (anticolonial) liberation, not conquest, thereby gaining internal Jewish legitimacy and international support. Therefore, from the early years, Zionism developed a dual identity. On the one hand, it evolved as a colonial project, attempting to maximize landholding and economic strength in the new colonies. On the other, it presented itself as anticolonial, attempting to "liberate" the homeland from the British in order to build a Jewish state (see Shohat 2001, 237–38).

The unfolding nature of the Zionist project spawned increasing Arab opposition, culminating in the 1936–39 "Arab revolt," which erupted over the growing Zionist threat to the Palestinian homeland (Said 1994; Salih 1988). The revolt was brutally put down by the British, who exiled much of the Palestinian leadership and imposed harsher controls over their political rights. The three-year revolt exerted a high economic, communal, and political price, disrupting Palestinian nation building and political institutionalization (Khalidi 1997). This occurred despite the attainment of some policy concessions, such as greater British control over Jewish immigration and land purchase. However, the main goal of the Arab revolt—halting the Zionist project—was frustrated as the clouds of murderous anti-Semitism were closing on Europe and Zionism was perceived as a highly moral rescue movement of a besieged, homeless, people.

As far as the Palestinians were concerned though, the righteousness of Zionism and the tragic plight of European Jews mattered little; Jews were perceived as foreigners whose presence in the land violated the natural rights of Palestinians (Said 1993, 1996). Palestinian suspicion was also fueled by the highly segregated manner in which Jewish society developed, separating itself almost totally from local Palestinians. This ethos of collective survival-revival, with an Orientalist colonial attitude typical to Europeans in settler societies (Shafir 1989), created a dual society, manifested in separate residential areas, education systems, cultural milieu, labor markets, and political organizations.

The rule of Hitler in Germany and the atrocities committed by the Nazis during the Holocaust (the Shoah) saw Jewish refugee migration to the land accelerating. For Zionists, the Holocaust illustrated the ultimate need to build a Jewish national state, and it reinforced the zeal and militancy of Zionist colonizers. The Holocaust also solidified the Zionist construction of the Jewish diaspora as a timeless void, a disastrous black hole outside history, leading to Jewish resurrection only in the Jews' own homeland. This view reinforced the territorial nature of the Zionist project (see Raz-Krakotzkin 1993).

Consequently, in 1947 there were already 610,000 Jews in Palestine, constituting 32 percent of the country's population. Jewish land holdings were more modest, covering 8 percent, mainly along the coastal plain and the northern valleys. That year, the United Nations proposed a partition of the land, awarding 55 percent of Palestine to the Jews, although this included the sparsely populated (and mainly Bedouin Arab) southern desert as land for the future absorption of Jewish refugees. The UN proposal was accepted by the Jews after a fierce debate but rejected by most Palestinian leaders and Arab states. A war broke out, during which some Arab forces fought alongside local Palestinians in an attempt to destroy the Zionist entity (Morris 1987).

The 1948 war, known to Jews as the War of Independence and to Palestinians as the Disaster (al-Naqbah), became a watershed in the territorial struggle over the land and the shaping of national identities. Jewish forces, better organized, trained, and equipped, managed to enlarge their territorial holdings, and at the end of the fighting they controlled 78 percent of the Land of Palestine/Land of Israel as defined by the British and the United Nations. Moreover, some 700,000–750,000 Palestinians fled or were driven out of the land by Jewish forces, and more than 420 Palestinian villages were demolished (Morris 1987; Khalidi 1997). A few thousand Jews also became refugees, finding haven in the main Jewish concentrations. The remaining parts of Palestine were conquered by Jordan (the West Bank) and Egypt (Gaza Strip) (see Figure 3.2).

The overall result amounted to a massive ethnic cleansing, whereby most Palestinians became refugees, dispersed throughout the Middle East and

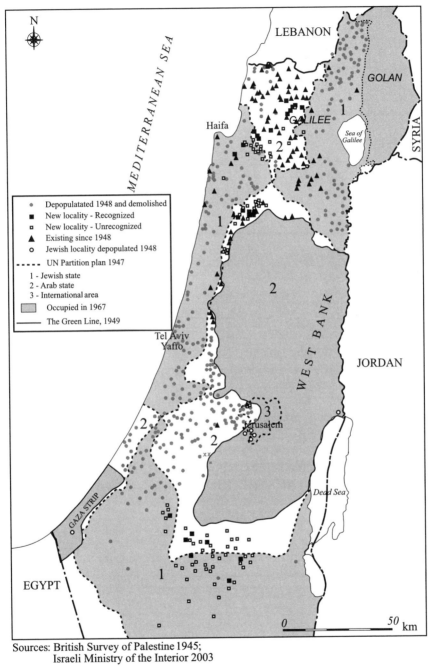

Legend:
- Depopulatated 1948 and demolished
- New locality - Recognized
- New locality - Unrecognized
- Existing since 1948
- Jewish locality depopulated 1948
- UN Partition plan 1947
  - 1 - Jewish state
  - 2 - Arab state
  - 3 - International area
- Occupied in 1967
- The Green Line, 1949

Sources: British Survey of Palestine 1945;
Israeli Ministry of the Interior 2003

Figure 3.2. Shifting Borders and Palestinian Localities in Israel

beyond, and were prevented from returning to their homes once the war ended. The Palestinian Naqbah, as well as the Jewish Shoah, became deeply etched in the collective memories of the two national movements as ultimate examples of their victimhood and righteousness.[3] The development of Zionist and Palestinian identities has since remained framed by the memories of immense collective losses, which formed a central spine of their collective narratives.

In terms of time/space conceptualizations, we can pause here and interrogate the "ethnically pure" image of the ideal nation-state, which has spawned both the UN partition plan and the disastrous events that ensued. Ethnic control over space and the "purification" of this space became the prime goal, buttressed by strong feelings of historical mission and justice. Notably, both Zionist and Palestinian discourses at the time aspired to enter history by achieving their own state; that is, *entering history through territory*. This illustrates that modern nationalism, propelled by the myth of the pure nation-state, inherently harbors the possibility of ethnic cleansing in situations of mixed geography.

In this context, space becomes paramount because it provides a concrete, achievable goal, and at the same time it distances rivaling groups from realizing their competing national-territorial agendas. Seizing and claiming sovereignty over contested space is closely tied to the denial of other claims to that space; that is, the Other's history, place, and political aspirations are presented as a menacing package to be rejected thoroughly. Indeed, in the following decades Israel attempted systematically to deny the existence of a Palestinian nation, constantly referring to Palestinian geographical dispersal and lack of past political independence in Palestine to refute Palestinian territorial claims (see Khalidi 1997).

The Israeli Ethnocracy: Judaization and Stratification, 1948–67

Following the 1948 war Israel was established formally as a democracy, with a parliamentarian system and with formal citizenship extended to all residents in the territory defined by the 1949 armistice lines (Figure 3.2). But at the same time, it evolved into a Jewish settling ethnocracy by launching demographic, geographic, and cultural strategies for the rapid Judaization of this territory. The structure of the Israeli regime and the rich and complex implications it had for intra-Jewish social and ethnic relations are discussed in detail in the following chapter. The focus here is on the main transformations necessary to understand the ongoing relations between Zionism, Palestinian nationalism, and the geography of Israel/Palestine.

As a Jewish state, Israel enacted the Law of Return, which allowed any Jews to immigrate to the country, thereby prolonging indefinitely the duration of the Judaization project. Simultaneously, during the first few years of independence, the state demolished more than four hundred Palestinian villages, nationalized Palestinian lands, and further confiscated large tracts of lands from the remaining Palestinian Arab population (Kedar 1998). At the same time, Jewish immigrants and refugees continued to pour into the country, increasing its population fourfold within the first decade of independence (or, in other words, replacing the Palestinian refugees whose total number was similar to that of Jewish newcomers by 1952). It should be remembered, however, that nearly all Jews arriving in Israel during that period were either refugees who had survived the Holocaust or emigrants from the Muslim world who were largely coerced by hostile Arab and Muslim regimes (augmented by Zionist activities) to leave their countries and who had little option but to settle in Israel (see Shiblak 1986; Shohat 2001).

This period illustrates one of the central points of this chapter, namely the elevation of space to an all-assuming kernel of national identity constructed through territorial struggle and socialization (Newman and Paasi, 1998). For Zionist culture, the "frontier" became a central icon, and its settlement was considered one of the highest achievements of any Jew. The frontier *kibbutzim* (collective rural villages) provided a model, and the reviving Hebrew language was filled with positive images drawn from religious myths of national redemption, such as *aliya lakarka* (literally "ascent to the land," i.e., settlement), *ge'ulat karka* (land redemption), *hityashvut* and *hitnahalut* (positive biblical terms for Jewish settlement), *kibbush hashmama* (conquest of the desert), and *hagshama* (literally "fulfillment" but denoting the settling of the frontier; for details see Yiftachel 1996, 1999b).

The glorification of the frontier was central to the construction of a "new Jew"—an ever ready settler-fighter who conquers the land with his physical strength and endless poetic love (Almog 1997). As shown well by Raz-Krakotzkin (1993) and Kimmerling (2001), the construction of the new Zionist Jew was premised on building a settling and militaristic national identity in negation and denial of two prominent Others—diaspora Jews and the local Arabs. The following song from Yoram Tahar-Lev, one of the most popular Zionist song writers, exemplifies the ethos of knowing, walking, settling, loving, and staking a claim to the land as a way of creating the new Zionist Jew.

Arise and Walk Through the Land

Arise and walk through the land
With backpack and stick
You'll surely find on the way
To the Land of Israel again.
The paths of the good land will embrace you.
She will call you as if to a bed of love.
And the groves of olive trees,
The hidden spring,
Still guard its dream,

Our ancient dream.
And red roofs on a hill
And children on the paths
In that place where we walked
With backpack and stick.
(Tehar-Lev 1980)

During the same period Palestinians were gradually emerging from the
1948 defeat and dispersal, and they began the task of rebuilding their national movement. This project had to overcome several major difficulties,
including the disenfranchised and stateless status of most Palestinians,
their geographical and political dispersion, the urgent economic and social needs of the refugees, the continuing denial by Israel of their collective
and individual rights, and the oppressive rule of most Arab governments
(Khalidi 1997; Tamari 1991).

   Like the Zionists, Palestinians expressed much of their sentiments in popular songs, which were quickly diffused as one of the main spines to hold up
a national spirit in the difficult conditions. Some Palestinian songs of that
period display a depth of desperation, mourning the lost land and shat-
tered collective life, and longing for a return. Another prominent type displayed a more militant call for uprising, struggle, and revenge. During the
same period, Rashed Hussein, a national poet, expressed national despair
by writing "My Palestine." The painful words were later turned into a song
and popularized throughout the Arab world by Abdullah al-Rawsheed.

My Palestine
My Palestine
I am one who will be livened by death.
I am one who chose the sunlight.
I shall die, but my death will bring me back to life,
My Palestine, my Palestine

I shall carry my soul on my palm
And throw it into the abyss of death.
My life will delight friends,
But my death will enrage enemies.

I shall encompass my land,
And for the al-Aqsa mosque
I shall sell my life and years.
I shall die and my death will bring me back to life
(Husscin 1965 quoted in Boullata and Ghossein 1979)

Fairuz, the enormously popular Lebanese singer of Palestinian origin, was
famous for devoting many of her songs to Palestine. Fairuz reflected and
created broad sentiments among the Palestinians about the loss of land

and the drive for return. Below is a famous song from the mid-1960s representing the more militant line:

Draw Your Swords!
Draw your swords! And blow the trumpets!
Now, now and not tomorrow!
Our bells of return will ring.
I shall never forget you, Palestine,
And your lands pull me, they pull me.
I am under your shadow, Nasrin.[4]
I am a flower, a thorn, and a rose.

We shall knock, we shall knock on the walls.
We shall receive the laurel leaf
And return the families to their homes.
Wiping fire with fire
The trumpets will blow aloud.
The bells will ring
For the stormy blood of the liberators.
(Fairuz and Rahbani 1960s)

During the 1960s Palestinian national activity was beginning to emerge in several Arab centers, most prominently in Egypt, which supported the 1964 establishment of the Palestine Liberation Organization (PLO). The PLO, which became the umbrella Palestinian organization, began during the 1960s to launch an armed struggle against Israel, with several raids against Israeli infrastructure facilities. The PLO's activities during that period were sporadic and had little impact on Israeli population or property.

The Palestinians remaining in Israel were totally separated during the 1948–67 period from their brethren abroad and were isolated in small geographical enclaves governed by military rule. Jewish settlements surrounded their localities, while more than half their private lands were confiscated by the state. But here, too, national resistance began to emerge during the 1950s and 1960s, most prominently among the Communist Party and the al-Ard (the land) movement, which effectively mobilized Arab youth and was subsequently outlawed by Israel in 1964 (Rouhana 1997; Zureik 1979).

Despite its "objective" weakness and geographical fragmentation, Palestinian collective identity began at this stage to display several distinct characteristics, centering around Palestinian dispossession, the land, and the struggle for its protection and liberation. The total belief in the superior national right over Israel/Palestine was a major driving force. This led to the emergence and glorification of key national-cultural symbols such as al-fida'i (the freedom fighter), al-balad (the village), al-falah (the farmer), al-ard (the land), al-zayt (the olive tree), and al-watten (the homeland). The main goals were articulated as al-awda (the return of the refugees), al-tahrir (national liberation), and al-istiqlal (national independence). These were disseminated through fledgling literature, poetry, and political discourses, which made constant use of national symbols (see Paramenter 1994). We can hence note, again, how national identity is reshaped through territorial conflict, and how laden it is with signs of active space, vis-à-vis a frozen notion of national time, to be recaptured only if space is fully controlled.

The renewal of collective Palestinian consciousness was impeded by competing political agendas, most notably pan-Arabism, and by the hostility toward Palestinian nationalism displayed by most relevant political powers, namely Israel, the West, and the Arab states (see Said 1993; Tamari 1991). Nevertheless, Palestinians did manage to regenerate a measure of national consciousness, albeit still weak and fragmented (see al-Budeiri 1998), centering around the PLO and the relished values that sustained the notion of homeland and liberation (Said 1993).

What followed soon was a further dramatic territorial transformation of Israel/Palestine. In 1967 Israel conquered vast Arab territories, including the West Bank, Gaza, the Sinai Peninsula, and the Golan Heights. This established the rule of the Jewish ethnocracy over the majority of Palestinians and over the entire territory of Israel/Palestine. The 1967 war also enabled the initiation of further Jewish settlement, this time in occupied territory, in violation of international law and the Geneva Convention. The major 1973 Arab-Israeli war in Sinai and the Syrian Golan left little mark on the Palestinian territories, but a new wave of Jewish settlement soon began to change their ethnic geography thoroughly, and with it the nature of the Zionist-Palestinian conflict.

Jewish Expansion and Palestinian Resistance, 1967–87: Settlement (Hitnahalut) vs. Steadfastness (Sumud)

A decade after the conquest of the occupied territories, the Israeli ethnocracy reached its peak. Following the 1977 rise to power of the rightist Menahem Begin and his Likud Party, Israeli policies began to create "irreversible facts on the ground" and prevent the possibility of the redivision of Israel/Palestine. The most conspicuous manifestation was the massive settlement program in the West Bank and to a lesser extent in the Gaza Strip. The rhetoric of Jewish survival was used once again and manipulated to justify the new settlement project on grounds of enhancing national security. The new settlers, many of whom aligned with rightist religious groups, also argued for the necessity of biblical lands to be settled as the "bedrock of Jewish national identity" (Newman and Herman 1992; Masalha 2000). Settlement was now placed in the midst of Palestinian population centers. Ancient Jewish time was thrust again into contemporary political moves by settling Jews at biblical sites, thereby shaping anew the nature of Zionist and Palestinian geographies and identities (see Figures 3.1 and 3.2).

The peace treaty signed with Egypt during the late 1970s ostensibly marked an opposite trend of Jewish contraction, including withdrawal from occupied territories (the Sinai Peninsula) and the significant self-dismantling of Jewish colonial settlements—for the first time in Zionist history. Yet the struggle over Israel/Palestine never genuinely included the Sinai. On the contrary, the peace with Egypt—the most powerful Arab state—actually enabled Israel to deepen its settlement and territorial control over Palestinian territories, particularly in the West Bank. It also allowed Israel to launch the 1982 Lebanon war, officially in reply to Palestinian attacks on Israel's northern border, but with the clear aim of destroying the PLO and dampening Palestinian hopes for consolidating a nation and achieving statehood in Palestine.

One of the most notorious incidents of the war—the massacre of hundreds of Palestinians in Sabra and Shatila Camps in Beirut by Christian-Lebanese militias supported by Israel—remains etched as a milestone in the sorry collective memory of Palestinian suffering and hence in Palestinian identity and mobilization. The impact of the Lebanon war on the politics of Palestine/Israel was not immediate; yet, in the long term it appears to have changed the course of events fundamentally. Israel not only failed to annihilate the exiled PLO leadership (thereby furthering its status) but was openly exposed as launching an aggressive war. This caused new and deep rifts between Israel's Arab and Jewish citizens, as well as within the increasingly polarized Jewish community (see Helman 1999).

Not satisfied with the slow initial pace of Jewish resettlement in the West Bank, the Israeli government initiated a new strategy in the early 1980s. In an attempt to attract middle-class suburbanites, it offered subsidized housing in new, well-designed localities located on confiscated Palestinian lands. These were situated in the occupied territories but in near proximity to the metropolitan areas of Tel Aviv and Jerusalem (Newman 1996). As shown in Table 3.1, the combined push and pull factors worked to increase quickly the number of Jewish settlers in the West Bank, which reached 129,000 by the end of the Likud's second term in 1984.

Massive Jewish settlement also created large segments in Jewish society with firm vested interests in the continued occupation of the territories. Jewish control and settlement in the territories also caused a major change in the representation of space: in the late 1970s Israel erased the Green Line (the 1949 armistice lines and the state's internationally recognized border) from official maps, atlases, and state publications. Despite certain remnants of the old border (Figure 3.2)—notably checkpoints on the roads entering the occupied territories—the Green Line has remained invisible in most Jewish public arenas, thereby facilitating the de facto annexation of Jewish settlements to Israel, and spawning greater frustration and militancy among the Palestinians. At this stage the Zionist goal was clear—to cement control over the entire greater Israel, that is Eretz Yisrael/Palestine (Naor 2001). This goal was candidly articulated by Israel's prime minister during most of the

TABLE 3.1. Jewish Settlers and Palestinians in the West Bank (Including East Jerusalem)

Year	Jews Outside Jerusalem	Jews in East Jerusalem	Total Jews[a]	Total Palestinians[b]	% Jews[c]
1976	3,000	23,000	26,000	0.66	3.7
1980	11,000	39,000	50,000	0.78	6.0
1984	48,000	81,000	129,000	0.91	12.4
1988	71,000	117,000	188,000	1.02	15.8
1992	108,000	146,000	254,000	1.15	18.1
1996	148,000	173,000	310,000	1.41	21.9
2002	218,000	176,000	416,000	1.78	23.3

a. Source: Israeli Central Bureau of Statistics (CBS).
b. In millions; sources: Benvenisti 1988; Foundation for Middle East Peace 1997; Palestinian Bureau of Statistics 2002; B'tselem 2002.
c. Of the total West Bank population.

1980s and early 1990s—Yitzhak Shamir, who stated in a Knesset (Parliament) speech: "This is our goal: territorial wholeness. It should not be encroached or fragmented. This is an a priori principle; it is beyond argument. You should not ask why. Why this land is ours requires no explanation. . . . Is there any other nation that argues about its homeland, its size and dimensions, about territories, territorial compromise, or anything to that effect?"[5]

A major focus of the Judaization project centered on al-Quds (East Jerusalem). The Judaization of the city is another telling example of manipulating Jewish history and identity for territorial gains. The Old City of Jerusalem (extending over a single square kilometer) is sacred to many Muslims, Christians, and Jews; indeed, it is the ultimate Zion. But following the 1967 war Israel incorporated some 170 square kilometers of surrounding lands (including some urban, rural, and vacant areas) and named the new entity "united Jerusalem." It invoked a most cherished Jewish symbol in order to gain Jewish land holding and marginalize the Arab residents of the city. Until very recently, the symbolic strength of Jerusalem and the superior power of Israel in the city have enabled the issue of a "united Jerusalem" to remain an untouchable taboo in the public discourse. That is, no leader or organized public voice was able to express support for the redivision of the city without being ridiculed or gagged. Similarly, the future of al-Quds as the future Palestinian capital has remained at the heart of the Palestinian consensus (Lustick 1999; Klein 1999, 2003; Sayigh 1997). Jewish settlement in East Jerusalem proceeded rapidly, with the construction of eight large settlements/neighborhoods, totaling some 206,000 Jewish settlers at the end of 2001. But Palestinian hold on the eastern city, although weakened, has not been fundamentally undermined. The official rhetoric of the Palestinian national movement repeatedly mentions al-Quds as the future national capital, and the existence of Islamic shrines on the Temple Mount (Har Habayit/Haram al-Sharif) has ensured continuing national and international support for a strong Palestinian presence (Klein 1999).

Jerusalem, then, has remained the geographical heart of the conflict, and a representative microcosm of the entire territorial conflict, as elaborated further in Chapter 11. Both Zionist and Palestinian cultures, which are intimately linked to the Jewish and Islamic religion, have sanctified and glorified the city. This is highlighted by the following poetic lines, widely known and cherished by their respective Jewish and Palestinian peoples. The two poems reflect and recreate the glorified status of Jerusalem by weaving in their lyrics frequent references to sacred texts and heroic pasts. But both poems also display the denial and exclusion of the Other— Jerusalem/al-Quds are purely Jewish/Arab. The Other is a present absentee, casting a shadow over the city, but is never allowed a voice, a name, or a rightful place in this binational, multicommunal city.

During the late 1970s and 1980s, Israel also continued relentlessly to expand its land control over the territories. In the mid-1980s it was estimated that 52 percent of the West Bank's lands were classified as Israeli state land (Benvenisti 1988; Shehadeh 1997). These lands were composed of (existing and planned) Jewish residential developments, other state lands, roads, Jewish agricultural land, army installations and training grounds, and industrial estates. This expansion was backed by a tight check over the development of Palestinian villages and towns, where hundreds of houses on private lands were demolished every year on the grounds that they were illegal or, more recently, a threat to the security of Jewish settlers. Other forms of Palestinian commercial or public development were stifled by the restrictive policies of military government, in effect ghettoizing the locals to their towns and villages and making them dependent on distant Jewish employment (Benvenisti 1988).

Palestinian resistance during the decade in question was weakened by the geographical and political split in its leadership between those inside (in the occupied territories) and those outside (the leading institutions of the PLO and other Palestinian organizations). Resistance was further restricted by Israel's political and economic oppression, a lack of effective Palestinian organization and resources, the frequent incarceration of local leaders, and the tacit legitimacy of the occupation within Israel (Ghanem 2000). If early Zionism was indeed a colonial movement of emigrants and refugees seeking survival, its later version became a calculated and exploitive state colonialism. The Zionist state was constantly using and abusing the survival and security rhetoric for goals of expansionist ethnocratic rule and for the dispossession of local Palestinians, while at the same time denying the

Jerusalem of Gold
Mountain air, clear as wine,
And the fragrance of pines
Stand in twilight breeze
With the sounds of bells
In the sleep of oak and stone.
Captured in her dream
The City waits desolate
With a wall in her heart.

Jerusalem of gold,
Of copper and light,
I shall be a violin to all your poems.

How the wells have dried.
The market square stands empty.
No one attends the Temple Mount
Inside the Old City.

And in the rocky caves
The winds are wailing.
No one descends to the Dead Sea
On the Jericho road.

For your name burns the lips
Like a resinous kiss,
If I forget Thee O Jerusalem,
All of gold.

We've returned to the wells,
The market, and the square.
The shofar calls on Temple Mount
And in the rocky caves
A thousand suns are shining.
We shall descend again to the Dead Sea
On the Jericho road.

Jerusalem of gold,
Of copper and light,
I shall be a violin to all your poems.
(Shemer 1967)

The Flower of All Cities
For you, the city of prayers, I shall pray,
For you, the city of beautiful homes, you
the flower of all cities.
O al-Quds, O al-Quds, the city of
prayers, I shall pray.

Our eyes will follow you every day
Searching for the places of prayer,
Embracing the old churches,
Erasing the sorrow of mosques.
O night of Israa[6] the path passed to the
heavens.
Our eyes will follow you every day and I
shall pray.

The faces of the child in the cave
And his mother Maria are crying
For the homeless and the abandoned . . .
For the defenders who died in the city
gates,
The martyrs of peace in the homeland
of peace,
And justice ceased in the gates
When the city of al-Quds fell.
Love retreated and the hearts of the
world settled on war.

The shining rage has come and I am
faithful,
The bitter rage has come and I shall
pass my sorrows.
Through all paths, they will come,
The horses of Godly fear, they will come
Like the face of the almighty God, they
will come.

The gate to our city will not remain
locked
and I am walking to pray.
I shall knock and open the gates.
I shall cleanse, O Jordan River, in holy
waters
And shall erase, O Jordan River
the traces of the savage foot.
The shining rage, O Jordan River, will
come
with the horses of godly fear,
Will crush the face of power.
The house is ours, al-Quds is ours.
With our hands, we shall return al-Quds,
With our hands, al-Quds, peace is
coming.
(Fairuz 1968)

relevance of the same security and survival considerations for the Palestinians (Said 1996).

Still, Palestinians never accepted Jewish occupation and expansion into what they perceived were but remnants of their historical homeland remaining in Arab control. The protection of land remained one of the highest values among Palestinians, and its sale was considered *tachween* (a traitorous act).[7] A most widespread form of resistance among Palestinians has become the *sumud*—literally steadfastness in hanging on to the land, the place, the homeland. The continuation of daily practices and rituals developed by hundreds of years of agrarian living, the desperate attempts to maintain normality, and the persistence in difficult circumstances came to characterize the Palestinian *sumud*. Until 1987 *sumud* was the Palestinians' main weapon against the expansionist Jewish settlement program, both in the occupied territories and within Israel proper (Shehadeh 1997). Tawfiq Zayad's famous song typifies this attitude:

We Are Staying Here
Here, on your chest
Here, like a fence
Here, in your throat
Like a piece of glass, like a Sabar[8]
And in your eyes
Like a storm from the fire
We are staying here.
(Zayad 1978)

During the same period, an expansive Jewish settlement policy was also implemented within Israel proper. The nationalist strategy of penetrating heavily populated Palestinian regions was carried out mainly in the northern Galilee, where sixty-two new Jewish settlements were built during the decade, and to a lesser extent along Israel's "hills axis" east and northeast of Tel Aviv, and in the southern Negev. In the north, this initiative continued the long-lasting "Judaization of Galilee" strategy. It also came as a response to growing resistance among Israel's Palestinian citizens, which culminated in a 1976 mass protest known as Land Day, during which six Palestinians were killed while protesting the confiscation of their land by the state.

Land Day itself has become a prominent Palestinian annual day of commemoration, providing another key example of the intimate intertwining between the geographical process—the discourses, development, and struggles over land—and the construction of Palestinian symbols and identity. The opposing forces of Jewish expansion and Palestinian national resistance gathered pace until they finally triggered a broad popular revolt—the 1987–93 *intifada*.

1987–2005: Between Uprisings and Territorial Compromise

The eruption of the *intifada* (the awakening) in late 1987 marked the beginning of a new phase in the territorial struggle over Israel/Palestine, which firmly refocused the conflict on the land and its residents and presented greater obstacles for the Zionist Judaization project. The new phase saw, for the first time, a period of relative parity in the territorial gains and losses of the two nations. Israel continued its Jewish settlement program, mainly in the West Bank, but also in Gaza, the Negev, and Galilee, but also reacted to violent Palestinian resistance by retreating from the main Palestinian cities. In 2005, as mentioned earlier, Israel created a precedent by evacuating twenty-one small Jewish settlements from the Gaza and Jenin regions, but at the same time accelerated the expansion of large West Bank settlements and hastened the construction of the separation barrier ("the Wall") inside the West Bank.

This phase begins in 1987 with the first intifada, which broke out first and foremost against Israeli occupation and against the unyielding Jewish penetration into Palestinian lands, but it was also a statement by local Palestinians against the ineffectiveness of the external Palestinian leadership headed by the PLO and Yasser Arafat (Ghanem 2000; Shekaki 2001). The *intifada* stepped up and organized resistance to Israeli occupation and lasted six years. It began in mass demonstrations, road blocks, labor and commercial strikes, and developed into sporadic violent attacks on Jewish settlers and Israeli residents within the Green Line. The *intifada* influenced Jordan to rescind in 1988 its annexation of the West Bank and declare it part of a future Palestinian state. It also caused a historic shift in the agenda of the Palestinian national movement, with the PLO declaring in late 1988 its acceptance of the existence of Israel. It launched a revised agenda of building a peaceful Palestinian state in the occupied territories. The Zionist reply to this move was to come five years later with the Oslo agreement.

Geographically, for the short term, the *intifada* also revived the Green Line (the official Israeli border effectively erased by Jewish settlement in the occupied territories). A new "geography of fear" was created with most Jews refraining from crossing the previous border, while Palestinians became increasingly barred from entering Israel proper (Portugali 1993). Jewish settlement in the West Bank and Gaza also slowed for a while, but it did not stop. It later continued with renewed pace, especially around Jerusalem. Another major event in the struggle between the two national movements was the arrival of some eight hundred thousand immigrants from the former Soviet Union during the 1990s, which strengthened Jewish economy and demography but also imposed new costs and tensions (Kimmerling 2001).

At the same time, it also became clear that the *intifada* imposed serious economic and political costs on Israel. The growing Jewish (Western-oriented) middle classes—whose wealth was significantly enhanced during the period of Jewish expansion—became concerned over Israel's increasing isolation and diminishing economic performance in the era of globalization (Peled and Shafir 1996). The costs of the *intifada* and the brutality needed to maintain the occupation were the major factors buttressing the large Israeli peace movement, which campaigned for territorial withdrawal (see Swirsky 2005). This movement was never clear enough about its precise territorial and political goals, but it did influence the decline of the rightist Likud in the 1992 elections and the rise of a less ethnocratic, more compromising Labor administration headed by Yitzhak Rabin.

On a more general level, the first *intifada* brought Israel into an acute crisis from which it has not yet recovered. The crisis was born of the conflict—for the first time in Zionist history—between the forces of expansionist ethnonationalism and economic development. Put differently, the ethnocratic identity project of Judaizing the homeland came into sharp conflict with the emerging new goals of Israeli elites—integration into the world economy, which necessitated the end of occupation. But territorial withdrawal seriously threatened the collective identity of Jewish settlers and their religious sympathizers, and it is also perceived by some to endanger the economic well-being of low-income (and mainly Mizrahi, Russian, and Haredi) Jews owing to the associated forces of privatization and liberalization (see Peled and Shafir 1996). The crisis has included heightened political tension, rounds of mass violence, two political assassinations, including that of Prime Minister Rabin (1995) and Minister Ze'evi (2001), and long periods of economic stagnation and social tension.

Still, in 1993 the decolonizing forces in Israel prevailed for a time, and the state signed the Oslo accord with the Palestinians, (temporarily) ending the *intifada*. The accord achieved, for the first time, mutual recognition between the two national movements and allowed the return of the PLO leadership to govern several autonomous areas to be transferred to Palestinian self-rule. The Oslo agreement sought to open the way for a gradual resolution of the conflict on the basis of a territorial redivision of Palestine. By 1993, the Palestinians appeared to have reasserted their collective power and articulated a clear territorial agenda of liberation from Israeli occupation and a vision of two neighboring states coexisting in peace. Zionism gained too by receiving broad international legitimacy, official Palestinian recognition, and laying the foundation for a period of rapid economic growth.

Let us take a short theoretical break and note the shortcomings of the main theories of nationalism to account for the case at hand. For example, the gaping chasm between the Jewish ethnocratic state and Palestinians generated much of the instability and conflict during that period; this runs counter to the observations of most nationalism theories, moving Israel further away from the nation-state ideal. In addition, the flat model of the nation, which generally assumes national territory to be a neutral geographical background to political developments, is also found wanting: it is impossible to understand the changing agendas of Zionist nationalism without dissecting the agendas into the discourses and interests of various ethnoclasses. That is, the changing territorial agendas cannot be fathomed without breathing life into the making of national space and accounting for the competing geographical interests on the national (territorial) agenda.

We turn back now to the Oslo accord, which, despite the high hopes, was only a five-year interim agreement and did not specify final territorial or political ends. It reflected the skewed balance of power between Zionists and Palestinians: the Palestinians recognized the state of Israel (and hence abdicated their claim to 78 percent of historic Palestine) but received in return a vague "recognition," and a concrete plan for a three-phase Israeli withdrawal from unspecified parts of the occupied territories. Central points of the territorial conflict, such as the future of Jerusalem/al-Quds, the plight of Jewish settlements, and the rehabilitation of Palestinian refugees, were shelved for later "final status" negotiations. What appeared to be leading to a historic compromise turned sour very quickly. The vagueness of the agreement encouraged opposition groups, from both Zionist and Palestinian sides, to launch a concerted attack on the possibility of political partition (Tamari and Hammami 2000).

Over a stormy period, Palestinian-Zionist violence reached new heights, beginning with the 1994 mass murder of Muslim worshippers in Hebron by a Jewish settler, continuing with large-scale anti-Jewish terrorism inside Israel, and culminating with the assassination of Israel's peace-leaning prime minister, Yitzhak Rabin, in November of 1995, by a Jew opposing Rabin's decision to transfer territories to Palestinian self-rule. In the words of the assassin: "Rabin had no right to relinquish any part of the Jewish historical and God-given homeland. He is therefore a traitor who deserves death."[9]

Likewise, Benny Katzover, a renowned leader of Jewish settlers in the West Bank and previously an active member of the settlers' Yesha Council, stated recently: "There are now between forty and fifty Jewish outposts spread around the hills of the West Bank, considered by some "illegal." But the issue is whether one leaves these hills to the Arabs, or whether Jews will live on them. That is the issue. The question of legality is secondary to Jewish control!"[10]

The counterpart to Jewish expansionists who vie to establish a greater Israel is Hamas, the radical Islamic organization established in 1988, whose Constitution declares openly a program to destroy Israel and reinstate Islamic control over the entire land. Recently, following pressure to halt attacks against civilians within Israel proper, Hamas leader and founder Sheikh Ahmad Yassin, declared in Gaza: "Hamas took on itself the liberation of the entire Palestine, from river to sea and from Ras al Nakura to Raffah. This is the overall goal. The liberation of Gaza and the West Bank is a fine goal, but without relinquishing the claim for any grain of soil conquered from us in 1948 and without recognizing the Zionist entity."[11]

As we can see, the rhetoric of the opposition groups, coming overwhelmingly from hard-core (Jewish or Islamic) religious circles, is spatially clear: the land cannot be divided; it belongs to us, and us only. Nevertheless, the Oslo agreement was partially implemented. It created a highly complex and convoluted patchwork of new ethnic geography, owing to the existence of Jewish settlements (Figure 3.3). Their existence, which breaches international law and convention, prevented the Palestinians from stretching their (limited) autonomy beyond an archipelago of disconnected enclaves. Security control over the land and external borders remained in Israeli hands. In 1996 Israel elected Binyamin Netanyahu—a right-wing Likud prime minister—who stalled the implementation of the Oslo agreement while accelerating Jewish settlement activity. Following international condemnation and economic downturn, Netanyahu was replaced in 1999 by Labor's Ehud Barak, who ran on a ticket of ending the conflict. This was the setting in the summer of 2000, when peace talks resumed between Israelis and Palestinians.

But under the guise of a peace process, another reality was brewing. Israel's promised phased withdrawal from the Palestinian territories as part of the Oslo process had been delayed by more than four years; settlements and an expansive network of bypass roads for Jewish settlers were being built rapidly; and the daily movement of Palestinians was tightly controlled by frequent closures (aimed ostensibly to prevent terrorism). At the same time, Palestinians continued to direct sporadic violence at Israeli civilians while building up large police and militia forces. During the period, and under the pressure of continuous closures and a sharp decline in employment in Israel, the Palestinian economy was steadily shrinking, unemployment was rising, and no concrete progress was apparent toward genuine Palestinian independence (Tamari and Hammami 2000). There was much talk of peace and a stubborn reality of a deepening, violent occupation.

Within this setting, a peace summit was convened in July of 2000 at Camp David, under the auspices of President Clinton of the United States. The summit failed to reach an agreement, although both sides made some notable breakthroughs on territorial issues. The Israelis offered, for the first time, to establish an "independent" Palestinian state, to withdraw from 80 percent of the West Bank (and 10 percent more at a later date), to dismantle most Jewish settlements, and to establish (limited) Palestinian sovereignty in Jerusalem. The Palestinians in effect rejected the offer but agreed to allow the continuing existence of several large Jewish settlements and to accept Jewish control over parts of conquered East Jerusalem.

However, these breakthroughs were not enough to prevent a deadlock. This was due largely (although not solely) to the Israelis' enduring belief that their presence on the land is natural and just, and to their denial of the root problems caused by the Judaization of the land. Israel continuously attempted to impose its perspective (albeit modified) on the main open issues

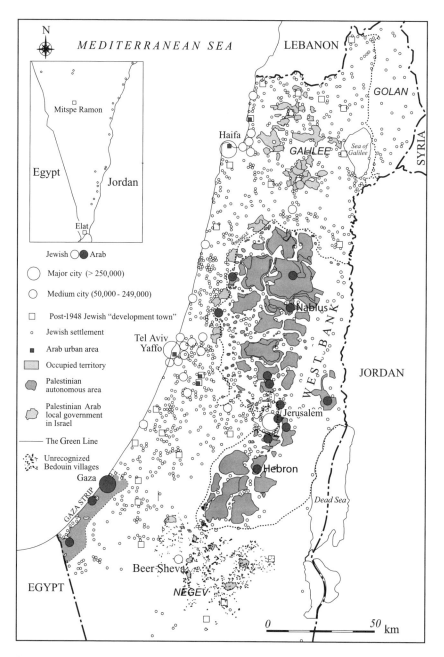

Figure 3.3. Ethnic Geography of Israel/Palestine, 2000

of the conflict. For example, transferring occupied territories to Palestinian control was represented as "Israeli generosity," and the main test for the feasibility of proposed arrangements was Israeli (not Palestinian) security. Accordingly, Israel's final status proposals rejected any mention of Israel's role in creating the Palestinian refugee problem, or the refugees' right of return; it still attempted to keep 80 percent of the settlers in the West Bank; and denied full Palestinian control over key Arab parts of al-Quds, most notably the holy Haram al-Sharif (Temple Mount).

Time-space configurations continued to be central here too. Israeli negotiators attempted to date the beginning of the problems in need of resolution to 1967, while Palestinians sought to address the roots in 1948. Hence, Israeli leaders and media portrayed a compromise over the 1967 territories as the only obstacle for peace. But in historical terms, most Palestinians felt they had already offered their full compromise to Zionism by recognizing Israel's right to exist securely on 78 percent of what they perceive as their historic homeland—"Palestine" as defined by the British Mandate. The Palestinians demanded that the remaining 22 percent be transferred to their full sovereignty (with minor modifications) and that 1948 issues, most notably the plight and property of the refugees, be addressed. Hence the consensual stand expressed by Faisal Husseini, the late Palestinian leader, in September of 2000: "There can be no compromise on the compromise!"[12]

But most Israeli Jews were led to think otherwise. Although in recent years many had reluctantly accepted the existence of a Palestinian nation, they still perceived the Palestinian state-to-be as an entity to be shaped by the needs and concerns of Zionism. Israeli Jews thus developed a convoluted, distorted debate about "how much land for peace?" Public discourse of the post-Oslo era was replete with arguments, agendas, and proposals of partial withdrawals, with Jews debating in their own exclusive bubble, showing little concern for the international or historical-geographical dynamic of the conflict (Falah and Newman 1995; Beilin 2001).

This view led most Israelis, including the leftist Labor camp, to equate "going all the way for peace" (Barak's oft-used slogan) with the annexation of many Jewish settlements in the occupied territories and a total denial of discussing the right of return for Palestinian refugees. In his recent memoirs of the Camp David peace talks, Israel's leftist foreign minister at the time, Shlomo Ben-Ami, boasts about the territorial achievements of his peace efforts: "The Camp David summit was a major Israeli achievement: for the first time . . . the Americans accepted . . . and Clinton stressed the importance of annexing 80 percent of the settlers to Israel . . . and a large Jewish Jerusalem under Israeli sovereignty . . . and we never, at any stage, agreed to the return of the Palestinian refugees."[13]

We can note again that the gaps between Zionists and Palestinians remained mostly spatial: the extent of Israeli withdrawal, the future location of the refugees, and the plight of Jewish settlements. Although the gap was not large in absolute terms, the attempts of Israel to dictate its position and the Zionist denial of its (partial) responsibility for creating the refugee problem lead to the collapse of the peace talks. This, coupled with the loss of faith Palestinians showed in their own ineffective and corrupt regime, caused the outbreak of the al-Aqsa *intifada* in late September of 2000 (Shekaki 2001). Typically, this uprising began following a (very geographical!) provocation—a public visit of the then opposition leader, Ariel Sharon, to the heart of the imagined Palestinian homeland, the holy Haram al-Sharif, for a purpose described in Sharon's own words: "To demonstrate Israel's undeniable sovereignty over the entire united Jerusalem."[14]

The visit was followed by Palestinian protest, Israeli repression, and a high number of casualties. This spawned mass Palestinian demonstrations, which confronted the main symbols of the occupation: road barriers, army camps, and Jewish settlements. The uprising began as a popular action, but it was supported (mainly tacitly) by the Palestinian leadership, which was seriously weakened at that stage following its failure to establish a legitimate state apparatus, accusations of widespread corruption, and its inability to extract any substantial gains from Israel since Rabin's assassination (Frisch 2003; Ghanem 2000; Sayigh 2001). The leadership was thus worried about its survival and sought new legitimacy in the face of popular criticism of "collaboration" with Israel and evidence of widespread corruption. This placed it in no position to try and put down the uprising, as demanded by Israel. However, it badly miscalculated the disastrous political and moral consequences of resorting to violence and later to terror (for the Palestinian debate on the issue of an armed struggle, see Frisch 2003; Sayigh 2001).

Significantly, the mass protest was joined for over a week by large numbers of Palestinian Arabs inside Israel, who fiercely demonstrated against their own oppression by the state. This resulted in the killing of thirteen Arab citizens (and one Jew), and in a notable deterioration of Arab-Jewish relations inside Israel to one of their lowest ebbs ever. Consequently, Palestinian Arabs in Israel appear to be gradually withdrawing from the state (Ghanem and Ozasky-Lazar 2001; Rouhana and Soultani 2003; Zreik 2003).

Unlike the first *intifada*, this uprising developed quickly into an armed guerilla struggle against the occupation, combined with escalating terror against Israeli settlers and civilians within the Green Line. The escalation of violence immediately after the peace summit toppled the government of Ehud Barak, who was replaced in landslide elections in February of 2001 by the rightist Ariel Sharon. Sharon received an unprecedented 62 percent of the popular vote, although the elections were boycotted by 82 percent of Israel's Arab citizens, who for the first time made a collective statement of their ability to disrupt Israel's political life and signaled their further disengagement from the Israeli regime.

Under Sharon, Israel stepped up significantly its attempts to put down the uprising by military means, spawning a vicious circle of violence and counterviolence. This culminated in near total reoccupation of Palestinian cities and in several operations causing widespread destruction in pursuit of "terror infrastructure." The cost was predictably high: by July of 2004, some 2,764 Palestinians and 902 Israelis had been killed, the Palestinian economy had shrunk by two-thirds, more than 3,500 Palestinian homes and commercial properties and more than fourteen thousand dunams of fields and industries had been destroyed.[15] A series of tighter closures prevented the Palestinians from the most mundane, daily movement (UNESCO 2002; B'tselem 2002). By the end of 2003, the Israeli economy too had shrunk for eight consecutive quarters, lowering Israeli average income by 9 percent, and causing unemployment and poverty levels to rise by 20 percent in the 2001–2 period, with a slight recovery during 2003 (Adva Center 2003, 2004).

The level of violence remained high for several years, with several fluctuations, reaching a peak in the spring of 2002 with the Israeli reconquest of the entire occupied territories. Since 2001, Israel has launched a campaign of targeted attacks (extrajudicial killings) of dozens of Palestinian leaders and key figures, including highly prominent personalities such as the general secretary of the Popular Front for the Liberation of Palestine (PFLP), Abu Ali Mustafa (assassinated in July of 2001), and the two leaders of the vastly popular Islamic Hamas—Sheikh Ahmad Yassin and Abed Aziz al-Rantissi (March and April of 2004). During 2002 and 2003 Israel made several deep invasions into Palestinian Authority areas and systematically destroyed Palestinian institutions, infrastructure, and property. At the same time, the Palestinians launched an unprecedented series of suicide terror attacks in Israeli cities and buses. This turn of events brought relations between Jews and Palestinians to one of their all-time lows.

In January of 2003, Sharon and the Likud Party won another set of elections with a sweeping majority, caused by a further swing of 7 percent to the nationalist right. The Israeli peace camp collapsed, losing 30 percent of its previous parliamentary power, mainly to parties classified as centrist. Despite a campaign by Islamic and nationalist movements, Arab citizens did not repeat the mass elections boycott, although their participation rate stood at a low 62 percent, and their support of non-Zionist (Arab) parties rose to 78 percent, signaling, again, the deepening of political polarization and the precarious relations between the swelling minority and the Jewish state.

During the period of Sharon rule, the Israeli government has continued actively to reshape the political geography of the country by further expanding its land control, while constraining Palestinian development. Palestinian resistance has been largely ineffective. Israel has continued with its tight military control, land seizure in security areas, and large-scale house demolition. On a structural level, Israel launched two major geographical initiatives—constructing a new wave of Jewish settlements, and planning and building a new security barrier (fence/wall) in the West Bank.

The new wave of settlements is concentrated mainly in areas with Arab regional dominance, mainly in the West Bank, but also in Israel proper (see Figure 3.4). In the West Bank, this wave of some ninety-five to one hundred new, small, outpost settlements (*ma'ahazim* in Hebrew) was designed deliberately to disrupt the reconciliation efforts between Israelis and Palestinians by making it increasingly difficult to imagine, let alone establish, a contiguous Palestinian state.[16] This move has been supported by a range of Israeli governments and leaders, most notably Ariel Sharon. Within Israel, thirty new Jewish settlements have been approved during 2002 and 2003, with the government using the traditional explanation for the allocation of massive resources: "The new settlements are aimed to ensure Jewish control over state land and to prevent Arab expansion and illegal building."[17]

The second major initiative has resulted in the construction of a major land barrier, known as the "separation fence," "barrier," or "wall," between Palestinian and Jewish localities on the western hills of the West Bank. The idea surfaced by popular demand, following an unprecedented wave of Palestinian terror in Israeli cities. But it quickly transformed into a tool for deepening Jewish territorial control. In a unilateral move, Israel chose the location of the barrier so as to include most Jewish settlement blocks in the West Bank, which stretched the planned route of the western barrier to 681 kilometers, and formed an act of de facto annexation (see Figure 3.5). The original barrier's route was approved by the government in October of 2003, with its cost estimated at $1.9 billion. It caused great anger among Palestinians and peace-oriented Israelis, as it left 16 percent of the West Bank area west of the barrier and required the confiscation of large tracks of Palestinian lands. The barrier's construction caused widespread damage to agricultural and natural landscapes and "trapped" close to fifty thousand disenfranchised Palestinians between the barrier and the Green Line (outside the Jerusalem area). Israel also surrounded the cities of Qalqiliya and Tul-Qarem with six-meter-high concrete walls, severely limiting their accessibility and potential growth. A similar wall has been built in East Jerusalem, closely following the municipal line imposed by Israel in 1967 as part of the colonization of "united" Jerusalem.[18]

By the end of 2004, less than one-third of the planned barrier (some 190 kilometers) had been built in the northern West Bank regions, mostly as a central, high, electrified fence surrounded by two tracks, ditches, and at times a secondary fence. The southern parts (in western Samaria) are more controversial, owing to Israel's desire to include large Jewish settlements deep in the occupied territories, thereby trapping scores of Palestinian localities between the barrier and the Green Line. In late 2003, the Israeli Ministry of Security approved the construction of an eastern security barrier,

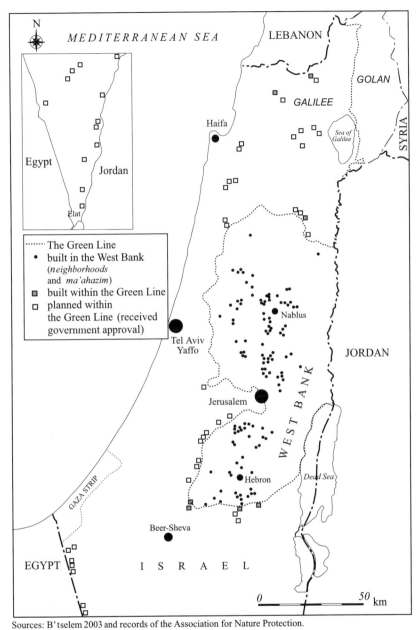

Sources: B'tselem 2003 and records of the Association for Nature Protection.

Figure 3.4. New Jewish Settlements, 2000–2003

attempting to further restrict Palestinian territorial control and stretching the plan to a length of 828 kilometers.[19] While the eastern barrier is yet to be budgeted or fully approved, its planning appears to be another step in the demarcation of fenced and controlled Palestinian enclaves to form the geographical basis for extremely limited Palestinian self-rule, to be titled a "state with provisional borders," and to form part of what I term the process of "creeping apartheid" (to be explained later; see Figure 3.5).

During 2003 and 2004 this route was subject to a fierce political, legal, and diplomatic struggle. Palestinians mobilized strongly both against the idea of creating such a massive barrier unilaterally and against the route cutting deep into the West Bank. The struggle bore some results, with both the Israeli High Court and the Hague International Court of Justice (ICJ) ruling in 2004 against the government plans to continue and build the barrier. The Israeli court, in response to a large number of appeals, decided in June of 2004 not to challenge the actual construction of the barrier but asked the government to minimize Palestinian sufferings and move the barrier closer to the Green Line.[20] The ICJ was far more critical of Israel, declaring in its July of 2004 decision (framed as a recommendation to the UN General Assembly) that the barrier and Jewish settlements in the West Bank contravene international law. It demanded that Israel dismantle the barrier and compensate the Palestinians for related damages.[21]

As a result, the government has amended the barrier's route, deciding in February of 2005 on a new plan, which brings the barrier close to the Green Line, while keeping on the western side four main Jewish settlement blocks and leaving 8.6 percent of the West Bank on the western "Israeli" side, as opposed to 16 percent in the previously approved route. The length of the western part was reduced by one-sixth to 580 kilometers. The new route leaves approximately 220,000 Palestinians on the western side of the barrier, the vast majority in the Jerusalem region. Yet, despite the improvement, which means that less Palestinians will suffer as a result of the barrier construction, the new route is still illegal under international law and practically untenable because of three deep "fingers" encroaching into the West Bank. These prevent the possibility of a viable, contiguous Palestinian state.[22]

Finally, during the 2002–5 period, Prime Minister Sharon promised to move toward establishing a Palestinian state with temporary borders within the initiative known as the "road map" promoted by President George W. Bush of the United States, the United Nations, the European Union, and Russia. The "temporary state" idea builds on the fact that for the first time in the history of the conflict there is a clear majority among both Palestinians in the West Bank and Israelis for a two-state solution (Shekaki 2001; Newman 2003).

The road-map strategy lost its momentum owing to a range of factors, first and foremost Israel's ongoing violent oppression of the Palestinians and

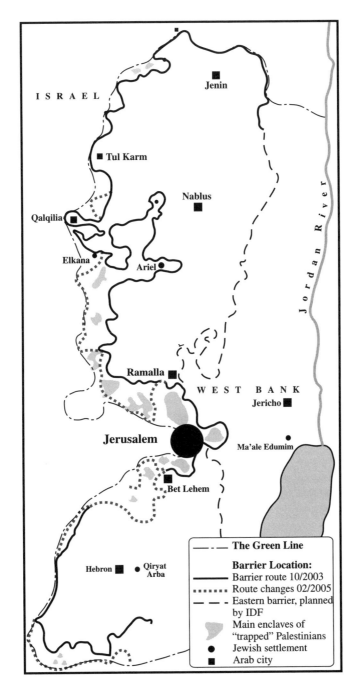

Figure 3.5. The Separation Barrier, 2003 and 2005

The following labels appear on the map:

ISRAEL

Jenin

Tul Karm

Nablus

Qalqilia

Elkana

Ariel

Ramalla

WEST BANK

Jericho

Jerusalem

Ma'ale Edumim

Bet Lehem

Hebron   Qiryat Arba

Jordan River

The Green Line
Barrier Location:
Barrier route 10/2003
Route changes 02/2005
Eastern barrier, planned by IDF
Main enclaves of "trapped" Palestinians
Jewish settlement
Arab city

expansion of settlements, as well as occasional acts of Palestinian terror and serious conflicts within Palestinian society and its leadership and a lack of a coherent Palestinian strategy. The world attention also moved to the U.S.-led invasion of Iraq. However, a step toward a temporary Palestinian entity was taken in the spring of 2004 with the Israeli government passing the "disengagement plan," according to which all Jewish settlements would be removed from the entire Gaza Strip and several small areas in the northern West Bank, while allowing limited Palestinian self-rule in Gaza. The plan indeed creates an important precedent, namely the willing removal of Jewish settlement, for the first time in the history of the struggle over Israel/Palestine.[23]

In November of 2004, the plan received new impetus with the reelection of George Bush to the U.S. presidency and the death of Yasser Arafat, who was considered by most Israelis and Americans to be an obstacle for Israeli-Palestinian dialogue and advancement toward political settlement. The election in January of 2005 of Mahmud Abbas (Abu Mazen) to the presidency of the Palestinian Authority has added momentum to Israel's partial withdrawal plans. Abu Mazen's long-standing position against violence and terror and persistant support of the peace process enabled several rightist Israeli politicians to support the disengagement plan.

But Israeli support for the plan was achieved only after packaging it with the construction of the security barrier in the West Bank. Tellingly, the government's decision to evacuate the Gaza settlements was approved at the same meeting as the new route of the separation barrier. It was also taken against the backdrop of continuing massive construction in the existing West Bank settlement, reaching 7,600 dwelling units in approval or the construction stage in 2005 alone.[24] Hence, the small withdrawal from Gaza and small areas in northern Samaria—significant as they may be in the history of Jewish colonial settlement—may not herald genuine decolonization but rather an adjustment of the Judaization strategy. While the government's new strategy has encountered fierce opposition from settlers' circles and from parts of the ruling Likud Party, it still aims to leave the majority of West Bank settlers in their place and continue to promote their settlements, infrastructure, and security.

Hence, the new strategy appears consistent with the political-geographic transformation of Israel/Palestine. I have conceptualized this process as "creeping apartheid," whereby the vast majority of territory and resources between Jordan and the Mediterranean Sea are controlled by Jews, while the Palestinians who comprise nearly half the population are constrained to several "self-governing" enclaves, covering around 15 percent of the land and lacking real sovereignty, freedom of movement, military power, control over water and air, and contiguous territory. This is a natural (though not inevitable) development of ethnocratic perceptions, driven by fundamental assumptions regarding the "natural" right of one group to control its (self-defined) homeland, while controlling other groups residing in the same political space.

This reality is "creeping" because (a) it is unfolding without any official declaration and open discussion; (b) Jews continue to settle in the West Bank; and (c) the ethnic stratification of civil status is diffusing into Israel proper, with greater segregation and new legal controls imposed on Israel's Palestinian Arab citizens. The separation barrier accelerates this process, driving Israel to relax its control over small pockets of territory, for the benefit of reinforcing its hold on other parts, hence deepening the reality of "separate but unequal." But the new Israeli "solution" may, at best, be only short-lived, as disgruntled Palestinians are likely to mobilize against the new spaces of oppression and destabilize the new spatial order. Hence, the prospects for ending the Israeli occupation peacefully still appear remote, being buried under the specter of mass violence, suspicion, and politics of hate.

A Brief Conclusion

No substantive conclusions can be offered at this stage, as the story of the Zionist-Palestinian struggle is indeed unfinished. But the brief account detailed in this chapter has highlighted the territorial focus of the struggle and its association with the ethnocratic logic of Judaization and its implications. The remaining unresolved issues of the conflict are indeed highly geographical in nature, namely the future of Jerusalem/al-Quds, the location of borders, the resettlement and rehabilitation of the Palestinian refugees, the future of Jewish colonial settlements in the occupied territories, and the rights of Palestinian Arabs and other non-Jews in Israel. Clearly, these issues stretch far beyond mere geography into critical aspects of memory, identity, economics, politics, and law. But it will be useful to remember that they are also directly related to the ceaseless spatial transformation of Israel/Palestine and are hence likely to preserve a simmering edge in Zionist-Palestinian relations during the foreseeable future. We move now to examine in more detail the connection between ethnic territoriality, national narratives, and the making of the Israeli ethnocratic regime—all developed in the next chapter.

Chapter 4

Debating Israeli Democracy

Following the historical-geographical account presented in the previous chapter, we now move to a more detailed analysis of the Israeli political system. The present chapter begins with a critical review of scholarly literature on the Israeli regime, which commonly classifies it as democratic. It pays most attention to one of the most influential interpretations of the Israeli regime—the "ethnic democracy" model proposed by Sammy Smooha (1990, 2002). Problematizing the democratic nature of the Israel regime will set the scene for the following chapters, which outline its ethnocratic characteristics.

The chapter highlights common blind spots in the work of many scholars committed to Israel's democratic classification. Typically, these scholars artificially separate Israel proper from the lands it has occupied and settled since 1967; they overlook the structural influence of Israel's ongoing connections with world Jewry; they ignore the creation and persisting influence of the Palestinian refugee problem; and they neglect to account for the role of religion in shaping the Israeli regime. Most scholars also ignore the dynamics of Israel's political geography and hence commit the error of *conceptual stretching* by classifying the state as a democracy.

When these key elements are taken into account, a different basic logic emerges as fundamental to Israel's regime structure—the Judaization of Israel/Palestine. The political-geographical perspective I offer here also highlights the need to include the entire area controlled and ethnicized by the state (namely, Mandatory Palestine between Jordan and the Mediterranean Sea) and the institutional and legal frameworks that have empowered this ethnic project in order to present a credible account of the regime, its crises, and its transformations.

The main argument advanced in this chapter is that a credible analysis of the Israeli regime, which takes into account the major forces operating on the territory and population under Israeli control, cannot conclude that Israel is a democracy, let alone a liberal democracy. Importantly, "democracy" is neither regarded here as ontological, nor treated uncritically. Hence, I view Israel as existing in the gray zone, with a mixture of democratic and nondemocratic regime structures, norms, and practices, best conceptualized by the ethnocratic categories developed throughout this book.[1]

The political-geographic angle highlights a major impediment to democratic rule under the Israeli regime as being rooted in the *decoupling of citizenship from geography*. As explained in the next chapter, this is a major deficiency, preventing the polity from creating a stable demos. Israel allowed Jewish settlers in the occupied territories (including East Jerusalem), now numbering around 450,000 Jews, to maintain full citizenship rights, including the right to be elected. At the same time, their Palestinian neighbors—controlled (directly or indirectly) under the same regime—are politically disenfranchised. Since the 1980s, the settlers have been the most overrepresented group in the Israeli government and in Parliament. They form one of the most influential lobbies in Israeli politics—all despite living outside the sovereign area of the state.

The empowerment of Jewish diasporas is another facet of decoupling citizenship rights and geography. Israel has incorporated world Jewry organizations as part of the regime, has allowed Jews automatic citizenship upon arriving in Israel, and has granted diaspora Jews superior land rights to those of the state's own Arab citizens. The citizenship of the Arab citizens inside the Green Line has also remained partial, suffering from many structural and legal forms of discrimination. This unequal system of rights was shaped to further the Judaization project and has put in train a process I have termed creeping apartheid, to be discussed further in the next few chapters. As a result of the blurred borders and boundaries, and the partial inclusion of peripheral groups, Israel has neither managed to create a firm sense of "Israeliness" nor a genuine Israeli (as distinct from Jewish) polity. This presents severe obstacles for the development of civil society and hence democracy.

But Israeli colonialism and discrimination against its Arab citizens are not the only tensions with democratic principles evident in Israel. The institutional role of the Jewish religion makes citizenship rights depend on one's faith and gender, with non-Orthodox Jews, "partial" Jews, and women having only a limited package of rights and capabilities. This is an anathema to any democratic theory. There are of course additional factors hampering the democratic nature of Israeli society, including the central role of the military in shaping Israel's public policies, state territory, and legal culture; the diminishing public accountability of the media; the recent retreat of the state from its welfare role, which has widened social gaps alarmingly, and the growing impact of capital and entrepreneurs on public decision making. These factors have often been absent from most accounts of the Israeli regime.

Debating the Regime

I begin with the fairly recent debate on the nature of the Israeli regime. Traditionally, analysis of the Israeli regime was dominated by an a priori acceptance of the democratic nature of the state. Until the 1990s, there were very few voices (see Jiryis 1976; Lustick 1980; Zureik 1979) that (only implicitly) challenged the democratic axiom. But during the 1990s, a debate began for the first time in academic and intellectual circles. The main triggers were worldwide discussions on democratization following the end of the cold war and the 1992 passing of two Israeli Basic Laws. These declared the state to be "Jewish and democratic" and enshrined several key human rights as part of a supposedly "modular" Constitution. The new laws and the "Jewish and democratic" legal phrasing regenerated the discussion over Israel's putative "Western and democratic" nature, which had been taken for granted by most Israeli and international scholars. Typical of this outlook was this statement by Aharon Barak (1998, 8), the active president of the Israeli High Court of Justice: "Our existence as a Jewish and democratic state with non-Jewish minorities who deserve full equality reflects our basic principles and values. . . ."

The mainstream of Israeli academia has followed, by and large, the High Court's line and considered the state to be a Western-oriented, liberal democracy, albeit with certain deficiencies. The works of Shmuel Eisenstadt, Asher Arian, Moshe Lissak, and Benny Neuberger are good examples of leading voices in this stream. While the first three present little critical analysis of the nature of the regime (as distinct from their in-depth social analysis), Neuberger has already identified "four stains" blotting the "copybook" of Israeli democracy, namely the lack of a Constitution, the occupation of Palestinian territories, the diminished rights of the Arab minority, and the lack of civil freedom on matters of personal status. However, he considers these "stains" to be relatively marginal, and Israel is still considered in Neurberger's analysis to be a liberal democracy. "We need, first and foremost," he states, "to check if it [Israel] fulfills the democratic liberal criteria. . . . On the structural and declarative level, the answer is positive" (Neurberger 1998, 8).

Ezrahi and Kremitzer (2001, 27), in outlining their platform for adopting a state constitution, go further by discerning the progression of the Israeli democracy from traditionalism to new liberal and multicultural formulations: "Recent developments caused Israeli society and its institutions to accommodate trends of pluralism and formalism, which contradict previous 'organic-familial' perceptions of society. In this context, Israel is undergoing exceptionally rapidly a process typical to national states based on organic conceptions, which have been transformed into multinational or multicultural democracies."

The two renowned experts on democracy present a sophisticated analysis, which highlights a range of difficulties in the acceptance of a new liberal-democratic constitution. These include the need to limit state power, restrain majority power, strengthen the value of the individual, separate religion and state, and reinforce procedural formalism (Ezrahi and Kremitzer 2001, 17–19). Notably, these lack reference to some of the structural difficulties highlighted earlier in the chapter and especially to the Judaization process. Moreover, later in their essay, Ezrahi and Kremitzer discuss the potential impact of the Jewish nature of the state on its democratic future:

In a near paradoxical manner, we can say that the state of Israel, which is supposed to represent the liberty of the Jewish people and the Jewish right for self-determination, *can only be a democratic state* [my emphasis]. According to this perception, not only is there no contradiction between the definition of the state as Jewish and democratic, but it is possible to find a necessary connection between the two. Only in a democratic framework can Jews of various opinions compete freely for the attitudes and sentiments of the public. Therefore, it seems like the state of Israel, like other democratic states, must enable the representation of many and changing identities, Jewish and non-Jewish alike. (17–19)

Ethnic Democracy?

The second, more critical approach toward the nature of the Israeli regime was advanced by leading scholars such as Sammy Smooha (1990, 2002), Yoav Peled (1992), Gershon Shafir (see Shafir and Peled 1998), Alan Dowty (1998, 2004), Ilan Saban (2000), and Ruth Gavison (1999, 2002) and defined Israel as an ethnic democracy. This model, first formulated by Smooha (1990), is aware of systematic inequalities between Arabs and Jews, particularly in the exercise of collective rights, and classifies the regime as a second-rate democracy. Yet it maintains that the state possesses an overall democratic framework, which guarantees basic civil rights. This setting, it is claimed, led to the articulation of the "Jewish and democratic" formula advanced over the years by the Israeli elites. It is claimed that the formula has even been accepted by the state's Arab citizens, thereby creating conditions for a reasonable measure of political stability. Smooha combines theoretical claims about the nature of democratic states dominated by an ethnic majority with a wealth of (mainly attitudinal) data. On the theoretical level, he claims that "ethnic democracy is a system, which combines the extension of civil and political rights to individuals and some collective rights to minorities, with institutionalization of majority control over the state. Driven by ethnic nationalism, the state is identified with a 'core ethnic nation' not with its citizens. . . . At the same time, the minorities are allowed to conduct a democratic and peaceful struggle that yields incremental improvement in their status" (Smooha 1998, 199–200; see also Smooha 2002).

When turning to Israel, Smooha integrates a critical examination of ethnic relations with a critique of past scholarship on Israel's political structure. After refuting common claims that Israel is a liberal or consociational democracy, and repudiating descriptions of the state as a nondemocratic colonial system, he concludes that it is an archetype of a newly defined regime type—ethnic democracy. "The democratic and Jewish characteristics of the state coexist; Israel proper qualifies as a political democracy on many counts. . . . It has thus far functioned quite well. . . . Israel defines itself as a state of and for Jews, that is, the homeland of the Jews only. . . . The state extends preferential treatment to Jews who wish to preserve the embedded Jewishness and Zionism of the state" (Smooha 1998, 205–6).

Even in the face of evidence to the contrary, Smooha has remained adamant. For example, following the turbulent events of 2000–2002, during which relations between Jews and Palestinian Arabs reached an all-time nadir, and in light of the collapse of other ethnic democracies in Sri Lanka, Northern Ireland, and Serbia, he still commented that "Israel flies in the face of lessons . . . demonstrating that ethnic democracy in a deeply divided bi-ethnic society is bound to fail. . . . The second-rate Israeli democracy looks robust and stable" (Smooha 2002, 427).

The model, as noted, created a lively scholarly debate, with several critical comments that are summarized elsewhere (see Rouhana and Ghanem 1998; Yiftachel 2001b). In the main, it received the support of a large number of scholars, including international analysts such as Claus Hanf, Alan Dowty, and Graham Smith, as well as notable Israeli scholars such as Yoav Peled, Gershon Shafir, and Ruth Gavison.

Shafir and Peled have given the ethnic democracy model its most substantial theoretical backing. In a series of widely quoted analyses (Peled 1992; Shafir and Peled 1998; Shafir and Peled 2002) they accepted the ethnic democracy classification and set out to examine how it maintains its stability in the face of the structural disparities. The key to this phenomenon lies in the institution of citizenship, which incorporates and at the same time separates. "Citizenship, conventionally conceived of as a civic mechanism of incorporation, is locked in battle, in multi-ethnic societies, with identity politics that seek to use particular criteria of membership as the bases of citizenship. These discourses are employed in competition over access to rights allocated by state and para-state institutions. Thus citizenship, instead of solely leveling status differences, can also function as a tool of stratification" (Shafir and Peled 1998, 408).

In a nutshell, they claim that ethnic democracy functions by the generation of three simultaneous citizenship discourses that demarcate differently the boundaries of the political community and the bearers of the collective good. These discourses work in parallel to produce a variegated "regime of incorporation," in which the civil status of each sector is legitimized and normalized, "allowing Israel to maintain a stable democratic regime in the context of an acute ethnic conflict" (128). The first citizenship discourse is liberal, encompassing Israel's Jewish and Arab citizens within one political community and focusing on procedural equality and individual civil rights. The second is an ethnonational discourse that demarcates the boundary of the political community around the community of Jewish descent, reinforcing its privileged position and actively incorporating peripheral Jewish communities. The third is a collectivist-republican discourse that defines full membership in terms of a civic virtue of active contribution to the Zionist collective good (typically entailing frontier settlement, military service, and a Western-secular orientation), thereby privileging the founding Ashkenazi community, which had itself shaped these republican goals.

Shafir and Peled also observe a historical dynamic of liberalization, in which the liberal discourse is gradually gaining strength, mainly owing to economic globalization, elite cultural transformation, and a process of decolonization in the occupied territories. Against this development, the republican and ethnonational discourses tend to decline. Hence, argue Shafir and Peled, the Israeli ethnic democracy manages to balance between its exclusive and inclusive drives. On the one hand, it incorporates marginal populations into a minimal citizenship (be it liberal or republican), while on the other, it marginalizes this population by excluding it from full, substantive citizenship, packaged with material, cultural, and political privileges. This enables the ethnic democracy to maintain its political stability while creating and preserving deep social disparities.

Shafir and Peled's analysis has been groundbreaking on many counts, and I endorse their observation of the long-term stratification of citizenship, as empirically supported by various chapters of this book. However, beyond their overreliance on the power of globalization and neoliberalism to shape social relations in a traditional ethnic society such as Israel, their analysis is questionable on two further counts. First, they implicitly project a certain equality between the three discourses, which are described as having their own, largely independent logic and trajectory. But I maintain that in Israel/Palestine, as in most ethnocratic societies, *the ethnonational discourse has been extremely powerful* and has largely dictated the content and boundaries of the other two discourses. True, other definitions of the collective good have been debated in the Israeli political arena, but they have never seriously challenged the tenets of Zionist and Palestinian ethnonationalism. Hence, the choice of the potentially universal yardstick of citizenship to analyze group relations in Israel/Palestine is limited in its ability to discern profound conflicts and transformations.

Second, the analytical categories used by the authors are misleading, falling into the trap of conceptual stretching, as explained below. In particular, their use of the terms republican and liberal is puzzling, as it overlooks the universal, inclusive nature fundamental to these two classical political terms. Both liberalism and republicanism, in their different approaches, aspire to create *equal citizenship*. Liberalism is not a credible category without (at least official) neutrality of the state and without a credible official discourse of "color blindness" in the treatment of all citizens by the authorities. Republicanism is premised on the integration of all citizens into the state identity and culture, forming the basis of what Habermas recently termed "constitutional patriotism." These democratic universal mechanisms are conspicuously lacking in the foundations of the Israeli state, which defines itself openly as Jewish and practices a range of Judaizing policies and practices that seriously impede the ascendancy of liberalism and/or republicanism. Hence the questionable use of these terms confuses more than assists in the understanding of the Israeli political system and erroneously enables its classification as democratic.

Gavison's (1999, 11) analysis goes in a slightly different direction but emerges with a similar analytical outcome. She lowers the definition of democracy by vaguely defining it as "a political system, which enjoys the consent of the main groups in society, and where all citizens enjoy the right to participate in the making of political decisions." Gavison focuses on the thinnest possible definition of democracy and hence avoids the question of unequal citizenship or the conspicuously undemocratic tyranny of the majority often produced by crude majoritarian regimes, even when all citizens have the right to participate.

Another supporter of the ethnic democracy model, Alan Dowty (1998), goes even further by claiming that a democratic system need not guarantee equal citizenship if it maintains democratic freedoms and a system in which governmental changes are made possible by a fair and inclusive electoral process. There are, of course, serious shortcomings with the reduction of democracy to such a procedural minimum, but we can observe that even that low standard is not attained in Israel. This is because Jewish settlers in the occupied territories participate in Israeli elections (and have often determined their outcome), while their Palestinian neighbors are disenfranchised. These elections, we must remember, have invariably debated the future of the occupied territories. Hence, Israel cannot even claim an open and inclusive electoral process and universal suffrage, which form the minimal possible prerequisite for democracy.

While a more in-depth analysis of the works of serious scholars such as Peled, Shafir, Gavison, and Dowty must await another occasion, it is significant to observe for our purposes here that they have accepted, without sufficient examination, the democratic nature of the Israeli polity and have given analytical support to the ethnic democracy model. How is that possible? The notion of conceptual stretching discussed in the next section may shed some light.

Meanwhile, we will make a small detour and observe that a group of critical scholars has emerged during the 1990s to challenge Israel's democratic definition. They include Majd al-Haj (2002), Uri Ben-Eliezer (1998), Lev Grinberg (2001), Baruch Kimmerling (2001, 2003), Yitzhak Nevo (2003), Ilan Peleg (2004), Asad Ghanem (Ghanem, Rouhana, and Yiftachel 1998), Nadim Rouhana (1997), Yossi Yonah (2001), and Elia Zureik (2001), to name a few. Their analyses range from an acceptance of the ethnocracy model to the definition of Israel as a theocracy, multicultural polity, imagined democracy, or seriously flawed democracy. Again, this is not the place to engage with their fascinating work in depth, except to note their contribution to the critical discussion of the democratic claim from a variety of angles, including the high level of regime centrality, the relative lack of political accountability, the weakness of the judiciary (until the 1990s), pervasive militarism, male dominance, and associated discrimination against women in most walks of life. Their work has made an important contribution to the lively and highly illuminating debate now taking place about the nature of the Israeli regime and the political programs needed for its reform and stabilization.

Democracy and Conceptual Stretching

In the framework of the critical approach that guides this book, we should not, of course romanticize the notion of democracy. As well shown by Mann (1999, 2004) it is a regime type, which reflects, among other things, the balance of power among various key groups, and has been formulated following centuries of fierce struggles among social groups. The meaning of democracy is also contested, as shown by the seminal works of Benhabib (1996), Kymlicka (2001), and Young (2002). Nevertheless, several key principles are commonly held as democratic and are pursued by most democratic regimes, at least in their official protocols. Without entering into the recent sophisticated debates about agonistic, deliberative, radical, or collaborative democracy (see Kymlicka 2001; Mouffe 1995), I will simply identify the fundamental principles perceived widely as democratic: (a) equal and inclusive citizenship; (b) popular sovereignty and universal suffrage; (c) protection of basic civil rights and minorities; and (d) periodic, universal, and free elections. Critically, the discussion over the achievement of these principles is premised on the assumption of the existence of a sovereign state within clear borders, a particularly problematic point in the case of Israel, to which I shall return.

The above principles present an ideal model, which is never fully accomplished. Hence, no state can claim to be a perfect democracy, and democracy cannot be treated as an ontological (yes/no) phenomenon. It is more fruitful to assess the extent of democracy in a particular state as a set of locations on an analytical continuum stretching between despotic and democratic poles. Democracy can be assessed separately on different societal spheres, such as ethnicity, class, gender, militarism, religiosity, centrality, transparency, or morality. Despite the inevitable variation most regimes display in the analysis of these spheres, it can be safely stated that certain states, especially in western Europe and North America, have managed to establish and sustain democratic regimes, a factor explaining their relative stability and prosperity.

At the same time, despite the complex understanding of democracy, we must acknowledge that below a certain level, and with structural and repeated deviations from basic democratic principles, as is the case in

Israel, democracy is no longer a credible classification. There is a need to search for new concepts, and in this book I offer ethnocracy and a process of creeping apartheid as more accurate and robust accounts of the Israeli regime (see Chapter 5).

I acknowledge that important democratic elements do exist within the Israeli regime, including periodic (though not inclusive) free elections, nonviolent government changes, a relatively free media, and an independent judiciary. The state's own legal-constitutional structure, defined by two 1992 Basic Laws as "Jewish and democratic," causes the state to restrain its own ethnicizing drive. Several civil rights are enshrined in Israeli law and the state respects, with few exceptions, the freedom of political organization and public protest. It is for this reason that the term open ethnocracy, as defined in Chapter 2, is apt for the Israeli case.

Moreover, the situation has not been unidimensional or static. Some of the constraints imposed on Israel's Arab citizens, especially during Israel's early years, did follow genuine security concerns. Several improvements have also occurred over the years in the situation of Israel's Palestinian-Arab citizens. The general moves toward relaxing government control and liberalizing and democratizing the Israeli regime have positively influenced the Arabs, at least until the October Events of 2000, when thirteen Arab and one Jewish citizen were killed. However, these improvements, important as they are, have not undermined the cornerstones of Israel's ethnocratic regime and have thus failed effectively to advance Arab-Jewish equality. In addition, they have not matched the rising levels of expectations among Israel's Arab citizens, thereby creating growing tensions between majority and minority (see Rabinowitz and Abu-Bakker 2002).

The recent works of leading democratic scholars, such as David Collier, Fareed Zakaria, and Jobani Sartori, sound a warning against the inflationary use of the term democracy to classify regimes. In particular, Collier and Levitski (1997), who draw on Sartori's (1987) work, note the constant use of "democracy with adjectives." They critique the use of most adjectives attached to the term democracy, such as popular, nonelectoral, bureaucratic, or transitional, because these distort the descriptive and normative meaning of the term. As such, they are part of a perilous phenomenon of conceptual stretching.

Zakaria (1997) adds the term illiberal democracies and argues that because "democracy" projects a positive image, it has been too quickly adopted by leaders and scholars to describe most regimes that hold periodic elections. Too often this comes at the cost of ignoring their routine abuse of human and minority rights. This allows such oppressive regimes to hide behind the legitimizing category of democracy while maintaining their control of minorities and abuse of civil rights.

It appears that the work of Smooha, Peled, Shafir, Gavison, and Dowty suffers from the same stretching. They have stretched key democratic terms, such as liberalism, republicanism, consent, and freedom, to fit an incompatible reality. This stretching was made possible by critical omissions and several blind spots in the debate over the Israeli regime, most notably overlooking its political geography, including the ongoing occupation and settlement of Palestinian territories, the role Jewish diasporas play inside Israel, the plight of Palestinian refugees, and the political role of religion. When these critical factors are omitted from the definition of the Israeli regime, it becomes possible to describe it as democratic. I suggest that instead of inventing new varieties of democracy (with inbuilt breaches of central democratic tenets) it is more analytically credible to analyze the democratic deficiencies of each state and work to close the gap between ideal and practice.

Critique

The following critique systematically addresses the main flaws in the ethnic democracy concept, covering the topics of civil inequality, problems in the definition of state boundaries, lack of minority consent, and ethnic exclusion. Together, these deficiencies cast doubt on the empirical and theoretical validity of the ethnic democracy model and on Israel's classification as a democracy. As noted, while the critique focuses on Smooha's work, it can be applied to most analyses of the Israeli regime.

ETHNIC DEMOCRACY AND CIVIL INEQUALITY

Equality between citizens is an essential characteristic of a democracy, often leading to popular consent. Indeed, equality and consent are often considered the main prerequisites of democracy, but both are absent from the Israeli state system. Israel never sought to achieve equal citizenship between Palestinian Arabs and Jews, nor did it seek the consent of its Arab citizens for the forceful ideological imposition of a Jewish state.

Israel's very regime structure makes equality between Arab and Jew impossible in practice and in theory. It is membership in the Jewish people, not citizenship in Israel, that is the chief criterion for the claim of state ownership. The state system is predicated on a constitutional arrangement that contradicts the conditions of equal citizenship and, therefore, democracy. The essence of this contradiction stems from Israel's very raison d'être. As argued elsewhere (Rouhana 1997), Israel embodies in theory, ideology, and practice Jewish state ownership in the sense that Israel is the state of the Jewish people regardless of citizenship. The state is structurally and openly biased in favor of one of its two main ethnic groups, hence emptying, to a large extent, the institution of liberal citizenship from its equalizing and legitimizing function claimed by Shafir and Peled.

Accordingly, Israel is an ethnic state in which the exclusive privileges of the dominant ethnic group are constitutionally grounded in a number of most important Basic Laws, including the Laws of Return and Citizenship and Basic Law: The Knesset (Section 7A), which defines Israel as the state of the Jewish people and limits the right to campaign for parliamentary representation to those accepting Israel's status as the state of the Jewish people (Kretzmer 1990; Rouhana 1997). This law was amended in 2002 to prohibit the candidacy of any party or individual who "supports (in action or speech) the armed struggle of enemy states or terror organizations." This has imposed greater restrictions on expressions of critical non-Zionist opinions and goals, even against Israeli occupation and conquest.

Following the enshrining of the concept Jewish and democratic in the 1992 Basic Laws, it has received near consensual status among the Jewish public. Consequently, legal, academic, and political discourses have constructed the term Jewish and democratic as an inseparable entity. Any activity against the Jewish nature of the state is now interpreted as an attack on democracy. For example, the attorney general, Elyakim Rubinstein, justified the charges he laid in 2002 against MK (Member of Knesset) Azmi Bishara by claiming that "democracy has to defend itself," although Bishara never expressed criticism of Israel's democratic features but, on the contrary, sought to strengthen democracy by promoting the agenda of a "state of all its citizens." Hence, the *Jewishness of the state has now become a precondition for its democracy* among the Jewish public, shrinking further the maneuvering room of non-Zionist (mainly Arab) political movements.[2]

Furthermore, as elaborated below, a number of laws that deal with most important issues, such as land ownership and control, education, and distribution of resources, openly privilege Jews. In addition, there are numerous regulations that do not use the term Jewish or Arab explicitly but which make it clear that preferential treatment of Jewish citizens is supported by statutory law and institutional regulations (Kretzmer 1990). These regulations cover a broad range of individual and collective state-supported assistance. Thus, Israel, by imposing ethnic affiliation as a condition for certain privileges, anchors the violation of equal opportunity in its own laws.

Unequal citizenship deprives Arab citizens of a meaningful state identity. Under the existing ethnic structure that so openly prefers Jew to Arab, and that sometimes treats Arabs as an internal or potential enemy, identification with the state is paramount to accepting constitutional and existential inferiority. Indeed, one of Smooha's fundamental theoretical and empirical claims is that the Arabs have undergone a profound process of Israelization (Smooha 1992), a conclusion that is based on conceptual and methodological pitfalls (Rouhana 1997). Israelization in the sense of accepting Jewish exclusivity and privilege and the Arab inferiority that comes with it, and in the sense of accepting Israel as the state of the Jewish people, is an illusionary identity at best and a distorted imposition at worst. The failure to offer—even theoretically—equal citizenship means that the only identity Israel can provide is, at its center, one that enforces inequality and exclusion.

The issue of consent is also directly related to the ethnically based constitutional inequality. A group's acceptance of unequal conditions violates not only its fundamental human quest for fairness, equal treatment, and equitable access to resources both intangible (such as identity, power, and belonging) and tangible (such as social benefits or access to high-ranking jobs) but also threatens its sense of collective worth and human dignity. Achieving equality is a vital need of the excluded ethnic group that has to be fulfilled if the group is to consent to the state system and develop a sense of belonging and attachment to the state. Achieving full equality is not only a basic group right but also a basic human need that no ethnic group willingly forsakes. Indeed, human needs theory considers equality and identity to be basic needs that cannot be negotiated, washed away, or repressed. Many argue that if these fundamental human needs are not fulfilled, the question becomes under what political circumstances crises will emerge—not *if* they will emerge. The October Events of 2000 were a stark reminder of the explosive potential of such crises.

As shown in a wide body of literature, there is little theoretical rationale, moral justification, historical evidence, or political foresight in expecting that a national minority should accept unequal status within its own homeland (Rouhana 1997; Yiftachel 2000b), especially when its minority status within the homeland is based on its recent collective dispossession (Zureik 1993). The ethnic democracy model tells us that the constitutional position of the subordinate group can only improve but never reach full equality. This "innovation" is actually a recipe for protracted social conflicts and not for their resolution.

Under such circumstances, inequality becomes a central issue of mobilization and political consciousness by the subordinate group. Its subordination can be maintained only if the dominant group is willing to use force as its ultimate means of control, thus violating one of the essential ingredients of democratic governance, as became evident in October of 2000. Other short-term appeasement is possible by, for example, improving the minority's share of public resources. But such improvements can hardly eradicate the source of the conflict. On the contrary, improved socioeconomic conditions can increase the political consciousness and collective expectations, thereby fueling the potential for conflict. Thus the viability of the model is, by definition, based on control and not on consent—a clear violation of democratic practice.

Ethnic Democracy: Boundaries, Ethnos, and Demos

What are the boundaries of the Israeli polity? This crucial analytical question has been conspicuously absent from the analysis of Smooha and most other analysts of Israel. These scholars have taken for granted the existence of political boundaries that define Israel proper by its pre-1967 borders. Closer examination reveals, however, that such an entity simply does not exist, since it is impossible to define Israel as a territorial unit and it is difficult to define the boundaries of its body politic. There are four principal reasons for this: the rupturing of the state's borders by colonial Jewish settlement in the occupied territories, the continuing political empowerment of Jewish diasporas, the essentializing impact of Israeli laws and policies toward Arab citizens, and the uncertain future of Palestinian refugees.

The construction of an unproblematic Israel proper is partially premised on viewing Jewish settlements in the occupied territories as temporary, or hoping for accelerated decolonization, as do Shafir and Peled. While we should not dismiss the significance of Israel's offers to withdraw from Palestinian territories, especially during the 2000–2001 peace negotiations, this temporary status has now lasted for more than thirty-five years and is not likely to end soon. During that period, some four hundred thousand Jews have settled in the territories (including al-Quds/East Jerusalem). This is not a mere temporary aberration but a structural factor that, beyond breaching international law and committing mass collective dispossession, also undermines the basic democratic principle of universal suffrage, as settlers remain fully enfranchised while their Palestinian neighbors have no say in Israeli policies that control their own regions. This has somewhat changed following the Oslo agreement, although most Palestinian residents and lands in the territories are still under Israeli control to various degrees, especially following the reinvasion of all of the Palestinian territories by the Israeli Defense Forces since the spring of 2002.

The significance of this undemocratic situation became clear in Israel's 1996 elections: counting only the results within the Green Line, Shimon Peres, the pro-peace Labor candidate who lost the elections by less than one percentage point, would have beaten Benjamin Netanyahu by a margin of more than 5 percent! This shows that the identification of Israel proper as a democracy is analytically misleading. The involvement of the settlers in Israeli politics is, of course, far deeper than simply electoral. They are represented by 16 Knesset members (out of 120) and 6 government ministers, including Prime Minister Sharon himself, whose official residence is in occupied East Jerusalem. The settlers have also held a host of key positions in the armed forces, politics, and academia since the late 1970s.

In addition, Jewish diasporas, represented by bodies such as the Jewish National Fund, the Zionist Federation, and the Jewish Agency, continue to hold executive political power in Israel based on covenants struck with the

Israeli government. Such bodies represent, and are funded by, world Jewry. They are charged with serving only the interests of Jews and are not accountable to Israeli citizens. World Jewry has also been involved with Israeli political parties and politicians, often influencing policy making and agenda setting. Hence, extraterritorial Jewish groups have amassed political power in the Israeli regime to an extent unmatched by nonresident groups in any democratic state.

Hence, Israel operates as a polity without borders. This undermines a basic requirement of democracy—the existence of a demos. The demos, as it was defined in ancient Greece, denotes an inclusive body of empowered citizens within a given territory. It is a competing organizing principle to that of the ethnos, where membership is determined by common origin. The term democracy means the rule of the demos, and its modern application points to an overlap between permanent state residency and political rights as a necessary democratic condition. Such overlap is the one and only way to enable the law of the land to be applied equally to all subjects. This necessitates the institutionalization of clear and permanent borders. In other words, the state should not only belong to all its citizens but also to them only. Smooha's ethnic democracy concept entails a problematic mix of two opposing principles of political organization—ethnos and demos—resulting in an oxymoron.

A major characteristic of Israeli policies toward the minority has entailed the vast appropriation of Arab land and its settlement with Jews, as fully elaborated in the following chapters. Jewish settlement activity has indeed slowed during the last two decades but has not ceased. Following the al-Aqsa *intifada* it has received a new boost with dozens of new settlements built (often without formal approval) in the occupied territories and thirty-two new ones, fully approved, in Israel proper. Laws and policies have continued to facilitate the transfer of land control, ownership, and use from Arabs to the Israeli state. Arabs are commonly excluded from purchasing or leasing land in most nonurban Jewish settlements, whose jurisdiction covers more than 80 percent of the country. Arab citizens are thus denied a basic democratic right of access to property and residential areas in their own state. This has essentialized the boundaries between Arab and Jewish citizens and polarized ethnic relations.

A third boundary overlooked by the ethnic democracy model is analytical: Where should we begin and end our analysis of the Israeli regime? Here Smooha, like most analysts, refrains from examining several other obstacles to democracy in Israel, such as pervasive militarism, low levels of regime accountability, and especially the political agendas of Orthodox and ultra-Orthodox (Haredi) Jewish groups. Here I contend that the historical accommodation between secular and religious Jews, despite the deep differences between the two communities, has been premised on their joint interest in the Judaization project. That is, despite the notable tensions between the groups, secular parties have made serious concessions to Orthodox parties. This has ensured the cooperation of the two groups in the advancement of the project of Judaizing Israel/Palestine, geographically, demographically, and religiously. Hence, it is analytically deficient to label Israel a democracy without examining the impact of Orthodox political agendas and practices on the principles of a democratic state. As further developed in the next chapter, the analytical boundary within which the regime should be examined definitely should include the relations between state and religion, which are overlooked by Smooha's model.

ETHNIC DEMOCRACY, MINORITY EXCLUSION, AND TYRANNY OF THE MAJORITY

Smooha, like most analysts of Israel, argues that a balance exists between universal democratic rights, which are extended to all Israeli citizens, and collective norms, which grant priority to Israel's Jewish citizens. Smooha makes this distinction between individual and collective rights a centerpiece of his model, although closer examination shows that the distinction is rather blurry, for two main reasons: (a) collective rights often express the accumulation of individual preferences for culture, residence, and development; and (b) the limitations imposed on collective rights violate individual rights in the above areas. This putative balance between full individual and limited collective rights provides the chief theoretical basis for the ethnic democracy model. It opens up, according to Smooha, avenues of upward mobility and integration for the minority mainly owing to its politicization and modernization under a (supposedly democratic and responsive) Israeli political system. In practice, however, several key spheres of Israeli society—ideological, symbolic, structural, and political—repress the mobility of the minority.

First, the political structure breaches another key democratic rule: the protection of minorities. Most political theorists, as early as de Tocqueville, have warned against the dangers associated with the *tyranny of the majority*. Crude majority rule is thus offset in most democracies by mechanisms that protect individual citizens and minority groups, including a constitution, a bill of rights, a bicameral parliament, or institutionalized ethnic compromises, such as power sharing, grand coalitions, cultural-regional autonomy, or minority veto. Nearly all of these are absent in Israel. Israel as a state and as a political system preserves the superiority of the Jews and the inferiority of the Arabs on several levels (see Ghanem 1998).

On the ideological and symbolic levels, as already mentioned, Israel's objectives, symbols, and policies promote the public Jewish-Hebrew culture, without recognizing the needs of the large Palestinian minority for public and symbolic expression of its identity as well. In contrast to the Jews, who treat the symbols, values, and institutions of the state as their own and see them as part of their heritage and a source of identification, the Palestinian citizens feel alienated from these exclusively Jewish and Zionist symbols.

Arabs are also involuntarily excluded from key Israeli institutions that are often designed to serve Jewish objectives and not those of the entire citizenry. This entails the marginalization of the Arabs in the arenas of political power and decision making, their nonconscription into the army, the nonemployment of Arabs in security sensitive jobs or in senior bureaucratic positions, the establishment of special institutions or departments to deal with Arabs, the inferior position of Arab education and public media, and the carefully designed exclusion of Arabs from the institutions governing land ownership and control.

This exclusion is also reflected on the executive level: there has only been one (minor) Arab (Druze) minister in the fifty-five years of Israel's existence; no permanent Arab judge has ever served on the Supreme Court; and no Arab parties ever been part of a governing coalition. The budgets of Arab local governments and the allocation of land and development programs to these municipalities have been consistently inferior to their Jewish counterparts.

Further, the politicization and modernization observed by Smooha to propel Arab mobility are partial and distorted (Rouhana and Ghanem 1998). Rather than portraying Arabs as an ethnic minority with upward mobility in the Israeli democratic state, it would be more appropriate to conceptualize their condition as a trapped minority (Rabinowitz 2001; Yiftachel 1999a), a minority in crisis (Ghanem 2000), or a community developing in a fractured region (see Chapter 7). None of these approaches assumes stable, normal minority-majority relations, as portrayed by most mainstream analyses of the political status of the Arabs in Israel.

Conclusion

We have seen in this chapter that despite a few dissenting voices, Israel is commonly defined as a democracy, often a liberal democracy, by a range of prominent scholars. But this definition is premised on partial and faulty foundations and suffers from conceptual stretching. In particular, serious empirical and conceptual flaws exist in the ethnic democracy model and in analyses of the Israeli regime that support that model, most notably the works of Peled, Shafir, Dowty, and Gavison.

Conceptually, the inclusion in the one term (Jewish and democratic or ethnic democracy) of two opposing principles such as demos and ethnos is questionable. This hybrid causes internal inconsistency (akin to expressions such as "hot ice") and a subsequent blurring of the system's structural ethnic stratification. This may lead to a distorted acceptance of constitutional and institutional inequality as part of a democratic system.

Moreover, most analyses have largely ignored the dynamics of Israel's political geography, which have caused the state to radically change its demography, alter patterns of ethnic territorial control, rupture state borders, incorporate Jewish and block Palestinian diasporas, and form strong links between religion, territory, and ethnicity. These are not minor details but fundamental forces in shaping every settler society, and especially one that continues to pursue an active program of ethnic immigration and settlement while still refusing to define its geographic and political boundaries clearly.

It is here that the distinction between *regime features and structure*, as outlined in Chapter 2, becomes useful to explain the common reference to Israel as a democracy. Several features of the Israeli regime indeed resemble the working of a democracy (for example, periodic elections, a reasonably autonomous judiciary, a relatively open media, and certain civil protections), but none challenges the undemocratic structure, which still encourages and facilitates the Judaization project. The focus on regime features, and silence over structure appear to have blinded most scholars to the genuine nature of the regime operating in Israel/Palestine.

In light of the clear inconsistencies, blind spots, and deficiencies shown above, the classification of Israel as a democracy may appear to function more as a tool for legitimizing the political and legal status quo than as a scholarly exploration guided by empirical accuracy or conceptual coherence. Instead of attempting to stretch and distort the democratic model to fit the twisted reality, it is analytically and politically more credible to reconceptualize the Israeli polity according to its major constitutive forces and frameworks of power. This is the task of the next chapter.

Chapter 5

The Making of Ethnocracy
in Israel/Palestine

Following the critical analysis of Israel's democratic axiom, this chapter describes the making of the state's ethnocratic regime. The focus is on the reciprocity of spatial transformations and ethnic relations. The chapter shows how the project of Judaization, that is, the spatial, political, and discursive forces associated with Jewish expansion and control over Israel/Palestine, has created the main bases of the regime, and it illuminates their impact on the shaping of ethnonational and ethnoclass relations.

Let us begin with the Qa'adan saga. During the1995–2000 period, the country's High Court of Justice was grappling with an appeal lodged by Adel Qa'adan, an Arab-Israeli citizen whose attempt to lease land in the suburban locality of Katzir was rejected on the grounds that he was not a Jew.[1] During the lengthy delays and deliberations, the Court's president, Judge Aharon Barak, known widely as a champion of civil rights, noted that this case was among the most strenuous in his legal career. In March of 2000, the Court handed down a historical decision claiming that past land policies unduly and illegally discriminated against Arab citizens. The court upheld the right of the Qa'adan family to lease state land but fell short on specific instructions to enforce the ruling, or specific instructions on how to force the locality to lease land to the Qa'adan family.

The decision caused shockwaves in Israel and prompted several people to claim that this decision meant "the end of Zionism as we know it," either approvingly or disapprovingly (see Vitkon 2001). Other analysts were more careful but still noted a fundamental change in the Israeli land regime (Kedar 2001). The issue entered the public arena, with several well-attended conferences and publications wholly devoted to the *Qa'adan* decision.

While analysts and the public fervently discussed the issue, actual reforms in the Israeli regime have not occurred as yet. The Qa'adan family continued to seek admission into Katzir, but its application was stalled time and again on procedural, administrative, and social grounds. In 2001, the Israeli Association for the Protection of Civil Rights filed an appeal for contempt of court against Katzir, but still the Qa'adans were not offered a block of land for three more years. In July of 2004, the manager of the Israel Land Authority, Ya'akov Efrat, sent a letter requesting Katzir to allocate land to the Qa'adans, although at the time of this writing, the land has not been allocated, and resistance still exists within the small Jewish locality.[2]

During 2003–4, new arrangements were planned by the Israel Land Authority to allow the transfer of state lands to the Jewish Agency and/or the Jewish National Fund (both registered as private companies). This would enable the construction of new Jewish settlements, neighborhoods, and suburbs while continuing the policy of legal exclusion of Arabs, returning conditions to a pre-Qa'adan state.[3] While the new land arrangements have not been finalized as of this publication, the fact that after five and a half decades of sovereign independence the state's highest legal authority still finds it difficult to ensure the fulfillment of a basic civil right such as equal access to state land provides a telling starting point for understanding the Israeli ethnocratic regime. In the pages below, I wish to present the ethnocratic prism through which the formation of Israel's regime and its ethnic relations can be explained. The chapter traces the making of the Israeli ethnocracy, focusing on the major Zionist project of Judaizing Israel/Palestine. It argues that Judaization is the major axis shaping relations between the Zionist and Palestinian ethnonations, as well as between the various Jewish and Arab ethnoclasses.

Historically, the phenomenon asserts that the closer a group is to the heart of the Judaization project (in its ideology and practices), the higher its political and economic status. Although this ethnocratic logic has been complicated in recent years with the emergence of other mobilizing societal goals, such as liberalization, globalization, and hyperreligiosity, the social structure created by Judaization is still highly evident and still determines much of the social hierarchy in Israel/Palestine. Finally, the chapter points to a process of *creeping apartheid* evident in Israel/Palestine over the last two decades. It argues that this is a logical (though not necessary) extension of the ethnocratic system, as the latter requires ever harsher measures to fend off the challenges against its segregative and stratifying logic.

As in previous chapters, the analysis below places particular emphasis on Israel's political geography and political economy. This perspective draws attention to the material-spatial foundations of social relations, holding that discourse, space, and development are intertwined in their process of transformation and struggle (see Lefebvre 1991; Massey 1993). The critical perspective taken here problematizes issues often overlooked among analysts of the Israeli regime, such as settlement, segregation, borders, development, and diasporas. Drawing these elements into the analysis broadens the notion of regime to incorporate the material and spatial as foundations for the shaping of politics and society.

Ethnocracy in the Making: The Judaization of Israel/Palestine

This book covers, as it should, the entire territory and population under Israeli rule. Prior to 1967, Israeli rule was limited to the area within the Green Line (the 1949 armistice lines), but after that date it covered all of Israel/Palestine, or what Kimmerling (1989) has called the "Israeli control system." This appears to be the situation even following the 1993 Oslo agreement and the al-Aqsa *intifada* (2000–2003); the areas under limited Palestinian self-rule have remained under (direct or indirect) Jewish control. Therefore, the appropriate political-geographical framework for the analysis of Israel/Palestine since 1967 is *one ethnocracy, two ethnonations, and several Jewish and Palestinian ethnoclasses.*

Because this chapter addresses ethnic relations, we should first outline the current demography in Israel. At the end of 2002, Jews accounted for about 81 percent of Israel's 6.6 million citizens and Palestinian Arabs about 16 percent.[4] Approximately 420,000 Jews resided in the occupied territories of the West Bank and Gaza, and an additional 3.4 million Palestinians resided in the territories. Hence, the population of Israel/Palestine was 52 percent Jewish and 47 percent Palestinian Arab (CBSa 2003).

Ethnic and religious divisions are also marked within each national community. About 38 percent of Jews are of Ashkenazi origin and about 40 percent are Mizrahi.[5] The rest are mainly recent Russian-speaking immigrants, who form an ethnocultural group gradually integrating into Israel's (Ashkenazi-oriented) mainstream. Orthodox Jews, whose religious identities are closely associated with strong communal-ethnic boundaries, amount to 15 to 17 percent of the Jewish population, half of whom are ultra-Orthodox (Guttman Institute 2000).

Of the Palestinian Arabs in Israel, 81 percent are Muslims (one-fifth of whom are Bedouin), 10 percent are Christian, and 9 percent Druze. In the occupied territories, 96 percent are Muslim and 3 percent Christian. In both the Jewish and Muslim communities, a major cultural division has also developed between orthodox and secular groups. About 15 to 17 percent of Jews are Orthodox, as are about 30 percent of Muslims on both sides of the Green Line. Finally, the recent phenomenon of labor migration has added a group of 300,000–400,000 residents to the area's population, almost half of them unauthorized (see Dellapergola 2001).

Typical to ethnocratic societies, many of these divisions have developed into ethnoclasses, that is, cultural collectivities bound by their material, geographic, and political positions. In the terms defined in Chapter 2, the European Jews (Ashkenazim) have constituted the charter or founding group that has occupied the upper echelons of society in most spheres, including politics, the military, the labor market, and culture. The Eastern Jews (Mizrahim) have been the largest group of later immigrants, recently accompanied by the large group of Russian speakers and a small group of Ethiopian Jews. These later immigrants are placed in a middle position, lagging behind the Ashkenazim but above the indigenous Palestinian Arabs (see Cohen and Haberfeld 1998; Elmelech and Lewin-Epstein 1998). As is typical in settler societies, the indigenous Palestinian Arab groups have occupied from the onset the lowest position in most spheres of society and have been largely excluded from its political, cultural, and economic centers. Following the first *intifada* and the economic closure imposed on the occupied territories, as well as the partial liberalization of the Israeli economy, a fourth "foreign" ethnoclass appeared, composed mainly of labor migrants. This is a growing and fragmented underclass that is largely denied political and civil rights.

A Jewish and Judaizing State

As described in Chapter 3, following the UN partition resolution, the establishment of Israel was achieved through war, first against the Palestinians, and later against invading Arab armies. The war in which Arab forces attempted to destroy the Zionist project resulted in widespread ethnic cleansing, which turned two-thirds of the Palestinians into refugees, most of them outside the boundaries of the Israeli state. This issue has not been settled to date and has constituted a central component in the shaping of Israeli policies and identities.

In 1948, Israel declared itself a Jewish state. In some ways, Israel's Declaration of Independence was quite liberal, promising non-Jews "full and equal citizenship" and banning discrimination on the grounds of religion, ethnic origin, gender, or creed. The central political institutions of the new state were established as democratic, including a representative parliament (the Knesset), periodic elections, an independent judiciary, and a relatively free media.

During the following years, however, a series of laws and practices enshrined the ethnic and partially religious, *Jewish* character of the state, rather than its Israeli character, as would be required by international standards of self-determination. Chief among these have been the state's immigration statutes, which made every Jew in the world a potential citizen but denied this possibility to many Palestinians born in the country. As shown in the previous chapter, a wide range of other laws and policies further anchored the Jewish character of the state not only symbolically but also as a concrete and deepening reality. These laws and policies have formed the bases of the Israeli ethnocratic regime as outlined below.

In 1964, the Israeli High Court handed down the Yerdor case, which declared "the Jewishness of Israel" as being a constitutional given (see Lahav 1997). In 1985, revisions made to the Basic Law on the Knesset added that no party would be allowed to run if it rejected Israel's definition as a state of the Jewish people, and in 2002, the law was further amended to disqualify any party or person supporting an armed struggle against Israel or any organization defined (by the same state) as terrorist. The combination of these laws created a structure whereby any democratic struggle to change the state's Zionist character would be almost impossible.

Further, the two 1992 Basic Laws defined the state as Jewish and democratic, thereby further enshrining the state's Jewish character and also coupling it with a democratic commitment. As argued below, this coupling is problematic not as an abstract principle but rather against the ongoing reality of Judaization, which has unilaterally restructured the nature of society through its wide-reaching policies and practices.

Therefore, I argue, the main structure of the Israeli regime, and hence the main obstacle to democracy, does not relate only to its declaration as being Jewish. This may be akin to the existing constitutional status of democratic states such as Finland as Lutheran, and England as Anglican. The deeply structural element lies in the parallel processes of *Judaization and de-Arabization* facilitated and legitimized by the declaration of Israel as Jewish and by the ethnocratic policies and institutions resulting from this declaration.

What are the main foundations over which the metagoal of Judaization was translated into laws, policies, discourses, and practices? Drawing on the framework offered in Chapter 2, I briefly sketch the six major regime bases typifying the Israeli ethnocracy. These have shaped relations between Jews and Palestinians, as well as the various ethnoclasses in Israel/Palestine.

- *Demography*: Given the goal of establishing a Jewish state in an Arab region, ethnic composition has been a most central concern. This caused imposition of tight controls over population status and movement. The lynchpins of the system have been the Jewish Law of Return, and the denial of the Right of Return for Palestinian refugees. Israel has also actively encouraged Jewish immigration and imposed strict constraints on the naturalization of other ethnic groups (al-Haj 2001; Kimmerling 2001; Shuval and Leshem 1998).
- *Land and settlement*: Given the establishment of a Jewish state in contested territory, Israel's land, settlement, and planning policies have consistently pursued the transfer of land control to Jewish hands, the settlement of Jews in all parts of Israel/Palestine, the segregation of Palestinians and Jews, and the restriction of Palestinian Arab settlement and development (Kedar 2001; Yiftachel 1999b, 2002). These structural geographical processes have also widened the gap between Jewish ethnoclasses. This is the central topic of the book, to be further developed in the remaining chapters.
- *Armed forces*: The legal means of violence, and especially the management of the army, police, and paramilitary units, have been dominated

by Jews. They have enjoyed a supreme status in Israeli decision making, elevating security concerns to unquestionable truth and shaping strong Israeli militarism (Ben-Eliezer 1995). Israel's Arab citizens have not been allowed to join the Israel Defense Forces (IDF) apart from the coopted Druze, and some Bedouins (Lustick 1980). The state's armed forces have also put into practice complex processes of integration and stratification among Jewish groups (Helman 1999; Kimmerling 2001).

- *Capital flow*: Policies guiding development and capital accumulation have also weighed heavily in favor of Jews. This has been evident in a range of policies, such as government developmental incentives, industrialization, the system of taxation, employment practices, and links with local and international (mainly Jewish) entrepreneurs. The state's recent liberalization and global outlook and subsequent retreat from market regulation have deepened the gaps between the state's ethnoclasses (Swirsky 1995). These forces have also provided a new discourse, which has often challenged the logic of the Judaization project and particularly the ongoing colonial hold on Palestinian territories (Shafir and Peled 2002).
- *The law*: Until the 1980s, the legal system, by and large, backed the main projects of the Zionist state in the key areas of citizenship, immigration, land and settlement, occupation, religion, and public culture. This included implicit support for the occupation and settlement of Palestinian territories (Hajjar 2005; Kimmerling 2001; Kretzmer 2002). With regard to civil law, religious regulations were adopted by the state that prohibited civil marriage, which deepened the chasm between Jewish and non-Jewish citizens. Since the 1990s, however, with the advent of judicial activism, the system has increased its independence and protection of civil rights, presenting a growing (though partial) challenge to the state's overt practices of Judaization.
- *Public culture*: The state's main symbols, such as the flag, anthem, ceremonies, and logos, all stress the Jewishness of the state. The Sabbath and Jewish holidays are observed by the state. This has been augmented by the use of Hebrew in nearly all bureaucratic and legal forums (despite Arabic also being an official language). Hebrew-Jewish public culture has also been diffused through place naming, mapping, road signs, and the shaping of public spaces.

Clearly, this schematic and very brief outline does not do justice to each of these critical areas of state-society relations. Neither can it elaborate on the complex ways in which these regime bases generally reinforce but at times contradict one another. Two points in particular require further attention: religion and resistance. First, as discussed in Chapter 2, ethnocratic regimes are often closely associated with the politics and institutions of religion. In most cases, this is due to the overlap between religion and ethnicity and their mutual reinforcement in the construction of ethnic boundaries. This has been the case under the Israeli regime, which has used religion as a centerpiece in the Judaization project. The institutions, regulations, and moral authority of Judaism have indeed been a major force in the making of the Israeli ethnocracy. Its influence has even made the Israeli state relinquish segments of its law-making sovereignty to religious institutions in the sphere of personal affairs (see Kimmerling 2001).

However, religion is not defined here as a regime base because qualitatively Judaism and Jewishness in Israel have mainly functioned as gatekeepers for the Zionist project and as main markers of excluded non-Jews (mainly Arabs), as discussed further below. But even this central function has diminished recently, with the arrival of hundreds of thousands of non-Jews (mainly from the former Soviet Union, who were allowed to enter Israel because of their kin relations with Jews) who have joined the Jewish-Zionist collectivity and have demonstrated the relatively subordinate position of religion vis-à-vis ethnicity in the making of the ethnocratic society.

Second, the dynamics of these regime bases have not remained unchallenged. Counterforces have gathered momentum, especially since the 1960s. These have emerged, first and foremost, from Palestinian populations, either external refugees (who formed the basis of the Palestine Liberation Organization), residents of the occupied territories, or Israel's Palestinian citizens. Other challenges emerged from Jewish marginalized groups, most notably the Mizrahim (see Shalom-Chetrit 2000; Shohat 2001). During the 1990s, the influence of globalization and liberalization began to erode the logic of Judaization and created severe tensions and contradictions in the ethnocratic system (Kedar 2001; Ram 2001; Shafir and Peled 2002). These have thrown the Israeli policy into its current political and economic crises but have not managed, as of yet, to change its ethnocratic basis.

We turn now to the dynamic political geography of the contested land ruled by the Israeli ethnocracy.

Judaizing the Homeland

Like the 1922 arbitrary British demarcation that became the Zionist and Palestinian homeland, the outcome of the 1948 war created Israel proper within the Green Line as a geobody to be sanctified as a new homeland. Subsequently, Israel entered a radical stage of territorial restructuring centering on the Judaization and de-Arabization of the new, smaller homeland. Some policies and initiatives were an extension of earlier Jewish approaches, but the tactics, strategies, and ethnocentric cultural construction of the pre-1948 Jewish *yeshuv* (settling community) were significantly intensified. This process was enabled by the aid of the newly acquired state apparatus and the international legitimacy attached to national sovereignty. The territorial transformation began, as noted, with the flight and expulsion of approximately 700,000–750,000 Palestinians during the 1948 war. Israel prevented the return of the refugees and destroyed more than four hundred villages (see Morris 1993; Nazzal 1974). The authorities were quick to fill the gaps with Jewish settlements inhabited by Jewish immigrants and refugees who entered the country en masse during the late 1940s and early 1950s.

As detailed in Chapter 6, the frontier became a central icon, and its settlement was considered one of the highest achievements of any Zionist. The reviving Hebrew language was filled with positive images about the redemption of land and making the desert bloom. The glorification of the frontier thus assisted both in the construction of a national Jewish identity and in capturing the physical space on which this identity could be territorially created (see Kemp 1997; Kimmerling 2001).

This cultural, political, and geographical orientation was premised on the historical myth, cultivated since the rise of Zionism, that "the Land" (Haaretz), that is the ancient Jewish homeland, belongs to the Jews and only to the Jews. A rigid form of territorial ethnonationalism developed from the beginning of Zionist settlement in order to indigenize immigrant Jews quickly and to conceal the existence of a Palestinian people on the same land. Popular culture, especially songs, ceremonies, public speeches, and literature, were used extensively to generate the new pioneering-settling culture.

The role of popular culture in Judaizing Israel/Palestine has also been central (for elaboration see Kimmerling 2001; Ram 1999; Shohat 2001). It will suffice to say here that it diffused the perception of the land as Jewish only, drawing on a mythical national discourse of forced exile in ancient times and a subsequent return to the homeland (Ram 1996). A parallel discourse developed in reaction to the Arab-Jewish conflict, and persisting Arab aggression toward the new state elevated the exigencies of national security to a level of unquestioned truth. These discourses blinded most Jews to a range of discriminatory policies imposed on the Palestinians, including military rule, the lack of economic or social development, political surveillance, underrepresentation, and—most importantly for this essay—large-scale confiscation of land and severe restrictions on settlement and development (see Kedar 1998; Zureik 1979).

Such sentiments were translated into a pervasive program of territorial socialization, creating an inseparable bond between Zionist Jews and their newly constructed homeland. This relationship was expressed in school curricula and most spheres of public discourse. Even after the establishment of a sovereign Jewish state, Jewish settlement remained a cornerstone of Zionist nation building. This project was aimed both at fending off Arab threats to Jewish land control and building the spirit of a new Jew, one deeply rooted in the homeland (Zerubavel 2002).

To be sure, the return of Jews to their ancestors' mythical land and the perception of this land as a safe haven after generations of persecution had a powerful liberating meaning, especially following the Nazi atrocities in Europe and ongoing Arab threats to Israel's security. Yet the darker side of this project was ignored during the construction of an unproblematic return of Jews to their biblical promised land. Few dissenting Jewish voices were heard against these Judaizing practices. Any opposition that did emerge was suppressed by Jewish elites.

Several commentators have noted that the intensity of the Judaization frontier has slowed down recently because of the global orientations of Israeli elites and Palestinian resistance (Ram 2001; Shafir and Peled 1998, 2002). This has been reflected by the emergence of a fierce struggle inside the Jewish society over the future of the occupied territories and by the election of two Labor-led Israeli governments promoting decolonization policies. But the governments of Rabin and Barak, together with significant economic and cultural forces, failed to implement the decolonization program. In other sections of Zionist society, the logic of Judaization is still fundamental to orientation and power and treated as the historical core of Israeli identity (see Newman 2001).

Consequently, since 1948, two parallel processes have developed on the same land: the visible establishment of democratic institutions and procedures, and a more concealed yet systematic and coercive seizure of territory by the dominant ethnic group. The contradiction between the two processes casts doubt on the pervasive classification of Israel in the academic literature as a democracy, a point to which I will return.

Prior to 1948, only about 8 percent of potential Israeli land was in Jewish hands, and about 5 percent was vested with the representative of the British Mandate. About a quarter of the remaining land was owned by Arabs, another quarter was in constant Arab use, and the rest was in sporadic use (Kedar 1998). The Israeli state, however, quickly expanded its land holdings and currently owns or controls 93 percent of the area within the Green Line. One-third of this land transfer was based on expropriating Palestinian refugee property. The remaining two-thirds of the confiscated land belonged to Palestinians who remained in Israel as Israeli citizens. At present, Palestinian Arabs, who constitute approximately 17 percent of Israel's population, own about 3 percent of the land, while their local government areas cover 2.5 percent.

A central aspect of the land transfer was its legal *unidirectionality*. Israel created an institutional and legal land system under which confiscated land could not be sold. Further, such land did not merely become state land—it became possessed jointly by the state and the entire Jewish people. This was achieved by granting extraterritorial organizations, such as the Jewish

National Fund, the Jewish Agency, and the Zionist Federation, a share of the state's sovereign powers and significant authority in the areas of land, development, and settlement. The transfer of land to the hands of unaccountable bodies representing the Jewish people can be likened to a black hole into which Arab land enters but can never be retrieved. This structure ensures the unidirectional character of all land transfers: from Palestinian to Jewish hands and never vice versa. A stark expression of this legal and institutional setting is that Israel's Arab citizens are currently prevented from purchasing, leasing, or utilizing land in the entire area of the regional councils, an area that constitutes around 80 percent of the country, as detailed in the next chapter. It can be assumed that the constitutions of most democratic countries would consider such a blatant breach of equal civil rights illegal. But Israel's character as a Judaizing state has so far prevented the enactment of a constitution that would guarantee such rights.

During the 1950s and 1960s, following the transfer of land to the state, more than six hundred Jewish settlements were constructed in all parts of the land. This created the infrastructure for the housing of Jewish refugees and immigrants who continued to enter the country. The result was the penetration of Jews into most Arab areas, the encirclement of most Arab villages by exclusively Jewish settlements (where non-Jews are not permitted to purchase housing), and the restriction of the Arab minority to specific small enclaves.

Settlement and Intra-Jewish Segregation

I turn now to the issue of ethnoclasses. Beyond the obvious consequences of the Jewish settlement project on the ethnonational level, it also caused processes of segregation and stratification among Jewish ethnoclasses. This aspect is central for the understanding of relations between the various Jewish ethnoclasses, especially Ashkenazim and Mizrahim. Notably, I do not argue that relations between Jewish ethnic groups are nondemocratic in the formal sense, but rather that the ethnocratic nature of Jewish-Palestinian relations has adversely affected intra-Jewish and intra-Palestinian relations. To illustrate the geography of these processes, I outline in more detail the social and ethnic nature of the Jewish settlement project, which advanced in three main waves following the establishment of the state.

During the first wave, from 1949 to 1952, some 240 communal villages (*kibbutzim* and *moshavim*) were built primarily along the Green Line. During the second wave, from the early 1950s to the mid-1960s, 27 development towns and 56 villages were built. These were populated, usually by coercion, by Jewish refugees and immigrants from North Africa. During the same period, large groups of Mizrahim were also housed in frontier urban neighborhoods, which were either previously Palestinian or adjacent to Palestinian areas. Given the low socioeconomic resources of most Mizrahim, their generally enemy-affiliated Arab culture, and their lack of ties to Israeli elites, the development towns and the neighborhoods quickly became, and have remained to date, distinct concentrations of segregated, poor, and deprived Mizrahi populations (Gradus 1984; Hasson 1981; Swirski and Shoshani 1985). This geography of dependence, achieved in the name of Judaizing the country, accounts for the evolution of Ashkenazi-Mizrahi relations to the present day.

During the last twenty-five years, the third wave of settlement saw the establishment of more than 150 small nonurban settlements known as community or private settlements or neighborhoods (*yeshuvim kehilatiyim*) on both sides of the Green Line. They were presented to the public as a renewed effort to Judaize Israel's hostile frontiers, using the typical rhetoric of national security, the Arab threat to state lands, and the possible emergence of Arab secessionism. In the occupied territories, additional rationales for Jewish settlement referred to the return of Jews to ancient biblical sites and to the creation of strategic depth. But despite the continuation of a similar Zionist discourse, a major difference characterized these settlements: they ruptured, for the first time, Israel's internationally recognized borders, a point to which I return below.

From a social perspective, those who were part of the third wave of settlement were mainly Ashkenazi suburbanites seeking to improve their housing and social status (see Applebaum and Newman 1991; Yiftachel and Carmon 1997). This trend has intensified during the 1990s and early 2000s, with a pervasive construction of new gated community neighborhoods, most adjacent to centrally located metropolitan *moshavim*. More than two hundred such neighborhoods have been built, hosting mainly the suburbanizing middle classes. During the 1990s, Jewish settlement activity in the West Bank accompanied the suburbanization trend, especially in affluent settlements close to the Tel Aviv and Jerusalem regions. Since the mid-1990s, and especially since the outbreak of the al-Aqsa *intifada*, these West Bank settlements have increasingly accommodated religious-national and ultra-Orthodox Jews of lower socioeconomic standings and less of the secular middle classes.[6]

"Fractured Regions" in Israel/Palestine

Notably, the different waves of settlement were marked by social and institutional segregation, sanctioned and augmented by state policies. A whole range of mechanisms were devised and implemented not only to maintain nearly impregnable patterns of segregation between Arabs and Jews but also to erect fairly rigid lines of separation between various Jewish ethnoclasses. Segregation mechanisms included the demarcation of local government and education district boundaries; the provision of separate and unequal government services (especially education and housing); the development of largely separate economies; the organization of different types of localities in different state-wide settlement movements that organized separate service delivery; and rivaling political affiliations according to historical ideological differences. This segregative tendency was augmented by an uneven allocation of land on a sectoral basis in which rural villages (especially *kibbutzim* and *moshavim*, and lately *kehilatti* localities) were granted larger land resources than their neighboring development towns or Arab localities. This disparity has become economically very significant since the early 1990s, when large tracts of agricultural lands were redeveloped for urban purposes. This topic is elaborated in the next chapter.

It may be apt at this stage to introduce the concept of "fractured regions," which provides a central element in the spatial-social making of ethnocratic settler societies. I contend that given the history of settlement waves, the relatively homogenous nature of each settling and indigenous locality, and the high level of institutional segregation, a political-geographical pattern of fractured regions was created. The main unit here is the region (see Paasi 1991)—a spatial and political entity denoting a scale of human organization between locality and state, normally combining a considerable number of localities and people and forming the foundation for geographically based identities and mobilizations (see Markusen 1987).

Unlike the ordinary meaning of regions, in Israel/Palestine these entities are fractured, that is, created with no territorial contiguity. This is due to the deliberate land and settlement policy that sought to prevent territorial continuity of Palestinian Arabs by settling Jews (mainly immigrants of low socioeconomic status) in the frontiers/peripheries. The resulting pattern is conspicuous in Israeli geography, society, and politics as non contiguous regions are institutionalized and reproduced through separate systems of education, planning, local government, political mobilization, and cultural orientation. These regional ethnoclass communities often mobilize for resources, power, and recognition, thereby reaffirming their existence as a community. Their spatial organization, as depicted in Figure 5.1, resembles chains of beads. The ongoing flows and interactions among the various ethnic localities and the uneven ethnic power relations work to maintain these regional identities vis-à-vis pressures for spatial integration.

While the situation is, of course, not static, several regional communities have established themselves through the division of space, most notably Haredi Jews, *kibbutzim, moshavim*, Mizrahim in development towns and deprived neighborhoods, Jewish settlers in Yesha (in the occupied territories), Russian immigrants, mainly in peripheral towns, Palestinians in the Galilee, Palestinians in the West Bank, Bedouins, and so forth. Figure 5.1 displays the translation of the concept to the ethnic and social geography of Israel/Palestine (for full elaboration of the concept, see Yiftachel 2002).

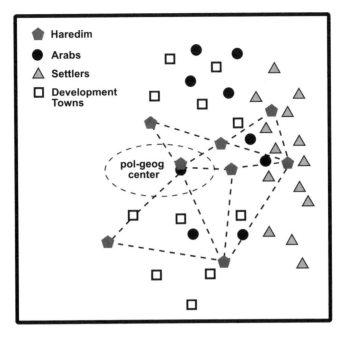

Figure 5.1. Fractured Regions: The Concept

Several main consequences can be discerned from the shaping of fractured regions in Israel/Palestine. First, this system of sociospatial organization has reinforced and legitimized the uneven segregation among ethnoclasses, augmenting the process of creeping apartheid described below. Second, the lack of geographical contiguity has considerably weakened the power of peripheral and regional communities, enabling the state to maintain an exceptionally centralized power structure (see Sharkansky 1997). Third, the system is fraught with tensions and conflicts as rivaling populations are deliberately spatially intermixed. This creates a situation of proximity and competition, which is highly susceptible to long-term conflicts. This has been most conspicuous in the occupied Palestinian territories, where two uprisings have erupted against Jewish control and settlement. However, it has also been evident, in various degrees of severity, in the shaping of relations between Israel's Arab and Jewish citizens, between (mainly Mizrahi) development towns and the surrounding (mainly Ashkenazi) *kibbutzim*, and increasingly between secular and Orthodox Jews.

Therefore, despite the strong integrative discourses of Zionism, layered and differentiated collective spaces were created, with low levels of contact between the various ethnoclasses. This has worked to reproduce inequalities and competing collective identities. Movement across boundaries has been further restricted by the power granted to most Jewish localities (built on state land) to screen their residents by applying tests of resident suitability and to use exclusionary zoning to maintain their middle-class character. This practice has produced communities dominated by Ashkenazim and upwardly mobile Mizrahim. The ethnoclass fragmentation and hostility currently evident in Israeli society can thus be traced, at least partially, to the specific nature of the Judaizing settlement program and its institutionalized segregation.

The manner in which space has been divided has thus contributed to a long-term stratification. The Ashkenazi founding group and its descendents occupy a dominant position in most societal spheres: the economy, culture, politics, academia, the legal system, and professional associations (Mautner 2000; Lewin-Epstein and Semyonov 1993). The link between the division of spatial assets and social stratification is, however, neither direct nor totally stable. There are other key factors that influence social standing, and such standing is subject to ceaseless struggles and oppositions. Yet, the spatial marginality of Palestinian Arabs and Mizrahim—created to a large extent by their position vis-à-vis the Judaization project—cannot be separated from their inferior social position.

The enduring structural gap is well illustrated by the following figures: mean income of Arab households ranged between 56 and 51 percent of Ashkenazi family mean income during 1988–2000, or between 77 and 71 percent of the state average. During the same period, Mizrahi mean household income ranged between 63 and 69 percent of its Ashkenazi counterpart. The gap would have been wider had it not been for the statistical inclusion of the vast majority of Russian immigrants with the Ashkenazi groups. Without the recent immigrants, the mean income of Arab and Mizrahi households would only reach 48 and 65 percent of the Ashkenazi mean, respectively (CBS-a 2001; see also Cohen and Haberfeld 1998). Similarly, persisting ethnoclass gaps are conspicuous in educational achievements. In 2000, 55 percent of youth in the twelfth-grade age bracket matriculated in cities with an Ashkenazi majority, as compared to only 29 percent in the (mainly Mizrahi) development towns and only 20 percent in Arab localities (Adva 2003). The standing of other ethnoclasses is more difficult to measure owing to limitations in data availability, but repeated surveys show that the ultra-Orthodox (Haredi) population and the southern Bedouins are the most deprived groups in socioeconomic terms (Adva 2003). These groups are also highly segregated geographically. Indicators among the Russian-speaking population are more mixed: while their income levels are relatively low (about 70–80 percent of state average and rising), their educational achievements and mobility in Israeli society are above average, indicating a process of rapid adjustment (see Horowitz 2003; Kimmerling 2001).

In this process we can also note the working of the ethnic logic of capital, noted earlier as a major force shaping ethnocratic group relations. Development closely followed the ethnoclass pattern prevalent in Israeli society. This created spatial circumstances for the reproduction of the ethnic gap between Ashkenazim and Mizrahim (and later groups such as Russian-speaking and Ethiopian immigrants) through location-based mechanisms such as education, land control, housing, social networks, local stigmas, accessibility to facilities, and opportunities. This was exacerbated during the 1990s because of the partial liberalization of the land market and the concentration of development in Israel's metropolitan regions. Given the concentration of Mizrahim, as well as Russian and Ethiopian immigrants, in regional or urban peripheries, ethnoclass disparities have widened, leaving some peripheries to face repeated economic and social crises (see Tzfadia 2001). Therefore, somewhat paradoxically, the programs of settling Jews in the periphery, putatively for national purposes, have caused a spatial-social structure of ethnoclass fragmentation instead of the desired national integration.

Figure 5.2 attempts to display conceptually the impact of the ethnocratic dynamics on Israeli society. It illustrates how the main ethnocratic strategy—the Judaization of contested territory and power structure—has also resulted in ethnoclass stratification within Jewish and Palestinian societies. It also shows how Zionist development has evolved over time, pursuing globalization and liberalization during the 1990s and being reinforced by massive immigration and partial Israeli-Palestinian reconciliation. This was accompanied by the blunting of the anti-Arab Judaization drive and has had a complex effect on social relations: it exacerbated the stratifying impact of public policies and amplified the process of creeping apartheid, but it has also opened new spaces for mobility and resistance, as discussed in the next few chapters.

Ethnocracy or Theocracy?

Some scholars claim that a growing influence of Orthodox Jewish groups is likely to lead Israel from ethnocratic to theocratic rule as a logical extension of ethnic control (see Greenfeld 2001; Kimmerling 1995; Nevo 2000). These claims are not without basis, as the longer ethnocratic principles rule over Israel/Palestine, the greater the potential role of religion in (a) imposing natural segregation between dominant Jews and subordinate Palestinians, and (b) forming a collective narrative to justify the unfolding reality of creeping apartheid. Both segregation and justification are necessary to maintain the system of disproportionate Jewish control and to marginalize rival civil agendas. Therefore, the more acute the ethnonational conflict, the more potent the political role of religion becomes. This observation is supported by the solid rise in the power of religious political

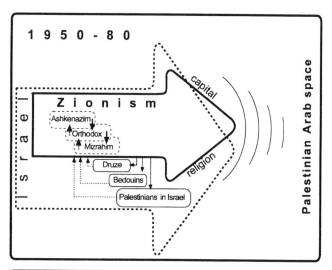

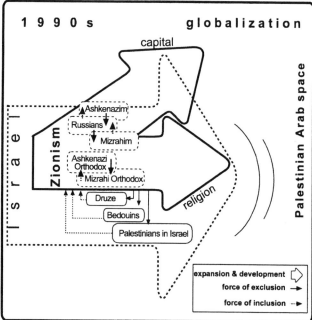

Figure 5.2. Israel's Ethnocratic Dynamics: Ethnonational Expansion and Ethnoclass Stratification

movements among both Jews and Palestinians since the occupation of the Palestinian territories and since the first *intifada.*

Despite its centrality, religion (as an institutional-political framework) has been secondary to ethnicity in the shaping of the Zionist project. This is quite typical of ethnocratic regimes, as explained in Chapter 2, and in Israel/Palestine it is more specifically due to the partial compatibility of Orthodox and secular (non-Orthodox) perceptions of contemporary Jewish nationalism. Regardless of past bitter disputes between the two camps, today they both take the rule of the Jewish ethnos in Israel as a given point of departure. Hence, the Orthodox campaign is set within the Zionist project and is mainly geared toward deepening the religiosity of the ethnocratic state, and reinforcing—by legal, political, and institutional means—the overlap among Jewish ethnicity, religion, and nation. In other words, Zionism allows the Orthodox and secular agendas to be promoted concurrently.

At some point, however, the simultaneous promotion of the two agendas creates severe tensions between the Orthodox and secular versions of Jewish nationalism. These clashes are exhibited in constant struggles over core issues such as state borders, the status of minorities under Jewish rule, legislation on personal affairs, the role of Judaism in shaping public spaces, the lack of military service by most of the ultra-Orthodox, and the nature of conversion to Judaism. These tensions existed among Jews in Israel/Palestine since the beginning of Zionism, but until the 1990s they were concealed to a large extent by the common goals of Judaizing Israel/Palestine and building a (vaguely defined) Jewish state.[7] Institutionally, the two camps regulated their relations through the status quo agreement, which maintained a de facto veneer of understanding on the character of Israeli public spaces and personal affairs. During the 1990s, greater tensions surfaced between Orthodox and secular Jews because the secular public began to pursue goals of liberalization, globalization, and democratization (Ram 2003). Against these new agendas, religious elements appeared to threaten the growing perception of Israel as a Western, Jewish, and democratic state. However, for most Orthodox individuals, the Jewish nature of the state is clearly superior to its Western or democratic orientation (see Peres and Yuchtman-Yaar 1999).

Accordingly, all Orthodox parties support the increasing imposition of religious (Halacha) rule in Israel. As stated by the late leader of the National Religious Party, Z. Hammer, who was considered a moderate: "I genuinely wish that Israel would be shaped according to the spirit of Torah and Halacha . . . the democratic system is not sacred for me" (Neuberger 1998, 41). Likewise, Rabbi Ovadia Yosef, the undisputed spiritual leader of the Sephardi Shas movement, which is considered less strict on religious matters than its Ashkenazi counterparts, declared recently: "We work for creating a Halacha state. . . . In such a state the courts will observe Jewish law . . . We have the sacred Torah, which has a moral set of laws, why should anyone be worried?"[8] During the 2003 elections campaign, Rabbi Yosef went even further by claiming that those voting for secular Zionist parties are "betraying the cause of Judaism." He added: "Only Shas can save Israel's Jewish character by introducing the Torah to the lives of your community and children," often using the biblical war cry "Those following God—to me!"[9]

Against this persisting rhetoric, it may be surprising that the actual political initiatives to impose new religious measures on Israelis have been relatively mild in recent times and are confined to the public (and not private) sphere. Given the gradual secularization of Israeli public space, most religious groups seek to protect the status quo agreement, which has remained for five decades a loose blueprint for secular-Orthodox relations. One of the major differences between the two camps revolves around the definition of Jewish identity. The secular interpretation attempts to define Jewishness as an ethnonational or cultural identity. This allows some mobility and flexibility in the definition of collective boundaries, especially with regard to the integration of other groups into the Jewish collectivity.

Orthodox groups, in contrast, attempt to define a more religious Judaism as an inseparable communal whole (with both ethnicity and religion defining the rigid boundaries of an enclosed human collectivity). The vagueness in the definition of the Jewish collectivity in Israel and the diverging interpretations of Jewishness and Judaism are at the heart of the conflict between the secular and Orthodox camps. If the meaning of "Jewish" is unresolved, how can the nature of the Jewish state be determined? And how can the nature of Judaization be agreed upon? As we shall see below, the differences are not only theological or ideological, but touch on the very materiality of Jewish existence in Israel/Palestine and on the question of occupation and settlement in the Palestinian territories.

But first, let us look further at the dynamics of Jewish ethnic boundaries. The 1990s witnessed a major shift in the de facto definition of Israeli Jewishness. As depicted in Figure 5.3, until the late 1980s, religion and ethnonationalism *overlapped nearly totally* in the legal and political definition of the Zionist nation. Judaism could be seen as an ethnic religion, and its structural influence was felt in a variety of regime bases, including immigration, land, and public culture.

There were several public and legal disputes about the question "Who is a Jew?" but they were confined to intrareligious disputes about the location of religious authority (in effect debating "Who is a qualified rabbi?").[10] These debates did not challenge the principle of an ethnic religion but rather dealt with the various *religious* interpretations about entry procedures into the collectivity. The main rivals were the Orthodox, Conservative, and Reform streams of religious Judaism. The argument revolved around the question of whose religious interpretation should determine automatic Jewish-Israeli citizenship. Therefore, until the 1990s, the Israeli public debate did not seriously challenge the overlap between religion and ethnonationalism. During the 1990s, Israel experienced what I call the eth-nicization of Jewishness.

Some 300,000–350,000 immigrants, mainly from the former Soviet Union, arrived in Israel, but they were not considered Jewish according to the Orthodox regulations used to determine Jewish identity. These immi-grants were members of Jewish families and hence were qualified under the Law of Return to receive Israeli citizenship. While they have maintained a lively Russian culture, they have gradually integrated into Jewish (mainly Ashkenazi) society (see Horowitz 2003). They are educated in Israeli schools, serve in the IDF, and are politically and socially indistinguishable from the large group of (properly Jewish) immigrants. Hence, since the 1990s, the de facto boundaries of Jewish nationalism in Israel have *broad-ened* to include ethnic Jews on the basis of their family ties. This has seri-ously undermined the previously clear ethnic-religious overlap and diminished the control of religion over entry into the Jewish collectivity. This highlights an ethnocratic paradox: in order to enhance the Judaiza-tion of Israel/Palestine (by immigration), Israel has actually undermined the status of Judaism in Israel (Figure 5.3).

This change may signal the decline (but far from disappearance) of reli-gion as a structural element in the making of the Israeli regime. Integrative forces from below continue to be generated by the highly mobilized com-munity of Russian immigrants, which has managed effectively to penetrate many aspects of Israeli life, especially academia, arts, politics, and the army.[11] Further, the mere existence of this secularizing force in Israeli-Jewish society, as well as the liberalizing and globalizing trends noted above, has caused a gradual shift among veteran Israeli Jews, who increasingly choose to bypass the religious establishment in the conduct of their per-sonal affairs. For example, in 2000, 49 percent of Israeli Jews supported the introduction of civil marriage and 70 percent supported the opening of shopping centers on the Sabbath, as compared to 38 and 59 percent a de-cade earlier, respectively (Gutman Institute 2000). The movement in the re-ligious direction has been much lighter, with recent data showing that between 1999 and 2002 (inclusive) an annual average of a meager 853 Russ-ian immigrants converted to Orthodox Judaism. This number represents less than 0.1 percent of this community. The low figure is even more strik-ing given the concerted efforts by the state and religious organizations to create mass conversion among Russian immigrants.[12]

The dramatic rise of the Shinui movement in the 2003 elections is yet another indication of the same trend. Shinui, which ran on a ticket of sec-ularizing the Israeli public sphere and fighting what this party often refers to as the "oppressive, corrupt religious establishment," increased its power from six to fifteen Knesset members. Its rise illustrates the phenomenon of

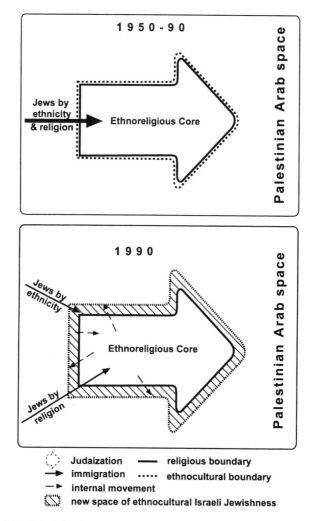

Figure 5.3. The Ethnicization of Israeli Jewishness: Immigration and Boundaries

moving out of the religious core into the fledgling ethnocultural definition of Israeli Jewishness (Figure 5.3). Significantly, Shinui also ran on a firm nationalist ticket supporting the strong-arm policies of the Ariel Sharon government vis-à-vis the Palestinians.

The ethnicization of the Jewishness process does not necessarily weaken the Jewish ethnocracy—it simply redraws its boundaries. The change is naturally subject to intense struggle between Orthodox circles that oppose the new ethnic-cultural boundaries of Jewish nationalism and the more liberal forces in Israel that are pleased with the new spaces offered for nonreligious

Jewish citizenship. Still, the partial secularization has not offered significant opportunities for Palestinian Arabs to integrate into meaningful membership in the Israeli Zionist community.

Against the ethnicization of Jewishness, and the subsequent piecemeal secularization of the Israeli public sphere, the challenge to democracy by the Orthodox agenda has become even more acute. This trend is clearly reflected in politics, with the Orthodox political camp growing stronger and more radical over the last two decades. It has risen from 16 Knesset seats (out of 120) in the 1981–84 Knesset, which was proportional to its size in the population, to 32 seats in the 1999–2003 Knesset.[13] While this number declined slightly to 30 seats in the 2003 elections, it is still nearly twice the proportion of Orthodox in the population at large. The rise in power of religious parties is only partially explained by demographic growth, which has been moderate. The main reasons lie in the ability of religious parties to provide a legitimizing narrative for Israel's Judaizing drive and in their resources and ability to mobilize popular support, often from nonreligious circles.

Notably for this chapter, the rising power of the Orthodox sector is closely associated with the political geography of Judaization. There are four main grounds for this connection. First, all religious movements in Israel, and most conspicuously Gush Emunim (Loyalty Bloc—the main Jewish religious organization to settle the West Bank), fully support settling Jews in the occupied Palestinian territories and using the military to occupy these areas. This is often asserted as part of a divine imperative, based on the eternal Jewish right and duty to settle all parts of the promised land and is generally detrimental to the collective and civil rights of Palestinians in these territories. Needless to say, this agenda commences a process of creeping apartheid and undermines even the possibility of democratic rule. It has already caused several waves of intra-Jewish religious-secular violence, including the assassination of Prime Minister Yitzhak Rabin in 1995.

Second, repeated surveys show that the Orthodox public in Israel is the most intransigent in its opposition to granting civil equality to Palestinians in general and Israel's Arab citizens in particular. This does not mean that the entire Orthodox public opposes democratic rule or that it is homogenous in its political views. However, nearly all opinion studies, as well as the platforms of the main religious political organizations, indicate that Orthodox Jews rank democratic values lower than the Jewishness of the state or Jewish control over the entire Israel/Palestine territory (see Pedahzur 2001; Peres and Yuchtamn-Yaar 1999; Smooha 1992).

Third, there is a discernable link between the rising power of Orthodox bodies and the rupturing of Israel's borders. Political analyses and surveys show that as the Judaization of the occupied territories has deepened, so have the Jewish elements in the collective identity of Israeli Jews at the expense of Israeli components (see Kimmerling 2001; Lustick 2002; Migdal

1996). This trend stems from the confusion of the meaning of "Israeli" when both state borders and boundaries of the Israeli polity are blurred. In other words, the encroachment of Israel's borders with settlement activity and the involvement of world Jewry in internal politics have eroded the territorial and civil meaning of the term "Israeli" and simultaneously strengthened the (nonterritorial and ethnoreligious) Jewish collective identity. This process has grave implications for democracy, principally because it bypasses the institution of territorial citizenship on which a democratic nation-state should be founded. In the Israeli context, it legitimizes the stratification between Jews (with full citizenship rights) and Arabs (second-class citizens), thus denying Arabs much of the status attached to their Israeli affiliation. Only the demarcation of clear Israeli borders and the subsequent creation of a demos—a territorial political community—can halt the ethnocratic ascendancy of Judaism over Israeliness.

Moreover, the Judaization project is perceived by many in the Orthodox camp not only as ethnic-territorial, but also as deepening the religiosity of Israeli Jews. This is based on interpretation of a central precept: All Jews are guarantors for one another. Here "guarantor" entails returning all straying nonbelievers to God's way. This mission legitimizes the repeated (although often unsuccessful and weak) attempts to strengthen the religious character of the state, that is, its laws and public spaces. The state's religious character is already anchored in a variety of areas: the Jewish Sabbath is the official Israeli day of rest, public institutions only serve kosher food, the importation of pork is prohibited, all personal laws are governed by the national rabbinate (which prohibits civil marriage), and most archaeological digs need approval from religious authorities.

In the face of persisting disagreement on the future of the occupied territories and the strengthening political polarization between secular and Orthodox Jews, it may be that the long-standing cooperation between the two camps is waning. The 1999 and 2003 election campaigns, for example, were marked by increasingly antireligious rhetoric not heard in previous campaigns, and, as noted above, a discernable rise of secular political parties demanding a more secular state. The antireligious campaign was met by a similar polarizing discourse among Orthodox Jews, highlighted by a vicious campaign during 1999–2000 to delegitimize Israel's secular and leftist Supreme Court, oppose the Law of Return (for allowing non-Jewish members of Jewish families to migrate to Israel), and continue efforts to enforce religious regulations in Israel's public spaces.

In summary, religion has played a central role in the making of the Israeli ethnic regime, but it has been subordinate to the exigencies of the ethnic nation. Yet the contested geography and religiosity of the Jewish state has seen the Orthodox and secular camps developing conflicting agendas. This has caused a dual process: while the public sphere has been secularizing from below, Orthodox parties have strengthened and radicalized.[14] They have gained support from the ongoing Zionist-Palestinian conflict, the military occupation of Palestinian territories, the absence of clear state borders, and the subsequent containment of Israeli civil society (Ben-Eliezer 2003; Kimmerling 2001). This bifurcating trend of secularizing public space and radicalizing religious politics is likely to create a simmering edge for future Orthodox-secular relations.

Finally, and back to the main topic of the book, we should observe that while the Orthodox-secular conflict is often portrayed as a clash over religiosity, it cannot be separated from the political geography of Judaization. In this context, it may be telling that the hegemonic Israeli discourse in politics, academia, and the general public tends to treat secular-religious matters separately from Arab-Jewish issues. This strategy of denial conceals the direct link between the secular-Orthodox conflict and the plight of Palestinian Arabs. This was vividly expressed by the 1995 assassination of Prime Minister Yitzhak Rabin by a religious Jew who claimed that Rabin had no right to relinquish territorial control to the Palestinians and no moral standing to use the vote of Arab parliamentarians to pass the Oslo agreement.

Hence, beyond matters of pure religion, a central topic of contention between Orthodox and secular Jews has been the Israeli occupation of Palestinian territories and the associated process of creeping apartheid. In other words, the recent polarization between secular and Orthodox Jews can be seen as part of the tensions and contradictions typifying ethnocratic regimes and as another facet of settler-indigenous relations. Indeed, the two camps are deeply divided on the desired extent of Judaization, geographically and religiously, and hence on the nature of future relations between Jews and Palestinian Arabs.

A Segregative Settling Ethnocracy

As we have seen, the project of Judaizing the state, spearheaded by Jewish immigration and settlement, has been a constitutive basis of the Israeli regime. Israel thus fits the subtype of settling ethnocracy defined in Chapter 2. But beyond regime definitions, we should observe the spatial pattern of segregation legitimized by the ethnocratic system. The prevalence of segregation has been exacerbated by the geographic nature of the Jewish settlement project, which was based on the principal unit of the locality (*yeshuv*). The Jewish settlement project advanced by building localities that were usually ethnically homogeneous and thus created from the outset a segregated pattern of development. The political, legal, and cultural mechanisms introduced for the purpose of segregating Jews from Arabs were thus also used to segregate Jewish elites from other ethnoclasses, thereby reinforcing the process of ethnicization typical of ethnocratic regimes.

To be sure, these mechanisms were used differently, and more subtly, among Jews, but the persistent gap between Ashkenazim and Mizrahim cannot be understood without accounting for the geography of intra-Jewish relations. In the main, Mizrahim were spatially marginalized by the Israeli settlement project, whether in the isolated periphery or in poor and stigmatized neighborhoods of Israel's major cities. This has limited their potential economic, social, and cultural participation.

There is a clear nexus connecting the de-Arabization of the country with the marginalization of the Mizrahim, who have been positioned—culturally and geographically—between Arab and Jew, between Israel and its hostile neighbors, between a backward Eastern past and a progressive Western future (see Shohat 2001). But, we should remember, the depth and extent of discrimination against Palestinians and Mizrahim have been quite different, with the latter included in Jewish-Israeli nation building as active participants in the oppression of the former.

A similar segregationist logic was also used to legitimize the creation of segregated neighborhoods and localities for groups such as ultra-Orthodox Jews, recent Russian and Ethiopian immigrants, and Palestinian Arabs, although the segregation of each group has different dynamics and social depth. Despite the differences between the various ethnic geographies, it is clear that the uneven segregationist logic of the ethnocratic regime has been infused into spatial and cultural practices. These have worked to ethnicize Israeli society further. Importantly, ethnocratic regimes do not only entail the dominance of a specific ethnic nation and ethnoclass but also *the dominance of ethnicity itself*, as a legitimate and mobilized category.

Of course, not all ethnic separation is negative, and voluntary separation among groups can at times function to reduce ethnic conflict. But in a society that has declared the gathering and integration of the exiles *(mizug galuyot)* a major national goal, levels of segregation and stratification between Jewish ethnoclasses have remained remarkably high. Referring back to our theoretical framework, we can observe the fusion of settler-society mechanisms (conquest, immigration, and settlement) with the power of ethnonationalism (segregating Jews from Arabs) and the logic of ethnic capital (distancing upper and lower ethnoclasses) in the creation of Israel's conflict-ridden contemporary human geography.

This process, however, is not unidimensional and must be weighed against countertrends, such as growing levels of assimilation between Mizrahim and Ashkenazim and increasing formal equality in social rights among all groups. In addition, solidarity among Jews in the face of a common enemy has often eased internal tensions and segregation, especially between Mizrahim and Ashkenazim, as both have merged into a broadening Israeli middle class. As mentioned earlier, the original Ashkenazi charter group has broadened to incorporate the Mizrahim, especially among the assimilated middle and upper classes. Yet, the ethnicization trend has also been powerful, as illustrated by the growing tendency of political entrepreneurs to exploit ethnic capital and to draw on ethnoclass and religious affiliations as a source of political support. In the 1996 elections, such sectoral parties increased their power by 40 percent and for the first time in Israel's history overshadowed the largest two parties, Labor and Likud, which have traditionally been the most ethnically heterogeneous.

Moreover, the situation has not been static. The strategy of Judaization and population dispersal has recently slowed in response to the new neoliberal agendas of many Israeli elites (Ram 2003; Shafir and Peled 2002). It has also encountered violent Palestinian-Arab resistance and strongly mobilized Mizrahi grievances, which in turn have reshaped some of Israel's territorial policies. Both Arabs and Mizrahim have progressed in their absolute (if not relative) socioeconomic standards, partially because of Israel's development policies. Likewise, Palestinian resistance in the occupied territories, culminating in the two *intifadas,* has slowed Jewish expansion in several regions, brought about the Oslo agreement, and achieved a measure of limited Palestinian self-rule.

These changes, important as they are, have still occurred within the firm boundaries of the dominant, ethnocratic Zionist discourse, in which Jewish settlement and control and the territorial containment of the Arab population are undisputed Jewish national goals, both within the Green Line and in large parts of the occupied territories. It can even be argued that the Oslo process has accelerated the process of Judaizing large parts of the occupied territories by legitimizing the construction of further Jewish housing, land confiscation for bypass roads, and the building of dozens of new (unofficial) settlements in the West Bank during the al-Aqsa *intifada.*

In this vein, the pervasive closures of the territories and the subsequent importation of hundreds of thousands of foreign workers to replace Palestinian labor are also part of the post-Oslo process of Judaization. Jewish-Israeli society is also torn, with large segments supporting the end to the Judaization policy and a withdrawal from the occupied territories. In this context the decolonization moves made by the Rabin and Barak governments were indeed significant for the shaping of Israel/Palestine. To date, these agendas have not been implemented, meaning that Israel is likely to stay, in the foreseeable future, an ethnocratic and colonial regime.

Creeping Apartheid: Judaization and Stratified Citizenship

As we have seen, the Judaization of Israel/Palestine has had many consequences, such as the eruption of violent conflicts between Jews and Palestinians; the making of less violent but profound conflicts between Mizrahi and Ashkenazi Jews, as well as between secular and Orthodox Jews; the creation of fractured regions on the social landscape; and high levels of segregation among ethnoclasses. A less visible, and far less analyzed consequence has been the advent of *creeping apartheid.* This is a logical (though by no means necessary) extension of the ethnocratic system because its rule requires ever harsher measures to fend off the challenges of disgruntled minorities. The legitimacy granted to ethnicity as a major organizing principle, coupled with separate and unequal conditions, has caused long-term ethnoclass stratification. This has seriously undermined the normative meaning of citizenship and fueled a constant process of dissent and insurgence. I title this process creeping apartheid because it is undeclared, and is being amplified by a sequence of incremental decisions about practices, such as the ongoing settlement of Jews in the occupied territories and the increasingly heavy-handed policies toward Arabs and non-Jewish immigrants in Israel.

The exigencies of Judaization, which as we saw include a range of immigration, land, military, legal, and cultural practices, have resulted in the emergence of several different and unequal types of citizenship. These are differentiated by their combination of legal and informal rights and capabilities. Within each group, and more conspicuously among religious collectivities, status is also stratified along gender lines, with men enjoying a superior position. The pattern of group membership under the Israeli regime appears to be shaped by three intertwined elements: ethnic affiliation; group spatiality; and levels of economic development.

The first component, ethnic affiliation, is often openly expressed in Israeli discourse, both in political rhetoric and official Communication, as noted on identity cards and ethnic (national) registration at the Ministry of the Interior. The registration provides a different citizenship package for each group. It is comprised of formal and informal components, such as the right to vote, rights of residence, physical mobility, accessibility to services and facilities, taxation levels, housing availability, army service, education, and the management of personal affairs.

Ethnic affiliations, and at times identification, are never established in isolation. They are intertwined with the two other components, namely the group spatiality (location, local attachment, and spatial control) and its levels of economic development. For example, the position of Jewish settlers in the West Bank cannot be determined solely by their ethnic/religious affiliation but must take into account their specific geography and level of resources allocated by the state. Likewise, the status of Palestinians in Israel is shaped by their (inferior) ethnic affiliation but also by their (favorable) spatiality and economic development, as compared to Palestinians elsewhere.

On this basis, I suggest that the process of creeping apartheid, evident in Israel/Palestine since the late 1970s, has constructed and institutionalized at least ten different citizenships, as shown in Table 5.1.[15] The table below presents a simplified picture because the position of each group is determined by a multiplicity of components and may not be easily captured by a single ranking. Positions may also change over time. It is nevertheless useful to present the following somewhat sketchy hierarchy of groups that has been established in Israel/Palestine.

TABLE 5.1. Stratified Group Position under the Israeli Ethnocracy

Mainstream Jews
  • Mainly Ashkenazi middle to upper ethnoclass
  • Peripheral ethnoclasses (mainly Mizrahi and Russian)
Orthodox Jews
  • Settlers in the occupied territories
  • Ultra-Orthodox groups in Israel
Pseudo-Jews*
	Upper
	Echelon

Druze
Palestinians holding Israeli citizenship
Bedouins
  • Galilee
  • Negev
	Middle
	Echelon

East Jerusalem and Golan Arabs Palestinians in the West Bank Palestinians in Gaza Labor migrants (foreign workers)	Lower Echelon

*Mainly immigrants from the former Soviet Union who qualify for Israeli residency under the Law of Return but are not recognized as Jews by the Israeli religious establishment

Let us elaborate on the second component—spatiality—that has been particularly central to this stratification on several counts. First, Zionism is still a settlement movement, emphasizing land, settlement, and spatial planning control as critical to the attainment of national goals. As shown elsewhere (see Chapter 7; Yiftachel 2002), the combination of settlement, ethnicity, and uneven development has created a pattern of fractured regions that connects chains of localities according to their ethnic affiliation and level of development and forms an important foundation for Israeli politics and identities.

In such settings, spatial elements are not simply background variables or determinants of economic value. They form the very basis of group identity, as evident, for example, in the case of the Negev Bedouins or the Jewish settlers. Further, location often defines legal categories according to which ethnicity is legitimized and reproduced by the Israeli ethnocracy. The rights of Druze or ultra-Orthodox Jews (for example, in education or housing) are attached to specific localities. This process constantly reinforces the spatiality of collective existence and at the same time emphasizes the uneven division and development of space that marks the groups as different and unequal.

Central components in shaping both the political and the everyday are determined by the group's location. This is critical to shaping the collective citizenship, premised on a policy of spatial repression. In general, the greater the repression is, the lower the group's citizenship status. Spatial repression is rife in Israel/Palestine, encapsulating a multitude of regulations that control movement, accessibility, development, and mobilization. Stark examples of such boundaries include the newly erected separation barrier in the West Bank and Jerusalem/al-Quds; road blocks between Palestinian cities (in the occupied territories); checkpoints on the Green Line (that screen only Arabs, not Jews); restrictions on residential mobility (as shown by the case of Qa'adan above, or in the case of providing housing for Jewish immigrants only in certain locations—see Chapter 10); and the inability to receive resources or services outside one's locality, as in the case of the Orthodox Jews or the Druze. Finally, with the ascent of economic neoliberalism and the gradual withdrawal of the state from social services, the market value of location has become central in shaping a group's economic position and hence its social status. In this sense, the events of the last few years, including the al-Aqsa *intifada,* the construction of the separation barrier in the West Bank, and the liberalization of the economy, have all worked to deepen the process of creeping apartheid—making ethnoclasses in Israel/Palestine more separate and unequal.

No great elaboration is necessary to realize that the prominence of separate and unequal processes poses serious consquences for the stablity, prosperity, and morality of society. Much knowledge has been accumulated about the disastrous potential of long-term ethnic oppression, particularly when it overlaps strongly with class and spatial cleavages, as is the case in Israel/Palestine (for an international comparison, see Gurr 2000). Hence, the system of unequal citizenship, which is preserved by various degrees of force and control, is bound to create ever intensifying waves of discontent and challenge. This is evident by repeated Palestinian rebellions in the occupied territories and growing alienation among Israel's Palestinian Arab citizens (see Rabinowitz and Abu-Bakker 2001) and peripheral Jewish ethnoclasses (see Peled 2001).

Conclusion: The Enigma of Distorted Structures

This chapter attempted to depict the nature of the Israeli regime from a political-geographic perspective, showing the significance of the ethnocratic project of Judaization, which provides a major axis for understanding the politics of Israel/Palestine. It has not only exacerbated the Zionist-Palestinian conflict but also created fractured regions on the social landscape, reshaped the relations among other ethnoclasses, and put in motion a process of creeping apartheid. To reiterate, I do not claim that the Judaization process can explain every facet of cthnic and social relations in this contested territory; rather, it is a central factor largely overlooked by the social science literature.

It should be reiterated that the Judaization process has also affected critical aspects not covered sufficiently in this book but nonetheless central to understanding the Israeli regime, such as militarism (Ben-Eliezer 1995; Helman 1999; Kimmerling 2001); male domination and the shaping of gender relations (Ferguson 1993); the high levels of regime centrality; bottled-neck communication between communities and politicians (Lehman-Wilzig 1990); weak or nonexistent accountability of public figures; and the weakness of civil society in the face of military, ethnic, or economic power (Avnon 1998; Ben-Eliezer 2003). These illustrate the growing distance between Israel's desired image as a Western democracy and the reality of skewed power relations and uneven geographies that are producing a system of creeping apartheid.

A key factor in understanding the Israeli regime thus lies in uncovering the sophisticated institutional settings that present themselves as enlightened but at the same time facilitate the continuing oppression of marginalized groups. Here we can observe that the legal and political foundations of the Jewish state have created a distorted structure that broadcasts a democratic and enlightened image. Once in place, this structure has become self-referential, reifying and reinforcing its own image and logic. It appears to have blinded the population from identifying the consequences of the Judaization process.

In many ways, the situation resembles the hegemonic moment observed by Gramsci, when a dominant "truth" is diffused by powerful elites to all corners of society, preventing dissension and reproducing prevailing social and power relations. It appears that this hegemony has reached even the most enlightened and putatively democratic realms of Israeli Jewish society. How can this enigma be explained? How can enlightened circles square the Jewish and democratic account with the enfolding reality of creeping apartheid? I suggest here a metaphor in which Israeli Jewish discourse is analogous to a tilted structure such as the Tower of Pisa. Once one enters the tower, it appears straight, since its internal structural grid is perfectly perpendicular and parallel. This is akin to the introverted discourse about the Jewish and democratic state: once inside this discourse, most Jews accept the Jewish character of the state as an unproblematic point of departure, much like the floor of the tilted tower. From that perspective, Judaization and its oppressive consequences appear natural and justified—or perhaps do not appear at all. This is the view held by most Jewish political movements. Hence, the deep chasm often portrayed between rightist and leftist Jewish camps (see Lustick 1988; Smooha 1998) concerns only the extent and brutality of Judaization and not the taken-for-granted existence of this strategy.

On the basis of this tilted foundation of our metaphorical tower, Israel has added laws and policies over the years that can be likened to the tower's walls. Given the tilted foundation, these walls could only be built on an angle, yet they appear straight to those observing from the inside. One needs to step outside and away from the tilted building and measure its coordinates against truly vertical buildings in order to discern the distortions and inconsistencies.

In the Israeli case, it is time for scholars to step outside the internal Jewish Israeli discourse and analyze the Israeli regime systematically against the straight principles of equal citizenship, democracy, and social sustainability. A particularly promising avenue is to explore in depth the bases of the Israeli ethnocratic regime, such as land and culture, to which the next two chapters are devoted.

Chapter 6

The Spatial Foundation: The Israeli Land System

This chapter begins the task of elaborating on the various spheres of the Israeli ethnocracy by analyzing one of its central regime bases—the land system. That system, as the title suggests, provides the spatial foundation for the establishment of ethnocratic society and geography, and puts into motion processes of domination and conflict on both ethnonational and ethnoclass levels.

The chapter presents a historical-legal account of the making and social consequences of the land system and of recent challenges to both the ethnicizing and liberalizing forces within the system. It uses the ethnocratic framework by first tracing the interrelations between the ethnonational settling project and the legal and institutional structure of the land system, and second by examining the impact of the ethnonational project on social relations within Israeli society. The chapter also uses analytical tools drawn from the emerging new field of legal geography and its critical examination of settler societies. We begin with an anecdote from a very visible legal land struggle.

En Route to the High Court: Landing Public Insults

In early 2002, the struggle over the control of agricultural land in Israel escalated dramatically in preparation for an expected watershed decision of the Israeli High Court of Justice.[1] The Court was about to rule whether Jewish farmer-settlers, who had leased state land for farming purposes, could continue claiming profits from urban redevelopment or whether a freeze should be placed on the redevelopment of farming land. During the preceding decade, more than four hundred thousand dunams of state agricultural land had been rezoned, with large profits pocketed by the farmers.

The main objector to the redevelopment process was the Democratic Mizrahi Rainbow (the Keshet), a nongovernmental organization (NGO) promoting social justice in the distribution of public resources, especially pertaining to economically deprived Mizrahim.[2] In January of 2000, the Rainbow launched a High Court petition against land redevelopment and the creeping privatization of public lands and has since been joined by high profile NGOs such as the Association of Civil Rights and the Nature Protection Association. The main defenders of the farmers' interests came from Ashkenazi circles, which have traditionally enjoyed privileged access to public resources. The agricultural lobby mainly includes representatives of collective agricultural localities (mostly *kibbutzim* and *moshavim*)[3] and large-scale land developers, who were partners in several recent lucrative redevelopments of agricultural land.

During January and February of 2002, a smear campaign was launched by several major landholders. Manipulating the public atmosphere charged at the time by violent Israeli-Palestinian hostilities, they claimed that the challengers were driven by "a secret goal of flooding the country with Palestinian refugees."[4] On large billboards, in newspaper advertisements, and in numerous media appearances, the speakers for the agricultural lobby ridiculed the Rainbow and its leading activists, claiming that they were "funded by unknown sources";[5] that they "aim to destroy the state of Israel"; that they "have become enemies and haters of Jewish settlement";[6] that they are "interested in nothing but big bucks to their own pockets"; and that "beyond the rhetoric of social justice they hide an anachronistic, destructive, leftist post-Zionist position" that "aims to dispossess Israel's impoverished farmers."[7] Attorney Shraga Biran, who represented *kibbutzim* located in the center of Israel, where price and demand for real estate were high, issued similar accusations in a brief submitted to the High Court: "The acceptance of this petition, God forbid, is the acceptance of a post-Zionist, antinationalist argument.... Would this honored Court accept an argument that property should be taken from the Jewish public in the name of the [Palestinian] right of return?... In a time of terrorism and bloodshed, this honored Court is asked to reject totally the petitioner's attempt apparently to erect a legal platform for the right of return and the movement of the refugees and displaced persons in the state's borders" (Biran 2002, 113).

Responses to the smear campaign were mixed. The Rainbow issued several strong statements refuting the allegations. But the responses of the main groups aggrieved by the conspicuous inequalities of the Israeli land system were particularly illuminating. The Development Towns Forum, comprising the mayors from most peripheral, and mainly Mizrahi, development towns, began to mobilize and support the Rainbow challenge, claiming that they have been discriminated against for years by the farmers' firm grip on national land. As stated by Haim Barbibai, mayor of the peripheral town of Kiryat Shemoneh: "Finally we have a group attempting to address the long-term inequalities of the Israeli land system; the accusation of their 'secret' goals to help the Palestinian refugees are nothing but a farce that aims to divert attention from the ongoing 'strangling' of our towns by the agricultural settlers; we will not change our resolve to support the Rainbow challenge or other initiatives that promote our rights."[8]

Leaders of the second main group deprived by the Israeli land system—the Palestinian-Arab minority—were more skeptical. For example, Hana Suyaid, mayor of the peripheral town of Ilabun and head of the Arab Center for Alternative Planning, commented: "It is interesting that the Rainbow claims to advance goals of social justice, but why is this limited to Jews only? They want to stop Jewish farmers and developers from making large profits but forget to mention that the original holders of the land were Arabs, and that they should be the main beneficiaries of any land redistribution; as usual, Jews fight among themselves at the expense of the Arabs."[9]

This escalating debate over land control is an appropriate preface to this chapter, which accounts for the making of the Israeli land system. As in previous chapters, the focus will be on the Judaization project as a major spine that shapes laws, policies, and institutions, and later it will turn to partial liberalization as a new engine behind changes in the system. The analysis will concentrate on Israel proper (within its 1967 borders) although the Judaization process has been highly conspicuous in the occupied territories, where 52 percent of land has already been declared (Israeli) state land, and where 145 Jewish settlements have been built, recognized, and supported by the Israeli state.

The analytical focus of this chapter is on the system of land ownership, zoning, and allocation. However, it also recognizes, of course, that land is but a part of an overall system of spatial control, which includes other arms of government, most notably urban and regional planning, housing, infrastructure, local government, and the military and security apparatuses. Given Israel's history of expansion and settlement, the land system has indeed assumed a major role in the production of ethnic space, but the interested reader is advised to explore this subject further in order to appreciate better the contribution of the entire spatial system (see Alterman 2002; Dery 1994; Yiftachel 1992a, 1997c).

The chapter shows how the Israeli land system has worked, first and foremost, to support the ethnonational project of territorial Judaization, and second, to facilitate an uneven allocation of land among Jewish ethnoclasses. In the latter part, the chapter accounts for the impact of the recent neoliberal shifts in Israeli society, which have started a process of quiet privatization whereby public lands are rezoned and redeveloped for the benefits of dominant groups. This regressive move has generated, for the first time in Israel's history, a concerted, multisectoral mobilization against the land system, culminating in the High Court challenge with which this chapter opened.

The Legal Geography of Settler Societies

The intersection of law and geography has recently spawned the new field of legal geography. The term first appeared in the 1920s, but it was only in the

1990s that a scholarly field began to emerge (see Blomely 1994, 2001; Delaney 2000; Forest 2000; Kedar 2003). The field draws strongly on the notion that "the legal and the spatial are, in significant ways, aspects of each other . . ." (Blomley, Delaney, and Ford 2001, xviii).

Legal geography asks questions concerning law and the making of cities (Fernandes and Varley 1998), segregation (Delaney 2000), globalization (Mitchell 2003), and informality (AlSayyad 2001). Recently, questions regarding land reform and restitution in post-communist countries (Marcuse 1995), as well as law and informal settlements and indigenous land in Brazil, South Africa, New Zealand, Thailand, and Trinidad began to be addressed (see Blomely, Delaney, and Ford 2001).

A notable stream has been critical legal geography, which stresses that geography is not an inherent result of natural phenomena or an inevitable outcome of market forces. Instead, legal decisions often mold human geographies. Critical legal geographers are concerned with "social, economic, and political inequality and seek to demonstrate how legal institutions, conventions and practices reinforce hierarchical social relationships" (Forest 2000, 6).

Critical legal geographers explore the reasons for and impact of law when it is predominantly used as a tool of domination (Blomely 2001; Kedar 2003). They argue that one of the main functions of law is to make uneven power relations seem acceptable and/or necessary (see Kennedy 1997; Minda 1995; Shamir 1990). The legal system, then, simultaneously privileges and legitimizes the interests of powerful groups, resting on the common perception of the law as a taken-for-granted foundation for relations between citizen and state. Hence, formalism and legalism, seemingly neutral and standing above social relations, actually constitute an important ingredient in the ceaseless construction of hegemony and legitimation (see Mautner 2000).

Researchers in the field often draw on critical geographical concepts (see Brenner 2004, Gregory 1994; Harvey 2001; Massey 1994) to demonstrate that legal structures constitute important building blocks in ordering and legitimating spatial/power hierarchies. They argue that legal categories and distinctions both shape and constrain group spatialities, that is, the combination of spatial rights, capabilities, and oppressions (Taylor 2000). Critical legal geographers stress that while law is implicated in the production and endurance of spatial inequalities, various rhetorical devices contribute to their legitimization and perpetuation. Thus, the articulation of allegedly technical formal rules and categories with meticulous legal distinctions can often conceal power-laden social relations that stand behind the invention and institutionalization of these categories.

The legal arena is implicated with the politics of space in many other ways, including the use of alienating legal and regulative language, within which only certain privileged voices can be heard (Shamir 2000); the selective interpretation of facts in the courts; and the omnipresence of background rules and assumptions that are never discussed but nonetheless serve to differentiate unequal social groups (Kedar 2003).

In settler societies, such as Israel, the founding group invariably receives preferential status, commonly expressed by privileged land rights. In most cases these are acquired by force and are subsequently translated into legal and institutional arrangements. The establishment of ethnocratic settler states usually entails the establishment of new property systems (Russell 1998). Ethnocratic land systems generally reproduce and reinforce social stratification, allocating the founders control over most land resources. Immigrants are usually urbanized and hence have little access to land, while the indigenous and alien groups are typically denied land control almost entirely.[10]

The land system also constitutes a legal-cultural order that reduces the necessity to use direct force. Critical legal geographers argue that dominant groups construct legal belief structures that justify racial and spatial inequalities through a complex professional discourse, while claiming to be objective and impartial (Delaney 2001). By reconstituting settlers' cultural biases and power relations into formalized rules such as property arrangements, law plays a significant role in the legitimation and endurance of ethnocratic regimes.

As recently exposed in an extensive comparative study by the United Nations, the legal system often imposes insurmountable obstacles for natives and other outsiders (Daes 1996). Settler states frequently regard native land as public land that can be disposed of by governments without the natives' approval or even knowledge (Singer 1992). As a result, many natives have become trespassers on their own land. Even if states recognize native possession, it is usually conceived to be only at the whim of the sovereign and may be revoked at any time (Daes 1999). Often, however, the settlers' legal systems deny altogether any recognition of native land rights even when the native group has been in possession of the land since time immemorial, as was the case with the doctrine of *terra nullius* (empty land), in force in Australia until 1992 (see Mercer 1993)

But the role of law and courts is not necessarily only regressive. The legal arena does possess important internal protocols of justice, universality, and equality. These often present opportunities for minorities and marginalized groups to exploit the tensions and inconsistencies between the internal legal discourses of equality and the persisting reality of discrimination. Further, during the last two decades a new international moral regime has established a conspicuous judicial presence. The discourses of human and minority rights have been institutionalized and actively pursued by a range of organizations, most notably the United Nations. This has strengthened the hand of minorities in dealing directly with their states and opened opportunities for mobilization within the international system (Howitt 2001; Sassen 1999).

Recently, for example, courts in Australia began to play an important progressive role in redefining indigenous rights to land. In the 1990s the Australian Supreme Court began to revolutionize the legal and political discourse by laying down its famous *Mabo* (1992) and *Wik* (1996) decisions (Hewitt 2001; Mercer 1993). The Court rejected the legal doctrine of *terra nullus* and recognized Aboriginal indigenous titles. Similar, though not identical, legal processes have been occurring recently in New Zealand and Canada (see Russell 1998). Notwithstanding the limitations of these legal decisions, they are significant in the gradual decolonization of the Aborigines (Hewitt 2001; Russell 1998). As shown by the multidimensional ethnocratic framework (see Chapter 2), however, legal victories are but a small step in a difficult process of achieving indigenous equality. Yet, such victories can enhance recognition and equality, as shown later in the case of Israel.

The Making of the Israeli Land System

The roots of the land and settlement systems can be traced to the early decades of Zionist land purchase and settlement in Palestine (see Kark 1990; Kimmerling 1983). However, 1948 was a major watershed, the profound significance of which is often overlooked by Israeli scholars. The 1948 war and the establishment of a state revolutionized the land system, strongly influencing social and political relations.

The 1948 war provided the initial setting for major Jewish land seizure. The flight and expulsion of Palestinians allowed Israel to distribute their lands (temporarily) among Jewish farmers and settlers. Ever since, a central goal of the Israeli land system has been to prevent a possible return of the refugees by settling Jews on the land and by legally and institutionally anchoring the land in Jewish hands. Significantly, most Jews who arrived in Israel before 1953 were themselves refugees or coerced immigrants with few other options. The majority of them were settled on land previously held or used by Arabs, as were approximately 350 out of the 370 Jewish settlements established during this period (Falah 2003; Golan 2001).

Similar to other settler states, Israel initiated a fundamental restructuring of the land system, resting on new, powerful legislation, institutions, and policies. Beyond the legal sphere, the Judaization project involved several major moves and transformations, such as the destruction of more than four hundred Arab villages, towns, and neighborhoods; the launch of intensive Jewish settlement; the placement of spatial restrictions on Arab localities and development; the Hebraization of the landscape; the parallel development of Jewish urban and occupation centers; and the redrawing of municipal boundaries in ways that ensured wide Jewish control (see Chapter 5; Benvenisti 2001; Kedar 1998; Kemp 1997).

Yossef Weitz, who was a central figure in the Zionist land-settlement establishment, was the long-time head of the Jewish National Fund's (JNF) Land Department and later the first director of the Israel Land Authority. The following quote from Weitz illustrates how the issue of ethnic land control engaged Israeli political thought even after the creation of a sovereign Israel. In 1950, he wrote, "Some theorists in the Hebrew public think that since the state was created, it controls all land . . . and therefore the land problem was solved by itself . . . and the land was redeemed. . . . The land is indeed state land, but there is one flaw with it. . . . Rights to that land belong to all the state's citizens, including the Arabs. . . . In this situation, we must ensure that most land will belong to Jews . . . and therefore we must continue with land redemption" (Weitz 1950, 143–45).

At the end of the 1948 war, Israel controlled an area covering approximately 20.6 million dunams of land, or 78 percent of British Mandate Palestine.[11] Land officially owned by Jewish individuals and organizations only amounted to approximately 8.5 percent of the state's total area (Kark 1995).[12] With the addition of British Mandate land inherited by Israel, this reached about 13.5 percent (2.8 million dunams). According to the vision of Weitz and other Zionist leaders, the Israeli state rapidly and efficiently increased the amount of land in its possession, transforming it into *Jewish-Israeli land.*

A totally new land system was thus established, based on national-collectivist principles that rapidly implemented the tenets of Judaization and expansion. At the conclusion of this phase, approximately 93 percent of Israeli territory (within the pre-1967 Green Line) was owned, controlled, and managed by either the state or the Jewish people (through the JNF). Taking into account private Jewish ownership, more than 96 percent of the state's landmass was Judaized during Israel's first decade. As illustrated in Figure 6.1, the making of a new land system was based on several key principles: physical seizure, nationalization, Judaization, establishment of tight central control, and uneven distribution. This was achieved in seven major steps, which shaped the character of the land system until the 1990s.

(1) *Expropriation of Palestinian-Arab lands.* It is estimated that before 1948, Palestinian Arabs owned between 4.2 and 5.8 million dunams of land in the territory that became Israel (Kark 1995).[13] The property of the Palestinian refugees was transferred to public/Jewish ownership. In addition, Palestinian Arabs remaining in Israel lost approximately 40–60 percent of their lands. The confiscation of Arab land began during the war under temporary emergency regulations. After a short period, the Israeli legal system began to legalize this

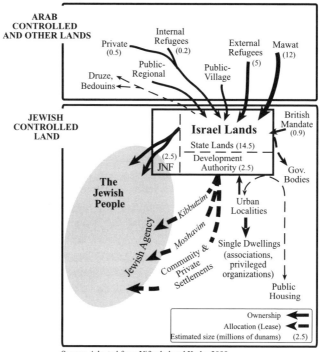

Source: Adapted from Yiftachel and Kedar 2000.

Figure 6.1. The Israeli Land System: Ownership, Control, and Allocation

transfer of land, mainly through the Absentee Property Law (1950), the State Possession Law (1951), and the Land Acquisition Law (1953) (see Kretzmer 1990; Lustick 1980; Kedar 1996, 1998).

In the early 1950s, a new phase of land transfer was based on settlement of title. This process deprived many Arab landholders of the right to retain their land, especially in the frontier areas of the Galilee and the Negev (Kedar 1998, 2001; Shamir 1996). In later phases, the legal focus shifted from expropriation of ownership to land-use limitations. This was achieved primarily through planning and zoning laws and by the strict containment of Arab municipal boundaries (Khamaissi 1992).

(2) *Land control by state-Jewish organizations.* The state created a legal and institutional structure, which transferred refugee land to management by and ownership of state and Jewish organizations. This was achieved by pooling all refugee land under a new entity, the Development Authority, and by establishing in 1960 the Israel Land Authority to manage these lands. Power in the Israeli Land Authority was to be shared equally between the Israeli government and the

JNF. Land allocation and management also involved the Jewish Agency. In this way, all public Jewish and state lands were managed together by a combination of world-Jewry organizations, causing the structural exclusion of Arabs (Kedar 1998).

(3) *State registration of British Mandate lands.* The British Mandate formally claimed ownership of approximately one million dunams of land. During the process of settlement of title, the Israeli state transferred millions of dunams into its ownership as state land, mainly in the Negev and Galilee. Much of the land transferred to state ownership during this formal process of registration had hitherto been unregistered.

A significant part of this land was transferred to the state as a result of classifying Bedouin-held land in the Negev and the Galilee as *mawat* (dead land) (Kedar 2001; see Chapter 8). The *mawat* categorization, operating in conjunction with Ottoman and Mandatory laws and their interpretation by Israeli courts, enabled the state to claim ownership of twelve million dunams of land (or 56 percent of Israel's landmass) that lacked ownership documentation. Much (though by no means all) of this land was previously held by Arabs. It also enabled the state to prevent previous Arab landholders from securing residency or cultivation rights. Simultaneously, crucial changes took place in adverse possession rules (which allowed unauthorized land users to gain possession), making it extremely difficult for Arab landholders to prove possession (Kedar 1996, 1998). The central role played by the Israeli Supreme Court in this dispossession prompted its labeling elsewhere as "judicial land redemption" (Yiftachel and Kedar 2000).

(4) *Transfer of land and power to the JNF.* During the early 1950s, the JNF more than doubled its land holding as the result of purchasing two million dunams of (previously Arab) agricultural land from the state. The financial details of this sale are not fully known, and some lands were returned to the state during the late 1950s (Golan 2001; Holzman-Gazit 2002). Following this transfer, the exclusively Jewish JNF became the largest owner of agricultural land in Israel, blocking the accessibility of Arab citizens to these lands.

(5) *Prohibition of land sale.* In 1960 Israel adopted the long-term policy of the JNF and declared that all state lands will never be sold,[14] thereby ensuring the perpetual ownership by state and Jewish organizations of all lands transferred to the state and Jewish organizations (Section 1 of Basic Law: Israel Lands, 1960).

(6) *Transfer of land control to the Israel Lands Authority (ILA).* In 1960, following years of negotiation, a final agreement between the state of Israel and the JNF was signed, creating the ILA. The ILA was charged with managing state, Development Authority, and JNF

lands, which cover 93 percent of Israel's pre-1967 territory.[15] Although it owns only about one-sixth of public lands, the JNF received equal representation (50 percent) on the ILA's executive board. The council consisted overwhelmingly of representatives from the founders' group (chiefly from the Jewish agricultural sector). Within the Israeli regime, the ILA enjoys a quasi-sovereign status, subordinate only to the state laws but not to the decisions of other executive bodies, including the government.

(7) *Uneven allocation of land.* The Israeli land system has had a major impact on the shaping of social relations by determining the allocation of the vast amount of public land under the ILA's control. The possession of virtually all nationalized land was allocated to Jewish residents and settlement movements. The ethnic logic of the system aimed, first and foremost, to minimize Arab control, but it has also deepened—through the same Judaization project—the gap between the Jewish Ashkenazi founders and Mizrahi immigrants (see Benvenisti 2001; Elmelech and Lewine-Epstein 1998; Law Yone and Kalus 1995; Yiftachel 1998b).

This manifested in all levels of land allocation—size, location, strength of possession, and potential for development. Figure 6.2 illustrates a central aspect of the uneven allocation—the size and location of municipal areas dominated by Jewish (and mainly Ashkenazi) regional councils. As we have seen, these regional councils have traditionally been dominated by protected agricultural land, but in recent years—with the process of commercialization and partial privatization—they have assumed a different role in holding the main land reserves for urban redevelopment. As such, control over large municipal areas, coupled with typical jurisdiction over local planning, has become increasingly meaningful in terms of material benefit. The administrative allocation of state land in the 1950s can now be translated into development power and profits, deepening ethnoclass relations in Israeli society.

The land allocation process also created and/or reinforced distinctive *legal categories* of land possession. Concurrent with the process of allocation, laws and administrative practices that define distinct, unequal arrangements for different groups were crafted. While these arrangements were formulated in seemingly neutral language (describing, for example, allocations to *moshavim,* development towns, *yeshuvim kehilatiyim* (community settlements), or seasonal agriculture, these spatial/legal categories usually denoted distinctive social groups. In Mizrahi localities, for example, such as the development towns or fringe urban neighborhoods, many residents who were brought to these localities by the state received public housing with very weak, terminable short-term contracts. Many landholders in the Arab sector

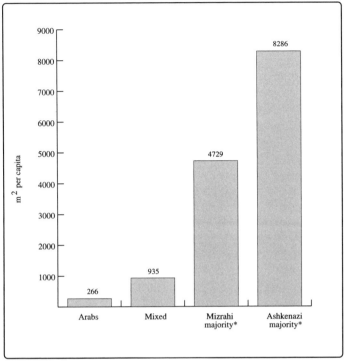

Not including the regional councils of Ramat Negev, Bne-Shimon, Tamar, Hevel-Eylot, and Mevo'ot Hachermon.

*Above 60%.

Figure 6.2. The Division of Nonmetropolitan Space in Israel

who could not prove land ownership were deprived of their land. Those holders who were not physically removed were categorized as trespassers (for example, some residents of the unrecognized Bedouin villages).

Lands in *kibbutzim, moshavim,* and community localities, which were usually populated by Ashkenazim, were transferred to residents in long-term legal arrangements (including inheritance rights) far preferable to those prevailing among dwellers of public housing.[16] The social-geographical differences between public housing tenants, Jewish farmers, and Arab farmers were transformed into distinct legal categories, which permitted the enactment of discriminatory laws while simultaneously maintaining a neutral facade that helped preserve the ethnocratic hegemony.

As detailed in the previous chapter, the gap between Ashkenazim and Mizrahim was further widened through the land policies, when some 160 new suburban settlements usually referred to as community localities *(yeshuvim kehilatiyim)* or private localities were established across the country, housing mainly middle-class Ashkenazim. They received considerable public resources, such as land, development rights, municipal status, and the ability to screen residents, thereby shifting resources from the public to private hands (Yiftachel 1997b; see also Carmon et al. 1991; Law-Yone and Kalus 1995).

Ethnospatial Regulations and the Dark Side of Planning

At this juncture, it is logical to ask how Israel succeeded in preserving Jewish spatial control. How did the state bypass democratic and market mechanisms through which Arabs could, at least theoretically, challenge this process? Much of the answer lies in the unidirectional nature of the process—from Arab to Jewish ownership but never back. Simultaneously, such land came under the partial control of the Jewish people through the involvement of international Jewish organizations in the ownership and management of Israeli public land. This situation was sanctioned in covenants, which were ratified as legislation, between the Israeli government and Jewish organizations, specifically with the JNF and the Jewish Agency (see Holtzman-Gazit 2002).[17]

Therefore, the powers delegated by the state to the JNF and the Jewish Agency became powerful tools in legal discrimination against Arabs, as it permitted them to continue a for Jews (only) policy while incorporating these organizations into the seemingly universal state system. The state thus utilizes Jewish organizations in a nondemocratic manner in order to bypass the institution of equal citizenship and all that it entails.

Jewish citizens residing in nonurban areas usually are allocated public land by a complex system. Initially, the land is assigned through a system known as the three-party lease, whereby three parties sign the initial land allocation contract: (a) the ILA as the public landowners' agent;[18] (b) the Jewish Agency, and (c) the Jewish locality as a collective (its legal entity is a cooperative). In order to lease (normally at a subsidized price and sometimes free of charge) an individual plot of land, a person must be accepted as a member of a cooperative that incorporates all residents of the community. The cooperative (often with participation of the Jewish Agency) has the power of selection and practical veto power over acceptance. A major rationale of this delegation of state power is to preclude Arabs from access to land.

As a result Arabs are barred in effect from buying or leasing land in approximately 80 percent of Israel's territory.[19] Given this institutional-geographical setting, regional councils have become a key actor in the control of Jewish space. These incorporate *kibbutzim, moshavim,* and community localities, whose residents belong mainly to the founding group. Such councils generally control local planning, which regulates land development. They play a central role in shaping the spatial processes taking place in Israeli society, such as suburbanization and suburban commercial development.

Concerning Israel's Arab citizens, the long-term effect of the measures outlined above can be summarized as follows.[20]

- The Arabs make up 16 percent of the state's population but own only 3.5 percent of the land area.
- The jurisdiction of Arab local authorities extends over 2.5 percent of the state's land area.
- Over half the land owned by Arabs in 1948 has been expropriated by the state.
- Only 0.25 percent of allocated state land has been distributed to Arab localities.
- Arabs are effectively blocked from acquiring or leasing land in some 80 percent of state land area.
- The Arab population has grown six-fold since 1948, yet the land under its control has halved.
- Since its establishment, the state has built more than seven hundred Jewish localities.
- During the same period, no Arab localities have been built (apart from twenty-one towns and villages to concentrate the Bedouins).
- Dozens of long-established Bedouin Arab villages, mainly in the south, are unrecognized, and the state plans to evacuate them.

The land system, therefore, was highly effective in creating a spatial foundation for the Israeli ethnocratic regime. It has worked effectively to Judaize lands and preserve Jewish institutional control through the placement of various geographical and institutional layers—settlement, municipal boundaries, development, and planning. It has laid the grounds for the massive Jewish settlement efforts (on both sides of the Green Line) and concentrated the vast majority of land resources in the hands of the dominant Jewish ethnoclass. This combined strategy forms a clear example of what I have termed the dark side of planning (see Yiftachel 1994), whereby the very same measures devised to improve living conditions and quality of life for the majority are used by the state to deepen its control over minorities.

But such a system can rarely remain unchallenged. Indeed, it has increasingly become the locus of antisystem grievances, most conspicuously expressed violently by the two Palestinian *intifadas,* which openly challenged Israel's land control in the occupied territories. But in Israel proper, too, challenges began to surface in the 1970s. First came the Black Panther movement, which for the first time in the state's history openly challenged Israel's Ashkenazi-dominated housing and social policies and protested in the name of marginalized Mizrahim.[21] This has had a lasting effect on Israeli politics (Shalom-Chetrit 2000). In 1976, Land Day was declared by Palestinian Arabs who lost their lands to the construction of the Jewish town of Carmiel. Land Day ended in the killing of six Arab citizens and has since become a national day for Palestinians in Israel and the occupied territories. Since the 1970s, land, housing, and development has been a major source of grievance for Israel's marginalized populations (see Yiftachel 2000b). It was only natural that more systematic legal and institutional challenges would surface, as indeed occurred with the *Qa'adan* case, detailed in the previous chapter, and with the battle over agricultural lands described below.

Therefore, the land system represents a fundamental basis of the ethnocratic regime. Yet it also exposes cracks in the system and provides opportunities for mobilizations necessary to transform the ethnocratic regime. Such transformations, whose end is yet unknown, began in the 1990s.

Sometime in the early 1990s, the Israeli land and planning system entered a new phase. Mounting pressures began to appear, caused, intra alia, by the gradual liberalization of the Israeli economy and land markets, an influx of mass immigration, a decline in agriculture profitability, and the continuing suburbanization of Israel's growing middle classes (Alterman 1995; Feitelson 1999; Gonen 1995). The pressures mounted most acutely on agricultural land because of the previous tight control over its development and because of its potential profitability.

The founding group, which held control over most agricultural land, was well connected with Israel's land administrators and main developers. These connections enabled it to propel a significant policy change in the shape of partial privatization.

According to the initial contractual terms of land allocation (reinforced in ILA Resolution 1, 1969), cooperative villages held land for agricultural use only (Vitkon 2001) and were prohibited from initiating commercial development or speculative price hikes. According to the contract, if agricultural land was rezoned, it should be returned to the state. Compensation was to be equal only to the value of agricultural investment made on the land. But in the beginning of the 1990s a profound change occurred in the status of agricultural landholders. Starting in 1992, the ILA passed a number of resolutions allowing rezoning and redevelopment of agricultural land, thus greatly increasing the property rights of agricultural landholders.[22] Contrary to the contract and ILA Resolution 1, landholders would now be able to rezone their land and acquire ownership over part of the redeveloped land. This increased the transfer of funds to the farmers by a thousand-fold, as compared with the previous regulation, and granted control over a large portion of Israel's land reserves to a small group.

The administrative setup was well geared to fulfill these interests, as the representatives of the farmers have traditionally functioned as the guardians of agricultural land while at the same time constituting the strongest force within key land policy institutions, such as the Committee for the Preservation of Agricultural Land and the various regional planning councils. Ideological changes, need, and opportunity led these guardians to make an about-face and support the rezoning of agricultural land for residential and commercial development. To be sure, this was not an abstract exercise, as most of the rezoned lands remained in their possession. Hence, the agricultural sector effectively transferred considerable resources (especially land and development rights) from the public to its own private hands. During the same period there was a visible increase in the prominence of land entrepreneurs, who were working with the farmers to accelerate the rezoning of land.

In addition, the perception of a shortage of accessible land for residential construction resulted from the wave of mass immigration totaling more than two hundred thousand people in its first year. Because a large portion of vacant land was in the possession of the cooperative villages, the ILA decided to provide holders with financial incentives to vacate their land. It justified this move by claiming it facilitated rapid housing construction for immigrants. It turned out, however, that there was no significant shortage and that the vast majority of construction on lands held by cooperative agricultural localities was not sold to immigrants (Alterman 1995; Tzfadia 2002a). Still, the rhetoric linking immigrant absorption and the opening up of new tracts of land played a critical role in advancing the interests of the founders, be they farmers or land developers.

This process helps illustrate how the central power bases of the Israeli ethnocratic regime work in conjunction with one another. Immigration policies intended to intensify the Judaization of the state worked in favor of adopting a new land policy (opening up land) as well as changing the regulative system. These changes would benefit the strong sectors in Israeli society and legitimize their lucrative use of public resources, such as land resources and planning permits.

Changes in the legal arena have also been influential. When Palestinian land was nationalized during the 1950s, no constitutional guarantee of property rights existed. Today, property rights, often acquired by force or political affiliation, have become constitutional owing to the 1992 Basic Laws, which treat property rights as a constitutionally protected baseline. This has concealed the manner in which some state lands have been obtained, namely the confiscation of Palestinian Arab land and its uneven distribution among the Jews (see also Gross 1998; Zalzberger and Kedar 1998).

Another critical aspect is the nondemocratic manner of formulating land policies. Critical decisions were not instituted by proper legislation but rather made behind closed doors and by nonrepresentative bodies. The founders in general, and the cooperative rural sector in particular, wield disproportional power in Israel's land policy forums and especially in the ILA. This body is not elected. It represents the Jewish people as a whole (through its connection with the JNF) and is, in essence, a powerful autonomous player within the Israeli power structure. Therefore, the work of these agencies in shaping the Israeli land regime function according to an ethnocratic logic that serves, first and foremost, the Zionist project but within that project favors the founders over the various groups of immigrants.

The conduct of decision making in small, semisecretive forums, coupled with the vague language of the ILA resolutions, prevented from the start the development of public debate on the future of this enormous public resource. This comes as no surprise. Ethnocratic regimes typically develop such mechanisms—camouflage, vagueness, and use of complicated professional terminology—to support the national and economic supremacy of the dominant group and to present obstacles for the initiation of public debate.

Regulations and Tribulations

An important precedent was set with ILA Resolution 533 in 1992. Chaired by Ariel Sharon—then the minister for housing responsible for land policy—the ILA determined that long-term holders of agricultural land would be compensated for rezoning based on the land's new (redeveloped) value and not on the value of their agricultural investment, as had previously been the case. The resolution also facilitated the purchase of agricultural land by members of cooperative agricultural localities for half the land's value. Such compensation could potentially total tens if not hundreds of millions of shekels if they could develop their entire agricultural holdings. Resolution 533 started a process that could make the temporary allocation of the 1950s permanent.

In 1994, following pressure from within the agricultural sector, Resolution 666 replaced 533. It differentiated, for the first time, between several types of agricultural landholders, mainly according to their location, whereby peripheral regions would gain more compensation while central areas, which were experiencing an unprecedented property boom, would have their earnings reduced. In addition, private agricultural companies, which hold lands in many of Israel's attractive coastal regions, were also included for the first time in the arrangements, enabling redevelopment.

Notably, the 1994 regulation remained silent on two sectors: Jewish seasonal cultivators (farmers with no long-term arrangements, who are mainly Mizrahim in peripheral *moshavim*) and the Bedouin Arabs in the Negev. Although these groups had cultivated state land for decades, they were not presented with any opportunity of capturing its redevelopment value. Hence, the legal categorization of land possession, among Jewish farmers on the one hand (among cooperative localities, private companies, and seasonal cultivators), and, more markedly, between Jewish farmers and the Bedouins on the other, caused a clear hierarchy of benefits. Cloaked in seemingly neutral terminology, this hierarchy ranged from the provision of excessive benefits to the founders and some of the immigrants (*kibbutzim* and *moshavim*) to a complete denial toward the weakest members of the indigenous/native group (the Bedouins).[23]

This began to generate disquiet among the discriminated groups. Several appeals claiming discrimination and improper management were submitted to the High Court. In 1996, the Court struck a significant ruling by rescinding Resolution 666 because of the conflict of interests of most decision makers at the ILA, who are also holders of agricultural land.

But still, the Court's judgment addressed procedural issues and did not touch on the claims of substantive discrimination or unreasonableness raised by disadvantaged groups. Subsequently, less than two weeks after the judgment, the ILA passed Resolution 727, which was identical to 666. The only difference was the physical absence of representatives of the farmers from the vote itself. The procedural flaw was corrected and Resolution 727 was in force for eight years, setting the platform for continuing rezoning and effective privatization of state land (see also Kedar 2003; Shachar 2000).[24]

During the same period, the ILA passed additional resolutions favoring agricultural landholders, including one dealing with locality expansion (Resolutions 612 and 737 of 1993 and 1995 respectively), which enabled *moshavim* and *kibbutzim* to redevelop agricultural land at reduced prices to offer housing for their maturing children. But as noted by the state attorney general, the implementation was often fictitious: construction approved for local youth was often turned into new commercial neighborhoods. This occurred chiefly near *moshavim*, which charged land purchasers full value and pocketed the difference (Rubinstein 2000).

The Ronen Committee

Opposition to the new land policies continued to surface. For example, the government attorney general, Elyakim Rubinstein, stated that people "reap unjust riches from state land by means of tainted exploitation of the ILA policy" (Rubinstein 2000, 14). The public debate became acrimonious in 1996, prompting Ariel Sharon (the minister of infrastructure who was responsible for land policy) in the rightist Netanyahu government to appoint the Ronen Committee to offer new solutions. The committee, which was the first of two important public committees to work on the subject, was headed by an economics and management professor and staffed by two other experts from the financial field. Its report, tabled in April of 1997, was significant because for the first time since quiet privatization had begun, an official, authoritative body determined that the holders of state agricultural land have no legal right of rezoning (Ronen 1997, 22–23). But the committee still encouraged privatization across the board, with some changes in the levels of compensation, favoring the periphery. The Ronen

Report was adopted by the government in the summer of 1997, after several stormy debates. However, while approving the practical privatization of lands in the urban sector, and offering a similar move in the actual built-up areas of rural localities, the government omitted the committee's recommendation regarding the privatization of agricultural lands. This was due to JNF opposition, as expressed by one of the official organs of this organization, the journal *Karka*, in 1998: "It appears as if the recommendations of the Ronen Committee are not driven by national-Zionist considerations; there is a danger that they will undermine the very [territorial] basis on which the state was founded. . . . The neglect of state land could lead to 'erosion' of the Green Line and even to its movement westward and then to Arab seizure of agricultural lands. . . ."[25]

In a telling episode, the ILA board met on the subject in late 1997 and was presented with a halachic (Orthodox Jewish) ruling, signed by several notable rabbis, that held that the new policy contravenes the basic law of Judaism. The proposed policy of privatizing agricultural lands was then rejected by the board. In this way, the ethnocratic logic found new means to defend the morality of continuing discrimination among citizens.[26]

Further, under the cloth of a liberal privatization approach, the Ronen Report contained no mention of the severe problems plaguing Arab farmers, such as lack of state land allocation, zoning and municipal restrictions, and a water shortage (Khamaissi 2001). This is a good example of liberal and legalized discrimination, which uses universal categories to conceal the troubling past and present of the Israeli land system. By using legal categories, such as rezoning or state lands, the state camouflages its discrimination and ignores the way in which these lands came under state control and the associated dispossession of the Arab citizens, as described above.

Moreover, the Ronen Committee ignored its mandate to deal with land and housing arrangements in distressed urban neighborhoods. It refrained from touching the important social issue, which mainly affects Mizrahi and Russian immigrants. Here, too, the universal language of privatization concealed the very different situations of urban holders of state lands, who remain virtually rightless. Overall, and typical of ethnocratic societies, the Ronen Committee focused on the property rights of the founders while neglecting the needs and concerns of indigenous and immigrant groups (for a detailed critique, see Kedar and Yiftachel 1999).

Despite this, the Ronen recommendations received a hostile response from the farmers, mainly owing to the reduced rights they offered to redeveloped agricultural lands. The agricultural lobby managed to torpedo the report's implementation while seeking new ways to receive practical ownership of agricultural lands.

At this stage, the Knesset became the main arena for land maneuvers, twice approving in preliminary readings the Farmers' Land Rights bill, once in 1996 and again in 1998. The 1998 bill, for example, allocated land for Jewish agricultural localities for 196 (renewable) years and allocated rezoning compensation at a rate of 100 percent to the landholders, meaning the effective transfer of full ownership rights (see Kedar and Yiftachel 1999).

Just before the 1999 general elections, a joint effort by public officials, environmental groups, and social justice organizations succeeded in preventing the passage of the Farmers' Land Rights bill. After this failure the ball was back with the office of the executive, which supported the transfer of agricultural land to its holders through the 196-year leasing contracts. This decision aimed to apply pressure on other decision-making bodies but remained mainly declaratory, as such moves require new legislation or ILA resolutions, none of which was forthcoming.

PUBLIC PROTEST

These blatant moves generated increased public protest against the hurried decisions made behind closed doors. A range of social organizations led by the Mizrahi Rainbow and the Israeli Association of Civil Rights, as well as by a large number of smaller, new organizations, initiated protests. During this period, organizations formed a coalition and initiated—for the first time—an intense debate in the Israeli media concerning one of the sacred cows of the Zionist state—the land system (see Yonah and Saporta 2000). The intense involvement of academic, media, and professional experts contributed to the growing public interest by exposing dubious, secretive, and at times corrupt land allocation and development procedures.

In light of the public disquiet, and in an unprecedented step, the ILA published the proposed privatization resolution on its internet site in March of 1999. Although the public was given only two weeks to respond, this invitation constituted an important step for improving the transparency of this public agency. The proposal's publication sparked a torrent of 191 responses from financial institutions, social movements, public bodies, and private citizens. Only four responses supported the proposal[27] while the remainder criticized it on social justice, planning, and environmental grounds (see Kedar and Yiftachel 1999). The nature of the public response and the allegation of improper decision making that favored a small group apparently made the ILA postpone the process indefinitely.

A stark comparison made during the public discussion was the unequal state treatment of the (favored) farmers, as opposed to the disadvantaged residents of public housing. The latter never managed to secure their property rights, although they had a similar legal status to the farmers (lessee) and were of much lower socioeconomic status. After a stubborn battle, public housing residents and their representatives in the Knesset succeeded in passing the Public Housing Law (1998) and were about to acquire rights to purchase, on favorable terms, the dwellings in which they had been living for decades. However, the law was frozen by the Netanyahu, Barak, and Sharon governments, demonstrating profound contempt of the large but marginal public-housing public.

Further criticism was leveled against the ongoing discrimination of Israel's Arab citizens. It was argued by several NGOs, such as Adalah, Adva, and the Center for Alternative Planning, that the privatization process would severely (although not completely) limit their access to privatized property, and in this way it would legally anchor the Judaization of lands originally confiscated from Arabs. It was also argued that the wording of the proposal denied Arab farmers the same rights to public resources as those granted to Jews. In addition, the critics continued, the proposal would seriously impede finding solutions to the property claims of Palestinian refugees, both external and internal.[28]

POLITICAL DEADLOCK, LEGAL STRUGGLE, AND MORE COMMITTEES

After the 1999 elections, in which Ehud Barak became the new prime minister, which represented a major swing to the left in Israeli politics, the Farmers' Land Rights bill was submitted again. Yet it continued to encounter the same opposition within the Knesset and the bureaucracy. The legislative path hit a deadlock during this period, which lasted until 2002. Critically, the ILA rezoning resolutions remained in effect throughout this period. This meant that parliamentary delays were working in favor of the landholders because a large portion of land reserves, estimated at four hundred thousand dunams between 1992 and 1999, continued to be rezoned for redevelopment. This gradual privatization generated a claim by several *kibbutz* lawyers that the rezoned land is no longer returnable to the state and is now protected as a basic right according to the 1992 Basic Laws.

In order to prevent this situation, the Rainbow and a group of academics petitioned the High Court of Justice in January of 2000 in an effort to rescind all ILA resolutions enabling the rezoning of state agricultural land.[29] The response of the Barak government to the High Court appeal was the appointment of another committee, this time staffed by powerful members of the Israeli bureaucracy, in order to "finally resolve the future of agricultural land."[30] The committee, which would supercede the Ronen Committee, was headed by David Milgrom, the treasury's chief of budgets. Serving with him were the directors of the ministries of infrastructure and agriculture, the director of the planning administration, the head of the ILA, the attorney responsible for civil affairs in the State Legal Service, and a government advisor on planning and development.

In light of the pending High Court petition, the Milgrom Committee generated wide interest. A group of *kibbutzim* and *moshavim* from Israel's central Cheffer Region, known as Granot, became particularly active and hired the high-profile lawyer-developer Shraga Biran to represent them in the High Court. Biran, who was also a main beneficiary of land rezoning through several large joint projects with agricultural localities, launched an all-or-nothing aggressive campaign, typified by the mudslinging episodes outlined at the beginning of this chapter.

The pressure mounted further in May of 2000 with the particularly damning report of the state comptroller (no. 50b), who noted with alarm the privileges of the agricultural sector, the pervasive commercial redevelopment of state lands, the rife land speculations, and the shoddy decision making and law enforcement practiced in these areas. This caused a wave of media reports with accusations of improper conduct of the ILA, farmers, and real estate developers.

While the political and legislative deadlock continued, the High Court petition became the center of attention, with several hearings drawing large crowds and broad media focus. In June of 2000, for example, the Court was debating a request for a temporary injunction to stop land rezoning because it was claimed that the lengthy delays in the case were working in favor of the land developers, who were continuing to push for redevelopment. Future delays, it was argued, would create further uncontrolled and illegal rezoning. In the debate, most judges exposed serious contradictions in the position of the state, which allows the uncontrolled privatization of its own lands without proper legislation or an appropriate public debate. However, with promises from the state to hasten the Milgrom Committee's report, the court refrained from issuing the injunction. Yet, the very public debate of a previously closed policy arena further shook existing land arrangements.

The Milgrom Committee tabled its recommendations in December of 2000. It took a similar pro-privatization line to the Ronen Committee but made it less attractive financially to rezone agricultural land. The Milgrom Committee also made a clear distinction, for the first time, between the locality built-up area known as the camp and the surrounding agricultural lands. The committee recommended that urban-like property rights be transferred to members of the cooperative villages in the camp area while keeping state ownership of agricultural lands, with firm long-term leases available to all farmers of state lands.

The agricultural lobby expressed disappointment and anger at the Milgrom Committee's recommendation and relaunched its legislative efforts for a new version of the Farmers' Land Rights bill. In February of 2001, following the failed peace talks with the Palestinians and the outbreak of the al-Aqsa *intifada*, the leftist Barak government collapsed and Ariel Sharon was elected prime minister. His government nonetheless included the Labor Party, and the new minister of agriculture, Shalom Simhon, a Labor representative of the *moshavim* movement, continued the policy and legislative efforts for the rezoning and transfer of property rights.

But the new legislative efforts were frustrated once again, both by political pressures and by the Knesset's legal advisors, who saw the proposed law as breaching the state's Basic Laws. Further, the JNF remained a main objector to the bill, which breached its compact with the Israeli state. The compact prohibits the sale of land by either side and places decision-making powers on land policies with the ILA and not the Knesset. During 2001 the debate between the state and the JNF reached a new crisis, with the JNF publicly threatening to withdraw from the ILA and the entire land system.[31]

In February of 2001 the attorney general also ruled that the Farmers' Land Rights bill contravened Israel's Basic Law: Israel Lands and the 1992 Basic Law: Human Dignity. Hence, the legislative path, despite its early successes, was heading into a deadlock again. However, the legal path was not more effective for the farmers: in November of 2001 the High Court finally issued a temporary injunction against the rezoning regulations. The noose was tightening around the unchecked privatization of land. The Court explained that the delay in the state's reply was no longer reasonable given the ongoing redevelopment of state agricultural lands. The Court gave a two-month period for deals to be finalized before the injunction would take effect. During this period, an unprecedented rate of deals was signed, channeling a record 725 billion NIS to the state coffers.

In August of 2002, a seven-judge panel of the High Court tabled its long awaited ruling, upholding the Rainbow's petition, thereby rescinding the three rezoning regulations—717, 727, and 737. The Court relied on a mixture of procedural and normative grounds to strike down the decade-old land arrangements. The legal argument was quite clear—the commercial and residential rezoning of state agricultural lands was illegal. The Court also commented on the social aspect by reasoning that there was no justification for the excessive financial benefits conferred by the rezoning on the *kibbutzim* and *moshavim*. The ILA, the Court added, is the public's trustee for state lands and must therefore manage these lands for the benefit of the entire public rather than awarding excessive benefits to particular sectors. Finally, for the first time in Israel's history, the Court also used a normative argument of social justice by stating:

the case raises the value of implementing distributive justice in land allocation by the ILA. This value is concerned with the just distribution of social and other resources. The duty to consider distributive justice is inseparable from the power of any administrative authority, which allocates scarce resources. The duty has been expressed by the wide-ranging ruling of this Court, regarding discrimination, freedom of occupation, equality of opportunity . . . even though it did not use in earlier rulings this term explicitly. (Bagatz 244/00, 18)

The significant nature of the decision and the use of an explicit normative language made this a true landmark decision. Like the 2000 *Qa'adan vs. Katzir* decision, it was hailed as historic because it broke down long-established practices of privilege and inequality. The Court did not re-frain from setting a new normative and civil framework for future land al-location, which will undoubtedly act as a precedent for similar questions concerning other public resources.

Following the Court's decision, the government adopted in September of 2002 the recommendations of the Milgrom Committee and began the separation between (developmentable) residential and (long-term leased and restricted) agricultural lands in the rural areas. In January of 2003, the ILA re-enacted two of the annulled resolutions (717 and 737) but this time with only little financial benefits to the farmers. The third controversial resolution (727), which allowed commercial development on agricultural lands, has of course been at the heart of the struggle and has not been re-formulated yet.

During spring and summer of 2003, another committee, this time headed by ex-treasurer Moshe Nissim, proposed transition regulation to re-place Resolution 727 until a new policy is formulated. Not surprisingly, the Nissim Committee, which was subject to persistent pressure by developers and farmers, recommended generous interpretations of the High Court de-cision and the Milgrom Report. The committee's recommendations called for allowing all rezoning initiatives of agricultural land that preceded the High Court's decision to continue, allowing rural households to register 2.5 dunams as private residential land, allowing three dwellings, and also allow-ing five hundred square meters of agricultural land to be redeveloped for commercial and/or industrial activities. Notably, however, these lands were to be confined to the locality's built-up area.

These recommendations clearly attempted to compensate the farmers following the High Court's decision. They generated, again, a heated de-bate, accusations of further transfer of public resources to the farmers, and threats by the Rainbow and environmental groups of further legal action. But despite the opposition of the attorney general, and despite wide public criticism, the ILA Council adopted the Nissim Committee's recommenda-tions in its meeting of August 5, 2003. At the same meeting, the ILA also approved a draft resolution that outlines the compensation criteria for all agricultural lands not included in the redevelopment areas. While the pro-posal is, again, fairly generous to the farmers (reaching up to seventy thou-sand NIS per dunam) it critically prohibits urban redevelopment on these lands. This is a significant development, relevant to the vast majority of agricultural lands. It is consistent with the recommendations of the Mil-grom Report and with the state's official planning strategy of protecting open spaces (Shachar 2000), and it may put a halt to the redevelopment at-tempts, at least for the short term.[32]

At the time of writing, then, the future privatization of land appears lim-ited to the built-up area of urbanizing rural villages or the very immediate vicinity. At this stage, the continuation of large-scale rezoning of agricultural land appears unlikely, although renewed pressures to transform agricultural land into urban developments are likely to emerge in the long term.

Finally, in May of 2004 the responsible minister, Ehud Olmert, appointed the Gadish Committee, which was composed of several high officials in the land, planning, and housing administrations, to reform the ILA. Simultaneously, two senior ILA officials, Shlomo Ben-Eliyahu (a member of the committee) and Gidon Vitkon, published a report recommending the separation of the JNF and the ILA as part of a wider initiative to liberalize the ILA, to "reduce the friction between the public and land officials," but also to enable the JNF to use land to "further national [Jewish] goals in accordance with its charter"—that is, leasing it to Jews only (Ben-Eliyahu and Vitkon 2003; Chapter 8).[33] While there is a certain emphasis on liberalization, the Gadish Committee reforms—if implemented—are not likely to significantly change the link between land control and ethnoclass stratification in Israel because the existing skewed distribution of the land forms a basis for the planned liberalization.

Further, the move to separate the JNF and the ILA possesses a danger of legitimatizing the exclusion of Arab citizens from JNF land, thereby deepening the ethnocratic nature of parts of the system at the same time it liberalizes others. This is likely to neutralize the impact of the High Court *Qa'adan* decision. The new institutional setting gained further impetus following another ground-breaking decision, this time by Israel's attorney general, Menahem Mazuz, who ruled in January of 2005 that Arab citizens cannot be excluded from the sale of JNF lands, which are administered by the ILA. His order specified that if Arabs seek to purchase JNF land, the state would compensate the JNF with alternative land of the same value.[34]

This ruling followed the attempted marketing of land in the Galilee city of Carmiel for Jews only during the summer of 2004. Several appeals to the High Court challenged that exclusion, which contradicted the *Qa'adan* ruling, and the attorney general wished to prevent a likely defeat by the state.[35] But, his decision did not only promote equality for Israel's Arab citizens but also institutionalized an arrangement of creating a rolling front of Jewish development, where the JNF and the state can exchange lands in order to facilitate the further Judaization of space, mainly in peripheral areas. It is also likely that given the high real-estate value of large reserves of JNF lands, which are located in Israel's central districts, the exchange would actually result in enlarging JNF's land reserves, causing further Arab-Jewish tensions. Mazuz's decision was greeted with some satisfaction among liberal circles, although most organizations, including the Association for Civil Rights, Adalah, and the Democratic Mizrahi Rainbow, commented that all institutional discrimination should end and that the struggle for this end must continue.

In overview, the struggle for reforming Israel's land system reflects an important change, namely the mobilization and public activism of groups that had hitherto been excluded. The active participation of academicians, civil rights activists, and professional experts in this struggle helped, for the first time, to challenge ethnocratic decision making and resource allocation practices. These constitute a discernable (albeit incipient) sign of democratization and popular empowerment. Yet the forces working to maintain the ethnocratic nature of the system are still strong and are likely to continue in their efforts to preserve their material assets.

Conclusion: Toward Reforms in the Land System?

The analysis discerned three main phases in the making of the Israeli land system: the Judaization of lands, the uneven allocation of land to Jewish ethnoclasses, and the partial privatization and rezoning of agricultural land. The first two steps reinforced Jewish dominance in Israel/Palestine and at the same time created ethnoclass stratification based on deep inequalities between the group of founders, immigrants, and indigenous/aliens.

This system was very effective in Israel's first decades of independence, mainly because of the weakness of adversely affected populations. But over time opposition began to surface, as shown by several notable outbursts during the 1970s and 1980s, reaching structural levels by the 1990s. They emerged from the Palestinian Arabs, public housing tenants, Mizrahim, and other immigrants residing in peripheral locations. The opposition also caused fierce reaction from the present holders of state lands, whose privileges were brought into question.

This opposition has rarely been coordinated, emerging as it did from outside the traditional political or administrative arenas. At times, new sociopolitical coalitions were formed, cutting across class, regional, and ethnic lines, as occurred in the struggle against the redevelopment of agricultural lands. While the opposition is still in its infancy, the creation of further coalitions to reform the land system may offer common social-justice agendas for diverse sectors and groups, with the effect of eroding the total domination of ethnocratic and recently neoliberal logics.

But to date, the institutional and policy response to emerging opposition has been far from promising. The main thrust of the authorities has been to tighten the ethnocratic logic, as shown by the 2002 government's decision to erect thirty-two new Jewish localities inside the Green Line and dozens more in the West Bank (B'tselem 2002). No parallel plans existed for new Arab localities (apart from further coerced concentrations of Negev Bedouins). Further, government efforts were made, as detailed above by my accounts of the Ronen, Milgrom, and Gadish Committees, to liberalize land administration, thereby enhancing the ongoing transfer of land resources to dominant leading ethnoclasses, especially to land developers. At the same time, public housing reforms, promised during the late 1990s, have remained frozen, and budgets for housing and development in the social peripheries have shrunk significantly (Adva 2003).

Returning to the model of ethnocracy, it is clear that the taken-for-granted status of the ethnocratic land system has recently been challenged from various angles. It is less clear, however, whether this challenge can transform and democratize the system, or whether it will cause, as most past challenges have, only a minor adjustment within the resilient ethnocratic system.

Part III
Ethnocracy and Its Peripheries: Palestinian Arabs and Mizrahim

Chapter 7

Fractured Regionalism among Palestinian Arabs in Israel

This chapter opens the third part of the book, in which the discussion moves from a state-level analysis to a greater focus on specific communities within the Israeli ethnocracy. Here we begin with the Palestinian Arab minority in Israel, which embodies the tensions and possibilities of the Israeli regime: a nominal commitment to democracy; structural and daily marginalization by an expanding ethnocratic state; long-term collective involvement with the ongoing Zionist-Palestinian struggles; and a process of identity formation, which is strongly influenced by the forces highlighted above.

The chapter's central argument is that the Palestinian Arabs in Israel are in the process of forging an *ethnoregional identity*. This identity is shaped, first and foremost, by the practices of the Israeli ethnocratic regime, which have caused the Arabs to become a striking example of a "trapped minority." The resultant regional identity is strongly influenced, in different ways, by Jewish and Palestinian nationalisms, and by the minority's marginalized, yet significant, civil incorporation into Israel. The establishment of a collective identity is framed by the Arabs' "fractured region"—a divided homeland territory within Israel, constrained and fragmented by deliberate land, settlement, and planning policies (see Chapter 5).[1]

The chapter covers in detail four main spheres in which the mobilization and collective identity of the Palestinian Arabs in Israel can be examined: geography, socioeconomics, extra-parliamentarian protest, and electoral behavior. The chapter also analyzes the impact of the violent October Events of 2000 and the al-Aqsa *intifada*. It identifies the emergence of a recent new stage in the asymmetric dialectics between Jews and Palestinians, resulting in the shrinking space of Arab citizenship in Israel (for a glossary of terms, see Appendix 1). The ethnoregional concept well explains this turn of events, including the post-2000 period, which appear to have accelerated the process of minority regionalization.

The regional perspective offers a new account of the mobilization and identity of the Palestinians in Israel. It responds to the failure of past scholarly approaches to describe and predict the developmental and political trajectory of this community. As noted in Chapter 4, most work on the Palestinian minority in Israel treats Israel unproblematically as a democratic nation-state, overlooking critical structural variables such as the occupation and settlement of Palestinian territories, immigration, refugees, capital, and the role of religion in shaping Arab-Jewish relations. These factors are critical for understanding the plight of Israel's Palestinian citizens.

Therefore, unlike most work on the subject, the analysis here does not treat Arab-Jewish relations in Israel as a separate sphere. On the contrary, I contend that the plight of Israel's Palestinian population is inextricably linked to the transformation of Israel/Palestine and the system of *creeping apartheid* gradually taking root in the areas under Israeli rule (see Chapter 5). Only if we consider the interdependence of the entire Israel/Palestine space, stretching from Jordan to the Mediterranean Sea, and account for the role of Jewish and Palestinian diasporas can we credibly fathom the strenuous processes shaping the place and identity of the Palestinian-Arab minority in Israel.

Minority Mobilization and Ethnoregionalism

Let me first touch briefly on several theoretical points on the position and identity of minorities within ethnic states. Social science literature has developed around two main debates, with the first focusing on the impact of nationalism (see Anderson 1991, 2001; Smith 1995; Kymlicka 2001; Penrose 2000), and the second on the potential role of citizenship and civil society (see Dahl 1989; Habermas 1996; Offe 2002; I. M. Young 2003). Knowledge from the two debates has rarely been combined, but there are some notable exceptions, such as the ground-breaking work of Hechter and Levi (1979) and later contributions by Hechter (2000), Keating (1988, 1996), McCrone (1993), Mikesell and Murphy (1991), Newman (1996, 2000), and Shafir (1995). These studies have shown that under certain circumstances, the most likely result of minority politicization in ethnic states is the emergence of ethnoregionalism. The term has been used in a variety of ways, but here I wish to define it as the mobilization of collective ethnic struggle within a state, aiming to channel resources to specific spaces; attain collective rights; preserve or build a collective identity; and challenge the state's ethnonational structure.

Ethnoregionalism is a dynamic consequence of a hegemonic ethnonational discourse superimposed over the existing grid of citizenship rights and group spatiality. It usually forms as a reaction to the often exclusive, expansionist, or exploitive nature of majority ethnocentric nationalism, which propels trapped minorities to campaign for goals such as territorial or cultural autonomy, self-determination, devolution of government functions, de-ethnicization of the state, power sharing, and socioeconomic equality (Keating 1996; Mikesell and Murphy 1991).

Ethnoregionalism is different from both ethnonationalism and civic mobilization on a number of counts, making it a distinct, durable, and meaningful political dynamic. It is distinct from ethnonationalism by its lack of explicit drive for ethnic sovereignty; by the self-perception of its territory as constrained, fractured, or divided; and by its attempt to reconcile ethnic and civil bases of identity. It is distinct from civil group mobilization by its emphasis on the protection of specific homeland spaces, by the promotion of a collective identity, and by the steadfast demands to restructure the foundations of the polity and not merely redistribute its material resources.

An ethnoregional campaign thus reflects a hybrid group identity, which emerges after a period of struggle within a state controlled by another ethnic group. This identity synthesizes ethnonational and civil motives, as illustrated by the growing number of such groups, including, for example, the Catalonians in Spain, the Tyroliennes and Slovenians in Italy, the Flemish in Belgium, the Hungarians in Romania and Slovakia, the Chinese in Malaysia, and the Welsh and Scots in Britain. This hybrid entity also appears likely to proliferate under the current world order of increasingly globalized norms of civil rights, which feature high on the agendas of ethnic and national minorities.

Further, ethnoregionalism is also a common response to the strategies of ethnicizing the homeland advanced by ethnocratic regimes. But the expansive homeland construction typical to dominant majorities often generates new campaigns among peripheral minorities in which they discover their own homeland as a source of identity and political power, within and across state boundaries. Yet unlike separatist nationalism—at times adopted by dissenting minorities—ethnoregionalism has the potential to reform the state from within. If minority oppression by the state persists, however, ethnoregionalism may turn into a program of open ethnic nationalism, as occurred recently in Nigeria, southern Sudan, Bosnia, and Sri Lanka (Connor 2002; Hechter 2000).

Ethnoregionalism is thus both a territorial reality and a political process, whereby a homeland ethnic minority re-imagines its collective identity as forming a region; that is, a specific territorial and political community, situated between local and state-wide scales. The region forms the base from which the minority challenges the privileged access of other groups to state power and resources and the legitimacy of dominant power structures. In most cases it is a distinct and lasting group identity that presents a notable challenge to the homogenizing myth of the nation-state order.

Palestinian Arabs in the Israeli Ethnocracy

Previous chapters have already outlined the history of Zionist-Palestinian relations. Here I shall add several details necessary for the framing of this chapter. The Palestinian Arab minority includes all Arabs with Israeli citizenship, who form a nonassimilating homeland community. In December of 2002, 1.02 million Arabs lived in Israel (not including East Jerusalem) in three main areas: the Galilee, the Triangle, and the Negev, as well as in several main urban areas (Figure 7.1). The Arabs in Israel belong to three main religions: 81 percent are Muslim (one-fifth of whom are Bedouin), 10 percent are Christian, and 9 percent are Druze (CBS 2003).

The historical and political background of Arab-Jewish relations in Israel is covered extensively elsewhere (see Chapters 3 and 4; Bishara 1999b; Ghanem 2000; Lustick 1980; Rouhana 1997). Several historical milestones should be reiterated here as shaping much of the collective memory, identity, and causes of mobilization among the minority. These include the Naqbah (the Disaster), connoting the period from 1947 to 1949 after the Arabs rejected the UN partition plan, when an ethnic war broke out. During or immediately after the war, 700,000–750,000 Palestinians were driven out of their homeland, and more than four hundred villages were demolished (Morris 1987). Other events included the imposition of military government on the minority until 1966, the massive confiscation of Arab land, and the general neglect of the impoverished Arab sector in Israel. Two further milestones were related to violence and collective loss. The first was Land Day in 1976, when six Arabs were killed while demonstrating against land confiscations, and the other was the October Events of 2000, during which the police killed thirteen Arabs protesting against Israeli policies toward the Palestinians.

The plight of the Arab minority has been strongly affected by a rapid process of Zionist-Jewish nation and state building. Israel has evolved quickly into a Jewish ethnocracy in which nearly all state resources, energy, and programs—with significant assistance from world Jewry—are aimed at furthering Jewish control. This ethnocentric orientation and the tragic plight of Jews during the preceding decades, especially in Europe, can explain the public legitimacy accorded to severe policy measures such as the imposition of military rule over the Arabs and the widespread confiscation of their land. The state capitalized on the scarring legacy of past Jewish traumas, on the enormous challenge of absorbing large numbers of Jewish refugees, on continuing security problems, and on genuine Jewish yearnings for forming a physically, culturally, and politically safe nation, and it proceeded to implement its ethnocentric nation-building policies, largely at the expense of Palestinian Arabs.

Arab-Jewish relations, however, have not remained static. Tied to a limited process of democratization, Israel has relaxed some of its control policies and practices over the Arabs, allowing their partial incorporation into Israeli society (Smooha 1992). However, despite this (slow) trend, the Arabs are still the least mobile and most politically, economically, spatially, and culturally marginalized sector among Israel's citizenry. Their inferior position was brutally reaffirmed during the October Events of 2000 described in more detail later.

In parallel, other forces have been at work, most notably Palestinian nationalism and Arab awareness of their civil status as Israeli citizens

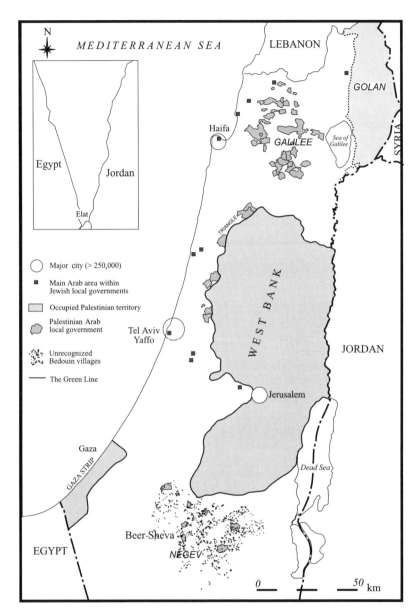

Figure 7.1. Arab Areas in Israel

(Hasson and Abu-Asba 2004). Palestinian nationalism, which emerged in full force following Israel's 1967 conquest of the West Bank and Gaza, has never explicitly embraced the Palestinian-Arab citizens of Israel, but it has still left a marked influence on their identity and status. It legitimized the contacts between the Arabs in Israel and national Palestinian leaders and caused the minority to voice strong support for and demonstrate in favor of Palestinian national issues. The Palestinian Arab community in Israel thus nurtured some of the most well-known Palestinian authors and poets, such as Emil Habibi, Mahmud Darwish, and Samih al-Khasem. As Rouhana (1997) shows, the Arabs in Israel were and are Palestinians, and the construction of their own identity is framed within their Palestinian past and present.

However, Israeli citizenship has also formed a main foundation of their identity, being gradually but steadily used as a framework of political, social, and cultural organization. Nearly all Arabs are bilingual and consume Israeli media and culture, and most professional Arabs attend Israeli academic institutions. Repeated surveys show that even if an independent Palestinian state were established in the territories, the vast majority of the Arab minority (80–95 percent) would prefer to stay in Israel (al-Haj 1993). The Arabs' increasing awareness and use of political rights draws heavily on Israel's claim to democracy and the associated political conventions (Smooha 1992). Although several scholars such as Rouhana (1997) and Bishara (2000) argue strongly that the Israeli part of their identity has remained devoid of any emotional or substantive bond, even they concede that the Israeli context has created a political community and hence had a significant impact on their identity and mobilization.

Four main factors are thus highlighted here as shaping the identity and struggle of the Arabs in Israel: Jewish nationalism, Palestinian nationalism, Israeli civic affiliation, and ethnic geography. However, research on the subject has rarely attempted to synthesize these factors as they are played out in the thick material and political setting of the Israeli ethnocracy, that is, within the political zone stretching over Israel/Palestine (see Rabinowitz 2001; Yiftachel 2002).

Instead, two leading interpretations of Arab orientation have dominated the literature: (a) politicization, which claims that the growing assertion and militancy of the minority reflects, first and foremost, a struggle for Arab civil equality within Israel and an acceptance of life as an ethnic minority within a Jewish ethnic democracy (Lehman-Wilzig 1993; Rekhess 1998; Smooha 1992, 2002); and (b) radicalization, which argues that the strengthening Arab struggle for civil rights masks a deeper process of Palestinian nationalism, implicated with profound disloyalty to the Israeli state, and that this is likely to lead toward Arab separatism and irredentism (Landau 1993; Shiftan 2002; Soffer 1991, 2001).

But as argued elsewhere (Yiftachel 1995a), the politicization-radicalization debate presents a false dichotomy because there is little evidence to suggest that the two are mutually exclusive (Yiftachel 1992a). Further, the analysis below shows that neither politicization nor radicalization can adequately explain the political mobilization of the Arab minority. Both approaches are too rigid and like most theories in the field fail to treat seriously the nuances and intertwining realities of nationalism, space and civic concerns, and the impact of Israel's ethnic geography.

Further, both leading interpretations have failed to describe credibly the development and mobilization of Israel's Arab citizens or predict the trajectory of Arab-Jewish relations. This is because their basic framework regarding geography, history, and political processes has been distorted. As explained in Chapter 4, a leading strategy of the Israeli academia has been to treat Israel unproblematically as a democratic nation-state in its pre-1967 borders. Hence, most scholars make a distinction between Arab-Jewish relations in Israel and key issues such as Israel's occupation and settlement of the occupied territories, continued oppression of the Palestinian national campaign, the active role of Jewish diasporas, the plight of Palestinian refugees, and the nature of public policies. It may be possible to imagine Israel as a democracy by leaving aside these factors, but the price, eventually, is conceptual collapse and serious social disorder, as occurred in October of 2000.

Palestinian Arab Identity in Israel: Fractured Regionalism

My central claim is that the impact of both Zionist and Palestinian nationalisms, and the civil affiliation of the Arabs with Israel, have combined to cause a discernable redefinition of Arab collective identity in Israel. Whereas before 1948 Arabs formed an integral part of a fledging Palestinian nation, and from 1948 to 1967 were isolated as Israeli Arabs, since 1967 they have been in the process of a collective re-imagining into an ethnoregional community of Palestinians in Israel. This community is caught in a fixed, controlled geography, positioned in a double periphery in both Israeli and Palestinian societies (al-Haj 1993). It reformulates its identity by using the main identity building blocks at its disposal: linked homeland localities, Palestinian attachment, and a recent history of political and economic struggles, events, and places within Israel.

Why should this process be interpreted as ethnoregionalism and not simply a drive for "better terms of co-existence" (Smooha 1992, 3), or a movement whose "next step means an attempt to secede . . . from Israel and be annexed to the Palestinian entity across the border" (Soffer 1991, 198)? I will show below that a third ethnoregional path has emerged among the Arabs and focus on four key dimensions that point to this new identity: a geography of Arab enclaves, an ethnoclass, public protest, and electoral polarization.

GEOGRAPHY

Ethnoregionalism is premised on a long-standing territorial base for minority mobilization and identity construction (Paasi 2000). A most striking feature of Arab geography in Israel has been its (forced) stability and containment. The Palestinian Arab areas shown in Figure 7.1 have been virtually the same since 1948, marking a stable Arab region. This is noteworthy given Israel's dynamic history of settlement and rapid geographical change among all other population sectors (Gonen 1995). The original Arab villages have, of course, grown, urbanized, and suburbanized, but there has been only scant Arab migration into non-Arab parts of Israeli cities (Falah 1996). As shown in Figure 7.1, the Palestinian Arab region is spatially fractured among various locations in the country's north, center, and south—a key feature to which I shall return later.

Because we have observed that ethnoregionalism denotes both a geographic reality and a political process, we must elaborate on the way in which this exceptionally stable geography was created and maintained. Here we draw the reader's attention back to Chapters 3, 4, and 6, which describe the Zionist state-building practices as characterized by a concerted drive to Judaize the country. Territory—above all else—has been the prime resource sought by the Zionist movement (Kimmerling 1983) and has generated an elaborate system of Jewish territorial control (see also Falah 2003).

As a result, 50–60 percent of Arab-held land in Israel was expropriated by the state.[2] The Arabs now own only 3.5 percent of the country's landmass and control 2.5 percent of the country's local government areas, yet they constitute 16 percent of the state's population. Following the transfer of land to the state, more than five hundred Jewish settlements were constructed on that land, in all parts of the country.

The result was the penetration of Jews into most Arab areas, the encirclement of most Arab villages by exclusively Jewish settlements (where Arabs are not permitted to lease land and housing), and the virtual ghettoization of the Arabs. In the process, Arabs have not only lost individual property but have also been dispossessed of much of their collective territorial assets and interests, because nearly all land transferred to the state (ostensibly for public purposes) was earmarked for Jewish use (see Kedar 2000).

Spatial control has also been imposed on the Arab minority through the planning process. Statutory outline plans have been prepared for most Arab localities by the Israeli authorities, commonly without the participation of the local community. The content of these plans, especially those prepared during the 1970s and 1980s, was marked by restrictions on the expansion of Arab localities. The main planning strategy called for intensification and densification of land uses within Arab localities, as well as encouraging multi-story structures. This was in sharp contrast to the planning strategy for Jewish localities in the same region, which were allocated ample land and encouraged to expand (see Falah 1989). In recent years some Arab municipal areas have been expanded, but the vast majority of regional land between Arab localities is still planned and used by Jewish councils, chiefly for the benefit of Jews.

In response to the spatial control imposed by land and planning policies, the Arabs staged an intense struggle. They rallied around several key issues, most notably land expropriation (as discussed further below), the enlargement of local government areas, and improvement of housing conditions, all with limited success (Yiftachel 1999a). Individual Arabs, especially in recent years, have also begun to move to Jewish towns and neighborhoods, at times demonstrating the ability to overcome intense Jewish opposition but usually being contained within Israel's urban areas by a combination of uneven public policies, social practices and prejudice, and their limited capital resources (Ben Artzi 1996; Rabinowitz 1997; Yacobi 2002).

In this context, it should also be remembered that the segregative Arab geography in Israel is also a result of voluntary processes, born of a commonly found isolation tendency among distinct ethnic minorities. Spatial segregation in such circumstances protects the minority from cultural intrusion and forms an organizational base for political mobilization (Peach 1996; I. M. Young 2002). In addition, and as is typical of homeland minorities, the geography of the Arabs in Israel has resulted from the strong Palestinian bond with their ancestors' land, embodied in the age-old custom of *sumud*: steadfastly staying on the land. Yet the present constrained and fragmented Arab region has been, in the main, caused by Israeli policies of dispossession, containment, and control.

In terms of collective identity, the spatial confinement of the Arabs has had some important effects. While being obviously restrictive and painful, it has provided a unifying experience, distinctive to that community, and has facilitated the creation of a dense local culture, framed by what Rabinowitz (1994, 117) has termed a "collective memory of loss." This spatial reality has erected visible and almost impregnable boundaries between us and them, in and out.

On this basis, Schnell (1994) documents the translation of the stark reality into attitudes and community formation. In his fascinating study of Arab territorial perceptions, he uses interviews, surveys, and the drawing of mental maps to find Arab sentiments of solidarity and comfort toward other Arab spaces, localities, and regions within Israel. Conversely, Arabs are usually indifferent, uncomfortable, or even hostile toward Jewish localities and spaces. Falah (2003) takes Schnell's analysis further by showing how Palestinian territoriality and identity has been shaped against the process of spatial and mental shrinking born of Israel's constant drive to de-Arabize the territories under its control. This has generated hostile attitudes toward the state and given rise to growing resistance and steadfastness among most Palestinians.

The result of these complex processes has been the creation and reinforcement of a fractured Arab region, which can be likened to a chain of beads connecting segregated spaces and localities by common perceptions, experiences, affinities, and functional agendas. Therefore, a fractured Arab ethnic region already exists in Israel, functioning to a large extent as one political, cultural, and social unit, while rooted in its own (constrained) homeland enclaves.

ETHNOCLASS

Ethnoregionalism is tied to socioeconomic disparities between region and state that generate a mobilization of discontent, rooted in what Markusen (1987) and Paasi (1991) saw as the necessarily material basis of constructing a regional community. In Israel, this has been combined with the ethnic logic of capital—a governing principle of ethnocratic regimes that is highly visible in the uneven patterns of resource distribution by Israeli authorities.

Historically, Israel constructed a hierarchical dual system of separate Arab and Jewish labor, described by Grinberg (1991) as split corporatism. This system derived its logic from the Jewish colonialist strategy of separating Jewish and Arab workers, which dates back to the beginning of the twentieth century (see Shafir 1989; Shalev 1992). Following independence, the system's first and foremost objective became the provision of employment for Jewish immigrants in order to avoid social upheaval within the then unstable Jewish society. Arabs were thus kept under military rule for eighteen years, during which their daily movement was restricted, effectively locking them out of the Israeli labor market. Further, their membership in the Histadrut—then Israel's all-powerful labor organization—was only granted (to loyal non-Jews) in 1959 (Shalev 1992, 49). Even in the 1990s, Arabs remained underrepresented in most rungs of Israel's labor organizations, despite their concentration among the country's working classes and the poor.

As analyzed by Zureik (1979), the Palestinian Arabs in Israel became subject to a regime of internal colonialism, whereby the majority exploits minority resources (such as land and labor) and uses the state apparatus to further its own economic position. The pervasive state expropriation of Arab land, the lack of development in Arab localities, and the simultaneous industrialization of Jewish Israel have caused a class transformation among the Arabs, from peasantry to a commuting proletariat (Haidar 1991; Schnell and Sofer 2000).

The late incorporation of the Arabs into the Israeli labor force and the practices of internal colonialism meant that their occupational opportunities were severely limited, not only by their stigma as Arabs in a Jewish state, but also by the fact that they had to enter the labor market from its lowest stratum. This disadvantage was amplified by their low levels of professional qualification, paucity of capital resources, peripheral location, and exclusion from many of Israel's security-related industries. As a result, Arabs have been incorporated into the Israeli economy mainly as "hewers of wood and drawers of water" (Semyonov and Lewin-Epstein 1987) and are concentrated in low-skill and menial labor, especially in agriculture, manufacturing, transport, and local public bureaucracies. Israeli capital, from the outset, was indeed governed by a conspicuous ethnic logic.

Since 1967, the partial incorporation of mass disenfranchised labor from the occupied territories, and most recently large numbers of temporary migrant workers who replaced the Palestinians, pushed Israel's Arab citizens up the occupational ladder, placing them in better paid and more managerial positions, albeit mostly in their traditional branches of the economy. However, despite the pervasive incorporation of noncitizens into the Israeli economy, and despite the Arabs' rise up the ladder, they are still highly constrained in an economy still stratified according to ethnic and national affiliations (Lewin-Epstein and Semyonov 1993; Shafir and Peled 2002).

This economic stratification has been translated into a concrete material reality. For example, in 1989, 39.8 percent of Arab households and 48.7 percent of Arab children lived under the poverty line, as opposed to 12.8 percent of Jewish households and 18.6 percent of Jewish children. The gap has even deepened slightly in subsequent years: in 2001, 44 percent of Arab households and 56 percent of Arab children lived under the poverty line, as opposed to roughly one-third of these proportions among Jews, who now include a vast community of recent immigrants.[3]

Income data, too, show that for the last fifteen years, Arab household income has consistently been approximately 65–73 percent of that earned by Jews (Adva 2002). Given household sizes, the ratio remained around 1:2 in income per capita over the last three decades (Adva 2003). Likewise, a recent survey of socioeconomic characteristics (CBS-a 2001) found that all sixty-three Arab localities are ranked in the bottom four deciles of Israeli localities, and more than half are in the lowest 20 percent. Finally, Arab localities have consistently formed the highest concentrations of unemployment, occupying in late 2002 the highest twenty-four places in the list of unemployment-affected localities (Adva 2003).

The material reality of Arab deprivation is not just statistical but is visibly grounded in their spaces, which form a central component of collective identity construction. Thus Khalidi (1988) claims that the Arabs have become a restricted economic region, directing most of their resources, entrepreneurship, and transactions into a confined Arab sector. This was largely supported by a later industrial study (Schnell and Sofer 2000), which found that although most Arab firms attempt to expand their trade into the Jewish industrial sector, they have remained constrained to specific menial niches and still perform some three-quarters of their transactions within Israel's Arab localities. Therefore, the situation of the Arabs in Israel confirms the overlapping of an economic niche, relative deprivation, and ethnic territory, together which constitute a firm foundation for ethnoregionalism.

PUBLIC PROTEST

Public protest generally reflects the changing nature and emphases of ethnic demands vis-à-vis the centers of power, especially the state. It also acts as a symbol and generator of collective identity. As noted by Lofland (1985), key protest events often find their way into the group's collective memory, thereby forming a key role in the shaping of its communal identity. As such, Public protest is a useful prism through which to study ethnic political mobilization.

The public voice of Palestinian Arabs in Israel only began to surface in the mid-1970s.[4] Prior to that, and owing to military rule imposed over their localities, as well as poverty, isolation, fragmentation, and peripherality, Arabs only rarely challenged the Israeli state and its policies. In the early years, the activities of the national al-Ard (the land) movement (which was subsequently declared illegal) and annual rallies staged by the Communist Party around May Day were the most notable occasions expressing antigovernment resistance.

Publicly conspicuous Arab protest erupted in 1976 as a head-on challenge to the Judaization project. The occasion was the first Land Day, which marked the point of significant entry of Arabs into Israeli public politics. A general strike and mass demonstrations against land expropriation in the Galilee took place, resulting in widespread clashes with the police and the killing of six Arab protesters. Since then, Land Day has been commemorated as a major annual event. Despite the traumatic events of that day, and the failure of the campaign to retrieve the land, the Arabs gained a presence in Israeli politics; they could no longer be ignored.

Following the first Land Day, Arabs began to marshal popular antigovernment sentiments and gradually built a well-organized and sustained civil campaign around the leadership of voluntary bodies such as the National Committee (of the Heads of Arab Councils), the Follow-Up Committee (composed of the National Committee, Arab parliamentarians, and other prominent leaders), and the Islamic Movement. The civil campaign came into full force during the mid- to late 1980s, combining past grievances with a future outlook, as displayed by the following statement by the mayor of Dier Hanna, a medium-sized Arab locality, during Land Day of 1983: "Israel has taken our land, surrounded us with Jewish settlements, and made us feel like strangers in our homeland. . . . The Jews do not realize, however, that we are here to stay, that we are here to struggle for our rights, and that we will not give up our identity as Palestinian Arabs and our rights as Israelis. . . . The more they take from us, the more we fight."[5]

The campaign progressed with dozens of planned events, a fairly coherent ideology of peace and equality, and a broad agreement among the minority about the cause and methods of struggling within the Israeli state. In 1987, the National Committee even published a ten-point manifesto that claimed to represent the goals of the entire Arab community, which articulated a vision of Arab-Jewish relations moving toward equality and stability, as well as greater Arab control over their communal life—including education, planning, and development. This vision expressed, for the first time, a coherent collective dissent by Israeli citizens to the tenets of the Jewish and Judaizing ethnocracy. It also created an umbrella under which most Arab political parties, ranging from national-secular, socialist, and conservative-religious, could coexist.

What did the Arabs protest against? Our analysis reveals three dominant issues: land and planning policies, socioeconomic conditions, and (Palestinian) national rights. What is striking is the continuing prevalence of all three issues in almost equal intensity: in the 1975–96 period, 33 percent of the total number of protest events were about land control and urban planning issues (such as boundaries, house demolitions, and zoning); 42 percent were about socioeconomic issues (such as budgets of Arab local governments, services, and infrastructure); and 25 percent addressed Palestinian national issues (mainly responding to events in the occupied territories and Lebanon). When we measured protest by intensity, however, land and planning issues were the basis for 33 percent of Arab protest, socioeconomic grievances 28 percent, and Palestinian national issues 38 percent.

The three protest topics have thus jointly and evenly dominated the mobilization of Arab mass politics. This lends support to the ethnoregionalism thesis: if Arabs were radicalizing and moving toward secession, the national cause would gradually prevail; conversely, if they were striving for full integration into the state as an ethnoclass, the socioeconomic strand would dominate. But continued concern of the Arabs for all three issues, and especially their persistent rallying to protect and expand their rights and power over land, all indicate a regional-level campaign grounded in Arab spaces and localities—in short, a campaign of a budding ethnoregional movement.

Another indication of the regional nature can be found in the communal leadership, which includes organizations positioned between local and state levels. Most prominent has been the National Committee, supported by the Follow-Up Committee, and—most recently—the Islamic Movement. These are all voluntary bodies that receive their support from a growing Arab focus on grassroots and village-based politics, illustrating a process of "Arab political encapsulation" (al-Haj 2002).

A more recent expression of the prominence of voluntary organizations is the rapid growth of Arab nongovernmental bodies (NGOs), which have taken a leading public role in the Arab struggle on a range of communal, professional, and legal issues. During the 1990s, several organizations received public prominence, including, among others, Adalah, a center for defending the minority's legal rights; Badil, a center for developing alternative plans for Arab localities; the Galilee Society, a coordinator of alternative health services; and the Regional Council for Unrecognized Bedouin Villages, an elected and professional body working for the recognition of dozens of Bedouin localities (see Chapter 8). A wide range of joint Arab-Jewish organizations has also been active in promoting Arab equality in Israel, including the Association of Civil Rights, the Negev and Galilee Coexistence Forum, Sikkuy, and Taayosh, to name just a few of the prominent organizations.

The minority has thus rallied behind these voluntary organizations, often in open defiance of the state, which has attempted to ignore, marginalize, or at times even disallow their activities. In some respects, Arab political organization and institution building thus often *bypasses* the formal procedures and institutions of state and local governance.

But to return to Arab protest, the Arab campaign began to wane and change during the 1990s. In every year except for 1994, levels of protest and mobilization were lower than the heyday of the late 1980s (although considerable protest activity continued). Arab protest has also changed its character: it is far more local, reactive, and sporadic, in contrast to the more programmatic and planned campaign of the 1980s. How can this decline and change be explained, especially in light of the persisting exclusion and deprivation of Palestinian Arabs in Israel?

Some claim that a combination of a pervasive process of Israelification, as well as improved government policies, especially during the Rabin/Peres government (1992–96), made the difference (Rekhess 1998; Smooha 2002). Others claim the opposite: Arab marginality within the Judaizing state has caused a prolonged crisis, distorted Arab development and confused Arab identity, all militating against the maintenance of an organized civil campaign (see Bishara 1999a; Ghanem 2000). My position is that the Arabs have hit the impregnable walls of the Jewish ethnocracy, which is still preoccupied with its own victimizations and fears, as well as its drive to Judaize Israel/Palestine. The ethnocracy is thus able to ignore the undemocratic nature of Arab exclusion and the political ramifications of the Arabs' visible and obvious deprivation (Yiftachel 1999a).

This structural impediment led to a prevailing feeling among Arab leaders that under the current settings the Israeli state is able to continue to reject or ignore Arab demands for equality (Bishara 1993, 2001). Hence, antistate protest has lost its appeal as a strategy to achieve political or economic change while other modes of operation have gained favor, including the strategic use of the Arabs' electoral clout (Lustick 1989) and the channeling of Arab energies into an internally oriented construction of political, social, economic, and cultural enclaves within Israel.

Most recently, the ongoing absence of Arab political gains generated demands for cultural and religious autonomy, and for turning Israel into a state of all its citizens. In the Israeli ethnocratic and Judaizing setting these basic, and even banal, democratic demands harbor genuine dissent against a unicultural state that often privileges world Jewry over the state's Arab citizens. They have generally caused an aggressive Jewish reaction bordering on panic, illustrating the obvious gap between Israel's self-representation as a democracy and its ethnocratic reality. Mainstream Israeli Jewish discourse (of both right- and left-wing parties) has quickly painted this demand as radical and subversive, as recently argued by A. Burg, a Labor MK considered leftist, and known for his pro-peace activities. In the following statement Burg marks the simple civic demand as dangerous and raises the shadows of past anti-Semitic persecutions: "The demands to turn Israel into a state of its citizens are symptomatic of the persistent desire by the Arabs, since 1948, to undermine the Zionist idea, which, we must remember, comes hard on the heels of generations of Jewish persecutions in the diaspora; we are not a normal nation because the majority of Jews live outside their only state; we therefore cannot become a state of all its citizens, or risk losing the moral meaning of our state."[6]

Against this attitude, the next act of public protest was a far cry from the organized and civil campaign of the 1980s and early 1990s. During October of 2000, thousands of Arabs flocked to the main roads to protest against Israel's policies in Jerusalem and throughout the country in what has been called the October Events ("Akhdath October" in Arabic), or the October *intifada*.[7] As described later in this chapter, the state's violent reaction to this outburst of minority frustration put in motion a process of negative dialectics, which now typifies the polarized Arab-Jewish relations inside Israel.

Arab collective identity has thus constructed, often unconsciously, the Arab region in Israel. The activity has generated a political and spatial entity between local and state levels, combining the various Arab localities into a statewide ethnic and political community. This region is formed as a clear site of resistance to Israeli policies, but it is also a painful reminder of the minority's current inability either to significantly change the nature of the ethnocratic regime or to secede from the state. This recognition is gradually developing through a crisis-riddled process, during which the Palestinian Arabs in Israel are being shunned by the mainstream in both Israeli and Palestinian societies and hence are developing their own regional space of identity and mobilization. The making of the Arab region is thus a response from below to the entrapment of the Arabs in Israel, offering a potential strategy of resource allocation, identity building, and solidarity within an alien state.

ELECTORAL POLARIZATION

Analysis of electoral behavior can further illuminate the minority's grievances, agendas, and changing identities. While processes of collective mobilization and identity formation are, naturally, complex and multidimensional, the electoral moment provides one of the major surface expressions of these processes at fairly regular intervals.

The most conspicuous electoral trend has been a gradual *polarization* between Arab and Jewish voters, particularly since the main Arab protest campaign began in the mid-1970s. Figure 7.2 shows that despite some fluctuations there has been a steadily growing level of Arab support for predominantly Arab non-Zionist parties, which have continuously posed a challenge to the existing Zionist nature of the state. At present, these parties include Hadash (a socialist-communist democratic bloc), Balad (a secular national-democratic bloc), and the United Arab Party (a conservative bloc linked to the Islamic Movement). While the level of the non-Zionist vote hovered around 20 percent until the 1970s, it rose to twice that rate during the 1980s and early 1990s, reaching 68 percent in 1996 and peaking at 79 percent in 2003.

To be sure, other factors such as religiosity, ethnicity, the economy, and location affect the vote of the large and diverse Arab population. Yet a genuine chasm is developing between the near total majority of Jews who support Zionist or Jewish parties (some 99 percent without much fluctuation), and the 80 percent of Arabs who prefer to vote for Knesset members who challenge—implicitly or explicitly—the Israeli ethnocratic regime. The gradual shift to the political left (defined in Israel as dovish positions on Israeli-Arab peace) is more striking when we consider that for decades the political organization of Arabs in Israel was under strict surveillance, that Arabs were punished for joining non-Zionist parties, and that they were not allowed to run in all-Arab parties until 1988.

Analysis of recent election campaigns lends further support to the regionalization argument by illustrating the emergence of a distinct and dissenting Palestinian Arab political identity within the Israeli state. The increasing non-Zionist vote obviously indicates growing opposition to Israel's character as a Zionist Jewish state. However, several other indicators point to a growing Arab drive to change the system from within. First, the electoral turnout, while declining (Figure 7.2), is still substantial compared to marginalized minorities in other ethnic states (Gurr 2000). A mass boycott of the 2001 elections, as discussed below, provided a warning signal of possible political disengagement from the state, but the return of 62 percent to vote in 2003 shows that a majority of Arab citizens still believes in the (slight) possibility of political change from within. The declining turnout among the Arabs in the 2003 elections was similar to a corresponding decline among Israeli Jews, reflecting a general sense of disillusionment

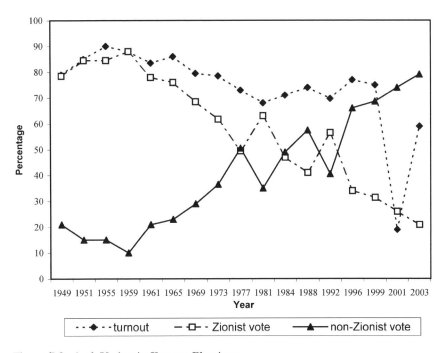

Figure 7.2. Arab Voting in Knesset Elections

with politics, above and beyond the ongoing marginalization of particular sectors.

Second, the platforms of three predominantly Arab parties have explicitly voiced since the mid-1990s their desire for a new political order in Israel. They have all used varieties of the slogan "a state of all its citizens" (first coined by Balad's leader, Dr. Azmi Bishara), which challenges Israel's self-definition as the state of the Jewish people and the structural preference given to Jews over the country's Arab citizens.

Further, since the mid-1990s, all three main non-Zionist parties have called for the first time for recognition of the Arabs as a national minority, as opposed to their current classification by the state as religious minorities. This is coupled with corresponding demands for further Arab control over planning, land, local government, and education, as well as for a more general cultural autonomy. These demands quickly became a standard goal among the Arabs, prompting further calls for a consociational and even binational state within the Green Line (Ghanem and Ozacky-Lazar 2003).

An equally significant aspect of the last three election campaigns was the participation, for the first time, of two previously rejectionist organizations:

the Muslim Movement and the Sons of the Village. The Muslim Movement, after a damaging split between the rejectionist northern and more pragmatic southern sections, joined with the Democratic Arab List under the new banner of the United Arab Party. The Sons of the Village, long one of the most nationalistic organizations among the Arabs, was the leading element in the Balad bloc, which has been the fastest growing (though only the second largest) party among the Arabs, reaching 19.8 percent in the 2003 elections, as compared with 26.9 percent for Hadash and 18.6 percent for the United Arab Party.

The decision of the two rejectionist organizations to contest the Israeli elections is significant for two principal reasons: (a) from their own previous rejectionist perspective, this step and its associated rhetoric amount for the first time to a *recognition* of the Israeli state; and (b) their decision to run was accompanied by a widely expressed agenda of *restructuring* the state from within. This agenda, and its links to both Israeli and Palestinian concerns, was articulated by Bishara, leader of the Balad Party, in a pre-election rally: "By running in this election we are of course accepting the existence of Israel, thus toeing the line with the Palestinian people who did the same by endorsing the Oslo agreement. . . . Our project addresses the next urgent goal: restructuring the Israeli political system, which is totally based on the definition of the state as belonging to the Jewish people more than to its own citizens. . . . Only by working to change the system can we achieve our status as a national minority, our need for cultural autonomy, and our fundamental right for genuine collective equality."[8]

Recent election campaigns also showed that the distance is growing between the Palestinian Arabs in Israel and the main Palestinian national leadership (now in Gaza and the West Bank). This was reflected by the declining weight given by Arab parties to the support of the Palestinian Authority, the PLO, and the PLO's chairman, Yassir Arafat. Another indication of this distance is the low profile that was kept by most of the Palestinian national leadership during campaigns since the mid-1990s, in contrast to the 1980s and 1992, when their impact was broadly felt among Arab organizations.

This trend was nowhere more expressed than during the 2001 prime ministerial elections, when Ehud Barak, the sitting prime minister who presided over the Israeli government during the October Events of 2000, was running against Ariel Sharon, arguably the bitterest enemy of the Palestinian people. Leading voices within the Arab community were pushing for a mass boycott of these elections, which presented the Arabs with no choice at all. The Palestinian national leadership (based in Ramalla) campaigned hard among the Arabs in Israel against the boycott, strongly preferring the more pragmatic Barak to Sharon. But the vast majority of Arabs (81 percent; or 90 percent without the Druze) did not vote, signaling their relative independence from both Israeli and (mainstream) Palestinian concerns.

This is the political space within which ethnoregionalism, as a movement of self-determination within a state, is now taking shape.

An incident during the 2001 election campaign starkly illustrated this trend. During a public meeting, the Palestinian minister of information and leading peace negotiator, Yasser Abed-Rabbo, attempted to convince the large crowd in Shefaamer (an Arab town in northern Israel) that boycotting the elections would surely bring Sharon to power and hence seriously risk the future of Palestinian society. This followed several other public attempts by the Palestinian leadership to discourage the boycott. However, Abed-Rabbo was received with hostility among both the speakers and the crowd. Jamal Zahalka, a leading member of Balad, responded to Abed-Rabbo: "This is our life, our future, and our agenda, not yours; let us determine our own politics. . . ."[9] Thus, the Arabs in Israel are distancing themselves at the same time both from the Zionist parties and from the immediate agenda of the Palestinian leadership. Although the solidarity with the Palestinians and their struggle continues to be strong, a new agenda is developing that reflects the long-term goals of an increasingly assertive Palestinian-Arab community within Israel (see Rabinowitz and Abu-Bakker 2002).

Finally, while there is still a range of political orientations (as shown in Figure 7.3), with large variation from the Arab mainstream notable among the Druze and to a lesser extent among the Bedouins, the electoral divisions among the Arabs are declining. This is to be expected in any large community. However, a growing consensus has been evident among all Arab parties regarding the minority agenda: equality and peace, with total Jewish withdrawal from the occupied territories, and a just solution to the refugee problem. This was reflected by the increasing number of votes for non-Zionist parties that hold these positions (Figure 7.2). The change can also be discerned within the two sectors traditionally closest to the Israeli state: the Druze and the Bedouin. In both sectors the number of votes for non-Zionist parties more than doubled during the 1992–2003 period. But the two communities are different: whereas the Druze still express loyalty to the Israeli regime, growing voices among the Bedouins have distanced themselves from the Zionist establishment. Overall, then, and with the possible exception of the Druze, the Arabs in Israel are carving a separate but increasingly unified political identity, which occupies the space between their Palestinian nation and the Israeli state.

The Shrinking Space of Citizenship: The October Events of 2000 and Their Aftermath

A chapter devoted to the Palestinian Arabs in Israel cannot close without taking stock of the period since the violent October Events of 2000 and the outbreak of the al-Aqsa *intifada*. This period developed a new polarizing discourse among both Arabs and Jews; marked increasing Jewish attempts

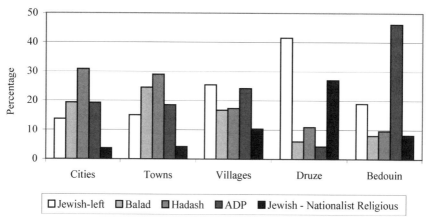

Source: Central Bureau of Statistics (CBS).

Figure 7.3. Arab Knesset Voting by Subsector, 2003

to marginalize the Arabs further; and saw a process of negative dialectics in which the growing hostility of one side exacerbates a similar discourse among the other (although this dialectical process is, of course, uneven, with the Israeli state and the Jewish public being more powerful).

What were these October Events and what was their impact? Following a provocative visit of Ariel Sharon to the Haram al-Sharif (Temple Mount) in Jerusalem on September 28, 2000, the killing of eight Arabs in Jerusalem the following day, and the wave of mass demonstrations in the occupied territories, Israel's Palestinian citizens joined the cause by demonstrating inside Israel. Several large rallies blocked main arterial roads inside Israel, and in other Arab centers, such as Nassrah, Sachnin, Arabeh, Jat, and Rahat, young Arab citizens threw stones at cars, police vehicles, and police personnel.

Like in the occupied territories, the state's response was quick and lethal. During the first three days of demonstrations, eleven Arab citizens were killed by the police, and two more were killed in demonstrations nine days later. A Jewish citizen was also killed by Arab demonstrators. It was the first time in Israel's history that snipers were used against Israeli citizens. Hundreds of Arabs and dozens of Jews were also injured.

Unlike in the occupied territories, however, where the combination of mass demonstrations and brutal state response developed into a sustained armed *intifada*, claiming nearly three thousand lives in its first two and a half years, the Arab population in Israel ceased the demonstrations in the face of the violent state oppression. Instead, it retreated to its towns and villages and began a period of internal debate, during which the relations of the minority with the state and with the Palestinian national movement were seriously reexamined.

The serious conflicts surrounding the October Events, especially the unprecedented police violence and the alleged role of radical Arab leaders, became the subject of the Or Investigative Commission, appointed in January of 2002 to analyze the eruption of the deadly violence. The commission interviewed dozens of key experts, minority leaders, and political figures, including all relevant ministers. Its final report, handed down in September 2003, constitutes a landmark in Arab-Jewish relations. It includes, for the first time, details and official recognition of the long-standing discriminatory practices by the state against the minority. The report contained an honest analysis of the tensions which led to the October Events, focusing on land, planning, economic, and cultural forms of discrimination.[10] It also condemned the violent treatment of the minority by the police and seriously criticized state and minority leaders for mishandling the situation. The report shied away, however, from recommending the indictment of police personnel allegedly responsible for the killing of demonstrating Arabs and from examining the impact of structural ethnocratic elements—such as the Jewish and Judaizing nature of the state and the brutal occupation of Palestinian Territories—on the situation of Israel's Palestinian citizens.

In response to the Or Commission Report, the government appointed a special committee, headed by the then justice minister, Yosef Lapid, to oversee the implementation of the commission report.[11] The Lapid Committee took a minimalist approach and only recommended several minor steps, such as the establishment of an authority for advancing the Arab minority, improving urban planning in Arab towns, and better integration of Arabs in the public service. Significantly, the Lapid Committee ignored key elements of the Or Commission Report, such as the misguided use of state violence against the minority, Arab land deprivation, and structural discrimination. It also devoted a major part of its report to discussing the role of local Arab leaders in allegedly worsening the tensions. Lapid's recommendations were therefore rejected by the majority of Arab citizens and considered widely as an attempt to bury recommendations of the Or Commission and to earn public opinion points from the political Right. In the ensuing period there have been some public, parliamentary, and legal attempts to force the government to implement more seriously the Or Commission Report, but without notable success. The issue appears to have been overshadowed, although it is bound to resurface as inevitable tensions between minority and state reemerge.

Most Arab opinions were hardened after the October Events, and new voices emerged that openly addressed radical options, such as the return of the Palestinian refugees, the restitution of land to internally displaced Arab citizens, Jewish-Palestinian binationalism, or ending the Jewish character of the state. Among Jews, too, an even harsher discourse emerged, which claimed that Israel had dealt too softly with its Arab citizens and openly advocated policy options such as population transfer, discrimination in resource allocation, further land confiscation, and Jewish settlement to control the Arab demographic threat, as discussed below. In short, a process of negative dialectics developed, reshaping Arab-Jewish relations within Israel (see also Rouhana and Soultany 2003; Zureik 2003).

This turn of events has demonstrated the inability of current approaches to explain Arab-Jewish relations. As earlier argued by Rouhana and Ghanem (1998), Yiftachel (1992b, 2002), and Rabinowitz and Abu-Bakker (2002), the common academic approaches treat Arab-Jewish relations in Israel as a normal case of majority-minority coexistence within a democratic nation-state (see Avineri 1998; Gavison 1998, 2002; Smooha 1992, 2002) and have been seriously flawed. This is not the place to repeat the critique developed in Chapter 4, except to reiterate the inability of most past theories to grasp fully the processes shaping Arab mobilization within Israel.

The October Events also highlighted the robustness of the regional approach. They showed the way in which the Palestinian Arabs in Israel are forced to carve a niche between the exclusionary Israeli state and the constrained and injured Palestinian national movement.

NEGATIVE (ASYMMETRICAL) DIALECTICS

In the wake of the October Events, and against the backdrop of intensifying Israeli-Palestinian violence, the thin layer of equal Arab citizenship eroded further. A clear expression was the increasing ethnocentric rhetoric by leaders and politicians and an escalating rhetoric of othering toward the Arabs. A notable step in this process was the indictment of MK Bishara, leader of Balad, the national-democratic Arab party, on a range of charges, such as supporting a terror organization, inciting violence, and endangering state security by organizing tours of elderly Arabs to Syria. The arrest followed his well-publicized September of 2001 appearance at the memorial service for the late Syrian president Hafez al-Asad, where he advocated continuing the resistance against Israeli occupation (*mukawamah*) through creating a unified Arab political position.[12]

This affair made conspicuous the discriminatory treatment of Arab leaders as the attorney general declined to press charges against Jewish leaders expressing more inciting statements. For example, MK Michael Kleiner claimed that leaders such as Bishara, who speak against their state, "are routinely put in front of a firing squad in most countries."[13] Rabbi Ovadia Yosef, the spiritual leader and political authority of the large Shas (Orthodox) movement, also declared in July of 2001 that Israel should "bomb the Arabs with missiles, through and through," and on another occasion he compared Arabs to snakes, who should all be annihilated. Yosef directed a public question at then Prime Minister Ehud Barak: "Why are you bringing them close to us? You bring snakes next to us. How can you make peace with a snake?" He added for bad measure, "They are all accursed, wicked ones. They are all haters of Israel. It says in the Gemara that the Holy One, Blessed be He, is sorry he created these Ishmaelites."[14]

These leaders, as well as other Jewish politicians, such as Ministers Avigdor Lieberman, Efraim Eitam, and Deputy Minister Gidon Ezra, who made inciting public comments about Israel's Palestinian citizens, remained untouched by the state's authorities. In contrast, during 2000–2003, three other Arab MKs—Taleb a-Sanna, Ahmad Sa'ad, and Abed al-Malik Dahamsheh—were charged with incitement following statements supporting the Palestinian *intifada* or the resistance of Palestinian Arabs in Israel to oppressive policies. Importantly, the negative dialectical process is asymmetrical. The power of the state and its leading politicians, attorneys, and bureaucracy is pitted against the minority, which is equipped with little political or economic leverage. In the face of the October Events the process of othering reached the highest echelons of Israeli leadership, including then Prime Minister Ehud Barak, who claimed in his 2002 testimony to the Or Commission that the riots of October 2000 "did not occur accidentally. . . . Bodies such as Balad or Sons of the Village . . . constitute extremist elements that pursue incitement against the state . . . and capture the Arab street."[15] By labeling the second-largest Arab party, which has a fully democratic platform, extremist, Barak, like many Israeli leaders, added a strong force to the process of negative dialectics.

However, the negative dialectics were also fueled by militant Arab discourse in Israel, with a range of combative statements made by political and community leaders. This trend has two main thrusts: Islamic and nationalist-secular. The former, headed by Sheikh Raed Salah, has mobilized Arab masses around religious-national agendas (such as the "al-Aqsa in danger" campaign, or the movement for boycotting Israeli elections), which work to delegitimize not only Israel's occupation of the Muslim holy places but Israeli sovereignty in general. The latter includes the various Arab national movements inside Israel that attempt to promote the thinnest version of citizenship, devoid of any attachment to the state. They view any state influence on the life and identity of the Arab citizens as disastrous. Zuhir Andreus, a renowned columnist and editor of the widely read *Kul al-Arab*, recently wrote in this vein: "Israelization is the most severe danger threatening the identity of Palestinians in Israel, and it turns them into a distorted group at present, and a frustrated group in the future. This forces us to act in wisdom now, so we do not regret it when it's too late."[16] Likewise, MK Bishara claimed in a public speech in May of 2003: "The alternative to our national democratic presence . . . is the danger of being recruited into the Israeli agendas. . . . They will push us aside and the last dam preventing Israelization will fall. . . . Our way is the only logical alternative to Israelization, which means marginalization."[17]

A further development has seen the surfacing of a new/old public discourse on a binational state in Israel/Palestine. This call has emerged from a group of intellectuals and activists who argue that it is now clear that Israel will never offer the Arabs equal citizenship, never evacuate the majority of West Bank settlers, and never allow the establishment of a truly independent Palestinian state. The conclusion is that only one scenario can lead to a fair and equal settlement to the conflict, including the division of space between Jews and Palestinians—the binational (Zionist-Palestinian) state. To be sure, this is still the view of a tiny minority, but it has become visible in the public discourse and appropriately from within Israel's Arab citizens who challenge the existing agendas of both Zionist and Palestinian national movements, each of which seeks its own ethnic state.[18]

Another force behind the Arab-Jewish polarization process has been the (often implicit) increase in support by Arab citizens for Palestinian terror. This included the first (and so far only) suicide bomber from a Western Galilee Arab town. While the numbers of actual participants in terror activity have remained very low, there has been a notable rise during the al-Aqsa *intifada*. For example, during the year 2000 only two groups suspected as supporting anti-Israeli terror were apprehended by the Israeli police, whereas during the first half of 2003 thirteen such groups were arrested.[19] The impact of the involvement of a few Arab citizens in terrorist activity, while negligible in security terms, has been substantial, with growing hostility among the Jewish public to basic Arab civil and cultural demands.[20]

The chasm between Jewish and Arab political space has thus widened significantly in the recent past, shrinking the ability of Palestinian-Arab citizens to mobilize within the confines of Jewish tolerance and Israeli law. This widening chasm appears as a new and openly antagonistic stage in the treatment of the minority by the authorities, which continue to intensify their push for Jewish control over most state resources.

JUDAIZING THE JEWISH STATE

Following the October Events, several high profile initiatives were launched to further the Judaization project, including legislative activity attempting to anchor the Jewish nature of the state; calls and plans to combat the demographic danger of the rising number of Arabs in the state (Hartzeliyya Forum 2001), plans for new Jewish settlement and new land policies; and new legislation restricting the free political expression and mobility of Arab leaders (for a thorough review, see Rouhana and Soultani 2003).

Three recent pieces of legislation are noteworthy. The first was an amendment to the Knesset Basic Law (1969) that prohibits the candidacy of any party or individual who supports (in action or speech) the armed struggle of enemy states or terror organizations. The second is the new Law against Incitement for Violence and Terror (2003), which specified harsh measures, including incarceration, for those supporting anti-Israeli violence.

These laws make it easier to disqualify or charge Palestinian Arab (and leftist Jewish) politicians running for the Knesset. The third, and most serious new legislation, enacted in July of 2003 and extended in July of 2004, is a temporary suspension of the Nationality and Entry into Israel Law (Temporary Order). The suspension prohibits Israeli residency or citizenship for Palestinians from the occupied territories who marry Israeli citizens. While the official reasons for the law were based on a security requirements, several Likud leaders openly described it as a tool to combat the demographic danger of the growing Arab population. As noted, demography has recently emerged as one of the central issues in the country's nationalist discourse, legitimizing the violation of human rights in the name of keeping a solid Jewish majority.[21] The three ethnocratic laws combine to seriously diminish the meaning of the Arabs' Israeli citizenship, adding fuel to the negative dialectical process.

The shrinking space of Arab citizenship became conspicuous during the 2003 election campaign, when the Knesset Electoral Committee disqualified MK Ahmad Tibbi, MK Azmi Bishara, and Bishara's Balad Party from running in the forthcoming elections. Hence, the effect of legislation mentioned above, which was created by a tyranny of the majority and without constitutional guarantees, was felt immediately. The Knesset also disqualified the Jewish candidate Baruch Marzel, who previously ran for the racist Kach movement. The political asymmetry of the balanced move was stark: Marzel was a marginal Jewish candidate, already convicted of racist behavior and advocating openly for an apartheid regime in Israel/Palestine. Bishara and Tibbi, in contrast, were the most prominent Arab leaders, who persistently advocated for more, not less, democracy.[22]

The disqualification was immediately challenged at the High Court, which reinstated the candidacy of Bishara and Tibbi in a swift decision, without issuing a report.[23] However, the thin layer of the upper judicial authority, while crucial for the 2003 elections, cannot gloss any longer over the deep ethnocratic currents now ruling Israeli politics that are attempting to minimize the appearance and influence of Arab political elements on the politics of the Jewish state. This was typified by the statement made by the minister of agriculture, Yisrael Katz, following the High Court's decision: "This is a regrettable decision. What other country in the world would allow its enemies to sit in its own parliament? The judges have lost touch with reality. And Bishara? He was nothing before, and we shall make sure he remains nothing after this ridiculous decision."[24]

The negative dialectics developed since October of 2000 have thus caused a notable shrinking of Palestinian Arab citizenship space, although the campaign of Arab leaders to remain included in the Israeli electoral process and their ability to win back their political rights testify that the space has not closed totally, providing a civil foundation for the development of the Arab region.

MANIPULATING GEOGRAPHY

Following the important (although ultimately deficient) attempt by the Barak government to stabilize Israel's borders in the Camp David and Tabba Summits, the manipulation of ethnic geography, with the goal of Judaizing Arab areas, has gathered pace once again. First and foremost, the idea of transfer has resurfaced. While the number of leaders openly supporting transfer is still small, several Knesset members and ministers have adopted the idea, often with (feeble) qualifications such as "if the need arises" or "only as a voluntary plan."[25] The aggressive transfer idea is now echoing aloud, growing in legitimacy in the view of the Jewish public.[26] Avigdor Lieberman, cabinet member and minister of infrastructure (lands), expressed sharp and controversial views on the subject: "There is nothing undemocratic about transfer; even in Europe millions were transferred from one place to another and it helped to bring peace. . . . The separation, like surgery, helps healing. . . . When I see Arabs going to blow themselves up in Haifa or Nahariyya, or Arabs who donate to terrorists' families—if it depended on me, they wouldn't have stayed here one minute, they and their families."[27]

Accompanying these voices are several variations on the theme, such as the vision revealed by the leader of the National Religious Party and cabinet member General Ephraim (Effi) Eitam. Intra alia, Eitam claimed that "the Arabs in Israel are a ticking time bomb. . . . They resemble a cancerous growth. . . . We shall have to consider the ability of the Israeli democracy to continue the Arabs' participation."[28]

In December of 2003, Binyamin Netanyahu, Israel's treasurer and former prime minister, similarly claimed: "If there is a demographic problem, and there is, it is with the Israeli Arabs who will remain Israeli citizens. If Israel's Arabs become well integrated and reach 35–40 percent of the population, there will no longer be a Jewish state but a binational one. . . . The Declaration of Independence said Israel should be a Jewish and democratic state. . . . Therefore a policy is needed that will balance the two."[29]

While these views are militant, they fall within the accepted boundaries of political debate developed in Israel during 2000–2003, with the obvious effect of shrinking further the ability of Palestinian citizens to find an effective political voice or strategy, beyond rhetorical provocations or withdrawal from the public arena. Lieberman, Netanyahu, and Eitam were far from being alone. Similar ideas, albeit with different geographical emphases, also came from the Labor Party. Most prominent has been a plan proposed in March of 2002 by the minister of transport, Efraim Sneh, to annex near-border Arab localities within Israel to the future Palestinian state in return for the annexation of West Bank settlement blocs to Israel.

These ideas received growing credence among Jewish publics, including support from prominent intellectuals and academics such as law professor

R. Gavison, geographer A. Soffer, and demographer S. Dellapergola. These leading voices all expressed a need to reshape Israel's borders according to ethnic principles.[30] The issue also presents a real dilemma for Israel's Palestinian Arab citizens, who have supported the Palestinian struggle for independence for decades and have increasingly reconstructed their own identity as Palestinian. But the persistent low support for the idea among Arabs (reaching 15–20 percent in most surveys),[31] demonstrates that a new political and social entity has been created inside Israel—the Palestinian Arab region, distinct from the frameworks of both the Zionist state and the Palestinian Authority.

Recent attempts to manipulate ethnic geography—typical to ethnocratic societies—stretch wider and deeper than debates over state borders. While less prominent on the public agenda, issues pertaining to planning, land, and development have pushed further the state's ethnocratic agenda since late 2000. For example, after a lull of several years, the state has again initiated large-scale Jewish settlement projects within the Green Line. In early 2002, sixty-eight new settlements were in the process of approval and eighteen began construction.[32]

In the meantime, seven new Arab localities were also approved, designed to concentrate Negev Bedouins into planned towns. As elaborated in the next chapter, the plight of the Bedouin community in the Negev continues to demonstrate the dark side of Israeli citizenship among the Arabs. Dozens of Bedouin villages, some in existence before 1948, others a result of state-organized transfers in the early 1950s, are now regarded as unrecognized and their residents as invaders. They are denied basic services and are pressured to move to a few planned towns in order to shift more land to state control. But as described in the next chapter, the oppressive reality spawned new forms of resistance, which uses the cracks and openings offered by the Bedouins' Israeli citizenship to combat, at times effectively, Israel's ethnocratic land and planning policies.

Conclusion: Palestinian Arabs, Ethnoregionalism, and the Nation-State

Any collective ethnic identity, and particularly that of the Palestinian Arabs in the contradiction-riddled Israeli environment, is slippery and dynamic. Nonetheless, the chapter analyzed four major dimensions of the collective behavior of the Palestinian Arabs in Israel—geography, class, protest, and voting—which point to the emergence of ethnoregional struggle and identity. Let us reiterate here our definition of a region—a spatial and sociopolitical entity between locality and state, which provides a basis for mobilization, identity, and challenge to the nation-state. Given this definition, an Arab region already exists in Israel, even if its political articulation is still in the making.

To be sure, regionalism among the Arabs in Israel is still nascent and mainly implicit. It may take years before it becomes the explicit goal of most Arabs in Israel, although leading intellectuals increasingly articulate such an agenda. Hence, the process has already been put into motion through the dynamics of local Arab governance, NGOs, statewide Arab networks, Arab economic activities, daily Arab social practices, and ongoing negotiated relations with both Zionists and Palestinians in the occupied territories and beyond. In the process, the Arabs are beginning to forge a profound challenge to the Israeli ethnocratic state.

The Arab struggle to define and empower their region provides a strategy of resistance against Israel's control policies and is the most effective way to break out of the entrapment of a marginalized minority in an ethnocratic regime. The Arab region has provided a collective core around which a newly defined ethnic identity has been formulated and re-imagined within the totally new circumstances prevailing since 1948. This identity is premised on the Arabs' national identity as Palestinians and their particular fractured political-geographical situation within the Israeli (Jewish) state—where the options of irredentism or separatism bear intolerable costs. It builds on the Arabs' Palestinian past, on their involuntary and partial civic incorporation into the Israeli political system, on the grievances generated by long-term deprivation, and on their geography of contained homeland spaces.

The regional consciousness also started to surface openly in recent years in political discourse, academic research, and the arts. This has been intensified following the October Events of 2000 and the al-Aqsa *intifada*, which have clearly deepened the chasm between Jewish and Arab citizens through the process of negative dialectics described above. Yet the carving of a separate (if constrained) collective space has not had the effect of merging the campaigns of the Palestinians in Israel and the occupied territories. Despite frequent displays of solidarity, the two have remained separate political movements, underscoring the emergence of a new Palestinian collective identity within Israel.

A poet and a political leader, the late Tawfiq Zayad (previously mayor of Nazareth) appeared to have captured some of the elements of the ethnoregional identity by expressing the salience of land, place, dispossession, and memory in group formation. These are coupled with underlying Arab hope, patience, and persistence generated by clinging to the homeland:

We guard the shades of our figs
We guard the trunks of our olives
We sow our hopes like the yeast of bread
With ice in our fingers
With red hell in our hearts . . .

If we are thirsty, we shall be quenched by the rocks
And if we are hungry, we shall be fed by the dust . . .

And we shall not move
Because here we have past, present,
And future. (Zayad 1983)

The understanding of Arab political mobilization in ethnoregional terms and a comparison with similar international cases also allows us to anticipate the likely shape of future Arab-Jewish politics. Arabs are likely to heighten their push for gaining recognition as a national minority, with associated cultural and (later) territorial autonomy; press for land rights; and campaign for the closing of Arab-Jewish social and economic gaps and for political and social equality (see also Ghanem 2000).

Clearly, the Arabs will not accept the ethnocratic character of the Jewish state, nor confine their struggle merely to "better terms of coexistence" (Smooha 2002). Using the ethnoregional framework, we can anticipate that the Arab struggle in Israel will intensify following possible Israeli-Palestinian reconciliation or broader peace in the Middle East and not subside as many assume. This will be particularly so if public policy toward the minority continues to be marked by control and marginalization. In such a context, Palestinian Arab regionalism within Israel is likely to seriously challenge and possibly destabilize the Israeli ethnocracy by intensifying the drive to democratize its ethnocratic character, equalize the distribution of public resources, and devolve the highly centralized structure of the Israeli regime.

Chapter 8

Bedouin Arabs and Urban Ethnocracy in the Beer-Sheva Region

On Independence Day 1998, while Israel was celebrating its fiftieth anniversary, the Negev Bedouin Arab community arranged a mass prayer in the city's abandoned hundred-year-old mosque to commemorate the Naqbah. The council allowed them to pray only outside the mosque, which was classified a "dangerous structure." But even the outdoor prayer was disrupted by a nationalist Jewish group, which blocked the path to the mosque and, to prevent the traditional Muslim kneeling, sprayed animal manure in the yard. After hours of local conflict, the Bedouins managed to conduct the prayer, using large plastic sheets to cover the manure. This was the last time the mosque grounds were used. One of the leaders of the Jewish nationalists was Eli Bokker, a Likud member of the Beer-Sheva City Council, who claimed: "The Bedouins should never forget: Beer-Sheva is a Jewish city. They can come here, work and shop, but that's it! The attempts to reopen the Beer-Sheva mosque are just a first step. Later they will start buying houses in the area and make the city more and more Arab. They have seven towns in the region—why do they need to come to Beer-Sheva?"[1]

This incident is but one dramatic event in the ongoing struggle over territorial and urban control between the Israeli state, local Jewish leaders, and Bedouin Arabs living in Israel's Negev (al-Naqab in Arabic). The Bedouin community forms part of the Palestinian-Arab minority discussed in the previous chapter, but because of its marginality it has received little scholarly or political attention. Most studies on the Bedouins focus on their unique culture and folklore or on the postnomad processes of modernization and urbanization (see Abu Rabi'a 2001; Abu Saad 1998, 2001; Meir 1997; Ben-David 1995). The present chapter takes a different angle by locating the plight of the Bedouins firmly within the making of Jewish settling ethnocracy in Israel/Palestine and the development of urban ethnocracy in and around the city of Beer-Sheva (Bir-Saba'a in Arabic) and the surrounding metropolitan region.

The emphasis of the book's previous chapters on the national scale leaves an analytical void on the urban scale—so central to the development of today's society. The urban scale is also central to the study of ethnocratic societies, because—potentially—it offers a more open and porous spatial-ethnic arena, where some of the ethnocratic boundaries and hierarchies may be undermined. The void will be partially filled in this chapter, which deals with the ethnic, economic, and political consequences of urbanization. It focuses on the ethnocratic city as an analytical entity, with its own constitutive forces and development trajectories. It shows how the Israeli settler society has constructed the Beer-Sheva region as an internal frontier and put in train an ethnocratic type of urbanization. This, in turn, has spawned the pervasive phenomenon of urban informality or illegality, which typify ethnocratic urban regions.

The analysis shows, however, that despite the potential of urbanization to erode ethnospatial exclusion and domination, and despite early signs of economic and cultural liberalization, Beer-Sheva's ethnocratic structure has not been seriously dented. Israel is still committed, in planning and practice, to the urbanization of the Bedouins into a small number of satellite towns. This runs counter to the wish of many Bedouins for a rural lifestyle and control over their ancestors' lands. As a result, growing mobilization and resistance among the Bedouins have produced alternative planning, thus creating a planning deadlock. This has caused the emergence of pervasive urban informality and growing ethnic conflicts in the northern Negev.

Theoretical Aspects: Urban Ethnocracy and Informality

The discussion of urban ethnocracy attempts to add a new dimension to the active scholarly debate over the remaking of cities in the era of globalization (see Brenner 2003, 2004; Friedman 2002; Sassen 2001; Marcuse and Van Kempner 2000). The scholarly debate, with few exceptions, focuses almost entirely on capitalism, globalization, liberalization, and development as the major forces driving urban transformation.

I have recently offered a more diverse conceptual approach, contending that three main engines combine to shape contemporary cities: (a) the logic of capital accumulation; (b) the drive for ethnic and national control; and (c) the evolution of modern governance. The interaction between these forces, as played out within the dense webs of local and institutional settings, often produces urban informality as a surface expression of the tensions and unresolved contradictions of these engines of spatial change (Figure 8.1). Informality is defined as spatial dynamics that are not shaped, controlled, or sanctioned by the state, including the concentration of undocumented immigrants and laborers, unauthorized housing, squatting, and trade. It forms one of the major components of most of today's metropolitan regions, mainly, but not only, in the less developed world (see, for example, AlSayyad 1994; AlSayyad and Roy 2003; Fernandes and Varley 1998; Pugh 1997).

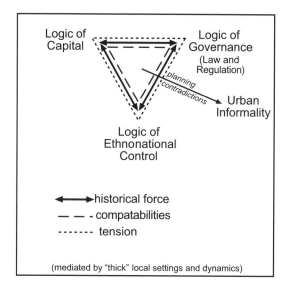

Figure 8.1. Forces Shaping Urban Regions

The Ethnocratic City

While the ethnocratic city is generally a product of the ethnocratic state, it does form an urban regime in its own right, which, in turn, shapes the major shifts, resources, and spatial transformations in the city area (for discussion on urban regimes, see Fainstein 1995; Lauria 1997). The ethnocratic city embodies the tensions and contradictions outlined throughout this book: on the one hand, it is officially an open and accessible space; on the other, it is segregated, controlled, and hierarchical. On the one hand, it is increasingly part of a globalizing culture and economy characterized by international migration, development bursts, and discourse on human rights, civil society, and democracy associated with late capitalism/modernity. Yet on the other hand, it is a product of the nationalist, expansionist logic of purified ethnic space. As we shall see later, urban informality becomes a common planning strategy in such settings, allowing both orderly and modernist planning to proceed while containing the tensions and preserving the control over the unplannable elements in these cities. In that sense, the ethnocratic city is a dynamic and uneven hybridity of what AlSayyad (1996) termed the colonial, the national, and the global urban orders.

Urban politics in the ethnocratic city often reflect wider ethnonational tensions and conflicts. Local politics usually revolve around struggles for space, economic resources, and political power, most commonly along ethnonational lines. But these cities never fully replicate the dynamics of the wider conflict, mainly because the urban arena is governed by a different combination of powers, regulations, and possibilities from the ones prevailing in nonurban regions. There are two main differences. First, in terms of sheer territory, urban areas are quite small. For this reason, national movements have generally emphasized control over the vast tracts of rural lands as a symbol of sovereignty rather than over the streets of contested cities. Second, exclusion and segregation of minorities is far less feasible or even desirable in urban areas. In the rural areas, the state (on behalf of the dominant ethnoclass) can legally and effectively marginalize and exclude members of ethnic minorities, as widely documented above in the case of Israel/Palestine.

But given the prevalence of a relatively open and increasingly liberalizing market system, and the need for cheap labor in proximity to major industrial and service centers, the urban areas in such states are more open and accessible. The need to ensure, at least on a formal level, the free flow of commerce and population in these urban systems opens up cracks and contradictions in the grids of ethnocratic control. Here we observe the coterminous operation of the various engines of urbanization: the ethnocratic city is developed both by the logic of capital and by the drive for reinforcing ethnonational urban control. Yet its development may create openings and spaces for minorities who draw on the democratic and liberal possibilities emanating from new spatial-political formations of modern urban governance. The presence of mobilized minorities challenges the hegemony of both ethnonational control and exigencies of capitalism.

How do ethnocratic states respond to this potential challenge? In general, they attempt to concentrate minorities in small areas, thereby minimizing their spatial control (McGarry 1998). Such policy often creates partial urbanization and ghettoization of near-metropolitan minorities, relocation of distant minority communities to major urban regions, and the creation of urban informality. In most cases, the ethnocratic state attempts to segregate between majority and minority, even in putatively open urban settings, although urban segregation generally assumes rather subtle, culturally based, voluntary, or market-led features.

The dynamics of the urban ethnocratic regime can thus be summarized by the following:

- The city is classified and represented as mixed, but it is dominated by one ethnonational group.
- Urban citizenship is unequal, with resources and services allocated on the basis of ethnicity, not residency.
- Urban politics are ethnicized, with a gradual process of ethnopolitical polarization.
- Housing and employment markets are officially open yet marked by deep patterns of ethnic segregation.

- Planning and development strategies reflect a deep ethnocratic logic, which is couched in professional, civil, and economic reasoning.
- Land and housing are allocated so as to minimize the control of minority members over urban resources.
- Municipal boundaries are gerrymandered to prolong spatial and urban control by the dominant ethnoclasses.
- The previous items generate urban-ethnic resistance, with the minority constantly challenging the prevailing order.
- Urban informality emerges as a conspicuous component of the metropolis and becomes a central part of the region's planning strategy.

The increasing occurrence and visibility of urban informality is linked directly to the concurrent working of the intertwined and opposing urban forces noted earlier (see Figure 8.1). These forces include the urbanizing logic of late-capitalist economies, particularly within a globalizing, and hence centralizing, urban system (see Sassen 1999; Marcuse and Van Kempen 1999); the ongoing drive for ethnic control over space; and the emergence of the city as the site of modernizing governance, with its emphasis on law and order, as well as rights, liberalism, and democracy. Nevertheless, the resulting urban order is never stable, as tensions arising from the interaction of these forces generate constant challenges to ethnic control and capitalist-generated inequalities. These emerge mainly from local minorities but increasingly also from migrant workers and long-term undocumented (illegal) residents.

In these unstable settings, a common planning response is to allow, to condone, and even to facilitate urban informality. Whole communities are thus left out of the planning process or are overlooked by the content of urban policies. Typically, such populations are mentioned as a problem, but their undocumented, unlawful, or even fugitive existence allows most authorities to ignore them as having full planning rights to the city (Lefebvre 1996). In other words, policy makers define urban informality as a method of indirectly containing the ungovernable. The tactic is avoidance and distant containment, but the result is the condemnation of large communities to unserviced, deprived, and stigmatized urban fringes.

Here lies a main feature of the urban informality as a planning strategy typifying ethnocratic urban regimes: it allows local elites to represent urban government as open, civil, and democratic, while at the same time denying urban residents and workers basic rights and services. Urban ethnocratic regimes draw legitimacy from this partial and distorted representation, which enables the preservation of their privileged ethnoclass position, and the maintenance of the ethnocratic system.

The use of planning to create, maintain, and facilitate urban informality is an example of its use as a form of social control. As discussed elsewhere (Flyvbjerg 1996; Yiftachel 1994), planning exposes a dark side of ethnocratic

societies. The agencies and tools originally designed to promote social reforms and amenities are used to contain and oppress marginalized communities. We turn now to the unfolding of these processes during the
transformation of Israel's southern Beer-Sheva region.

Israeli Planning: Negev, Frontiers, and Mixed Cities

Israel's first state-wide plan, headed by national planner Arie Sharon (1951,
3–7),[2] stated clearly its intentions of Judaizing the country's peripheries:

Nations all over the world attempt to decentralize their population, so they do not
become dependent on central congested cities. . . . In Israel this task is more urgent but also easier. . . . Urgent, because Israel holds the world record with 82 percent of the population in three main cities. . . . Easy, because unlike Britain, we do
not require to move existing populations, but simply to settle new immigrants in
the country's empty regions. Israel can thus decentralize its population [read, Jews]
to the north, Jerusalem corridor, and Negev regions, as the only rational way to
develop this country. . . .

Chapters 3, 5, and 6 showed how the combined discourses of nationalism,
modernity, and professional planning put in train an exclusive form of
Jewish territoriality, aiming to disperse the Jewish population, and to
conceal the past or present existence of Arabs. The frontier and internal
frontier became central icons, and the planning and implementation of
frontier settlement was considered one of the highest achievements of any
Zionist. The southern Negev, in which Beer-Sheva is located, became one of
Israel's prime frontiers, prompting David Ben-Gurion, the long-time leader
of the Zionist movement and Israel's first prime minister, to claim: "The
people of Israel will be tested by the Negev. . . . Only by settling and developing the Negev can Israel, as a modern, independent, and freedom-seeking
nation, rise to the challenge that history put before us. . . . All of us—veterans and *olim* [new immigrants], young and old, men and women—should
see the Negev as their place and their future and turn southwards. . . ."

In a similar spirit, Yossef Weitz, chairman of the Jewish National Fund,
the main Zionist arm of land purchase and settlement, declared on January 19, 1948 at the Mapai Conference, "The Hebrew state will have to em-
bark on a wide settlement strategy in its first three years . . . [a] big part of
it in the Negev. . . . In the Negev we'll be able to implement immediately
our development laws, according to which we shall expropriate land according to a well-designed plan . . ." (Weitz 1950, 367).

Significantly, the frontier was also a live concept in mixed Arab-Jewish
cities, where the government continued to promote the need to build
Jewish housing in, or immediately adjacent to, Arab urban neighborhoods.
In the plans of most mixed cities, specific goals appear about keeping the
Jewish character or combating the danger of increasing Arab population,

which might create a demographic threat to the city (see Yacobi 2003 for a comprehensive survey of these plans).

This planning rationale received stark physical expression in mixed urban areas such as Akko, Haifa, Jaffa, Ramla, and Lod, where high-density Jewish neighborhoods were rapidly constructed around the small Arab enclaves left in what were previously Arab cities. The treatment of urban Arab neighborhoods as internal frontiers into which Jewish presence should expand turned all mixed Arab-Jewish cities in Israel into urban ethnocracies. Arab presence was thus delegitimized and constantly portrayed as a danger, causing deep patterns of planning discrimination. This has spawned the emergence of various degrees of urban informality, from whole neighborhoods unseen by urban authorities (such as the railway locality in Lod), to recognized neighborhoods, which nevertheless receive inferior levels of services and planning, and whose residents are often excluded from the city's communal life and policy making. The Beer-Sheva urban region, to which we now turn, illustrates yet another kind of Israeli urban ethnocracy.

THE BEER-SHEVA REGION: ETHNOCRATIC MANAGEMENT AND URBAN INFORMALITY

Beer-Sheva was established by the Ottoman Empire at the beginning of the twentieth century as a small urban service center for the Bedouin Arab population of the northern Negev (al-Naqab). It remained a small Arab town of five to six thousand inhabitants until its conquest by Israel in 1948. Since then it has turned into an icon of Israel's efforts to settle, develop, and Judaize the internal frontier. Beer-Sheva became a Jewish city, and it has remained to date a focal point for repeated planning and development strategies to create and maintain a Jewish majority in the northern Negev.

Beer-Sheva was planned by the Israeli authorities as an arch example of a modern, national city (see AlSayyad 1996; Gradus 1993). During the 1950s and 1960s Israel developed a series of garden cities, mainly north and west of old Arab towns. The garden neighborhoods were typified by high-density, low-standard public housing blocks and large, mainly empty and underdeveloped, open spaces.

The vast majority of the population who settled in the town were immigrants from Muslim countries (Eastern Jews, or Mizrahim), who—as detailed in Chapters 5 and 9—were marginalized during the 1950s and became the social, economic, and political outcasts of Israeli-Jewish society. Beer-Sheva was planned as the capital of southern Israel and became what Gradus and Stern (1980) termed the Negev regiopolis, the center of a series of small frontier towns and agricultural settlements. Part of this regiopolis has been a large and loosely settled Siyag area (the fence—see below), northeast of the city, into which most of the Bedouin Arabs of the Negev were forcefully moved during the 1950s, as discussed below.

During the 1980s and 1990s the city began to suburbanize, with the middle classes moving either to new low-density, higher-quality neighborhoods or to relatively wealthy satellite towns mainly north and east of the city. A further transformation occurred during the 1990s with a massive influx of migrants arriving mainly from the former Soviet Union and Ethiopia, who congregated in several newly built neighborhoods, chiefly in the city's western areas. The city of Beer-Sheva itself and its regional setting have thus become dominated by binational and multicultural ethnoclass divisions, many of them expressed spatially (Gradus and Blustein 2001).

In parallel, the Beer-Sheva region increased its functioning as an economic and administrative center, servicing a large region in the northern Negev. It began to attract private capital, initially Israeli and recently international. The city underwent a physical restructuring during the late 1990s, gradually developing a modern central business district that replaced the old Ottoman-Arab city center. At the beginning of the third millennium, the Beer-Sheva regional economy is still based mainly on traditional sectors such as minerals, labor-intensive industries, and governmental employment. But with the onset of incipient processes of restructuring and globalization these sectors have been falling in their importance, while electronics, computing, and sophisticated service industries have begun to rise (Gradus, Yiftachel, and Livnon 1998). Nonetheless, the Beer-Sheva region can still be regarded as a peripheral, medium-sized planned urban center, which only now begins to link to the national and global economy (Gradus, Yiftachel, and Livnon 1998; Lithwick 2000).

Our attention here, however, will focus on the Bedouin Arab parts of the Beer-Sheva urbanizing region, north and east of the city (Figure 8.2). These have not been included in the Beer-Sheva plans but rather are administered by a different set of authorities and institutions. Consequently, the Arab localities enjoyed very little of the economic or physical development of the region, while increasing their dependence on its urban functions. This caused the classification of many such settlements by the region's planning authorities as illegal, unrecognized, or spontaneous. At the end of 1999, the illegal localities accommodated an estimated population of 65,000–70,000, with no planned recognition. A further population of the same size currently resides in impoverished and partially planned Bedouin towns.

The Beer-Sheva region has thus developed into an urban ethnocracy. Multiple sets of boundaries segregate citizens who reside in the same city region on the basis of their ethnicity. This strategy works mainly on the ethnonational level, aiming to facilitate the expansion and control of the dominant Jewish Zionist group. The high levels of uneven segregation in the region are testimony to the ongoing difficulties in achieving civil equality, mobility, and democracy, despite the formal openness of the city.

Returning for a minute to our theoretical point on the interaction of economic, civil, and ethnic engines shaping urban space, we can discern in

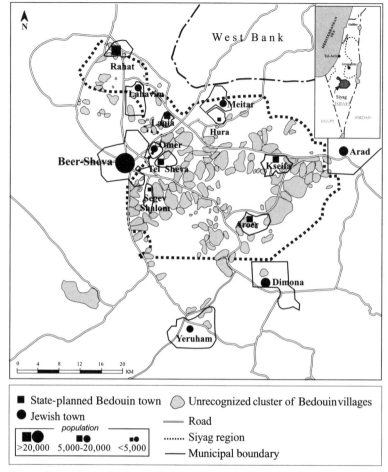

Source: Israel Land Authority (report to metropolitan planning team, 2003).

Figure 8.2. Jewish and Bedouin Localities in the Northern Negev

Beer-Sheva a clear, though not absolute, dominance of the last. The segregated nature of urbanization around Beer-Sheva was caused by Israel's drive to Judaize the region (which would have been impossible without planned and institutionalized segregation). But at the same time, the Bedouin Arabs in the region did gradually urbanize and have become an influential, although marginalized, part of the Beer-Sheva city region (see Lithwick 2000). The prevalence of illegality and massive informality among Bedouin Arabs is hence, first and foremost, a result of Israel's drive to maximize Jewish land control in a predominantly Arab area, and not necessarily the result of dictates or exigencies of capital accumulation, be it local or global.

However, these ethnocratic forces, which have prevailed in Beer-Sheva for decades, are being challenged gradually, and the logic of capital and democracy may begin to exert some pressures on the shaping of the urban region. The challenge appears mainly in the form of Arab resistance to the dictates of the state and its planners, as we shall see below. As in most other ethnocratic societies, the expansion and development process has amplified and created disparities on other levels, most notably among internal Jewish and Arab ethnoclasses, such as Mizrahi and Russian Jews, or real Bedouins, *falaheen* (agricultural Arabs), or *abeed* (ex-slaves). While this process is a central aspect of the ethnocratic society, the scope of this chapter does not allow its proper analysis. Hence the chapter will concentrate on the ethnonational level, that is, the relations between Negev Jews and Arabs, who in turn are part of larger Jewish Zionist and Palestinian Arab national collectivities.

The Bedouin Arabs and the Judaization of the Beer-Sheva Region

Some 140,000 Bedouin Arabs reside in the northern Negev, mostly within the Beer-Sheva urban region (Figure 8.2). Until the 1948 establishment of the state of Israel, the livelihood of this previously seminomadic community relied on cattle, herds, rain-fed agriculture, and commerce (Ben-David 1997). During and immediately following the 1948 war, some 80–85 percent of the Negev Arabs either fled or were expelled by Israeli forces to Egypt, Jordan, and the West Bank. Approximately 11,000 remained in Israel and were transferred to an area named the Siyag (fence), which is known for its low agricultural fertility and is located immediately northeast of Beer-Sheva. Twelve tribes were relocated into the Siyag, joining six tribes who had already lived there. This area stretches over a tenth of the Negev, and was controlled by military rule until 1966 (Figure 8.2). No stone or concrete building activity was allowed in the Siyag, forcing most tribes to erect localities of shacks and tents. The mass transfer to the Siyag area and the restrictions imposed on the Bedouin Arabs make a striking example of a trapped minority.

The Siyag's infertile lands, the shrinking grazing and agricultural space, and its urban proximity have dramatically transformed the lifestyle of Bedouin Arabs. From controllers of the desert region, they became fringe dwellers of a growing, modernizing Beer-Sheva city region. At the same time, the military government, which severely restricted their mobility outside the Siyag, further hampered their (already limited) ability to compete in the Beer-Sheva labor market. During the first decade of inhabiting the region, most of the Bedouins in the Siyag returned to a traditional self-sustaining lifestyle but later began to seek employment and commerce with the surrounding Jewish population (Falah 1983).

The enclosure of the Arabs in militarily controlled areas was officially justified on security considerations, but it resulted in preferential treatment of

Jewish immigrants into the area, who could gain employment with little competition from local Arabs. The immigrants were mainly low-income Mizrahim who were settled by the government (often against their will) in the peripheral Negev during the 1950s and 1960s. Their absorption into the labor market was particularly important for the authorities, who aspired to create an integrated Jewish Zionist nation and to minimize intra-Jewish political and social tensions (Gradus 1984; Meir 1997; Yiftachel 1998a, b).

As detailed in Chapter 6, nearly all lands held by Negev Arabs prior to 1948 were declared by the government to be state property. In a series of legal moves, the land was declared to be either dead (in legal terminology *mawat*, that is, unregistered and uncultivated), or absentee property, belonging to refugees who left the state during the 1948 war. These legal classifications gave the state permission, under its own laws, especially the State Property Act (1951), to nationalize the land (for details see Ben-David 1995; Kedar 1998; Lustick 1980). Given the self-declared nature of Israel as Jewish and the active involvement of worldwide Jewish organizations (such as the Jewish National Fund and the Jewish Agency) in the official state apparatus of land administration, the declaration of these areas as state lands meant their exclusive use by Jews. Indeed, the lands were subsequently allocated to some fifty Jewish settlements that were established in the Beer-Sheva metropolitan region, mainly to small development towns and communal rural villages whose farms stretch over most lands previously held by Palestinian Arabs.

The classification of the vast majority of the Negev as state land blocked virtually any possibility of its registration in the name of Arabs, who held it for generations (Kedar 1998). In addition, Israel's Land Acquisition Law (1953) expropriated the land of every person who was not residing upon, or cultivating, his or her land on one decisive date (April 1, 1952). Because the vast majority of Negev Bedouin had been forcibly removed from their land prior to this date, they lost their rights to land even when possessing documented proof of ownership (Babai 1997). In this way, the pre-1948 Arab community of the Negev—refugees and locals alike—lost more than 95 percent of its landed property. As mentioned earlier, this was reflected in the bitter statements made in 1998 by Hassan Abu-Quider, a Bedouin activist who was protesting against Israel's land policies: "Only in one instance shall the Bedouin Arabs get their full and equal rights in the Jewish state: only if miraculously we'll stop occupying, needing, or using any land. Then we shall receive what we truly deserve—full air rights . . . (minutes of meeting with A. Burg, then chairman of the Jewish Agency, December 6, 1998).

But local Arabs did not accept this legal situation. Those who became Israeli citizens have submitted some 3,200 legal claims to their expropriated lands, based on traditional Ottoman or British records that attested to their past holdings. To date, however, not even one Arab claimant has been awarded full ownership rights. The Israeli legal system consistently followed legal precedents,[3] and refused to award ownership without documented proof of individual title (Shamir 1996). At the same time, the state recognized partial holding rights for the Bedouin Arabs, either in accordance with land arrangements practiced before 1948, or in accordance with regulations agreed upon by the state and the traditional Arab elites after the transfer to the Siyag (Babai 1997; Ben-David 1995; Shamir 1996). However, these rights have remained vague, thus depriving the Arabs of basic development and planning capabilities.

Five decades later, the tension involving Bedouin-Arab land ownership is still a central issue in the Beer-Sheva region. Ninety-five percent of Arab claims to land have not been settled; these claims cover approximately eight hundred thousand dunams (Mena Committee 1997). Half of these lands are in areas settled by Jews. The compromises reached so far between Negev Arabs and state only to thirty thousand dunams. This low figure reflects not only the slow pace of the Israeli legal system but also the steadfast Arab resistance to state policies. The Arab opposition has attempted to link the settlement of land disputes with forced relocation into seven planned towns within the Siyag, as detailed below. The most common response among Bedouin landholders has been the *summud*. As described in Chapter 3, this Palestinian strategy entails a steadfast hold on community land, values, and political goals while resisting oppressive state policies. The two sides have thus found themselves in a political, legal, and planning deadlock, causing widespread urban informality in the Beer-Sheva region.

It should be reiterated that the forced concentration of Arabs in the Siyag was an integral part of a broader state policy to Judaize the entire disputed territory of Israel/Palestine. It followed the same logic as Israel's policies elsewhere of concentrating the Arabs and dispersing the Jews (see Yiftachel 1996). In the Negev, however, Israel recognized virtually no Arab land rights. In other areas, such as the Galilee and the Triangle, Israel respected Arab private ownership, based on British documentation. But even in these regions the state often used its powerful planning capabilities to expropriate private Arab lands.

Following the population transfer, the Siyag was neglected by planning authorities for twenty years. In several key regional plans, either in the Negev or the Beer-Sheva metropolitan area (including the 1972 District Plan, the 1991 Negev Front [Kidmat Negev] Strategy, the 1995 Beer-Sheva Metropolitan Development Plan, and the 1998 Renewed District Plan), the areas of Bedouin-Arab informal settlements were either left blank, as if they were empty, or designated for public uses such as sewage plants, recreation forests, or industrial zones. No settlement, agricultural, or industrial plans were prepared for this region, causing the emergence of widespread forms of urban and rural informality. Dozens of spontaneous Arab localities evolved and are characterized by tin shacks, cabins, or tents. The vast majority of these spontaneous localities are denied basic infrastructure and services such as electricity, running water, and roads. Their numbers have grown to some 65,000–70,000 people, constituting Israel's largest marginal and deprived community.

During the same period, parallel arms of the Judaization strategy continued to operate in the region, establishing some twenty Jewish towns and rural localities around the Siyag, thus creating an Arab enclave. Later, Jewish development also penetrated into the Siyag, first when the Nevatim airport was built in 1978 (resulting in the forced resettlement of some seven thousand Arabs [see Fenster 1996]), and later with the establishment of Jewish suburban localities, such as Meitar and Livna (Figure 8.2), and the expansion of older Jewish settlements. Most recently, a new wave of Jewish settlement has emerged as a reaction to the October events of 2000. Since 2001, construction has begun on the suburban settlements of Eshkolot, Meitarim, and I'ra—all in the southern slopes of the Hebron Mountains around the Green Line but still in commuting distance from Beer-Sheva.

Consolidating Urban Ethnocracy: Bedouin Arabs and the Dark-Side of Planning

A further step in the effort to Judaize the Beer-Sheva region was the launching in the mid-1960s of a plan to urbanize the Siyag's Bedouin-Arab population. The first mention of the plan was in August 1959 when Ben-Gurion announced in the Knesset a general five-year plan for the Arab sector in which "the government will bring down legislation to move and concentrate the Bedouins into permanent settlements." An intense policy debate ensued with two main positions: Moshe Dayan, then minister of agriculture and a dominant force in shaping Israel's policy toward the Arabs, supported the urbanization of Bedouin Arabs into mixed cities, mainly Beer-Sheva, Jaffa, Lod, and Ramla. Yigal Alon, then minister of labor, and a central government member with strong ties to the Bedouin communities, pushed for a more gradual urbanization strategy, mainly in the southern Siyag (Boymel 2000; Falah 1983).

Eventually, the latter strategy prevailed (although segments of the Dayan plan were also implemented with the settlement of some four thousand Bedouins in Lod and Ramla. In the Negev, seven towns were established into which the region's Arabs were supposed to relocate—Rahat, Laqiya, Hura, Tel Sheva, Kusseifa, Aru'er, and Segev Shalom (see Figure 8.2). The government's aim was to further decrease Arab land control and to concentrate the region's Arabs permanently in urban localities. It attempted to implement a top-down Judaization and modernization program for the Bedouin Arabs through the lure of modern services such as housing, roads, schools, clinics, and electricity.

The Arabs who agreed to relocate into the towns received heavily subsidized plots of state land and access to roads, water, and electricity. But these benefits depended on the Bedouins' cessations of all disputes over lands elsewhere in the Negev. The deal, therefore, was clear: accept fully registered, planned, and (partially) serviced blocks of land in a new Bedouin-Arab town (and withdraw all claims against the state) or remain in an illegal, unserviced locality, subject to the constant danger of house demolition and exposed to a wide range of legal penalties.

As a result, most Arabs who actually relocated into the towns were land-less *falaheen* (farmers) who lived for generations under the protection of Bedouin tribes. The new towns allowed them to bypass their social inferiority within Bedouin-Arab society by breaking centuries-old forms of patronage and dependence. These *falaheen* achieved political dominance in several towns and modernized (or significantly improved) their living standards. The state's urbanization policy, not accidentally, deepened the tensions between the various Arab ethnoclasses. By allocating privileges and resources (such as cheap, serviced lands) to the landless and weaker group, the state's urbanization policy distressed the upper echelons of the Negev Bedouin Arab society (Meir 1988).

Because of the low social status of most urbanizing Arabs, and despite their promise of modernization, the planned towns quickly evolved into pockets of deprivation, unemployment, dependency, crime, and social tensions (see Abu Saad 2003; Lithwick 2000). Although one should not underestimate the power of modernization to form a foundation for social and political mobilization, relocation to the towns also set in train destructive processes of social disintegration (Meir 1997). The towns positioned the Arabs in spatial isolation with little opportunities for local mobility or development (Abu Saad 2003; Lithwick 2000). The seven towns thus became, as potently described by a Bedouin activist, suburban ghettos.

By relocating the Arabs into these peripheral towns, and by separating them municipally from the stronger Jewish areas, Israeli planners laid the long-term structure for the creation of urban ethnocracy. This segregation was coupled by a total lack of services for the Arab population, such as schools, religious facilities, or community centers, within the main Beer-Sheva city area (Figure 8.2). As a result, only around 3,500 Arabs now reside in Beer-Sheva, and they are spread over a number of distant neighborhoods, without notable residential, cultural, or religious centers (Negev Center 1999).

The uneven separation imposed by the region's planners and leaders has created a near total Arab-Jewish segregation. While not all segregation is negative, and many Bedouin Arabs actually wish to remain in homogenous localities to protect their culture and communal cohesion, this highly segregated human landscape has ensured the control of Jews over the economic, political, and cultural resources of this binational metropolis. Thus, the Beer-Sheva urban ethnocracy unevenly incorporated the seven planned Arab towns and a large number of unrecognized (informal) Arab localities.

Israel's strategy to remove the unrecognized villages and coerce the migration of their inhabitants into the planned towns was accompanied by a range of pressure tactics. On the institutional level, special government authorities were set up especially for this task, including the Authority for the Advancement of the Bedouins (note the Orwellian connotation), the Implementation Authority, the Green Patrol, and Rotem, a police unit for law enforcement among the Arabs. These groups were geared, at least in part, toward the goal of concentrating the Bedouin Arabs in the planned towns and controlling their informal spaces.

The state also initiated a series of other pressure tactics to urbanize the Bedouin Arabs. These have included:

- strict nonrecognition of existing settlements located outside the planned towns;
- denial of most municipal services routinely provided to other citizens (water, electricity, telephone, health and public services, and accessible educational services);
- intensive legal penalties against unauthorized homes;
- actual demolition of some 1,300 homes and structures in 1990–98 (Negev Center 1999);
- the frequent issuing of eviction notices and fines in order to remove Arab invaders from state land;
- delay of land settlement proceedings, which have often lasted more than three decades and are intended to make Arabs give up the hope of winning back lands;
- heavy environmental restrictions on grazing and the subsequent seizure and destruction of most Bedouin herds;
- the poisoning of fields planted on disputed land; and
- activation of the state's tax authorities against problematic Bedouin Arabs.

On a planning level, beyond pervasive neglect, the state simply ignored the existence of these villages. This has been another clear example of the dark side of urban planning—the ability to use planning tools to retard and control a population instead of improving its quality of life and living environment. Planning documents by and large represented the Bedouin localities as blank spaces on all official maps and plans (see Figure 8.3).

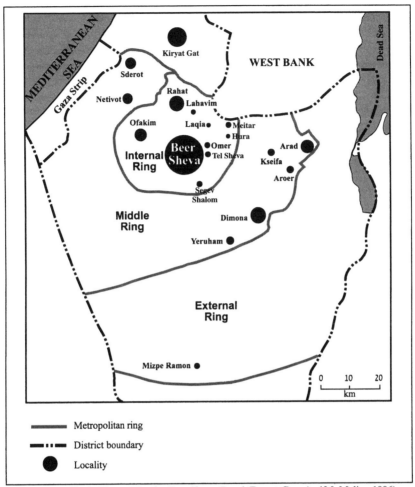

Source: S. Assif, ed., *Master Plan for Beer Sheva, Part 1* (Ramat-Gan: Assif & Maliss, 1996).

Figure 8.3. Representation of the Northern Negev in the Beer-Sheva Metropolitan Master Plan

The state's drive to concentrate and urbanize the Bedouin Arabs was reinforced by two other reasons. First, the state was worried that the Siyag might form an Arab land bridge between the West Bank and the Gaza Strip, thereby threatening the contiguity of Jewish land control. Second, the state was concerned about the costs involved in recognizing, planning, and servicing dispersed populations. The use of planning to control a weak minority was thus justified by geopolitical and rational-economic reasoning.

POLICY ENFORCEMENT AND A PERSISTING SHADOW CITY

Despite the consistent, harsh, and often violent pressure exerted by all Israeli governments since the 1960s to implement the seven-towns strategy, only 55 percent of the region's Arabs have actually moved into these towns. A significant, and rapidly growing, group has remained on the land in the illegal or unrecognized semiurban localities.

Let me reiterate that the illegal Arab localities exist in their places today either owing to their residence in the area in 1948 or as a result of forced government relocation, in other words, not through any form of illegal invasion. Hence, their treatment by state authorities is a testimony to the deep discrimination associated with the ethnocratic state and its urban extensions.

These state policies have caused the creation of a shadow city that is very physically visible but without legitimacy, recognition, or proper planning. This situation spawned growing alienation among Bedouin Arabs and recent mobilization either toward Palestinian nationalism, or—more commonly—Islamic traditionalism and new tribalism (Abu Saad, Yonah, and Kaplan 2000). To illustrate, in the 1999 elections, the United Arab Party associated with the Islamic movement (The Arab List) received 64 percent of the Arab vote in the south, eight times higher than any other party, while the rest of the votes went mainly to parties supporting Palestinian nationalism. This somewhat changed in 2003, when the national parties doubled their size, although the United Arab Party was still the largest. As discussed in the previous chapter, a notable new phenomenon has been the growing boycott of Israeli elections, supported by the more radical sections of the Islamic movement, which reached a significant 48 percent in the 2003 elections, four times higher than the average until 1999 (Negev Center 2001; CBS-b 2003).

Because building permits are granted only for areas with municipal status and approved plans, an absurd situation has developed in the region. Since most Bedouin Arabs continue living in unrecognized villages, all construction—even in a settlement that has existed for centuries—is considered illegal. A vicious cycle is set in motion: municipal status is denied, no plans can be approved, and all buildings are deemed illegal. Policy makers then refrain from granting recognition and municipal status, which may be seen as folding to criminal elements that violate state laws, thereby forcing the Arabs to continue to build illegally, and so forth.

The problem of unauthorized Arab building has caused growing tensions across the entire state of Israel. In 1987 the government adopted the recommendations of the Markowitz Report, which introduced an interim classification of gray zones. De facto recognition would be granted to thousands of unauthorized buildings in Arab settlements, while all permanent building activity in these zones would be continue to be outlawed. Although eighteen years have passed since the adoption of these recommendations, this temporary policy is still in force, disallowing permanent (stone and wood) construction in unrecognized localities. The policy has been enforced with rigor, with some 1,800 home demolitions in the Arab sector between 1987 and 2000.

Concurrently, the Arab population has grown by about 53 percent (Negev Center 2002), thus creating unbearable pressures on the typically small temporary homes. The gray-zone policy has thus forced the villages to become the most run-down localities in Israeli society—frozen as clusters of unserviced, dilapidated dwellings in neglected environments, with high residential density and grave poverty.

Finally, a qualification is in order: the distress of the Arabs in the region does not stem only from Israel's planning policies. It is also part of a traumatic transition of a traditional, seminomadic community into a modern, industrial age. This has been accompanied by geographic uprooting and monumental changes in community structure, family relations, and gender roles (see Fenster 1998; Meir 1997), which have caused a severe internal crisis. This is reflected in rising crime rates, poor economic and educational achievements, and paralyzing political divisions (Abu Saad 1998; Falah 1983; Lithwick 2000). Still, the state's planning policies, with their emphasis on de-Arabizing the region, have played a major role in deepening this communal crisis. We turn now to several recent examples of such policies and to the organized Arab resistance that has emerged against them.

ETHNOCRATIC MYOPIA AND LOCAL RESISTANCE

A telling example of Israel's ethnocratic dynamic is the March of 2000 decision by the Israeli minister of the interior to expand the municipal boundaries of the Jewish suburban town of Omer, abutting Beer-Sheva to the east. The minister nearly doubled Omer's municipal area, annexing en route several Arab illegal localities accommodating some four thousand people (see Figure 8.2). Omer's mayor defined these Arab residents as trespassers despite a documented local history of some communities stretching back to the Ottoman period.

Following the annexation, Omer's mayor refused to extend the well-developed services of this wealthy town to its new Arab residents, claiming that they needed to leave the area according to government policy.[4] Local Arabs and some Jewish residents of Omer have since begun a political and legal campaign against the forced annexation, which may lead to the evacuation of Arabs from their forefathers' land, or alternatively, to serious violence. This conflict attests to the region's continuous ethnocratic planning policies that pressure the Bedouin population to relocate into permanent towns.

Like Omer, most other councils whose municipal areas cover the unrecognized villages have ignored this population in their planning or service provisions. These councils include Bnei Shimon, Merhavim, Har Hanegev, Arad, and Dimona (Figure 8.2), where Bedouin-Arab residents have never had the right to vote. These Arab residents, many of whom inhabited the area before the Jewish councils were established, have thus become transparent. This denial of a "right to the city" (Lefebvre 1996) seriously taints the meaning of their local and Israeli citizenship and now forms the platform for gradual centrifugal withdrawal from the state and its institutions (Meir 1997).

In another policy arena, various Israeli governments have periodically announced new efforts to eliminate the Bedouin problem. In 1997, the Netanyahu government announced a new strategy to increase the pressure on Arabs to relocate into the seven planned towns. The strategy included measures to contain the spread of the scattered Arab population, prevent further invasion into state land, and tighten the enforcement of the state's planning and construction laws.[5]

The three years following the introduction of Netanyahu's plan were accompanied by the construction of four new Jewish settlements in and around the Siyag. These small suburban-like satellites were built according to a recent plan titled the Hebron Ring, under which ten more Jewish settlements are planned for the next decade. The Hebron Ring plan expresses clearly, once more, the ethnocratic and discriminatory nature of Israeli policies in the region: Bedouin villages hosting more than one thousand inhabitants are often asked by planners to relocate into the towns because they are too small, while at the same time Jews are allowed to establish smaller localities.

Another discriminatory aspect of the policy is the link between land ownership and planning rights. The authorities deny planning and infrastructure to the Arabs in the region, officially owing to land disputes with the states. However, as shown in Chapter 6, land disputes also exist between Jewish localities and the states, but planning in these settlements proceeds normally and communal facilities are duly provided. This ethnic difference illustrates again the discriminatory coexistence of a light side and a dark side of the Israeli planning system.

This systematic inequality has not escaped the eyes of residents in the informal localities who have increasingly mobilized and organized to counter the Israeli Judaization strategy. A number of bottom-up planning initiatives have recently been launched that aim to influence the planning in Arab areas. In the mid-1990s, locally drafted plans were prepared for a number of unrecognized villages (such as Darijat, al-Sayyad, and Umbattin—all localities northeast of Beer-Sheva) and presented to the public as alternatives to state plans and as an expression of new Arab assertiveness vis-à-vis the authorities. While none of these plans has been approved, the plans influenced the public discourse and raised consciousness among Jewish circles for the need to change the plight of the informal dwellers.

Another notable bottom-up initiative was the 1998 establishment of the Regional Council for Unrecognized Bedouin Villages (known as al-Una), a voluntary body representing most villages. In December of 1999 it submitted a plan for the recognition and long-term planning of forty-five villages as an amendment to the recently approved district plan.

Finally, the Alliance of Bedouin Organizations has been formed. It coordinates a range of self-help and NGO programs for community empowerment, education, and legal representation of the Beer-Sheva informal sector.

The Bedouin Arabs have also begun to launch proactive legal action, which aims to find cracks in the Israeli legal structure in order to oppose the discriminatory nature of Judaization policies and their contradiction to the tenets of law and planning. Most notable are two recent challenges to the High Court, one against the recent regional outline plan on the grounds that it ignores Bedouin Arab citizens, and the other against the decision to enlarge Omer municipal boundaries and annex rightless Bedouin communities. Both have had positive consequences for the Bedouin struggle. The first forced the government to make an official commitment to include Bedouin concerns, opinions, and representation in the new plan now being prepared for the region, while the second nearly totally canceled the municipal expansion of Omer, which encroached into Bedouin-held lands. Several other appeals have been submitted subsequently by Adalah and the Association for Civil Rights on issues covering water, health, education, and infrastructure.

The problem of implementing official plans for the area, in conjunction with grassroot pressure, has recently begun to influence the Negev's planning authorities, which may be the first signs in the weakening of the Jewish ethnocratic rule. In a significant symbolic move, the metropolitan development plan of Beer-Sheva (adopted in 1998) defined the region as a "binational metropolis." While this definition has remained declaratory, it reflects some legitimacy of the Arab existence in this urban region. Furthermore, in October of 1999, the district committee approved an amendment to district plans that added—for the first time in thirty years—three new Arab towns.

This has broken the seven-towns-only strategy, which has guided Israeli policy in the region for three decades and has been the source of numerous conflicts and tensions. During 2002–4, the authorities released several statements emphasizing their willingness to make planning concessions, most prominently by Prime Minister Ariel Sharon (in what is known as the Sharon-Livni Plan), and by David Cohen, the new chief administrator of the southern district. The new strategy calls for recognizing/building seven new planned Bedouin towns. This was backed in January of 2003 by a new governmental decision allocating 1.4 billion NIS for the plan.

However, most of the money was allocated by the government to law enforcement (a code name for house demolition). No consultation was conducted with the local Bedouin communities, which by and large rejected the plan, because—just like previous plans—it would force them to give up their land. Jaber Abu Kaf, chairman of the Regional Council of Unrecognized Villages (2000–2004), commented that "there is much noise and talk about 'solving' our land problem and investing in the Bedouin sector, but the essence of this plan is still to move us off our lands and to continue to control us as aliens, refugees, or simply unseen in our own homeland."[6] Hence, the new plan is not likely to receive wide support, except for breaking the state's rigid seven-towns-only planning concept.

But developments of an opposite, more accommodating nature have also taken place, with the ceaseless campaigning of Bedouin and other civil organizations for Bedouin rights. Significantly, after a long struggle, in August of 2004 the first unrecognized village—Darijat, located some twenty kilometers northeast of Beer-Sheva—was officially recognized and marked on Israel's official settlement maps. This was the first village (as distinct from a town) to be recognized, ending the official strategy that all Arabs in the Negev must urbanize.

The recognition of Darijat was also significant because the village exploited well the cracks in the Israeli system, thereby paving the strategy for other communities: it worked from below by demonstrating evidence about its existence on the land well before 1948, by building social facilities (such as a school and a health clinic), and through a series of planning appeals and court challenges. Despite long delays and bureaucratic rigidity, the state could not uphold the policy of nonrecognition in the face of these developments. Clearly, the recognition of Darijat is but a drop in the ocean and may even be used by the government to demonstrate its putative progressive activity on the matter, hence stalling progress on a wider scale, but it is still a significant precedent in the long Bedouin-Arab struggle for recognition.

In a related move, and most significantly, new planning principles were articulated in 2003 by the metropolitan planning team for Beer-Sheva, headed by Shamay Assif, who was replaced in mid-2004 by Moshe Cohen. In its preliminary report, the team described the future of the region as a binational metropolis. The new draft plan is expected to be released in late 2005. Early reports from the planning team reveal new goals vis-à-vis the indigenous Bedouin population.

The point of departure for planning the area scattered with Bedouin villages is the existing situation . . . and not some end-state plan drawn three decades ago. . . . The role of the metropolitan plan is then to foster the communal-cultural uniqueness of the Bedouin population while developing the paths for its integration in the making of the metropolis. The space defined in the (former) metropolitan plan for establishing new Bedouin villages . . . offers an opportunity to sever the vicious circle of mistrust and sanctifying the conflict itself. . . . [7]

The issue of informal settlement in the Beer-Sheva region has thus entered a new stage, with the old seven-towns strategy deeply discredited, but with no agreed upon new policy to direct near-urban development among the Bedouin Arabs. The planning direction, however, is quite clear—further concession and recognition of the informal Bedouin villages, although this is typified by a piecemeal, partial, and reluctant approach. The ethnic map of the region is still determined by the contours laid down during the 1950s, with Jews concentrating in the region's central, northern, and western parts and Arabs mainly in the east (Figure 8.2). Even in the unlikely event that Israel recognizes most of the Arab illegal settlements, urban citizenship will continue to be unequal. The right to the city will continue to be hierarchical, with Jews enjoying greater access and powers, and various forms of informality, old and new, are likely to persist, albeit in a more controlled and orderly manner.[8]

In the meantime, new forces have begun to play a role in the shaping of the Beer-Sheva urban area, most notably the gradual globalization and liberalization of Israel's economy and culture. In an indirect way, the large-scale Russian immigration can be seen as part of this process, as can the employment in the Negev of tens of thousands of immigrant laborers, mainly from Asia, Africa, and Eastern Europe.

Several multinational companies have also located in the Beer-Sheva area, and some Israeli companies have been sold to international investors. But so far the structural economic and cultural changes have left little mark on the region's Arab population and geography, except for creating greater competition in the lower rungs of the labor market. No significant openings or opportunities have appeared for the region's Arabs to overcome their structural marginalization and to emerge out of the shadow city as an integral part of the metropolis. The liberalization and mobilization potential of the new urban order are yet to be realized in the ethnocratic city.

Conclusion: Polarization or Coexistence?

This chapter continued the in-depth exploration of the Israeli ethnocracy by focusing on the Beer-Sheva urbanizing region and the relations between the Israeli settler state and local Bedouin-Arab communities. It outlined the role of Israeli policies in de-Arabizing, Judaizing, and developing the Beer-Sheva region, and it focused on their impact on the unseen parts of the emerging metropolis—the unrecognized and informal Bedouin localities.

The chapter also developed the concept of urban ethnocracy and discussed its impact on the emergence of urban informality or a shadow city. It showed the power of the authorities to classify, impose boundaries, and declare illegality for the purpose of marginalizing an entire ethnic sector. Ethnocratic cities, it was shown, exhibit a clash of logics between the forces of globalization-liberalization and a persisting drive for ethnic domination and segregation. Hence, the promise of the city as a liberating setting is not fulfilled in the urban ethnocracy. Instead, it becomes another arena where ethnonational dominance is institutionalized and reproduced.

Yet, urban dynamics do provide some openings for minority mobility and resistance and are likely to generate further challenges to the ethnocratic order. Signs of these processes have surfaced in the Beer-Sheva region and are expressed by growing mobilization of the Bedouins and more effective challenges to Israel's policy, which are emerging from public debates and professional-legal circles. This has led to a deadlock: the state continues to pursue a policy of coerced urbanization (recently on slightly improved terms) while the Bedouins practice *sumud*—steadfastly remaining (illegally) on the land and resisting state policies. This signals a profound cultural-political transformation—from seminomadic tribes a century ago to highly territorialized communities hanging on to their claimed lands.

Given this setting, what is in store? In several important ways, the northern Negev can become a prism of Arab-Jewish relations in Israel/Palestine. Given the acute level of the crisis, the deep poverty, the social chaos, and the gradual minority withdrawal from the state, time is very short for finding a path forward. The failure of past policies seems, finally, to have made some impact, prompting the state to develop new strategies. But is it too late? The mobilization and persistence of the Bedouin's struggle over their unrecognized localities is a testimony to the declining power of the state to implement its policies. Further, there is no guarantee that a revised strategy to concentrate the Bedouins, even on improved terms, would be more effective. The recent attempts by the state to offer more towns for the Bedouins appear to use the same faulty logic of planning as control, forming a clear case of too little, too late.

Therefore, a totally new approach is needed, pursuing recognition and a sense of security for all communities residing in the region while allowing the Bedouins to maintain control over their lands. All Bedouin villages that conform to the general standards governing Jewish development in Israel (in size, land area, distance, from metropolitan centers, and so forth) should be approved. A variety of locality types ranging from small family farms, to semi-urban villages, to large modern cities should be offered to the Negev Arabs, as they were similarly offered to Jews.

Beer-Sheva can, and should, become a binational and multicultural metropolis, de jure and de facto. If it takes this course, it may provide an example for the rest of Israel/Palestine about the possibilities of new ethnic relations in their joint homeland. If it fails, however, it will remain another ethnocratic urban region, contributing to the deepening of *creeping apartheid* and ethnic conflict, and using none of the possibilities offered by the urbanizing future of Israel/Palestine.

Chapter 9
Mizrahi Identities in the Development Towns: The Making of a "Third Space"

Land of Milk and Honey

You who left the distant village,
You who were respected in the Maghreb,
You left property, and brought a fez,
You left much wealth, to fulfill a vision . . .

You who immigrated from the green village,
You who they called *Lala shuk*,
You left everything there,
You brought just a kaftan and a red polar,
But you realized a dream . . .

You who were filled with belief,
You who brought the *mimuna* festival,
You wanted to be alike; you changed your names,
Jojo is worthless, Frecha is a disgrace,
You licked the honey, it was not always sweet,
The milk spilled, but you didn't cry over it,
With all the hardships, the language, the walls,
You planted roots and bore fruit.
(Oliel 1992)

The above song, by the Israeli band Sfatayim (Lips), whose members are natives of a southern development town, serves as a fitting opening to this chapter. The song's lyrics (and tune) expose the duality, ambivalence, and bidirectionality of Mizrahi (Eastern) identity. On the one hand, the Mizrahim (plural form, denoting Jews from Arab and Muslim countries) experienced hardships, discrimination, and confinement to peripheral towns, mainly during the 1950s and 1960s. But on the other hand, they came to terms with, and even sustained, the Zionist settlement project that marginalized them in Israeli society. This duality constitutes the backbone of Mizrahi identity in Israel's development towns.

This chapter is the first of two chapters covering the peripheral development towns. The first focuses on place and identity among Mizrahim in the towns, while the second (Chapter 10) deals with local politics and collective mobilization. These chapters continue to pursue one of the main goals of the book—to look from the periphery toward the ethnocratic center. The present chapter explores more deeply the transformation experienced by the Mizrahim by investigating patterns of identity formation, which means focusing on key aspects of collective identity, namely, the role of a hegemonic state, cultural traditions, ethnoclass stratification, and intergenerational transformations. The chapter first examines these issues from a theoretical perspective and later details an empirical survey conducted to understand the attitudes of Mizrahi residents in development towns over a range of spatial, cultural, socioeconomic, and political issues.

This chapter argues that the settlement of Mizrahim in peripheral towns led to the creation of a trapped identity. Entrapment—that is, a situation in which a group faces significant obstacles for mobilization against its marginalized position—is typical to immigrant, and not indigenous, minorities. Hence, the predicament and social processes experienced by peripheral Mizrahim are very different from the ones experienced by Palestinian Arabs, as discussed in the previous two chapters. One of the main differences lies in their entrapment within the Israeli ethnocratic project, as opposed to indigenous groups, who are trapped outside that project.

The discussion shows that a number of salient factors molded Mizrahi identities in the towns, including discriminatory state policies, partial inclusion into the Zionist nation, persisting Jewish-Arab tensions, continuing Judaization of Israel/Palestine, deepening socioeconomic stratification, and the decline of the welfare state. Thus, the identity of the Mizrahim in the towns crystallized in the gray areas between Jew and Arab, inclusion and exclusion. The Mizrahim's ambiguous space has caused their entrapment. On the one hand, the group cannot assimilate into the mainstream of society, yet on the other hand, it is unable to mobilize a competing communal project. It is thus left in an ambivalent, twilight zone, creating what Bhabha (1994) termed a third space.

Within the overall ethnocratic approach, this chapter stresses the settler-immigrant nature of society as a central force shaping Mizrahi identity. As noted earlier in the book, the settlement-immigration process functions as a mechanism for turning new immigrants into relatively weak and assimilating communities, sandwiched between a powerful founding or charter group, an excluded and dispossessed indigenous population, and, most recently, groups of aliens or foreign workers (see Stasiulis and Yuval-Davis 1995; Kimmerling 2001).

Yet the relationship between the founding group and immigrants is never totally dominated by the former. The interaction between the two groups creates Bhabha's third space, where new hybrid identities and social dynamics are created. The metaphorical and physical third space is molded by uneven power relations, thereby reflecting the infusion and impact of hegemonic values and practices. But the third space also creates a platform for later social and political mobilization, premised on the partial inclusiveness owing to the assimilation project. In this process, localities and regions become central to the process of identity formation. It is there that the materiality of social life takes shape, ethnic and social networks are built, and a process of spatial socialization ensues to give meaning and concrete shape to the immigrants' values, memories, goals, and interests (see Paasi 2000).

Typical of immigrant-settler societies, the only available path for marginalized immigrant groups remains individual assimilation into the dominant culture. Concomitantly, the dominant group represses potentially challenging identities by applying discriminatory spatial and economic policies and by generating derogatory discourses in key public arenas, such as education, the media, the arts, and politics. Hence, the entrapment of a marginal group inhibits the development of alternative spaces for identity formation. My study shows that Mizrahim in the development towns find themselves in such an entrapped position and subsequently develop an identity that is smothered, fragmented, and confused.

The data analyzed in this chapter are derived from an attitudinal survey conducted in 1998 among North African immigrants in six representative peripheral development towns, three in the north (Shlomi, Ma'alot, and Bet Shean), and three in the south (Kiryat Gat, Ofakim, and Dimona). The survey consisted of 294 in-person interviews, which examined the attitudes of residents over a range of subjects connected to feelings about place, identity, and position in Israeli society.

In order to trace longitudinal trends, the survey focused on families living in the towns for at least two generations. Half of the respondents were first-generation Israelis—born and raised in North Africa; the other half were these immigrants' children—born and raised in Israel. The project examined only non-Haredi (ultra-Orthodox) families, chiefly because the problem of accessing that population, which is estimated at 4 percent of the towns' population (CBS-a 2000).

Data collection relied on a closed questionnaire administered in face-to-face interviews, using quantitative analytical tools. This method has some drawbacks: it is often blind to subtleties of sentiments; it makes researchers unable to reflect on the experience and feel of a place; and unlike open interviews, it downplays the ability of interviewees to articulate their own emotions. However, this methodology does have the capacity to represent a wide spectrum of participants and trace broad social trends as a basis for macro-scale comparisons and generalizations. Being fully cognizant of both the advantages and disadvantages of this research method, I chose an attitudinal questionnaire as the principal research tool, supplemented by several in-depth open interviews of local leaders and residents. Before discussing the results of the survey, a brief historical and geographical account of the development towns and the plight of the Mizrahi immigrant-settlers is necessary.

The Development Towns

The planned establishment of the Israeli development towns in peripheral regions is not unique. After World War II this was a broadly accepted planning strategy, practiced in states such as the United Kingdom, the Soviet Union, Ireland, India, Spain, and Malaysia. The new towns had a twofold purpose: economically they were intended to serve as regional centers of growth and development, and socially they were to provide for a range of educational, cultural, health, and housing needs (Golani 1976). These towns were supposed to create opportunities for social and class integration, thereby reducing the likelihood of out-migration (Gans 1973). Meeting these requirements necessitated coordination of building plans, employment, and social services (Phillips and Yeh 1987). For the most part, this was not achieved. Further, given the logics of capital and political forces, the new towns, especially in peripheral areas, often became nodes of neglect and marginality. They turned into low-demand, low-prestige localities, drawing low-income immigrants and other marginalized groups (Harvey 1993).

In Israel, as detailed in Chapters 3, 4, and 6, twenty-seven development towns were established during the 1950s and 60s, mainly in the peripheral north and south. The official discourse gave several main reasons for this massive project: population dispersal, decentralization, immigrant absorption, and integration of the exiles, all routinely replicated in academic literature (see Shachar 1971; Efrat 1989; Lipshitz 1991; for a critical view, see Kemp 2002). The establishment of the twenty-seven towns was the outcome of the first national outline plan.

This important policy document was named after Arie Sharon, head of the Planning Authority in the prime minister's office from 1948 to 1952 (Sharon 1951). Sharon sought to provide Israel, anticipating the absorption of 2.5 million people, with an urban plan (Kark 1995). This plan created a pyramid with five primary types of settlement in a hierarchical relationship. One major category missing from the urban landscape prior to the founding of Israel was Jewish middle-sized towns and urban centers with populations ranging from six thousand to sixty thousand (Sharon 1951; Troen 1994). These communities came to be called development towns (Figure 9.1).

By creating a national community around the project of settlement and peripheral development, the Sharon Plan intended to advance the Judaization of territory and to assist in the process of nation building. By the mid-1960s, it had steered about two hundred thousand immigrants to the development towns, the vast majority being Mizrahim (Efrat 1989). In a classic case of planning from above, most residents were brought to the towns from temporary immigration camps (*ma'abarot*) or directly from Israel's ports and were lured by the supply of inexpensive public housing

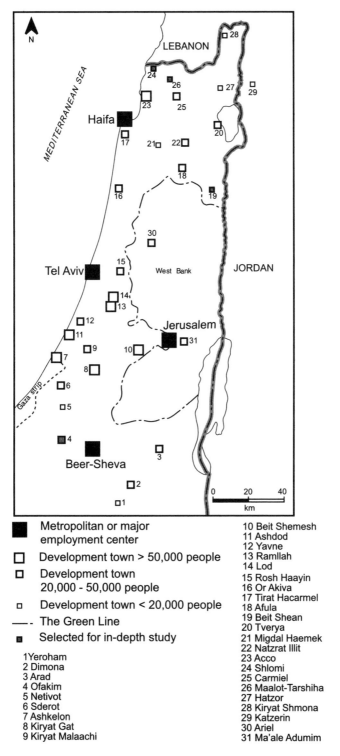

Figure 9.1. Israeli Development Towns, 2003

(Swirski and Shoshani 1985; Law Yone and Kalus 1995). The immigrant Mizrahi population, now residing in the towns, has remained largely segregated both from more established Jewish groups (mainly in rural settlements or older towns) and from the local Arab population, which remained the target of control and containment

A major goal of the Sharon Plan, along with other contemporary institutions, was to advance the national goal of integration of the exiles. Like the policy of population dispersal, this policy was intended to enhance nation building. It was the Israeli version of the American melting pot, but it was aimed only at Jews (Shuval and Leshem 1998). If the policy of population dispersal (that is, Judaization of space) aimed to maximize the overlap between the state's territory and Jewish control, the melting pot policy aimed to maximize the overlap between Jewish population and Zionist culture. The values and practices that all Jews were urged to adopt were drawn from the dominant Ashkenazi culture. The Mizrahim were subsequently pressured to shed their Arabic and Middle Eastern culture and adopt a new Israeli (read, Ashkenazi) identity, marked by a high level of secularity, militarism, collectiveness, nationalism, and European orientation in the arts, politics, gender, and labor relations (see Shohat 1997; Zerubavel 2002). These principles called for the uprooting of any diasporic remnants (Raz-Krakotzkin 1994) and pressed for exchanging the previous Jewish communal identity, defined chiefly by religion and ethnicity, for a national identity defined by territory, modernity, secularity, and quasi-Western values (see Hever, Shenhav, and Motzafi-Hallar 2002; Yonah and Saporta 2002). This belief, we must remember, was imposed on the longest established Jewish community which became the largest Jewish group in Israel.

Moreover, the implications of the population dispersal strategy partially contradicted the strategy of ingathering the exiles, since it created interethnic (Ashkenazi-Mizrahi) gaps through policies of uneven development (see Cohen 1970; Spilerman and Habib 1976; Swirski 1989), thereby legitimizing patterns of segregation and inequality. Over time, as shown in Table 9.1, this created a distinct ethnic geography of inequality. Given the high concentration of Mizrahim in the development towns, reaching 85–90 percent during the 1960s and 1970s (Efrat 1989), the association between Mizrahi identity, peripheral location, and economic deprivation became highly conspicuous. This spawned pervasive sentiments of resentment among peripheral Mizrahim and generated, in later years, a new politics of anger and difference (see Peled 2001).

As elaborated in the next chapter, during the 1990s the demography and physical structure of the towns changed dramatically with the arrival of mass immigration from the former Soviet Union and (to a lesser extent) from Ethiopia. Once again, the towns became the center of cheap housing construction owing to government politics of land allocation and financial incentive to developers. Consequently, most peripheral towns absorbed

TABLE 9.1. Selected Socioeconomic Criteria of Development Towns

Indicator	Dev. Towns	Israel
North African and Asian origin (1983)[1]	81%	44%
Percentage of immigrants (2000)	64%	39%
Mean salaried income (monthly)[2]	5,520 NIS	6,494 NIS
Ownership dwelling (percentage of households)[3]	66%	73%
Percentage of labor force unemployed[3]	11.2%	6.9%
Percentage of population receiving a disability allowance[3]	10.2%	4.2%
Percentage of households with cars	45%	56%
Percentage of employed persons in manufacturing[4]	30.1%	19.5%

1. CBS-a, 1983 Statistics 1983.
2. Israel Social Security 2000 (http://www.btl.gov.il).
3. CBS-a 1995.
4. CBS-a 1998.

large groups of low-income immigrants, straining their social services and employment opportunities. As shown by Tzfadia (2000), the process of negative selection continued during the 1990s, widening the gap between the socioeconomic level of the towns and mainstream Israeli cities (Table 9.1). Because the Israeli mean includes the Arab sector, generally more impoverished than the development towns, this intra-Jewish gap is even more pronounced than appears in the figures. Given the size of development towns, reaching 800,000 by 2000 (CBS-a, 2001), the ongoing negative selection dynamic became central to the reshaping of Israeli identity and politics.

Empirical Explorations

IDENTITY AND PLACE

Localities never exist in a vacuum but are constructed through their material and discursive settings. A place is constituted through the attachment of historical, social, and cultural meaning (See Harvey 1989; Tuan 1977; Taylor 1999). The omnipresent matrices of power result in the creation of hierarchical systems of places, in which marginality and centrality are ceaselessly constituted, maintained, and transformed through cultural, political, and economic practices and the accompanying discourses of prestige and stigma (Massey 1993; Shields 1991).

The importance of power relations in place making is conspicuous in the data. To begin, the survey shows that the places known as development towns were created by reluctant pioneers who had no other residential choice at the time (see Figure 9.2). More than half of this population was taken to the peripheral towns by the authorities straight from the ship or temporary immigrant camp (ma'abarah) with little opportunity to object. The

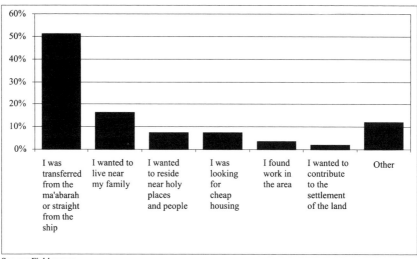

Source: Field survey.

Figure 9.2. Locational Choices: What Is the Most Important Reason for Your Living in the Town?

story of the forced dispatch of Mizrahim has already been told by a collection of local narratives (Shelly-Neuman 1996). The data verify this phenomenon and further attest that the collective memory of forced settlement has become central to peripheral Mizrahi identity formation.

The resentment of forced settlement does not dominate the sentiments of town residents. An ambivalent perspective is detectable in other responses. For example, most respondents (63 percent) claim that the establishment of the towns in the 1950s was necessary. But at the same time, the majority (57 percent) also believes that the state's policy toward the towns is discriminatory, particularly in comparison to the state's treatment of nearby (mainly rural Ashkenazi) *kibbutzim* (see Table 9.2). Two puzzling questions then arise: How were geographically, economically, and culturally discriminatory policies instituted without arousing serious opposition? Moreover, how was it possible to gain the consent of Mizrahi residents for such policies, as is partially reflected in the survey?

One answer to this puzzle can be derived from the prevailing hegemonic order of the settler society, which incorporates the immigrants (as inferior, but nonetheless, as members) of the nascent settling nation while simultaneously excluding the indigenous population. In Israel, the definition of the Zionist nation as Jewish and the ongoing expansion into (historical,

TABLE 9.2. Describe Your Feelings about the Town You Live In (Distribution of Answers in Percentages)

My Town Is:	Among All Respondents	Among the First Generation	Among the Second Generation
Friendly place/Unfriendly place	85	88	83
	9	11	8
Safe/Dangerous	71	74	67
	10	8	12
Has good population/Has bad population	64	72	57
	16	8	24
Improving/Regressing	62	67	58
	19	19	19
Attractive/Ugly	59	66	54
	21	17	25
Developing/Frozen	56	63	49
	23	22	23
Connected to country/Isolated on periphery	52	57	47
	23	20	26
Something I am proud of/ Something I am ashamed of	49	56	43
	21	13	29
Favored/Neglected	38	45	34
	34	25	42
Liked by the country/Disliked by the country	34	40	29
	35	24	45
Has a high quality of life/Has a low quality of life	31	32	30
	40	34	45
Rich/Poor	13	16	11
	49	47	51

Note: The table is based on an aggregation of the consecutive score data (1–7): 1–3: negative; 5–7: positive; 4: apathetic (not included in the table).

claimed, or lived) Arab space, in which the Mizrahim participated, has worked to incorporate Mizrahim into the collective identity, thereby preventing them from undermining the hegemonic order created, at least partially, at their expense. (For an expanded discussion see Shalom-Chetrit 2004; Yiftachel 1998b, 2000b).

In Israel, the hegemony of Zionism, including its settlement and security practices, is taken for granted and viewed as unavoidable and unquestionable. According to the survey, this is the common perception in the towns, despite some bitterness about the past, and despite some notable local variations. There is no real attempt to question the importance of the idea of settlement in general (a central component of Zionist hegemony), and the establishment of development towns in particular. Indeed, 63 percent of the survey participants claimed that the development towns are important for state security. The concept of security, as has been discussed extensively elsewhere, is one of Zionism's hegemonic proto-ideas (see al-Haj and Ben-Eliezer 2003; Ezrahi 1996; Kimmerling 2001).

The survey shows that localism, as a center of identity formation, has perhaps emerged in order to reconcile the tension between the Zionist esteemed value of settlement and the actual deprivation of the Mizrahim. Their shared fate, daily life, common origin, and similar economic class have created a clear sense of belonging to the development town. To some extent, this is a countermove to negative images commonly produced about the towns in the general Israeli public; these images have frequently served as an impediment to mobility and development (Avraham 2000).

The images constructed by the locals depict the development town as an arena for building their lives and not a stigmatized periphery. It is a social environment and a site of socialization through daily practices and interactions, which create a sense of place and security (Agnew 1987). Places are areas of contestation and are perceived differently by different people. Hence, the sense of place and identity is never homogenous or stable but is subject rather to ongoing challenges (Davies and Herbert 1993). In regard to the Israeli development towns, previous anthropological research has already (indirectly) considered the subject of local identity through the analysis of local symbols and sacred rituals, which are claimed to have created positive local sentiments (see Ben-Ari and Bilu 1987).

The current survey aimed to explore, in more depth, the nature of local sentiments in development towns. Thus, interviewees were asked to score pairs of contradictory adjectives describing their town on a scale of 1 to 7. The main findings are displayed in Table 9.2.

It can be immediately discerned from the table that the majority of respondents believe their town is friendly, safe, accommodating of decent populations, and improving. These indicators of solidarity, which can be termed positive local sentiments, stem in part from a certain local pride that has developed over the years in development towns. This has been reinforced by the discourse of local newspapers and, as observed above, by the development of local cultural symbols that enhance local identification (Ben-Ari and Bilu 1987). In addition, the emergence of capable local leadership has managed to wrest control of the development towns from external party functionaries, further increasing local pride and identification (Ben Zadok 1993).

However, even in small localities, often associated with consistency and continuity, identities are constantly challenged (Massey and Jess 1995). They are contested by internal dissatisfaction and unrest, and by the images, views, and practices of other groups, particularly when a place has entered the national consciousness as marginal and stigmatized. This may cause the emergence of resistant identities, born out of conflict and inequality between disgruntled groups and the centers of power (Castells 1997). Respondents were acutely aware of the development towns' negative image among the general Israeli society, 74 percent felt that their town is disliked by the rest of the country (see Table 9.2). Because local residents continue to attempt to create a different narrative of place, the emergence of significant resistant identities is yet to occur. As indicated in the table, respondents describe their town as safe and friendly and believe that despite its problems it is an excellent place in which to live.

The intergenerational prism offers another angle to analyze local sentiments. While members of both generations feel solid affinity with the towns and exhibit positive local sentiments, the younger generation views their towns with a more critical eye. This is particularly true when the question of the status of the towns in Israeli society is examined in a series of questions, such as "Are the development towns connected to the country or isolated on the periphery?" "Are development towns favored or neglected?" and "are development towns liked or disliked?" The responses show a tendency among the younger generation to see the development towns as more disliked by the country (45 percent), as neglected (42 percent), and as isolated on the periphery (36 percent). (The differences are significant at [$\alpha < 0.05$].) In other words, while the younger generation has a greater desire to integrate into the Israeli center and avoid the identity trap, it is also more aware of the difficulties of integration and mobility.

However, it is not enough for local residents on the periphery to construct a positive narrative about their place. Difficulties stemming from planning failures (Efrat 1989), discrimination in the allocation of resources (State Comptroller 2000), unemployment, an inferior education system, and cultural stigmas are well known to local residents. In the absence of promising economic prospects (Gradus and Livnon-Blushtein 2001; Razin 1991), a desire to emigrate has been pervasive in the towns despite local attachment. Of the surveyed participants, a high percentage (63 percent) expressed a desire to leave the development towns, mostly in the direction of Israel's central regions. This phenomenon is more prevalent among the younger generation, as discussed further below.

IDENTITIES IN PLACES

As illustrated above, local group identities are never constructed in isolation but are embedded within their environments and are shaped through interactions with other groups, places, and forces, in a process labeled spatial socialization by Paasi (2000). Accordingly, relationships between town residents and other Israeli groups are intimately linked to the policy strategies of population dispersal and integrating the exiles, and they are shaped by the partial contradiction between them. The policies created spatial proximity and economic dependence between the towns and the surrounding populations (Razin 1991), especially the *kibbutzim,* who were the elite group of Israeli society and a major cultural symbol of the new, modern, Western-oriented,

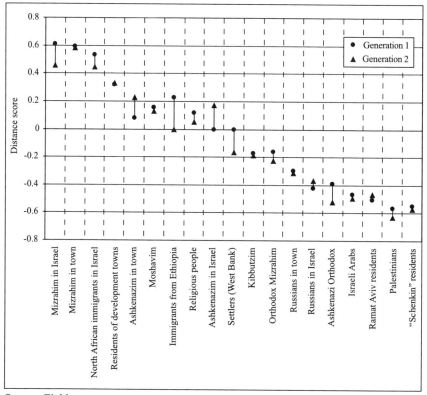

Source: Field survey.

Figure 9.3. Intergroup Distance: Describe Closeness/Distance toward Specified Groups

Zionist Israeli (Shohat 1997; Zerubavel 2002). Other groups influencing the development towns are local Arabs, Russian immigrants, and ultra-Orthodox Jews who became geographically adjacent during the settlement process. The daily interactions and power relations between these groups had a major impact on identity formation in the towns.

A clear indication of the nature of these interactions is reflected in Figure 9.3, where respondents were asked to indicate their perceived closeness/distance to/from other groups in Israel/Palestine. The index of perceived distance was built on values ranging from 1 (most close) to 7 (most distant). The distribution of responses is plotted in Figure 9.3.

The chart portrays a stark social perception, in which identification is related to geographical proximity and power position. Town residents expressed proximity to their own community (Mizrahim in the towns and in Israel) and also to other nearby groups (such as Ashkenazim in the towns).

Perceived distance is larger, but not extreme, toward socially distant local groups (such as local Russian and Haredim, and even, to a lesser degree, settlers in the occupied territories). The perceived distance to the Palestinians is matched by similar sentiments of distance and remoteness from two localities symbolizing Western-oriented, Ashkenazi elites in Israel—residents of Ramat Aviv (an affluent Tel Aviv neighborhood) and Sheinkin (a bohemian Tel Aviv inner-city area). Figure 9.3 is a clear reminder of the social fragmentation and stereotyping rife in Israeli society and the entrapment town residents feel, being distant both from the higher echelons of Israeli society as well as neighboring Palestinian Arabs. However, between these poles emerges a more variegated picture, which may open some possibilities to new perceptions, based on geographical proximity and the development of regional interests.

The sentiments of closeness/distance displayed in Figure 9.3 assist in defining collective identity by nuancing the process of othering according to a range of positive and negative group criteria. In general, town residents feel closeness toward Mizrahim in the town and in other parts of the country, highlighting the emergence of a fractured region connecting isolated islands of Mizrahim. Residents of the towns also showed relative apathy toward the West Bank settlers, other religious groups, and the *kibbutzim*, despite often sharing the same geographic district with the last group. The perceived distance, and even hostility, toward the icons of Israel's Ashkenazi elites (Ramat Aviv and Sheinkin) reflects the wide ethnoclass disparity that has developed between these groups. It is noteworthy that the *kibbutzim*—once themselves part of the Israeli elites—are perceived as closer to the towns. This is probably partially because of their geographic proximity and their recent decline in status.

Interviews also revealed that the perceived distance embodies more than the wide (and widening) economic gap and conspicuous geographical remoteness. It also reflects very different cultural orientations, whereby the periphery perceives the elitist groups as supporting globalization, Americanization, and post-Zionism, and hence a deliberate diminution of Zionism and its major achievements (see Ram 2003; Regev and Seroussi 2004; Silberstein, 2002). These orientations, which rest on educational, economic, and cultural capital of the Israeli elites, threaten the Mizrahim in the development towns by devaluing their main resources for mobility in Israeli society—national affiliation. As will be discussed below, these sentiments reflect not only the marginality of town residents from the agenda of the Israeli centers, but they can also serve as a guide to the Mizrahim's visions of the desired future of Israeli society.

Beyond the national factor, the perceptions of distance outlined in Figure 9.3 can be discerned as moving along two main axes: geography and ethnicity. Geographically, town residents tend to feel closer to residents of nearby localities. This is illustrated by the greater sense of closeness to

Ashkenazim and Mizrahim in "my town" than to their counterparts in the rest of the country. The impact of ethnicity is also conspicuous. Other Mizrahim (as well as Ethiopians, who are often represented in Israel as belonging to an Eastern culture) ranked higher than most other groups. Cross-regional ethnic affinity reminds us of the social and cultural geography of fractured regions that typify settler societies in general and Israel in particular, whereby regions are constructed of chains of settlement without territorial contiguity. Yet, they form a framework for mobilization based on ethnic affiliation and common political goals (Yiftachel 2001a). Thus, three major factors—ethnicity, place, and socioeconomic standing—combine to create the hierarchy of perceptions toward social distance.

Finally, the intergenerational angle reveals that sentiments toward other groups in Israel/Palestine have remained quite stable over time. Within this overall stability, we can observe that respondents born in Israel feel somewhat closer than their parents to Ashkenazim in the locality and elsewhere and to residents of Tel Aviv. In other words, they feel closer to the country's elitist groups, indicating their greater desire and ability to integrate. The same group also shows greater proximity toward Russian immigrants and toward local Mizrahim, indicating their solidarity with peripheral groups, which are geographically and economically similarly placed. The identity of town residents is also well reflected in perceptions on the future orientation of the state, as discussed later.

NATION, CULTURE, AND PERIPHERALITY

As already mentioned, relations between centers and peripheries are rarely dichotomous. Instead, their interactions often produce a third space in which new identities and dynamics take shape. The third space is never a product of equal interaction but rather reflects a skewed, often confused, and always constrained site of identities. Identities emerge from an uneven encounter of centers and peripheries and are often unnoticeable to the naked eye (Bhabha 1994). This dynamic is critical in the development towns, where residents have had to negotiate, first and foremost, with the Zionist (Ashkenazi) perception of religion and nation, as articulated by Kimmerling (1999, 340): "The main characteristic of the social order in Israel is the Zionist hegemony. This hegemony is expressed in the taken-for-grantedness of the equivalence between the Jewish religion and nation. It is common to both the Right and to the Left, to Ashkenazim and to Mizrahim, to the poor and to the rich, to women and to men, to the religious—in their degrees and hues—as to the secular."

Indeed, the vast majority of respondents (95 percent) defined themselves in the survey as Zionists. As noted by Kimmerling, this is manifested in a total acceptance of the inseparability of Jewishness and Israeliness, that is, between religious and national identities. Figure 9.4 shows that the most

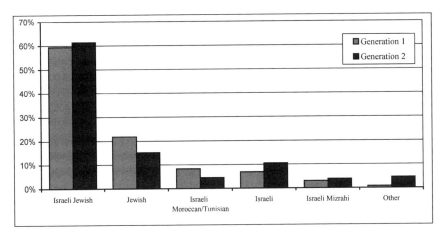

Source: Field survey.

Figure 9.4. Collective Identity: Which (One) Definition Describes You Best?

common self-definition by respondents was Israeli Jew (60 percent). This definition is stripped of communal-ethnic (*a'dati*) affiliation. This reflects a prevailing sense of belonging to a national group and not to an ethnic minority. The first choice of Israeli Jew is far higher than the average in Israeli Jewish society, which stands at only 18.5 percent when faced with exactly the same range of options (Smooha 1992, 78).

Notably, 19 percent of respondents in the towns chose not to use the title Israeli and simply used Jewish as the most appropriate category, as opposed to 17 percent among Israeli Jews at large. Hence, the label Israeli on its own received weak support, being selected by only 8 percent of respondents. This is only a quarter of the 36 percent of Jews in Israel who selected this category (Smooha 1992), indicating a sentiment of marginality that prohibits peripheral Mizrahim from perceiving themselves as simply or fully Israelis. Surveys among other marginal groups, such as Haredim (ultra-Orthodox), Russian speakers, or Palestinian Arabs, have also shown low support for the category Israeli (see al-Haj and Leshem 2000). That category enjoys its strongest support among the Ashkenazi middle classes (see Kimmerling 2001).

Finally, communal-ethnic categories such as Israeli Moroccan/Tunisian or Israeli Mizrahi were selected by only 10 percent of the respondents, although this is far higher than the national average, where less than 1 percent identified themselves as members of a hyphenated identity. For example, only 7.5 percent of Russian speakers in Israel identified themselves as Russians and 1.6 percent as Israeli Russians, although they have immigrated to Israel in the last decade. The categories of Jew, Israeli, or Israeli Jew were selected by 80.7 percent of the Russian immigrants; most of them (45 percent) preferred the Israeli category (see al-Haj and Leshem 2000).

The weakness of the state category (Israeli), in comparison to a religious-national category (Jewish), may indicate certain unease with Zionist hegemony, especially its secular, state-oriented elements. Such self-identification creates tensions with the orientation of powerful groups in Israel, although a major confrontation is averted by the ambiguity of Zionism itself toward Israeliness. As reflected in the towns, in recent years, the categories of Jewish and Zionist have overshadowed Israeli as a single dominant category (Kimmerling 2001). The reduced identification with Israeli also marks the ongoing difference between Mizrahim and mainstream Israeli society. Mizrahim place greater importance on tradition and religion (hence the popularity of the Jewish category). This is reflected by the 60 percent of respondents who identified themselves in another question as traditional (*messorti*—a category denoting partial observation of religious rules), this being twice the proportion among the Jewish Israeli public (see Peres and Yuchtman-Yaar 1998).

These figures correspond well with another set of responses focusing on the issue of ethnic-national-religious collective attachment (Figure 9.5). Here, the vast majority of respondents (64 percent) see themselves, first and foremost, as part of the Jewish people, and only 4 percent identify first with the Moroccan/Tunisian ethnic community. Other notable groups of respondents stress only one dimension of the national-religious combination—23 percent emphasize the national, while 9 percent prefer religious affiliation.

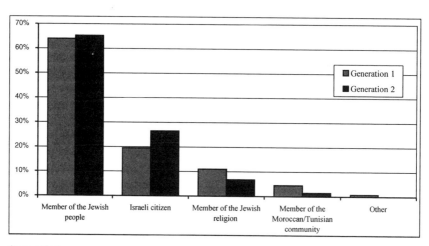

Source: Field survey.

Figure 9.5. Collective Affiliation: Which One of the Following Affiliations Is Most Suitable for You?

The intergenerational prism reveals here, again, a high degree of similarity, with more than two-thirds in both generations supporting combined national-religious identification. Intergeneration differences appear at the margins, with a larger proportion of the older generation identifying exclusively with the Jewish religion and a larger segment of the younger generation leaning toward an Israeli identity, which reflects their greater (although still partial) integration into Israeli society. The greater integration is also marked by the use of the term Mizrahi mainly among the younger generation. This is an Israeli-made term, designed originally to mark the difference and by implication the backwardness of Oriental (Mizrahi) Jews. Recently, this term has resurfaced as a more positive locus around which Mizrahi identities are formed anew (see Shohat 1997; Hever, Shenhav, and Motzafi-Hallar 2002).

These self-definitions are linked to the respondents' cultural preferences, to which we shall return, as well as to their perception of the future of Israeli society. Overall, we can trace a strong desire to integrate into the mainstream of Israeli Zionist society, but this desire is tempered by some critique, especially regarding the erasure of their ethnic culture and the attempt to secularize the Mizrahim. Hence, 77 percent of respondents supported a state with a traditional Jewish character, 12 percent supported a religious state, and only 8 percent advocated a more secular state. Thus, we can trace some elements of what Castells (1997) claimed to be resistant identity, which builds itself in opposition to society's dominant frameworks and values, although such identity has not gathered pace to form any noticeable backbone of coherent consciousness in the towns.

ARAB-JEWISH RELATIONS

Given their long-term support of rightist Jewish parties, especially the nationalist Likud and Orthodox-nationalist Shas, it is not surprising that Mizrahim often hold hawkish positions on Arab-Jewish relations. This has been reinforced by the elections of 2003, with right-wing voting in development towns reaching 74.5 percent (compared to 56 percent statewide and 66 percent among Israeli Jews). This pattern has been relatively stable in the towns since the early 1980s, with the main fluctuations evident internally within the rightist camp, between the two main parties—Likud and Shas (see detailed discussion in Shalom-Chetrit 2004).

Several explanations for this pattern have been advanced in the mainstream literature, including Mizrahi memory of oppression in the Arab world, coupled with a desire to turn these relations upside down (Peres and Smooha 1981) and with an alleged leaning toward authoritative, traditional, and hence irrational nationalist culture (Shamir and Arian 1997; Seliktar 1984). Other approaches stress more rational behavior, including a reaction to the discriminatory policies suffered by the Mizrahim at the

TABLE 9.3. What Should Israel's Policies Be toward the Arab Citizens?
A Comparison with the General Israeli Jewish Public (Percentage)

	Support in Towns	Support in Israel
1. The Arabs will live in Israel as citizens and accept their position as a non-Jewish minority in a state belonging to the Jews.	50	26
2. The Arabs will live in Israel as a national minority, recognized by the state, and enjoying proportional representation.	16	23
3. The Arabs will live in Israel as a minority with equal civil rights.	14	24
4. The state should make the Arabs live outside Israel.	12	20
5. The Arabs will live in Israel in Arab cantons with autonomy in internal matters.	3	7

hands of Israel's Ashkenazi elites (Smooha 1993) or hostility toward the Arabs based on labor-market competition (Peled 1990, 2001). Most recently, Shenhav (2004) traces the political orientation of the Mizrahim to Zionist practices, both in recruiting Jews in Arab countries and in creating a clear distinction between old (mainly Sephardi religious) and new (mainly Ashkenazi secular) Jewish communities in the Land of Israel. These practices, as well as later state policies in the field of education and public culture, constructed the Mizrahim as mainly religious and nationalist.

The missing links in these explanations are the dynamics of a settler society and the typical ethnoclass stratification produced by the new ethnic geographies of the settlement process. In such a setting, the immigrant group finds itself in constant tension with both indigenous and founding groups. Given its inferior position vis-à-vis the dominant ethnoclass, the immigrant group attempts to minimize the difference between the two groups. But its opposition to ethnic discrimination is complicated by its own ethnic prejudice vis-à-vis indigenous groups. This leads to the adoption of rightist nationalist positions, which attempt to locate the immigrants as political partners to the founding ethnoclass and raise their communal and political status. For the immigrants, then, nationalism constitutes important political capital. Let us now examine respondents' attitudes toward Arab-Jewish relations.

Statements 2, 3, and 5 in Table 9.3 present various variations of dovish orientation (advocating Arab-Jewish reconciliation and equality), while statements 1 and 4 are more hawkish (hard-line control). The first statement is closest to the mainstream Zionist position and is supported by 50 percent of respondents, almost twice as high as in the general Israeli public (based on Smooha 1992). A total of only 33 percent support conciliatory policies toward the Arab citizens, as opposed to 54 percent among the general public. Twelve percent support the extreme right-wing option

TABLE 9.4. What Should the Nature of Permanent Israeli-Palestinian Settlement Be? (Percentage)

	Support in Towns	Israeli Jews*
Keeping the territories with Palestinian autonomy	66	36
Israeli control to the Jordan River	15	30
A Palestinian state within 1967 borders	12	15
Democratic-secular state between river and sea	2	5
Other	5	14

*Based on Arian 1997.

of a transfer—forcing Arab citizens to leave the state—although this was lower than the Israeli mean.

The strong support for a hawkish line in statement 1 is also echoed by responses to a question about Arab and Jewish attachment to the land. The vast majority (79 percent) supported the perception that Israel is only the Jews' homeland, while 21 percent defined it as the shared homeland of Arabs and Jews. Other questions, which explored the settlement and Judaization of Galilee and the Negev, received vast support among respondents, with only 3 percent opposing such ethnocratic policies. These responses attest again to the power of Zionist hegemony, reflecting the unchallenged assumptions that these mixed Arab-Jewish regions are part of a Jewish state and hence should be Judaized. It is likely that the recent shift to the right of Israeli public opinion, following the 2000–2003 al-Aqsa *intifada*, has made this pattern even more conspicuous in the towns.

But the hawkish position prevalent in the towns is relatively moderate, as reflected by several indicators. For example, on the long-term resolution of the Zionist-Palestinian conflict, most respondents expressed opinions corresponding with the centrist and moderate factions of the ruling Likud Party (Table 9.4). The support of more extreme right-wing options, such as Israeli control to the Jordan River, received only 15 percent, being markedly lower than the 30 percent support among the general Israeli Jewish public. Likewise, support of what is perceived as a far-leftist position, namely a Palestinian state in the 1967 borders, was supported by only 12 percent of respondents, constituting only half the national average.

Hence, the position of the Mizrahim can be described as moderate right—they support preserving the inferior status of the Arab citizens and Israel's continued control over Palestinian territories, with Palestinian autonomy. Full Palestinian independence and equality for Israel's Palestinian-Arab citizens received only marginal support. This nationalist orientation—typical of lower, middle-class, immigrant settlers—forms an important backbone to their national, religious, and ethnic identities.

It may be useful to return briefly to the broader settler-society perspective and to echo Said's (1992) insights into the pervasive stigmatization of indigenous cultures by the discourses and practices of settling groups. In order to weaken resistance to the colonizing efforts and to legitimize the colonial dispossessing process in the eyes of the settlers, Zionism has systematically worked to demote and marginalize Arab Islamic culture, which was portrayed as backward, primitive, corrupt, lazy, and at the same time, dangerous and cruel (see Shohat 1997). This construction trapped the Mizrahim—themselves a product of Arab and Islamic societies—in a position of weakness and susceptibility to the overt dictates of dominant Ashkenazi Zionist culture. Castells (1997) observes that such marginalization is often the platform for the surfacing of resistant identities, which are shaped in opposition to dominant frameworks of power in order to unsettle and transform society.

However, the domination-opposition dialectic, which moves between total acceptance of the dominant identity to complete rejection, does not provide a satisfactory account of the Mizrahim's identity dynamics given their position as members inside the ethnocratic settling project. As mentioned, it is a third space of hybrid identities, which combine elements of dominant and marginal cultures, that explains the position of the Mizrahim. Yet, as Bhabha (1994) shows, identity in the third space is never settled because the power dynamic, which constitutes this metaphysical and real space, prohibits the possibilities of full integration or total separation.

To investigate these dynamics in greater depth, and to penetrate below the surface of declaratory political or identity positions, the Mizrahim in the towns were asked in more detail about their cultural preferences. Here the main issue is between the ever present temptation of assimilation and the desire to maintain an ethnic identity. Both forces are evident in the protocols of every immigrant community, including large and spatially concentrated groups such as the Mizrahim in the development towns.

Cultural Preferences

In attempting to pinpoint cultural preferences, a list was prepared of key personalities in key cultural fields, each symbolizing specific orientation and association with other groups in Israel. Respondents were asked to identify three of the ten personalities toward which they feel affinity and affection. This revealed a wide range of cultural preferences (within the limits of the lists prepared) whose emerging pattern would then sketch the towns' collective cultural orientation (Figure 9.6).

By and large, cultural preferences in the towns, especially among the younger generation, are relatively close to the Israeli Jewish mainstream. The most popular musicians, authors, and public personalities generally come from the established (mainly Ashkenazi) circles of Israeli society. To illustrate, singers such as Arik Einstein and Nurit Galron, and songwriters Naomi Shemer and Ehud Manor, who represent Western-oriented cultural

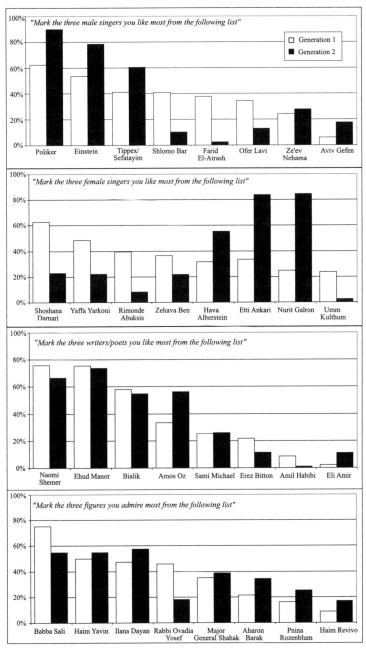

Source: Field survey.

Figure 9.6. Cultural Preferences and Collective Orientations

elements dominant in Zionist society, all ranked very high. Likewise, Haim Yavin and Ilana Dayan—two prominent Ashkenazi television personalities—and Major General Amnon Shahak (at the time the IDF's chief of staff) were ranked very high by the towns' residents. The dominance of Ashkenazi Israeli culture is perhaps most prominent among writers: beside Shemer and Manor, respondents also ranked highly Haim Nachman Bialik and Amos Oz, again, two prominent Ashkenazi authors.

Yet, as noted above, the cultural pattern is more complex, displaying a diversity of orientations in almost every category. Among the writers we also find Mizrahim such as Sami Michael and Erez Bitton, each receiving reasonable support. The pattern was more prominent among musicians, with Etti Ankri, Yehuda Poliker, and Tippex[1] (with popular lead singer Kobbi Oz) ranked very highly. These represent Mizrahi singers who write and sing about the country's social peripheries, using mainly Western-style music, with occasional Mizrahi tunes. While these singers have entered the Israeli mainstream and hence are popular among the general public, their selection also indicates affection for local artists and especially for those emerging from the development towns, such as Etti Ankri (who grew up in Ramla) and Kobbi Oz (who hails from Sderot).

Solid, if not overwhelming support is also given to artists using Mizrahi music, and combining elements of Western and Eastern styles. Shlomo Bar, Zehava Ben, and Ofer Levi are among the leading musicians of this genre. Among the singers we should also observe the low ranking of Aviv Gefen, a popular rock-pop singer among Israel's young generation (himself Ashkenazi and linked closely with the Tel Aviv music scene). His low ranking may be linked to towns' general aversion to conspicuous markers of Ashkenazi elitist culture, as was observed earlier with the perceived alienation between the development towns and places such as Ramat Aviv and Sheinkin.

The intergenerational differences in cultural preferences were found to be more consistent and distinct ($0.05 > \alpha$) than any other intergenerational comparison (Figure 9.6). The findings of the comparison show a clear tendency of the younger generation to prefer personalities and artists identified with the local Israeli output, less with the Mizrahi canon, and above all not with Arab artists. There is a clear tendency of the younger generation to prefer artists and figures identified with the Israeli mainstream, represented, as noted, by Arik Einstein, Yehuda Poliker, Nurit Galron, and Hava Alberstein, and prominent figures such as Major General Shahak, the president of the Supreme Court, Aharon Barak, and the celebrity Pnina Rozenblum. Their sympathy for Tippex shows a wish to exit marginality and approach the center by combining local and international cultural components. It is also related to the general success enjoyed by Tippex, currently one of the leading Israeli pop groups.

By contrast, members of the older generation display two major trends: first, a greater affinity for the main pillars of Zionist culture; and second, ongoing attachment to Mizrahi Arab culture. The firm link to Zionist culture is illustrated by the very high support given to Arik Einstein, Shoshana Damari, and Yaffa Yarkoni—all linked to the main building blocks of Zionist culture. The high ranking of Damari combines the support of mainstream culture with the Yemenite-Mizrahi flavor of Damari's music, making her the most popular singer among the first generation. Links to the Mizrahi and Arab cultures are also reflected in the relatively high ranking of Shlomo Bar, a Moroccan Israeli singer who has imported North African music and popularized it in Israel. Arab cultural icons, such as legendary Egyptian singers Umm Kulthum and Farid al-Atrash, and author Amil Habibi, did not rank high, but their mere existence among the favorites, in the face of systematic stigmatization of Arab culture in Israel, is worthy of mention.

These patterns point again to the partial effectiveness of the Israeli strategy of ingathering of the exiles. Immigrant cultural transformation, while evident, is rarely complete. Indeed, pockets of Mizrahi and Arab cultures surface time and again, even among the younger generation. The making of a hybrid third space is perhaps most prominently evident by the high ranking, among both first and second generations, of the late Baba Sali, the famous rabbi and *tzadik* (man of virtue). Beginning in the 1970s, Baba Sali made himself a focal point for local-popular-religious culture, drawing on the North African blessing tradition. Baba Sali (now replaced by his successor-son Baba Baruch) forms a prominent node of local-religious-ethnic identification, highlighting the emergence of new forms of Jewish ethnicities standing both inside and outside Israeli culture and thriving on the social and geographical periphery.

Clearly, these cultural preferences should not be analyzed in isolation, as if culture is a set of pure, stylistic orientations. Rather, as Jackson (2000) well explains, culture is always embedded in material, spatial, and power relations, expressed in our case by the cultural oppression of the Mizrahim during the 1950s, their geographical marginalization, and their economic dependence. While cultural oppression denied the validity and worthiness of many Mizrahi-Arab cultural values and practices, the geographical segregation, paradoxically, worked to preserve that culture. Hence we can discern a somewhat confused cultural mixture and an incomplete, ambiguous process of identity transformation.

It must also be noted that other immigrant groups arriving in Israel during the late 1940s and 1950s also suffered from a policy of cultural erasure, especially Holocaust survivors from Eastern Europe. However, they were far closer to the dominant Ashkenazi Israeli culture, housed in more favorable locations, and received more substantial economic support than the Mizrahim. Further, because their traditional culture was never stigmatized to the same extent as Mizrahi culture, they were able to integrate more successfully into the Israeli mainstream (see Segev 1999). The situation appears to be quite different in regard to the mass wave of immigrants from the ex-Soviet Union during the 1990s. Here, tolerance in Israeli society appears to have increased, and the Russian culture, which was never seen as directly threatening Israeliness, was allowed to thrive and integrate into Israeli society (see al-Haj and Leshem 2000; Kimmerling, 2001).

In this comparative vein, the plight of Mizrahim in other locations should be mentioned. As well shown by Weingrod (1995) and Lewin-Epstein, Elmelech, and Semyonov (1997), housing location was a key factor in determining the material success of second-generation Mizrahim, favoring those residing in Israel's main cities, especially the Tel Aviv and Haifa metropolitan regions. Benski (1993) also shows that the combination of class and special factors created a ladder in which the upper steps are characterized by Ashkenazi networks prominent in Israel's main urban centers, the bottom steps are Mizrahim at the peripheries, and the middle steps are where the two groups assimilate, chiefly in Israel's growing suburban rings.

Seemingly, the imposition of a new ethnic identity appears to be one of the main victories of the Zionist ethnocratic project. The creation of this new identity involved the de-Arabization of the Mizrahim, the near total erasure of their cultures (Shohat 1997), the nationalization of their politics, and their assimilation into Israel's economy and expanding middle class (Smooha 1993). But as Benski (1993) and Yonah (2001) show, Mizrahi identity has been preserved at the social and economic peripheries, not as a distinct cultural orientation but as a diffused sense of origin and solidarity fueled by persisting marginality and hardship.

Hence, the oppressive nature of the Zionist project appears to have partially backfired on the Ashkenazi founders, who left space for the legitimate expression of Mizrahi identity and community. The third space created between host and original cultures turned hostile to the dominant Ashkenazi group. The Mizrahim, not assimilated into Israel's middle class, channel their frustration and mobilization power into a variety of protest, political, and cultural movements, most notably the religious-ethnic movement Shas (for details see Peled 1990, 2001; Dahan-Kalev 2000; Shalom-Chetrit 2000). Much of the energy fueling these movements is rooted in negative sentiments toward the Ashkenazi elites. These sentiments are still evident at the beginning of the twenty-first century and are a major factor in the inability of Israel's dominant (and mainly Ashkenazi) classes to make political and social coalitions (or partnerships/associations) with the mass Mizrahi electorate at the periphery.

It can also be suggested that the spectacular success of the Shas movement in the development towns during the 1990s lies precisely in its ability to offer a way around the Mizrahi entrapment by developing identities and politics that bypass the ethnocratic-Ashkenazi logic of Israeli society. However, even Shas is not building a Mizrahi project but rather emphasizes the religious (Sephardi Orthodox) orientation of the Mizrahim. In this way it manages to penetrate the Israeli power centers with the legitimizing force of Judaism, which forms an effective basis for gaining state resources. Thus, Shas provides a broad base for political mobilization by linking communal and economic frustrations with the religious components of Mizrahi culture, previously repressed in Israel. But Shas, too, is careful not to build an explicit ethnic-cultural project of "Mizrahiness" (*Mizrahiyut* in Hebrew, meaning open Mizrahi cultural orientation), which still has no legitimacy in Israel. This is illustrated by its refusal to adopt the Mizrahi identity, preferring instead the more religious Sephardi label.

"Dust Heights" as a Conclusion

The song "Dust Heights," whose lyrics appear below, was written in the mid-1990s by Kobbi Oz, the leader of Tippex who is from the development town Sderot. The song provides a telling conclusion for this chapter; by articulating the pain of the rejected, the marginalized, and the forsaken it connects to the next chapter, which deals with public protest. This ironic song begins with a country-western tune and moves gradually into a soft Arab-Mizrahi warble. The lyrics scorn and tease the empty promises attached to one of Zionism's highest values—the settlement of the frontier. With irony and sadness, Oz points to the role of the Mizrahim—not hero settlers but downtrodden, helpless immigrants thrown into the desolate periphery.

Yet, despite the protest expressed in the song, it is not militant or confrontational but rather resembles a biblical lament—sad and quiet—with empathy to the people whose unfortunate fate made them outcasts in "Dust Heights." There, in the desert, the Mizrahim conduct their daily, difficult lives and continue to long for a fulfillment of a dream. Which dream? Apparently not the original messianic dream of redemption, nor the Zionist dream of settling the frontier, but now a dream of getting on the road from nowhere to the coveted heart of the Israeli mainstream. In the midst of these conflicting sentiments of frustration, marginality, and lure of inclusion lies the ultimate Israeli third space—the development town.

Dust Heights
It's not impressive, the ministers thought.
There are empty patches on the map,
Down there a settlement is missing.
So the powers send an order down:
"We'll build a town
And bring some people
So they fill with their lives all the new houses."

It's good, plenty of dots on the maps
And the media promised good exposure.
So the ministers ordered in a sleepy voice
And went to look for other "emergencies."

A second-rate clerk made the distance
To announce the opening of the new town called
Dust Heights . . . dust . . . dust . . . dust . . .

In Dust Heights at dusk
People gather along the central path,
Remembering dreams of the forsaken
Solidarity of the downtrodden.

They paved a road, black and narrow,
Cutting deep into the desert.
At the edge, they built some homes
As if they threw around match boxes.
Coffee shops with drunken men
And others just locked up at home
And each and every one just dreams
About a day they will get on the road to/from nowhere.

In Dust Heights at dusk
People gather along the central path,
Remembering dreams of the forsaken
Solidarity of the downtrodden.
(Oz 1995)

Chapter 10

Between Local and National: Mobilization in the Mizrahi Peripheries

This chapter builds on the analysis of Mizrahi identity and sense of place presented in the previous chapter to study other central elements—public protest and political mobilization—in the making of Mizrahi communities in the towns and in Israeli society. Mizrahi mobilization in the towns emerged against a background of geographical marginality, persisting deprivation, and demographic instability. A recent period of mass immigration from the former Soviet Union coupled with repeated economic crises associated with Israel's globalizing, neoliberal, economic policies has further destabilized the towns.

This chapter focuses on two central arenas of collective mobilization: extraparliamentary protest and local election campaigns. These provide useful vantage points from which to examine the changing patterns of mobilization and identity. Notably, different voices are raised in the two arenas: public protest is aimed outside, to the ethnocratic state and its loci of power, while local election campaigns are aimed inside, to the local community.

The chapter shows that the public protest by Mizrahim in the towns has voiced demands for a fairer share of Israel's public resources, falling within the legitimate boundaries of the (Zionist) ethnocratic discourse. In local election campaigns, however, the Mizrahim have often raised a more combative political voice, focusing on competition against the large number of Russian immigrants who arrived during the 1990s. Local election campaigns often digressed from the boundaries of accepted Zionist discourse by questioning the core ethnocratic values of immigrant absorption and population dispersal. What explains the different agendas and discourses?

I argue that the nature of political mobilization is rooted in the intertwined influences of place, identity, and class. The dynamic role of place is a central point in my analysis. It emerges as a major source of communal identity and political power, constantly reshaped through social processes (see Agnew 1987; Massey 1996; Paasi 2000). Further, place and identity are composed of several layers, most notably national and local. The former pertains to the formation of the Israeli-Zionist nation and the critical role of the development towns in the ethnocratic expansion of Jewish space, whereas the latter focuses more on the actual town and may be indifferent to national imperatives.

While the towns were created as peripheral and impoverished places in the attempt to Judaize the land, they have also become a significant—and threatened—ethnic and political resource. The Mizrahi voice is thus pitched differently at the two arenas: it demands resources from the state and economic forces, while attempting to maintain control over the local turf. Hence, my examination also reveals some cracks in the Zionist nation-building project: Mizrahi Jews in the periphery are developing alternative outlooks and voices (especially, but not only, ultra-Orthodox Sephardi), which aim to transform the nature of Zionism from within, while using the development towns as a major source of power. This has yet to present an open challenge to the Ashkenazi-dominated Israeli state, but the level of consent awarded to state dictates is gradually declining.

A basic assumption underlying this chapter holds that the goals of an eth-noclass and its identities are constantly reshaped by material and political circumstances. At each time/space configuration, an ethnic group will make use of what it considers to be the correct identity to advance its interests through public mobilization. This is particularly salient when an immigrant group resides in a community whose ethnicity is regarded as having a low social status—and especially a group whose identity, I contend, is trapped at the margins of an ethnocratic settler society.

The connection between patterns of mobilization for protest in development towns and the entrapment of their Mizrahim is central to the claims of this chapter. As already discussed in the last chapter, trapped identities emerge in the gray areas between the centers of authority and wealth and the excluded margins. Trapped communities have few alternative paths for identity development or political mobilization except the oppressive structure established by the state. The main open option is inclusion at the national center, but this comes at a heavy price of structural inferiority (see Swirski 1989; Shohat 2001).[1] However, no group would accept a trapped position as final and would search for ways to undermine the oppressive setting. Such an attempt is likely to emerge first on a local level, when interests are immediate and concrete. It is on the local level that the group may begin to exploit small cracks in the national hegemony.

To substantiate these claims, the chapter reports on two research projects. The first focused on acts of public protest in the towns, while the second studied local election campaigns. The first analysis explores the position of peripheral Mizrahim in the national place, identity, and politics, while the latter examines their mobilization in the local urban turf, particularly vis-à-vis the large influx of Russian-speaking immigrants in recent years. Prior to giving a detailed account of development town mobilization, I will outline some of my theoretical approaches.

Ethnic Mobilization and Protest

Substantive literature exists on ethnic mobilization and protest (for reviews, see Blumer and Solomon 2001; Gurr 1993). In this chapter, I draw briefly on three major approaches[2] most appropriate to the study of peripheral Mizrahim: relative deprivation, resource competition, and the politics of identity.

Relative deprivation is defined by Gurr (1970) as a gap between expectations (or sense of entitlement) and capabilities within a given political system. Changes in the social, political, or demographic structure can widen the gap between expectations and capabilities, leading to dissatisfaction, a sense of relative deprivation, competition for resources, and political mobilization. A sense of deprivation often fosters tensions between the group and state authorities. This plays itself out as a competition over economic, cultural, spatial, and political resources (Esses et al. 2001). Economically, this creates competition for housing (Barkan 1986; Johnston 1982; Knox 1982) and jobs (Olzak 1992; Bonacich 1972). Beyond these, the conflict over political resources is associated with an ability to organize both within the system, typically through voting, and outside it, in mobilizing extraparliamentary protest (Taylor 1993; Nagel 1986).

Protest by deprived minorities can range from rhetoric to violence. The groups adopting a strategy of militant or violent protest are usually homeland ethnic minorities or indigenous peoples. In contrast, immigrant groups usually adopt less militant strategies, their identity is more malleable, and hence the threat they pose to the established order is less acute (see Yiftachel 2001b).[3] Gurr and Harff (1994) note that immigrant mobilization often emanates from an ethnoclass identity, highlighting the link between ethnic origins, current material conditions, and political mobilization (Gurr and Harff 1994).

The politics of identity extends the theory of deprivation to mobilization aimed at nonmaterial gains. The politics of identity, above all, seeks to achieve recognition (Taylor 1995). This refers not only to accepting one's own identity, but to having others acknowledge the collective as different (Fincher and Jacobs 1998). At the same time, the politics of identity seeks to gain power on the basis of collective identity. This transforms collective identities into a resource for organizing and mobilizing political support, particularly in cases of collective deprivation (Herzog 1994).

The politics of identity intensifies at times of structural change, such as the entry of a substantial group with a different ethnicity, culture, language, or occupation. The multiplicity of identities in one location fosters the politics of identity, as groups and individuals become aware of the mo-bilizing potential of ethnic difference (Fincher and Jacobs 1998; Jackson and Penrose 1993). To enhance its power, each community mobilizes its members through the construction of difference as a convenient platform for reinforcing ethnic and racial solidarity. This does not take place in iso-lation but by groups in constant relation with other groups and interests (Comaroff and Comaroff 2000; Wilmsen 1996).

The politics of identity is also based on a sense of belonging to a place, since—beyond the ethnic culture—this is the resource most available to those organizing ethnic protest. During this process, local identities are created or renewed, reflected in phrases such as "my neighborhood," "my community," "my city," "my school," and "my turf." These identities attach themselves to the familiar and the spatial, in opposition to processes of globalization, which threaten uncertainty and fragmentation (Castells 1997).

Ethnic political mobilization can also be achieved via institutionalized mechanisms, such as political parties or other social movements. In frag-mented party systems, such as Israel's, ethnicity and place are major bases for rallying political support. This is especially true when the ethnic candidate or party promises benefits to group members—jobs in the public sector or an "open door" to public officials. Accordingly, the group homogeneity vot-ing model assumes that voters who belong to certain ethnic groups tend to vote for a party or candidate of the same ethnicity, especially if that group is relatively small and distinct from the rest of the population spatially, cultur-ally, and socially. The more an ethnic group maintains its distinct identity and religious or cultural institutions, the more likely its members will vote the same way. In contrast, if and when an ethnic group becomes assimilated into the general community, it is less likely to exhibit uniform voting pat-terns, even when ethnicity remains a symbolic general basis for group iden-tity and mobilization (Landa, Copelano, and Grofman 1995).

The mobilization of immigrants in Israel must also be set against their role and position in the Israeli ethnocracy, which has placed the Mizrahim, as already observed, in a twilight zone, being both within the Zionist proj-ect and positioned on its peripheries. The ambiguity of immigrant marginalization-inclusion is typical to settler-immigrant societies and trans-forms them into an ethnoclass (or a cluster of ethnoclasses) situated be-tween the founders and the indigenous. In due course, other immigrant groups join the project and create new axes of ethnoclass tensions and struggles. Through this spatial-economic process, immigrants become trapped, as it were, between the founding group to which they cannot eas-ily join and the excluded natives. Their identity thus develops at several si-multaneous layers (see Yuval-Davis 2000)—a quest for full integration with the founders at the national arena alongside an emphasis on difference at a local level. We turn now to the case itself.

Mobilization in the Development Towns

The Creation of a Mizrahi Ethnoclass

The development towns built by Israel during the 1950s and 1960s are the setting for this chapter. The towns became the main tool for implementing the policy of (Jewish) population dispersal and creating a Jewish majority in the Galilee and the Negev. Between 1953 and 1963, twenty-seven development towns were established as medium-sized peripheral urban centers. The towns were populated through the provision of public housing to (mainly Mizrahi) homeless and dependent immigrants who had little other residential choices (Efrat 1989; Lewin-Epstein, Elmelech, and Semyonov 1997; Tzfadia 2000). Most of the few Ashkenazim sent to the towns found their way to the center of the country, leaving the Mizrahim behind in the development towns.

Thus, paradoxically, the concept of population dispersal undermined another central concept of the Zionist project, the ingathering of the exiles, as the segregated new towns were virtually entirely populated by Mizrahi immigrants (Tzfadia 2002a). Over the years, these immigrants were subject not only to social, political, and cultural marginalization but were also at an acute economic disadvantage (Etkin 2002). The economic profile of all the towns relied on heavy and traditional industries, cheap labor, and constant job instability (Razin 1996; Gradus and Einy 1984; Gradus and Krakover 1977). The existence of towns distinctively inferior to mainstream Jewish-Israeli society and a common patronizing behavior toward the Mizrahim spawned widespread sentiments of alienation and social marginality (Shohat 2001).

The underdevelopment of the towns therefore contributed significantly to the persisting gap between Ashkenazim and Mizrahim in Israel, as analyzed in Chapters 5 and 6. This phenomenon generated various scholarly accounts. One perspective, drawn from neo-Marxist thought, views the settlement of Mizrahim in development towns as a pool of cheap labor for the rapidly growing Israeli economy (Shafir and Peled 1998; Bernstein and Swirski 1982). A complementary analysis regards the establishment of development towns as a means used by the dominant Ashkenazi group to advance the ethnocratic territorial goals of Zionism. In other words, by transforming the Mizrahim into a settlement force, the territorial interests of the dominant ethnoclass were served, creating a Jewish majority in previously Arab regions. During the process, these regions were also transformed from glorified frontiers to stigmatized peripheries (Hasson 1998). At the same time, the distancing of Mizrahim from the economic and political centers enabled the dominant Ashkenazi group to maintain its dominance, in different ways, over both Mizrahim and Palestinians (Swirski 1989). How did these circumstances affect the patterns of protest of Mizrahim from development towns?

PUBLIC PROTEST

The analysis covers 1960–98, during which 345 acts of protest took place in development towns (see Figures 10.1, 10.2).[4] Public protest in the towns has been relatively persistent and consistent, if not intense. Apart from one exceptionally active year (1989), public protest remained without the volatility and direct challenge to the settler-ethnocratic regime. This stands in contrast to far more intensive and often fluctuating levels in nearly all other organized sectors of Israeli society, notably the Arab citizens and Jewish settlers (Herman 1996; Lehman-Wilzig 1990). The relative detachment of the towns from the major political struggles of Israeli society was conspicuous in the early 1970s, when the Black Panthers movement mobilized many Mizrahim, especially in Jerusalem's poor neighborhoods, but managed to rally only scant support in the towns.

What about the fluctuations in protest? These, I found, were almost entirely influenced by two related factors: macroeconomic conditions and public policies. We can observe waves of protest surfacing during every period of economic hardship and restructuring in Israel, which usually hits peripheral groups hardest. This occurred during the mid-1960s, the late 1970s, the mid-1980s, the late 1980s, and the mid-1990s, when many demonstrations, rallies, and media activities in the towns objected, at times fiercely, to the rise in unemployment, the decline in services, and the emigration from the towns during these periods. And conversely, during periods of government investment in the towns and growth in local employment, such as the early 1980s (when a neighborhood renewal project was established in development towns), or

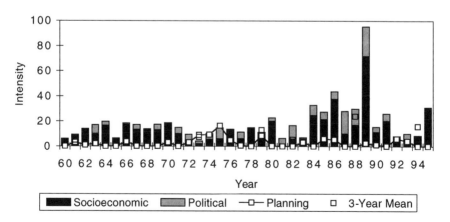

Figure 10.1. Protest Intensity in Development Towns, 1960–95

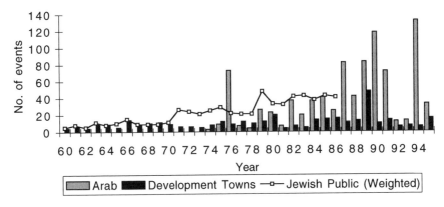

Figure 10.2. Public Protest in Israeli Sectors

the early 1990s (the massive building for Russian immigrants), the towns remained relatively calm.

What did peripheral Mizrahim mobilize against? Despite the large number of events in and about the towns, I discovered that the range of issues has been quite narrow. The findings show that protest in development towns focused primarily on economic themes, especially employment and wages: 62 percent of the acts of protest dealt with economic issues, 22 percent with political issues, 11 percent with planning issues, and 5 percent with other issues.

The narrow focus of protest is especially conspicuous in comparison to other groups in Israeli society who have campaigned on a range of matters pertaining to the national agenda, including Israel's relations with Germany; Arab-Israeli wars; the occupation and settlement of Palestinian territories; nature protection; and religious-secular, Mizrahi-Ashkenazi, and Arab-Jewish relations within Israel; as well as matters pertaining to resource distribution and service provision (Lehman-Wilzig 1990). This relatively limited focus and the consistent shunning of topics considered ideological illustrates the entrapment of peripheral Mizrahim within the Israeli settling ethnocracy. This setting silenced their voices on issues at the base of the oppressive system and gave them only limited options with which to challenge their marginal position, leading to the emergence of a fairly docile ethnoclass identity.

The virtual absence of public objection among peripheral Mizrahim against continuing Jewish settlement in the occupied territories is striking. This has clearly deprived the towns of material and human resources. Instead of objecting to ongoing settlement activity, the Development

Towns Forum (an umbrella forum of mayors often voicing the towns' collective concerns) accepted towns from the occupied territories (Ariel, Ma'ale Edumim, and Katzrin) into its ranks, thereby indicating indirect support for the continuation of Jewish settlement. Why do leaders of towns support further Jewish settlement activity? This, I suggest, reflects the dependent and insecure position of peripheral Mizrahim within the Israeli ethnocracy, cornering them to take a territorial-nationalistic and pro-settlement (that is, anti-Palestinian) position. This impedes their ability to voice opposition and challenge policies that clearly affect them adversely.

This collective identity, as also observed in the previous chapter, is marked by a strong desire to assimilate and integrate into the core Israeli culture, a pervasive feeling of deprivation vis-à-vis the national center, and a drive for improving the towns' low socioeconomic position. These factors, especially economic deprivation and social alienation, have recently given rise to a range of political movements, which promote local patriotism and especially Mizrahi Jewishness (Ben-Ari and Bilu 1987). Most notable has been the successful ultra-Orthodox Shas movement (Peled 2001; Shalom-Chetrit 2004).

Returning to the topic of protest, why did Mizrahim in the towns avoid raising ideological and controversial issues? Moreover, why did no significant political opposition emerge from the deprived towns? I point to Mizrahi entrapment within Jewish settler society as the key explanation. The Jewish settling ethnocracy institutionalized the superiority of the Ashkenazim in most spheres of society, creating a dependency of the Mizrahi ethnoclass on the Ashkenazi center. Thus, we should view the issues of public protest not through the narrow lens of protest and its motivations, but within the broader context of a society that is fractured and stratified in both class and ethnic terms. This society was built by a powerful Zionist-Ashkenazi hegemony, which has worked to overlap Zionism, Israeliness, and Ashkenazi identity. This power structure undermined every attempt to challenge its legitimacy and left no alternative other than protest against the discrimination and deprivation in the distribution of material resources.

In overview, the nature of public protest reflects a profound transformation of identity on a national-state level: from peripheral ethnicity or ethnicities to a *deprived ethnoclass*. This transformation has occurred under the force of the settling Jewish (de-Arabizing) ethnocracy, which has wiped out Mizrahi culture while settling Mizrahim in frontier regions, thus spawning the emergence of a relatively uniform, marginalized (and mainly Mizrahi), ethnoclass in the towns and across the state. In other words, the identity of peripheral Mizrahim as reflected in their protest activities is most identifiable in terms of their national peripheral socioeconomic and geographical position, and not through a distinct cultural or ideological stand. This, as we shall see, changes in the local arena, where we focus on local electioneering.

Here the new immigrants from the former Soviet Union (the Russians) provide a major focus.

Structural Change: Russians in the Development Towns

Some 911,000 immigrants from the former Soviet Union arrived in Israel from late 1989 until the end of 2001 (Ministry of Immigrant Absorption 2002). Like most previous waves of immigrants, the majority of Russians did not arrive in Israel for ideological reasons but to improve their security and quality of life (al-Haj and Leshem 2000). The economic and social beliefs of immigrants were the product of Communist socialization but also of exposure to Western culture after the disintegration of the Soviet Union (Lissak and Leshem 2001). The will of the Israeli elites to absorb such a large mass of immigrants is related to their (Zionist) desire to maintain Jewish majority over the Palestinians, to their aspiration to preserve a secular majority over a growing ultra-Orthodox population, and to their wish to reinforce the country's European culture. In these senses, the arrival of the Russian immigrants served primarily the interests of the secular Ashkenazim.

Unlike previous waves of immigrants, the Russians arrived in Israel when capitalist and individualist values were on the ascendancy. This created some space for norms that are different from, though not contradictory to, the core Zionist ideology and eroded the collective will to instill a uniform national culture (Kimmerling 2001). Instead, higher importance was placed on providing the immigrants with housing and employment. This was reflected in a new policy labeled direct absorption, whereby an immigrant is awarded a package of benefits and financial aid for a limited period to cover all social and housing needs. This is vastly different from the absorption policy prevailing during the 1950s and 1960s, when the state directed immigrants to public housing and prearranged employment (Hasson 1992).

But the government remained a key actor, shaping the location of immigrant absorption through the construction of large-scale projects of affordable housing and employment at the state peripheries, especially in the development towns (Tzfadia 2000). These policies contributed to the settlement in the towns of some 130,000 Russians, many of economically and socially disadvantaged backgrounds (CBS-a 1998). The rapid growth brought about not only an increase in the towns' populations but also significant changes in their ethnic composition. Spatially, most of the Russians settled in new neighborhoods, which became spaces distinct from the older urban sections and sometimes constitute a town within a town. Demographically, the towns lost their distinct Mizrahi character and at present accommodate 25–40 percent Russians (Tzfadia 2000).

The pattern of isolationism-integration adopted by the immigrants contributed greatly to creating a distinct social category—the Russians.

Although most of these immigrants came from a variety of subcultures, some from Asia and others from Europe, the great majority speak Russian and tend to see themselves as belonging to this category. Above all, this is how they are perceived and categorized by mainstream Israeli society. Thus, clear ethnic and cultural boundaries were drawn around the new immigrants, who emerge as a distinct group within an increasingly multi-cultural Israel (Kimmerling 2001).

These boundaries were accepted and reinforced by the founding of two immigrant political parties with a clear Russian character—Yisrael b'Aliyah (Israel in immigration/ascendance) and Yisrael Beitenu (Israel our home). The two parties (and especially the former) performed well in national elections, attesting to the success of the Russians in acquiring political power as a distinct group (see Figure 10.3). The success of the parties also demonstrates their ability to convert their numbers and organizational skills into political power in order to maximize their access to resources and budgets, which were also used to buttress the ethnic walls (Kimmerling 2001).

Figure 10.3, which documents the fluctuation in support of national-level parties, demonstrates the constantly shifting waves of political domination in the towns. Until the 1970s, the Labor bloc was dominant, replaced by Likud during the 1980s and early 1990s, and then by the religious-Mizrahi bloc (strongly headed by Shas with less, but constant, support for the NRP—the National Religious Party, or the Mafdal) in the late 1990s. In the wake of the violent al-Aqsa *intifada*, which brought to the fore national issues at

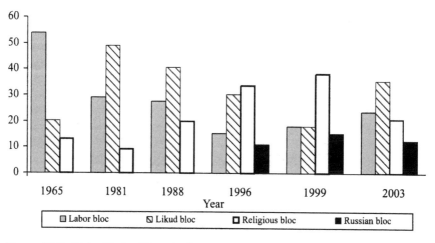

Figure 10.3. Major Voting Blocs in the Development Towns, 1965–2003 (Percentage)

the expense of sectoral-ethnic concerns, the Likud returned to a position of dominance during the 2003 elections, although the religious-Mizrahi and Russian blocs have remained significant. These figures show that over the years the towns' residents have constantly voiced frustration toward and disappointment in their political leadership, which has caused them to shift their political loyalties. The figures also demonstrate the recent structural change in towns' politics and the rise of ethnic politics as reflected in local elections and discussed below.

The encounter in development towns between the two social groups—the Russians and the Mizrahim—quickly led to competition over economic resources, which were already in short supply. This competitive drive was intensified by a sense of relative deprivation among the Mizrahim in light of the benefits bestowed upon the Russians, such as housing assistance (in new neighborhoods), tax breaks, and help in finding jobs, and a feeling that Israeli society is more indulgent toward Russian culture than it ever was toward Mizrahi immigrants. The Mizrahim have also observed that the housing benefits for the Russians are in excess of what they, the veterans, receive at present.

Welfare services became a major arena of contest in the early stages of absorption. The direct absorption policy decentralized the absorption functions, which had previously been handled by the central government, leaving most of the absorption work to the local authorities, including the provision of welfare services. The gap between demand and supply led to competition over the available services from the earliest stages of absorption. Later, the Mizrahim and Russians began to compete over employment, which has been notoriously scarce in the development towns (Lipshitz 1992). The struggle over these resources was conducted alongside other efforts of cooperation. It illuminated to both groups the importance of control over place as a means of acquiring not only economic but also political and cultural resources. The next section deals with control of place as reflected in local voting and electioneering.

LOCAL ELECTIONS

I begin by comparing statewide local election results in 1989, 1993, and 1998.[5] Later, this section focuses on the Mizrahi-Russian tension during the elections in two development towns in the southern periphery of Israel—Ofakim and Kiryat Gat.[6]

In most local elections, Israel's many political parties combined into several main blocs: Labor;[7] Likud;[8] Russian immigrant parties, local parties, small national parties, and religious parties. The religious bloc is divided into Shas—a Mizrahi ultra-Orthodox party founded in the 1980s following a split within the ultra-Orthodox circles between Mizrahim and Ashkenazim—and other religious parties.

The municipal council elections held on November 10, 1998 brought to a climax a number of dynamics that had begun in Israel in the 1980s, including the diminished power for the large parties and increased support for sectoral, ethnic, local, or independent parties (Goldberg 2001). In development towns, however, these processes were particularly salient, as the boundaries between the sectors were clearer and personal familiarity with the candidates carried greater weight, if only because these are small towns.

As can be noted from Figure 10.4, the key dynamics in the development towns were as follows. There was a significant drop in the election of Likud members to the councils—from 30 percent in the 1989 elections, to 22.6 percent in the 1993 elections, to 13.6 percent in the 1998 elections. In parallel, there was a significant drop in support for the Labor Party, especially in the 1993 local elections. In 1993, Labor won an average of 27.9 percent of the municipal council seats, while winning only 13.8 percent of the seats in 1998. In contrast to the diminishing power of the many "mother parties" (usually Likud and Labor, which have affiliated local parties), there was a slight increase in the power of the local parties in comparison to the previous elections in 1993.

In the 1989 elections, the local parties won 28.1 percent of the council seats, 22.3 percent in 1993, and 26.2 percent in 1998.[9] More importantly, the local parties became the dominant bloc in most councils, indicating the *increased importance of place* over national or statewide political concerns. Nevertheless, the local bloc is also rather fragmented and hence often ineffective. Together with increased support for the local parties was a sharp increase in the power of the Russian immigrant bloc, which captured 13.9 percent of all the municipal council seats in development towns. This achievement turned the immigrant bloc into the third largest, after the local and religious blocs. The immigrant bloc is composed primarily of Yisrael b'Aliyah, the national immigrant party, but also Yisrael Beitenu and other local Russian parties. The great homogeneity of the immigrant bloc enhanced its power, in contrast to the splintered power of the local parties and the partial fragmentation of the religious parties (Shas, Agudat Israel,[10] and other religious factions).

The roots of this keen ethnic electoral struggle, beyond the feelings of relative deprivation and competition over resources, relate to the existence of two distinct identities in a small, isolated place. The multiplicity of groups in a small place tends to sharpen the politics of identity and thereby reconstruct and even essentialize difference (Jackson and Penrose 1993). The struggle between Mizrahim and Russians to define which identity will be dominant in the small place is intertwined with the struggle over political power and local resources and is hence shaped by broader fields of influence, which determine distribution of resources and construction of identity.

In the development towns we can discern the existence of two major hegemonic influences. On the one hand, there was an internal-local hegemony, which characterized development towns prior to the municipal council elections, when Mizrahim enjoyed overrepresentation in local decision-making circles and the Russians had almost no voice (in the 1993 local elections, the Russians won 0.7 percent of the seats in the municipal councils even though the Russians comprised more than 25 percent of the towns' population). On the other hand, from a broader perspective of ethnic relations in Israel, the development towns remained in the margin of direct Ashkenazi domination. Some view this setting and interpret state efforts to settle large numbers of Russians in the towns as an attempt to undermine their Mizrahi identity (see Shalom-Chetrit 1999). Therefore, the conflict between veterans and immigrants in elections was also a reflection of the struggle of Mizrahim to protect their spatial bases of political and cultural power in Israel. This was most noticeable in the campaign of the Mizrahi-local movements, to which I shall return.

VETERANS AND IMMIGRANTS: KIRYAT GAT AND OFAKIM

The main tension between Mizrahim and Russians is generated by the desire of the Mizrahim to preserve their overrepresentation in the municipal councils and by the opposition of the Russians to that privilege. As found in previous empirical work, the power of the development town, in the opinion of its Mizrahi residents, derives from its ability to provide a relatively autonomous political space (Yiftachel and Tzfadia 1999). Within this setting, both the Mizrahim and the Russians seek to increase their control over local resources. Unlike the Russians, however, the Mizrahim perceive much of their cultural identity to be linked to the development towns (see Ben-Ari and Bilu 1987; Yiftachel and Tzfadia 1999). In this sense, the local government is perceived as having the ability to protect that identity, reflecting the importance attached to control over place; as Castells notes, protection of cultural identity is related to and organized around a particular territory (Castells 1984).

The intensity of the conflict differed from town to town, in keeping with two main factors: the relative size of the Russian immigrant community and its level of local organization. To illustrate the differences in intensity, two development towns in the south of Israel were selected: Ofakim, which had a low-intensity conflict, and Kiryat Gat, with a high-intensity confrontation. Prior to the arrival of the Russians, the two towns had much in common. Both were established during the 1950s in the southern periphery of Israel in order to Judaize the Negev, function as urban centers for agricultural settlements, and supply housing for Jewish immigrants. Mizrahi Jews mostly populated the two towns, and their economies were based on labor-intensive industrial development.

Typical of peripheral towns, the narrow economic base could not guarantee a decent standard of living. In 1997 the average income of wage earners in Ofakim was 77 percent of the Israeli average, while in Kiryat Gat it reached 80 percent. Other parameters also reflected socioeconomic weakness: a high rate of unemployment, a high rate of out migration, and low educational achievements. However, in the long run some differences emerged between the two towns, reflected in different growth rates, which saw Kiryat Gat reaching a population of 25,400 in 1983 and Ofakim reaching only 12,600. The difference was exacerbated when in 1993 a large Intel plant was established in Kiryat Gat, whereas two years later Ofakim lost one of its major employers, the large Uman textile factory.

The influx of Russian immigrants to Kiryat Gat and Ofakim caused a dramatic change to the towns' ethnic compositions. In December of 2001 the Russians constituted 27 percent of the population in Ofakim and 29 percent in Kiryat Gat (Ministry of Immigrant Absorption 2002). Other indicators show that the groups of immigrants residing in both towns are similar: about 23 percent of the immigrants in the two towns arrived from the Asian republics of the Soviet Union; 25 percent of the adult immigrants have an academic degree certificate, and 25 percent of the immigrants are elderly (sixty-five and over) (CBSa, 1998). The most important data on Russian immigrants in the two towns is that the Russians were conspicuously underrepresented in both local councils until the recent elections.

A major source of tension between the Mizrahim and Russians in the towns is the sense of relative deprivation felt by many Mizrahim. Hava Sultana (herself a Mizrahi) from Ofakim, who headed Veterans and Immigrants: The Hope of Ofakim, a joint party of newcomers and former residents running for the town council, expressed this clearly: "The tension between new immigrants and veteran residents is a product of the discrimination. The immigrants received more than Ofakim residents could attain. . . . It caused unrest . . . expressed as hostility toward them. This feeling grows because this is a small town and there is frequent contact between the two groups. . . . The fact that the new immigrants are foreign, different, is not what caused the frustration and tension. . . ."

In the local election of 1993 Sultana's party won one out of eleven seats on the town council. In both Ofakim and Kiryat Gat, then, the immigrants had negligible representation in the local government (Figures 10.4 and 10.5). However, this situation changed in the 1998 elections, as it became clear that immigrants were the single largest bloc in both towns.

The similarity in relative proportion of the immigrant population in each of these towns does not correlate with the power they gained in local elections. In Ofakim, two immigrant parties ran for the council: Yisrael b'Aliyah, the national immigrant party, and Veterans and Immigrants: The Hope of Ofakim, the joint immigrant-veteran party, headed by Hava Sultana. The Yisrael b'Aliyah Party won 13.3 percent of all the seats in the

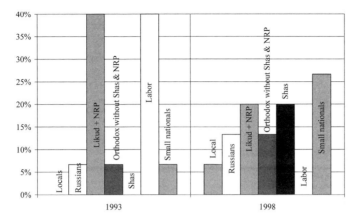

Figure 10.4. Composition of the Municipal Council in Ofakim, 1993 and 1998

council (two out of eleven members) and the joint party did not pass the qualifying threshold required to have a seat in the council.

In Kiryat Gat four immigrant parties competed for the municipal council. Yisrael b'Aliyah, the national party, won 10.5 percent of the council seats (two out of nineteen). Among the three local immigrant parties, Atid Ha'Ir (Future of the city) won 15.8 percent of the vote, or three council seats; the Bukharian party won 10.5 percent of the vote, or two council seats, and Kiryat Gat of the Immigrants did not pass the qualifying threshold. All told, the immigrant parties won seven out of nineteen council seats. More importantly, Alexander Wechsler of the Atid Ha'Ir immigrant party also ran for mayor, garnering 31 percent of all the valid votes, just

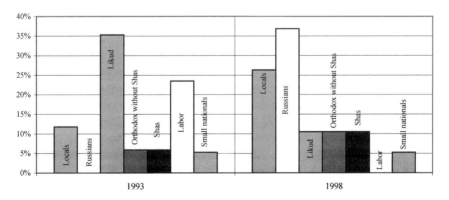

Figure 10.5. Composition of the Municipal Council in Kiryat Gat, 1993 and 1998

behind Albert Erez, the head of a local party called Mifneh (turning point) in Kiryat Gat, who won 34 percent of all the valid votes for mayor. According to Israel's electoral laws, a candidate cannot win an election unless he or she gains at least 40 percent of the vote. This often requires a second round of elections involving the two top candidates, which in this case would have meant that Erez and Wechsler would have had to run again in the second round. However, an unprecedented compromise agreement was signed by Erez and Wechsler on November 16, 1998, which prevented a second round, which would have caused heightened tension and possible violence. The compromise agreement saw Erez continuing as mayor and Wechsler becoming his deputy with new and wide responsibilities.[11]

The elections in Ofakim and Kiryat Gat differed from each other. In Ofakim, almost no tension was evident between the Mizrahim and Russians, as the Russian vote was split. Those immigrants who settled in Ofakim prior to 1993 and the elderly immigrants living in protected housing in a new immigrant neighborhood tended to support the rightist Likud-NRP coalition. This bloc was headed by Yair Hazan, the mayor during the years 1989–93 who was responsible for the absorption of many immigrants. Perhaps it was this function during his first term of office that won him votes of the elderly immigrants in these elections (Hazan was reelected mayor in 1998). Other immigrants supported Yisrael b'Aliyah, which was poorly organized and lacked leadership. The implications of this split among the immigrants can be gleaned from the words of Yair Hazan, the current mayor of Ofakim, who granted an interview on October 2, 1998, about a month before his election:

Because they [the Russians] don't have leadership and the immigrant vote is split . . . they pose no threat to control [of veterans in the Ofakim city government], and therefore there is no ethnic tension in town. . . . Immigrant parties are not trying to undermine the dominance of the Mizrahim, they want to enlarge their share of the local pie. . . . They have no leadership because they are economically and communally weak, with a high percentage of elderly and single parents. . . .

In Kiryat Gat, in contrast, although the immigrants split their vote for the council into three separate parties, they united in support of Alexander Wechsler for mayor. Because of his political experience—he had immigrated to Israel in the 1970s and was active for many years in the Likud Party—Wechsler was able to unite the ranks of immigrants. Despite his declarations that his party represents veterans as well as immigrants, the Mizrahim called it the Russian party. To rally immigrant support, Wechsler stressed the division between the veterans and the immigrants, with emphasis on the distress of the newcomers. In other words, Wechsler took advantage of political ethnicity to gain power. In one of his speeches, Wechsler said, "I do not deny the fact that there is a schism and polarization in the town. . . . The polarization was here even before the elections. The new immigrants live in ghettos here, in an atmosphere of 'us' versus 'them.' "[12]

The awareness of the Mizrahim in Kiryat Gat that their control over their place was in jeopardy created considerable tension, which also turned into violence. The tension reached a peak after the first round of voting in which it became clear that a second round would be required between Erez and Wechsler. There were incidents of violence, as dummy bombs were placed near Wechsler's home, threats were made, and knives brandished.

All of this took place in the context of continued stereotyping, with Russians being labeled as Mafia gangsters and prostitutes, and as lacking any connection to Judaism. These stereotypes were reflected in the following excerpt from the local newspaper *Ma Nishma* after the agreement was signed between Erez and Wechsler: "On Tuesday morning, after the agreement was signed between Erez and Wechsler, suddenly all the local massage parlors and branches of the Russian Mafia were 'closed.' Wechsler was acknowledged by his opponents to be Jewish, and all's well that ends well."[13]

The elections in Kiryat Gat thus revealed the underlying tension between the Mizrahim and the Russians. As observed earlier, this conflict peaked when the Mizrahim felt that their control over the town was at risk. Several statements by Mizrahi residents in Kiryat Gat appeared in the local press after the agreement, illustrating tension:

N.A.: The compromise is a wise move. An atmosphere of hate was avoided. . . . If Wechsler had been elected, there would have been a Mizrahi uprising. . . .
T.B.: During the final week of the campaign, there was an atmosphere of war. . . .
A.V.: A split and rupture between the Mizrahim and Russians . . . reflected in extremist invective and physical and verbal violence. . . .
M.B.: Had there been a runoff, the ethnic tension would have erupted. . . .

Ofakim and Kiryat Gat represent the spectrum of ethnic tensions between the Mizrahim and the Russians, which was evident to varying degrees in most development towns. Even in Ofakim, where the intergroup tension was never violent during local elections, the potential for violence existed had the Russian immigrants posed a threat to Mizrahi dominance. It was the different organizational ability of the immigrants that appears to have determined the intensity of conflict. In general, the more organized the Russians were, the more intense local electioneering became.

In November of 2003 another round of local elections took place. This time, ethnic tensions in Kiryat Gat subsided to some extent and intensified in Ofakim. However, in neither location did ethnic issues dominate the campaign, although they were still prominent in campaign discussions over education and public space. The foremost issue was the severe financial crisis of both local councils (similar to many across the state, especially in the periphery), along with the lack of economic and educational opportunities. In Kiryat Gat, the two major parties representing Russian immigrants lost 42 percent of their power (from seven to four seats). In Ofakim, the Veterans and Immigrants Party disappeared from the scene, and the new Ofakim Shelanu (Our Ofakim) list, which identifies with Russian residents, received two seats of the council's thirteen. There were still slogans and local advertising concerning local ethnic issues, but they were not as prominent as in 1998.

The declining role of internal ethnic issues in the 2003 elections is due to several external factors, including the economic crises in the towns, which created a common interest in the two communities, and the al-Aqsa *intifada*, which received overwhelming attention in state and local media and worked to bring closer Russian and Mizrahi Jews. In addition, five years on, further contacts were made between the communities, and a process of urban integration gained some momentum. Critically, however, this occurred without threatening Mizrahi dominance in the towns. Indeed, the two new mayors elected in 2003—Avi Asraf in Ofakim and Aviram Dahari in Kiryat Gat—are Mizrahim, representing the continuing dominance of veterans in the towns despite the massive demographic change. Yet, we must remember that once the external factors, such as the economic crisis and Israeli-Palestinian violence, subside, the Russian-Mizrahi issues are likely to resurface as major issues, given the differing views the two groups have on the towns' character and public culture (see Tzfadia and Yiftachel 2004).

In general, the elections in the development towns reveal a Mizrahi protest against the Russians, but this appears to have remained at the local level. The same action appears impossible on the national arena, given the persisting hegemony of Zionism. This impossibility led the Mizrahim to adopt a new strategy in order to defend their control in the towns, that is, a religious-national strategy.

According to this strategy the Mizrahim undermined the connection between the Russian immigrants and the Israeli Jewish nation by claiming that most of the immigrants were not real Jews. Since belonging to the Israeli Jewish nation is defined by Jewish religious law, and since many of the immigrants were not recognized as religious Jews, the Mizrahim could exploit an advantage in the field of national belonging and gain with it a high moral ground on the local level. By adopting this strategy, Shas, the Mizrahi ultra-Orthodox party, presented a powerful (if racist) counternarrative to the growing claims of Russians in the towns. Such counternarratives have occurred in several towns, including an incident, which received wide media attention in November of 1999, during a demonstration against the opening of nonkosher Russian grocery shops in the development town of Bet-Shemesh.[14] Rabbi Shmuel Bennizri from Shas preached to a local Mizrahi audience: "The Russians brought to Bet-Shemesh the diseases from

Russia. Heaven forbid, the following biblical text is turning into a reality: when ye entered, ye defiled my land, and made mine heritage an abomination [Jer. 2:7]. They [the Russians] inundated the land with tens of thousands of non-Jews, and they inundate the land with shops of abomination. Just after the town has developed, the devils raised their heads and inundate Bet-Shemesh with their abominations."[15]

Hence, Shas and the Mizrahim have used the national Zionist discourse, which includes people according to their connections to (ethnic) Jewishness, but they have modified that discourse to reflect the local religious circumstances, where the Mizrahim enjoy an advantage. This has allowed them to use an aggressive, essentialized rhetoric to maintain their control in the towns. But, notably, this strategy is another sign of the Mizrahi entrapment: despite the various attempts to restrict immigration, they find it very difficult to challenge the pro-immigration (ethnic) Zionist ideology, so they emphasize the issue of religious boundaries. This gave them a high moral ground within the very national project, which continues to marginalize them. We can observe this as a strategy adopted by the trapped ethnoclass, which illustrates the multilayered nature of its collective identity.

Conclusion

Building on the analysis of identity carried out in Chapter 9, the present chapter explored public protest and local electioneering in the development towns as additional aspects in the making of a peripheral Mizrahi ethnoclass. Two prevailing voices emerged from these two arenas. First, the arena of public protest has consistently broadcasted outward a plea for social and economic equality. This emanated from the towns' continuing deprivation as compared to the rest of Israel's Jewish society. As I have shown, the disgruntled nature of the voice emerging from the towns can be partially explained by the relative deprivation theory. But the relatively docile nature of the protest should be further explained by the Mizrahim's trapped settings within an ethnocratic settler society. These settings prevent the peripheral Mizrahim from challenging the very system that created their structural marginalization.

However, the second voice emerged in local electoral campaigns. There, the Mizrahim in the towns spoke in a different tenor, aiming inward and stressing the need to control their space, while (indirectly) questioning some of the major tenets of the ethnocratic Zionist state, such as the unconditional encouragement of Jewish immigration to Israel, population dispersal, or the unquestioned homogeneity and solidarity of all Jews. Here we can witness the relevance of theories of resource competition and the politics of identity to explain ethnic mobilization in the towns, which at times became more militant and less in line with the accepted norms of Israeli Ashkenazi hegemony.

Drawing on the findings and on the attitudes expressed in Chapter 9, we may describe peripheral Mizrahi identity, like most collective identities, as being built of various layers (see Yuval-Davis 2000). The national layer stresses an active, loyal participation in the national (and Ashkenazi-dominated) Zionist project. This perspective works to blur the differences between the towns and mainstream society. It hence traps the peripheral Mizrahim on the margins of Jewish society, giving them no real ability to challenge the oppressive system that created their structural deprivation but on which they also depend.

But the internal layer of Mizrahi identity is being shaped during the last decade vis-à-vis the new influx of Russian immigrants. Here we noticed a more militant stance, which works to differentiate Jewish identities and assert Mizrahi control over their (threatened) towns. The prominence of Shas in both Kiryat Gat and Ofakim, as in most development towns, highlighted the search for new resources, especially religious affiliation, as a tool in the ethnic competition.

Given the role of religion as a cornerstone of Israeli Jewish identity (see Chapter 5), the Shas movement has developed a strategy that attempts to bypass the ethnocratic entrapment of the Israeli settler society, with its emphasis on settlement, militarism, and secularism. By emphasizing religion, traditional values, and ethnic (Mizrahi) memory and solidarity, Shas was also able to present a powerful counternarrative to the Russians in the towns and effectively link local Mizrahi politics with a national agenda of "integration through difference" (see Peled 2001).

The local conflicts documented above illustrate the power of place and identity in mobilizing ethnic communities, often in contradiction to the broader national agenda. While this trend is still relatively minor, it should not be regarded as trivial, because, as observed at the outset, it is rooted in the resistance to the hegemony of Ashkenazi Israeli forces. Peripheral Mizrahim in general, and the new identification with the Sephardi-religious Shas movement in particular, are clear illustrations that cracks have opened in the Ashkenazi-dominated ethnocracy, at least among its Jewish peripheries. To be sure, these are not signs of the pending collapse of the ethnocratic system—far from it. Rather, they signal the persistent force of emerging contradictions, the diverging logics of group mobilizations, and the inevitable long-term instability of the ethnocratic regime.

Part IV
Looking Ahead

Chapter 11

A Way Forward? The Planning
of a Binational Capital
in Jerusalem

The struggle over geography in Jerusalem/al-Quds is complex as it is not only about soldiers and cannons, but also about ideas, about forms, about images and imaginings.[1]

This chapter continues the focus of Part III on specific communities and places by concentrating on Jewish-Palestinian relations in the Jerusalem/al-Quds metropolitan region. It also moves the book to a different phase by discussing the future of ethnic relations in Israel/Palestine.

Peace between Israelis and Palestinians is generally associated with the establishment of a Palestinian state over the territories conquered by Israel in 1967, including East Jerusalem/al-Quds. But even some who support the establishment of a Palestinian state over all of these territories have reservations about the repartition of Jerusalem/al-Quds between two states, which is a likely result of such a resolution to the conflict.

The aim of this chapter is to propose a different model for Jerusalem/al-Quds, which may alleviate the need for a scarring repartition of the metropolis, with the associated border checkpoints, fences, interethnic hostility, and economic decline. It argues that a binational, multicultural city may form a better option for the entire metropolitan region (including West Jerusalem), based on planning, social, economic, and even political grounds.

The nature and scope of this book prohibit an in-depth examination of possible futures for the city, or Israel/Palestine. Yet, the conceptual and empirical analysis of the previous chapters could be assisted by short examples of rethinking the future. The present and following chapter launch such a discussion, attempting to connect the main findings and critique outlined above and the possibilities of designing anew the political and ethnic space for Jews and Palestinians. This may provide some ideas for a different, more peaceful future for Israel/Palestine.

This chapter focuses on Jerusalem/al-Quds because this city is one of the main (if not the most critical) bones of contention between Zionist and Palestinians. The city also demonstrates starkly the political and physical consequences of the Israeli ethnocratic regime, providing ample examples of things to come if the process of creeping apartheid outlined in previous chapters were to continue. Moreover, Jerusalem/al-Quds also symbolizes the center of Zionist and Palestinian nationalism and harbors deep layers of meaning, yearning, and pride for both peoples, hence becoming a genuine sacred cow. Typically to most sacred (core) issues in the Zionist-Palestinian conflict, it has been silenced or ignored by Israel, thereby prolonging and intensifying its potency. Since one of main approaches taken in this book is that core issues must be analyzed, demystified, and openly discussed as the only way to achieve analytical and political progress, Jerusalem/al-Quds is a particularly apt place with which to start such a process.

Within the above context, the city has been frequently described as the biggest obstacle for peace. It is commonly argued that Jews and Palestinians have been thoroughly mixed in the urban geography created by the Israeli occupation, which prevents the possibility of repartition. At the same time, equal coexistence is ruled out by Israel's ethnocratic policies, which continue to seek (illusionary) Jewish control over united Jerusalem. This necessitates ever increasing control and oppression of the Palestinians of East Jerusalem and generates escalating Palestinian resistance.

As part of a protracted conflict, the city has become a mythical emblem for the national identity of both Zionists and Palestinians, with the associated goal of total ethnic control over its landscape and resources. But is this zero-sum perception a necessary product of the two sets of national aspirations? This chapter argues differently. It seeks a path of binationalism in Jerusalem/al-Quds that will both enhance the national projects of Zionists and Palestinians, while laying the planning and economic foundations for a thriving metropolis.

In this way, the chapter offers a novel approach. It claims that instead of being a flashpoint of conflict and an insurmountable obstacle for peace, the Jerusalem/al-Quds region can become a catalyst for Palestinian-Zionist coexistence. This may even lead to a "Jerusalem first" strategy in order to diffuse this sensitive issue and radiate the principles of Zionist-Palestinian equality and nondomination across the land. This possibility runs counter to most thinking about the city and the conflict, but I argue that the logic of structural forces shaping the metropolitan region around Jerusalem/al-Quds will always present the option of a binational, undivided, and federated metropolis as simultaneously realistic and visionary.

Two notable difficulties with the proposed model should be mentioned here: the recent violence and decline in Jewish-Palestinian trust, and the dominant way of thinking among policy makers on the future of Jerusalem. First, the 2000–2004 period, with the outbreak of the second *intifada,* and intensification of interethnic violence, especially in Jerusalem, has sunk Jewish-Palestinian trust to a point approaching an all-time low. Naturally, this presents serious difficulties for a model based on the sharing of geographical space and political power.

The latest round of violence is of particular relevance to our analysis because it erupted in the heart of holy Jerusalem—the Haram al-Sharif or Har Habayit—and has since been symbolically labeled the al-Aqsa *intifada*.[2] This has anchored the current conflict both within al-Quds and with the deepest religious layers of the bleeding Zionist-Palestinian conflict. Further, one of Israel's main responses to the uprising has been the construction of a massive wall, cutting through the West Bank and al-Quds (Arab Jerusalem). This is a major urban barrier that not only intensifies hostility and deepens the current apartheid logic of governing the city but also physically ruptures the fabric of urban life. At the time of writing (summer of 2004), the wall had been declared illegal by the International Court of Justice.[3] The new structure wreaks havoc on the lives of the city's Arab residents while presenting new obstacles for the planning of an undivided, thriving, metropolitan region.

The second difficulty is the prevailing opinion among leaders and experts interested in peace that a repartition of the city is a necessary evil. This is also a prominent feature of most peace plans—from Clinton's outline plan of 2000, through the Saudi and Arab League initiative of 2002, and the road map proposed by an international quartet in mid-2003. In other words, there are no organized political forces raising and discussing the vision of binational urban governance; hence, such an option does not appear as a genuine peace option in both Israeli and Palestinian mainstream discourses.

The response to these difficulties lies in distinguishing between short- and long-term strategies: while in the short term, ongoing Jewish colonialism, the construction of the massive wall, and low levels of trust create patterns of (unequal) separation, the need to plan and develop the metropolitan region jointly remains intact. Given the shared environment, economy, landscape, markets, and infrastructure, the concept of a shared metropolis is likely to remain relevant and to seek implementation on various levels of urban life. Hence, the existence of a contiguous mixed, urban geography in Jerusalem/al-Quds is a major (if often underresearched) factor, and its long-term management is best served by the model proposed here.

The chapter first sketches the development of Jewish-Palestinian relations in the city; it then briefly draws on international cases of divided capitals. Finally, it proposes a binational democratic and decentralized model for the capital region of Jerusalem/al-Quds, where formal sovereignty is held jointly by Israel and Palestine.

Jewish Ethnocracy and the Jerusalem Region

The question of Jerusalem/al-Quds cannot be separated from the broader Zionist-Palestinian struggle over the Land of Israel/Palestine. As explained in Chapters 3 and 6, the events and processes unfolding in the city since 1967 illustrate vividly the existence of a Jewish ethnocracy. This regime stretches over the entire Land of Israel/Palestine and finds a striking expression in the ethnic dynamics taking place in Jerusalem/al-Quds.

Typically to ethnocratic urban regimes (see Chapter 8), the purpose of the (Jewish-controlled) Jerusalem leadership was to expand Jewish control and to ethnicize the city's landscape and political structure. But at the same time, under most ethnocratic regimes, urban areas frequently form the flashpoints of ethnic tensions, as exemplified in the cities of Belfast, Montreal, Sarajevo, Nicosia, Beirut, and Kuala Lumpur. These cities became focal points for both ethnocratic regimes and for challenges to their oppressive practices (for international comparison, see Bollen 1999, 2000).

Moving to the Jerusalem/al-Quds context, it is noteworthy that despite the Israeli Zionist rhetoric of a unified Jerusalem, the Jerusalem/al-Quds area has become since 1967 an exemplar of an ethnocratic city. This policy is presented by both state and city authorities and has persistently promoted a project of Judaization. This attitude became formal and transparent within Israeli political discourse as well as the media, as exemplified by the following news report from 1997: "Prime Minister Netanyahu, the mayor of the city of Jerusalem, Ehud Olmert, and the minister of finance, Ne'eman, will meet on Friday to discuss the revolutionary proposal of Olmert. According to the mayor's proposal, the city of Jerusalem will get a special national priority in order to struggle against the demographic decline in Jewish population in the city."[4]

As documented widely,[5] Israel has used its military might and economic power to relocate borders and boundaries, grant and deny rights and resources, move populations, and reshape the city's geography for the purpose of increasing Jewish domination (for historical-geographical analyses, see Bollen 2000; Dumper 1996; Khamaissi 1997, 2002; Klein 1999; Nitzan-Shiftan 2004). Two central Israeli strategies have been (a) the massive construction of an outer urban ring of Jewish settlements (satellite neighborhoods), which now host more than half the Jewish population of the city, and (b) a parallel containment of all Palestinian development, implemented through housing demolition and the prevention of immigration or population growth in the city.[6]

Israel's ethnocratic management of the city has meant that despite a clear binational reality prevailing in the Jerusalem/al-Quds region, with approximately equal proportions of Jewish and Arab inhabitants, urban governance has been totally dominated by Jews. Palestinians in the metropolitan region were divided into two main groups: (a) residents of the enlarged Jerusalem municipality, who were placed under Israeli law[7] (in a move erroneously described by Israelis as annexation) and given Jerusalem residency rights (but not Israeli citizenship); and (b) those in adjoining localities who remained in the occupied territories, with no residency or movement rights in the city.

Palestinians have also been excluded from the city's forums of decision making—most notably city hall—owing to their refusal to accept the imposition of Israeli law, or the distorted municipal boundaries imposed on the city to ensure Jewish control. This weakness has meant that Israel has progressed quickly to Judaize large parts of the al-Quds urban area and the surrounding hills, with only little and ineffective Palestinian resistance to this move. This Judaization process has taken place while Israeli decision makers and state leaders portrayed the city, seemingly innocently, as reunited, integrated, modern, and even democratic (see Hasson 2001; al-Haj 2002; Nitzan-Shiftan 2004; Kallus 2004).

This approach relates to the Palestinian residents of East Jerusalem as an inevitable fact that should be kept quiet and passive, as expressed by the previous mayor of Jerusalem, Teddy Kollek, who governed the city for twenty-nine years and was considered dovish within Israeli Jewish circles: "So, I do not want to give them the feeling that they are equal. I know we cannot give them a sense of equality. But I want, here and there, when it does not cost so much, and when it is just an economic effort, to give them, anyway, the feeling that they can live here. If I will not give them such a feeling we will suffer."[8]

The unilateral management of the city has also meant that economic development and services were nearly entirely geared toward the needs and aspirations of the city's Jewish population, leaving the Arab neighborhoods in a state of neglect and underdevelopment. The result has been a gradual physical decline and stagnation in the city's Arab sectors, the cutting off of Arab Jerusalem from the Palestinian hinterland, and the subsequent exodus of Palestinian businesses north and south of the city. At the same time, development occurred at a breakneck pace in the city's ever expanding and modernizing Jewish areas.[9] However, the city's Palestinian community continued to grow through natural increase and has struggled to maintain residential construction activity vis-à-vis a restrictive Jewish city hall and often in defiance of the city's rules and regulations.

Concepts and Cases of Ethnically and Nationally Mixed Spaces

The proposal is based on extensive knowledge available in fields such as political science, urban planning, political geography, public policy, and ethnic relations of the principles of stable and legitimate management of deeply divided cities (for reviews, see Bollen 2000; Lustick 1996; Yiftachel 1995a). These are usually based on principles of political equality that necessitate the ending of belligerent occupation. Such principles would transform urban *ethnocracy to democracy,* that is, introduce ethnic power sharing, broad participation in decision making, representation of all major parties in the city's landscape, and proportionality in the allocation of public resources, including land, infrastructure, public facilities, and ongoing capital flow. At the same time, most of the approaches to the management

of ethnically and nationally mixed spaces call for maintaining and fostering ethnic and local autonomy and stress the importance of institutionaliz-
ing local democracy (see Lijphart 1984; McGarry and O'Leary 1993, 2000;
Kymlicka 1992, 2001).

Several comparative examples may prove useful for constructing a
shared future for the Jerusalem/al-Quds region. One is Brussels, which has
been delineated an autonomous binational province as part of the Belgian
constitutional changes, which were undertaken during the last two decades. Belgium has been transformed from a unitary state into a bi-ethnic
federation, with large-scale autonomy awarded to Dutch-speaking Flemish
and French-speaking Walloons in their respective regions. Within this new
state structure, Brussels has remained a joint capital city, belonging to both
Walloons and Flemish. It has a separate constitutional status and is governed according to the principles of power sharing and accommodation
between the two groups. Brussels' urban affairs are administered in a decentralized fashion as a cluster of cities, where local matters of planning,
development, and education are determined by local communities.

Brussels also resembles Jerusalem because of its high international status
as the administrative hub of the European Union. Although tensions between Flemish and Walloons have not disappeared under the new arrangement, and despite the excessively rigid and overregulated structure of
Walloon-Flemish relations, the Brussels region appears to be functioning
reasonably. It has gradually moderated the scope and level of conflicts between the two groups and institutionalized ways of resolving ethnic urban
tensions (see De-Ridder 1996; Murphy 1988; Bollen 2000).

A further relevant example is that of Chandigarh, India. Nehru, the legendary Indian prime minster, promoted the building of this city during the
early 1950s. It was the capital of the state of Punjab and was planned by Le
Corbusier as a modern, open, government center. But during the early
1960s, ethnonational pressure by the Sikhs caused the partition of Punjab
into two states—Haryana to the south and Punjab to the north. Yet, the
peoples occupying the two states both wished to maintain their capital in
the internationally acclaimed city of Chandigarh, which was geographically
close to their new border.

As a result, a city region was carved out as an autonomous region, officially controlled by the Indian federal government in New Delhi but in
practice self-governed by the multiethnic residents of Chandigarh, who periodically elect their representatives to city hall. Chandigarh functions simultaneously as the capital of two states and even some of the government
buildings, such as the Supreme Court and Parliament House are shared,
with different wings of these buildings designated for Punjab and Haryana.
Like Brussels, Chandigarh has an internal decentralized structure, with
most urban affairs being determined on a local, sector (quarter) level. Neither Brussels nor Chandigarh are identical to Jerusalem/al-Quds. Indeed,

Chandigarh has many features unique to its Indian setting. Yet it offers a very useful example of a capital city shared by two states with a history of ethnic tensions and separatism. The two states have managed to sidestep their territorial and ethnic tensions and manage jointly a city cherished by both peoples (see Singh 1994; Kalia 1999).

Both Brussels and Chandigarh, then, illustrate the ability of two neighboring ethnic groups residing in their homeland to share a capital city with a reasonable degree of stability and prosperity. Further, and equally important, the arrangements in the shared city have assisted in stabilizing and democratizing the broader scene of ethnic relations far beyond the boundaries of the cities in question. Clearly, the level of national sentiments and recent hostility between Jews and Palestinians may surpass that of the two comparative cases, but let us not forget the very recent bloody history of the Indian subcontinent in general and Punjab in particular,[10] and the long-term suspicion between Flemish and Walloons, to show that these are indeed deeply divided urban regions that found a path (imperfect as it may be) toward reconciliation and coexistence.

The strategy presented below for the Jerusalem/al-Quds region also draws on the many ideas, plans, and proposals already formulated by experts and activists for Jerusalem/al-Quds. Notable among these have been the options prepared by the Jerusalem Planning Center at the Orient House[11] and the Jerusalem Institute for Israel Studies, as well as by experts in the field (see Abu Odeh 1992; Benvenisti 1996; Khalidi 1992; Klein 1999).

Toward a United Capital Region for Jerusalem/al-Quds?

The proposed strategy would enable the Jerusalem/al-Quds region to function as one metropolis, yet reflect the collective aspirations and ethnonational identities of the two peoples. The proposal is presented here at a sketchy and conceptual level of detail; I recognize of course that its details must be further worked out for it to become implementable.

The main components of the proposed strategy, as expanded below, seek to transform the city from ethnocracy to democracy by redesigning its political geography. Key steps include the following:

(a) the declaration that the capital region belongs equally to Palestinians and Israeli Jews and hence the ending of Israeli occupation;

(b) the demarcation of an autonomous capital region to be placed under joint Israeli and Palestinian sovereignty, which would function as the capital(s) of both Israel and Palestine and as a modern, democratic metropolis;

(c) the establishment of an umbrella entity, the Capital Region Authority, to oversee the development and planning of the metropolitan region;

(d) the creation of a set of new local municipalities to manage most aspects of urban life in the various quarters, towns, and villages that make up the metropolitan area; and

(e) the demarcation of a small area around the Old City and the establishment of (a religious) Holy City Council to manage this area.

These steps will create a binational, multicultural city, shared on equal terms between Israelis and Palestinians, while allowing the many communities and localities to express and enhance their identity and character. The metropolitan region would be administered by a decentralized, federal-type urban regime and governed openly and democratically (see Figures 11.1, 11.2).

A WORTHY MOVE?

Why should Israelis and Palestinians prefer this option? Why should they head toward a joint urban future, which may be fraught with tensions and rivalries? Should they attempt to create a shared polity and society with a group toward whom they may feel mistrust, anger, and fear? Does the

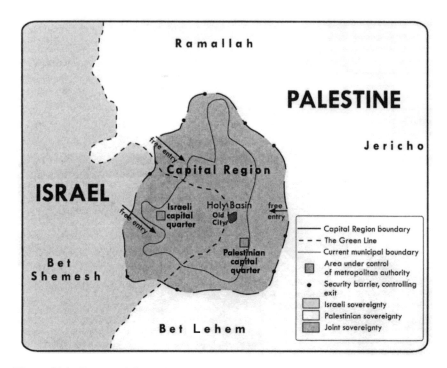

Figure 11.1. Proposed Capital Region: Main Features

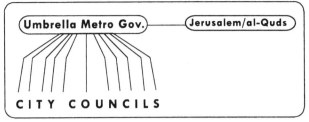

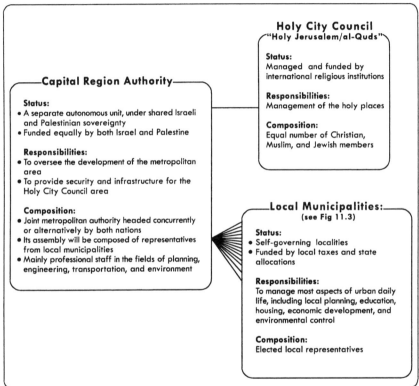

Figure 11.2. Capital Region Authority: Administration Model

model sketch a risky recipe for endless conflicts and struggles between mutually suspicious collectivities? These hesitations have intensified following the 2000–2003 al-Aqsa *intifada*, the associated rounds of firmer Israeli oppression of the Palestinians, and attacks of counter-Palestinian terror, very frequently in the heart of Jerusalem.

Yet, I claim that despite the unavoidable difficulties and risks associated with any period of profound transition, and despite the ongoing tensions between Israelis and Palestinians, which are not likely to disappear quickly, the decentralized one-city approach—which protects the rights of both Jews and Palestinians for self-determination, development, and equality— is preferable to interstate partition on several grounds. First, it appears that the two states would benefit from the new arrangement. They would have the entire Jerusalem/al-Quds region, with its enormous symbolic and economic resources, as officially part of their sovereignty. Even under the arrangement of a shared space, their position on the question of Jerusalem is likely to improve both domestically and internationally.

I also argue that maintaining a united city would enhance greatly its chances for economic development and prosperity. Given the momentum of the world's globalizing economy, and the potential for a diminishing role of state borders, an integrated Jerusalem/al-Quds region is likely to attract international investment and become a true cosmopolis (Sandercock 1998). Its functioning as an integrated urban region would also enhance the volume of tourists, forming a central and growing driving force of the city's economy. Its division would definitely hamper such prospects.

Further, collective and personal security is also likely to be enhanced under the new arrangement. On a collective level, the mutual recognition of Palestine and Israel in the capital city of its neighboring nation would undoubtedly ease both Israeli-Palestinian and Middle Eastern tensions and alleviate security threats deriving from the city's contested status. Likewise, personal security would be augmented, mainly because both states (with their well-developed security apparatuses) would have the highest of interests to maintain law and order in their political capitals.

Finally, on a broader level, achieving peace with a united capital region would send a message of genuine reconciliation to the rest of Israel/ Palestine and beyond. That said, the injustices of the past will keep surfacing, and claims and counterclaims for the city are likely to linger for generations and to be accompanied by possible outbreaks of violence. The legacy left by the manipulation of the term united Jerusalem during the last three decades, which only thinly covered a reality of forceful conquest and domination, is also likely to hamper efforts to built trust in a shared city.

Yet, the proposal outlined here for the city entails genuine unity, both geographically—by including the entire metropolitan region (in contrast to the current distortion of urban boundaries by Israeli authorities)—and politically—by incorporating equally into the political structure the city's Jewish and Palestinian collectivities. This reality is likely to gradually change attitudes and increase mutual Jewish-Palestinian confidence. Such a process might transform both people's consciousness toward the other as well as toward their own territoriality.

Hence, it may be that instead of viewing the future of Jerusalem/al-Quds as an obstacle to peace, as has been traditionally the case with policy makers on both sides, a united Jerusalem/al-Quds can become a catalyst for Jewish-Palestinian reconciliation. The model of a shared Jerusalem may form a reference point for groups elsewhere in the Land of Israel/ Palestine, where frameworks for just, equal, and democratic coexistence between Israelis and Palestinians need to be invented and implemented creatively.

PUTTING FLESH ON THE BONES

In more detail, the proposal entails the delineation of the entire Jerusalem/al-Quds metropolitan region—to be known as the Capital Region—as a separate and autonomous political unit under shared Israeli and Palestinian sovereignty. It would stretch from al-Birrya in the north, Ma'aleh Adumim in the east, Beit Jalla in the south, and Mevaseret Zion in the west, where some 850,000 people reside, in almost equal proportions of Palestinians and Jews. The area would be placed officially under joint Israeli and Palestinian sovereignty and be managed by a joint Capital Region Authority, headed concurrently (or alternatively) by a Palestinian and an Israeli. The Capital Region Authority would be a thin political institution. Its assembly would have representatives from the region's local governments and from the Israeli and Palestinian ministries. Its main staff would be professional, in the fields of engineering, planning, transportation, and the environment.

The urban region would include two capital precincts, which would host the Palestinian and Israeli government quarters. The Israeli government precinct would remain in its place (which would probably be enlarged), while the location of the Palestinian precinct would be chosen by the Palestinian people and the al-Quds community. Some possibilities include the Sheikh Jarrakh, Wadi Joz, or Jabel Mukabber areas. The city as a whole would be mutually recognized as a state capital by Israel and by Palestine. This would guarantee the eternal rights of both peoples in the city and slow the disastrous demographic and geographic competition between Israelis and Palestinians underway since 1967.

The name chosen here to describe the metropolitan area—the Capital Region—purposely steers away from using the names Jerusalem and al-Quds. This in order to avoid the manipulation and distortion of spatial representation through which the two sides have attached the names of Jerusalem/al-Quds, with their immense symbolic powers, to areas that had never been part of the city. This approach has been highly evident among Israeli-Jewish policy makers and shapers of the public discourse, which imposed the name Jerusalem on a large number of localities in the city's eastern, northern, and southern hinterlands.

This manipulation and distortion occurred with the unilateral expansion of the Jerusalem municipal area in 1967 over localities such as Shua'fat, Beit Hanina, and Sur Baher, and with the building of new Jewish settlements on surrounding (and often distant) hills, such as Gillo and Ramot, now considered part of Jerusalem. The manipulation was further evident in later years with the invention of new terms and entities—such as Greater Jerusalem and the Jerusalem envelope, which covered much larger areas and acted as signposts of Jewish control over outlying areas—cynically employing the cherished term of Jerusalem. Given the sanctity of Jerusalem in Jewish religion, culture, and history, the effect of this geographical distortion was twofold: to legitimate the Judaization of Arab areas renamed as Jerusalem, and to freeze, silence, or marginalize any critical voices, which were portrayed as supporting the division of Jerusalem.

The name Capital Region thus aims to take the sting out of the religious, historical, and political mega-importance attached to anything with (real or manipulated) association to Jerusalem (or, to a lesser extent, to al-Quds). The new plan hopes to create a mainly administrative and professional entity, which would govern the city's everyday affairs and future development without constant reference to heroic or tragic national narratives, or to sacred religious and historical sites.

As a parallel step, the proposed plan would delineate a small area covering the Old City and the immediate vicinity to be called Holy Jerusalem/al-Quds.[12] This small area, stretching about three square kilometers, would be the only locality in the metropolis to carry the names of Jerusalem/alQuds. This would be historically credible in the eyes of many, as the area in and around the Old City truly reflects the location of the sacred and cherished Jerusalem/al-Quds to whom Jews, Muslims, and Christians have developed a special religious and national bond.

Therefore, and unlike other proposals for the area (most notably the one associated with Abu Mazen and Beilin), the present plan aims to reduce radically the extent and scope of Jerusalem/al-Quds. We perceive this as a long-term step in desanctifying and diffusing the potential of these names to invoke hard-line religious and national narratives. As plainly evident during the last three decades, these narratives have destructively hardened political positions and caused the escalation of a negative dialectic between Jews and Palestinians in the city and beyond. Let us contract Jerusalem/al-Quds to their appropriate and credible proportions.

Under the proposal (see Figure 11.3), the small area designated as Holy Jerusalem/al-Quds would remain formally under joint Israeli/Palestinian sovereignty, but all responsibilities for its religious, economic, and planning management would be transferred to an international religious Holy City Council consisting of equal Christian, Muslim, and Jewish representation. It is expected that the management of the area would largely preserve the religious status quo and hence face relatively little pressures of redevelopment.

The responsibility for security and infrastructure, and hence the official sovereignty, would remain with the Israeli/Palestinian Capital Region Authority, but this would have little impact on the actual management of the

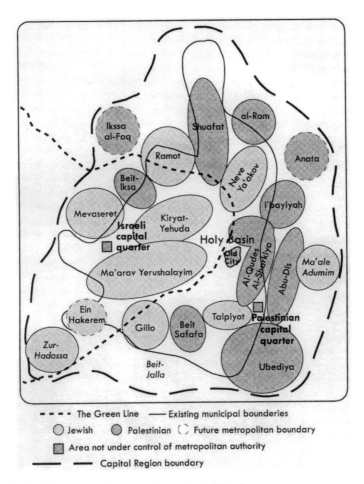

Figure 11.3. Cities in the Proposed New Capital Region

many holy places, interreligious affairs, and tourism, which would be controlled by the proposed Holy City Council. This arrangement would allow both Israeli and Palestinians symbols of sovereignty (such as flags and signs) to be hoisted over key points, such as the Haram al-Sharif or the Wailing Wall, while the actual running of the Old City would be managed by bodies external to the Israeli or Palestinian states.

GOVERNING URBAN COMMUNITIES

A lynchpin in the proposed model is the tier of local municipalities, where most urban governance would take place. This would ensure that over time, matters considered at present as national or religious would take a less explosive form as urban issues. The municipal tier would form the backbone of the region's communal, local, and urban planning management. Whereas the umbrella Capital Region Authority would be mainly made of professional experts, and the Holy City Council made of mainly religious figures, the local municipalities would perform the full range of urban governance, including local planning, education, housing, economic development, environmental control, and the daily procedures of urban democracy.

Accordingly, each municipality would govern a population of around 30,000–50,000 residents. An effort would be made to arrange the metropolis into quarters and towns, which would reflect the various religious, denominational, historical, local, and ethnic characters of the multitude of communities in the capital region.

At times, this would simply entail the recognition of long-standing, or geographically distinct, communities, villages, or towns as self-governing localities. Such places may include, for example, Beit Hanina, al-Azariyya, Beit Safafa, Mevaseret Zion, Gillo, or Ramot. But in other places the structure would need to amalgamate several neighborhoods of similar complexions and create new local councils as centers of urban government and communities. The redesign of municipal entities would attempt to create blocks of neighborhoods as a way of reducing the current frictions between radically different populations (such as secular and ultra-Orthodox Jews) over the shaping of public spaces.

The naming of the new local councils would also be important. The guiding principle is to select symbolic names, which may reflect or help create new local attachments and characters. These are some of the preliminary and suggestive names appearing in Figure 11.3: Ma'arav Yerushalayim (for secular Jewish neighborhoods); Kiryat-Yehuda (for the Orthodox Jewish areas); Al-Qudes Al-Sharkiya (for the inner Arab neighborhoods); and Ikssa al-Foq (Upper Ikssa, for future Arab suburban neighborhoods in the region's northern parts).

Local autonomy also affects the sensitive issue of sovereignty. Whereas officially, sovereignty would be shared over the entire metropolis between Israel and Palestine, each municipality would also have the autonomy to attach itself, legally, culturally, and symbolically, to one of the two states. Hence, it is perfectly possible Israeli law would preside over councils with a Jewish majority, and Palestinian law over councils with an Arab majority. Other symbols of sovereignty, such as flags, street scapes, festivals, or educational programs, would be adopted by each council as it sees fit. Hence, it is likely that full effective Palestinian and Israeli sovereignty would prevail in the region's councils and neighborhoods without jeopardizing the working of an open, fully accessible metropolis.

What would be the political association of the Capital Region with the Israeli and the Palestinian states? The city's Palestinian and Israeli residents would be full citizens of their respective national political communities. As such, they would vote for their respective parliaments and be subject to the respective Palestinian and Israeli legal systems. The entire city region would be open to Israelis and Palestinian Jerusalemites for work, residency, and leisure. In case border controls would be required by any of the two states (and in the hope that such controls are not necessary), these would be placed on exit points from the city. This arrangement would ensure that the Israeli and Palestinian states would be able to control movements into their sovereign areas without compromising free entry from the two states into their capital cities.

The special status of the Capital Region Authority would be further expressed in its autonomy and responsibility in areas such as infrastructure, metropolitan transport, and environment. But in order to diffuse potential tensions with both the Israeli and Palestinian states and with the city's municipalities, as already mentioned, the Capital Region Authority would concentrate on professional matters and would oversee the smooth functioning of the region's urban systems. It would have its own set of portfolios (for environment, planning, transport, infrastructure, and the like), and a Capital Region police force.

The Capital Region Authority would not draw on local taxes but would be funded equally by the Israeli and Palestinian states. Beyond the financial resources of the Authority, a special long-term fund should be established for the purpose of affirmative development, that is, development that aims to reduce inequalities. This is necessary, as the Jerusalem/al-Quds area is rife with disparities, most notably between Jewish and Palestinian neighborhoods but also between the wealthy and the poor groups among each national community.

This special affirmative development fund, which may be drawn from international sources, is imperative for the improvement of Arab-Jewish relations, in that it would gradually rectify the effects of decades of neglect and discrimination that left the city's Arab areas in a grave state of repair and underdevelopment. The fund would also enable the city to increase residential opportunities for its Palestinian residents, who have been highly constrained by Israeli policies. This would be achieved by either constructing new Arab neighborhoods or compensating Arabs for property lost through unilateral confiscation or expropriation.

In sum, the institutional and geographical arrangements outlined above would create a federal-like metropolis, which can be described as a cluster of cities. This suits well the current wisdom in metropolitan governance and planning, which emphasizes the advantages of a decentralized form of urban management while still fostering an overarching regional identity. This approach is compatible with the national aspirations of both Israeli Jews and Palestinians, but it also seeks to strengthen local democracy and identity (see Barlow 1996; Marcuse and Van Kempen 2000; Sandercock 1998).

Are Israeli Jews and Palestinian Arabs ready to take the challenge and risks associated with turning Jerusalem into a genuinely shared city? Are they willing to compromise on the notion of exclusive de jure ethnonational sovereignty for the economic, cultural, and environmental welfare of the city? Would they abandon the drive to create ethnocratic and counterethnocratic spaces governed by violent ethnic control in their national capitals? This is not clear. Recent trends, especially since the outbreak of the al-Aqsa *intifada,* indicate greater closeness, manifested in political hostility and the construction of physical barriers, most prominently the wall. But in the long term, it is argued here, Jerusalem will remain a loosely shared metropolitan region, in which Jews and Palestinians will most likely create long-term patterns of urban interactions, thereby producing a binational urban space on a daily basis.

I am fully aware of the difficulties and hardships tied to the implementation of a shared metropolitan strategy, but I maintain that a transformation from ethnocracy to equal coexistence is possible and even necessary. This will require a major transformation on the part of the policy makers and perhaps the rise of new, brave leadership. These could finally lead to the establishment of an undivided city, which would fit the description of Jerusalem in the sacred texts as both a city of peace *(ir shalom)* and a city of a united whole *(ir shalem),* thereby forming a model for the rest of Israel/ Palestine and beyond.

Chapter 12
Epilogue: A Demos for Israel/Palestine?
Toward Gradual Binationalism

Having discussed the ethnocratic forces and processes present in Israel/ Palestine, can we imagine a path forward in which national and ethnic communities in this troubled land enjoy greater legitimacy, security, peace, and equality? As a way of concluding the book, and drawing on its main theoretical arguments, this chapter will reintroduce the concept of the demos (a legitimate, inclusive, and stable political community) as a key factor in the drawing of a new political geography of peaceful coexistence. The main contention is that a theory and praxis of the demos are necessary to transform *ethnocracy into democracy* and begin healing the deep injuries marring ethnic relations in Israel/Palestine. This and other observations about the desired transformation outlined in this chapter follow the insights offered by the critical analysis of ethnocracy presented throughout the book.

This epilogue will start with a short overview of the book and then outline six possible scenarios for the creation of a demos (or "demoses") in Israel/Palestine. It will conclude by elaborating on the preferred option, labeled here "gradual binationalism," and on the nature of a transformed Israeli regime, characterized as moving from a centralized settling ethnocracy to a multicultural decentralized democracy.

The Book: Overview

The book consisted of four major parts. The first developed the concept of ethnocracy. It showed that, theoretically, ethnocratic and settler regimes establish themselves with the main project of ethnicizing contested territories and loci of power. These regimes emerge through a time-space interlocking of three major forces—colonialism, ethnonationalism, and capitalism. They typically devise powerful mechanisms of state control over territory and the oppression of minorities. These are augmented by their construction of the (mixed) state territory as their exclusive ethnic homeland and by constructing a typical ethnoclass hierarchy dominated by a powerful charter group and including also upwardly mobile immigrants, indigenous peoples and alien groups—all occupying the contested space.

The prominence of the ethnos over the demos in the making of such so-cieties, and the expansionist nature of the ethnic logic, with its associated structural segregation and inequality, stand as barriers to the institution of a full democratic regime. While several ethnocracies claim to be demo-cratic, the critical analysis offered in the book distinguished between regime features and regime structure and demonstrated the confinement of democratic practices to the relatively superficial level of regime features. Given the above, ethnocratic regimes are often characterized by chronic instability, marked by institutional instability, intense (and often violent) intergroup conflict, and repeated economic crises.

The book's second part analyzed Israel/Palestine, focusing on the Zionist project and the transformation and policies of the Jewish state. The analysis treated the entire Land of Israel/Palestine as one analytical unit subject to the powers of one regime. It began by tracing the manner in which Zionist and Palestinian nationalism became deeply territorial-ized, although Jewish and Palestinian diasporas remain critical to the conflict. Several chapters then analyzed the ways in which Israel's Judaiza-tion (and de-Arabization) project, first inside Israel proper and later in the occupied territories, has profoundly affected the relations between Jews and Palestinians, as well as between various Jewish and Palestinian-Arab ethnoclasses, setting in motion a process I have termed *creeping apartheid*. This part also explored in some depth the spatial and cultural infrastructure of the Israeli ethnocratic regime by examining the land system and tracing the construction of the Zionist homeland discourse in popular music.

The book's third part used more focused lenses to analyze the processes of entrapment and identity development among peripheral ethnoclasses, often as a reaction to the practices of the ethnocratic regime. First, it ac-counted for the emergence of *fractured regionalism* among Israel's Palestin-ian citizens and examined the plight of the southern Bedouin community. In the Bedouin's case, an *urban ethnocracy* has developed around the city of Beer-Sheva, with widespread informality and illegality undermining previ-ous forms of coexistence. A couple of chapters traced the mobilization of Mizrahim in peripheral development towns and unraveled a collective identity *trapped* between Ashkenazi dominance and Mizrahi cultural and economic marginality. This section emphasized that entrapment is never static; rather it leads to the formation of a third space on the margins of Jewish-Zionist society.

The book's fourth part turns the analytical lense toward the future, with Chapter 11 focusing on the planning of another urban ethnocracy—the Jerusalem/al-Quds region—and developed the concept of a binational, multicultural city as an exemplar for the entire Israel/Palestine. The pres-ent chapter completes this part by discussing the future political geography of the land and by advocating a scenario defined as *gradual binationalism*.

Scenarios for the Future Political Geography of Israel/Palestine

Many conclusions can be drawn from the analyses presented in the book. On a theoretical level, these may deal with the roles of space, planning, history, violence, and public policies in shaping ethnocratic societies. On a more local scale, they may address territory, culture, resources, and ethnic relations in Israel/Palestine. While these topics will no doubt form the focus of many future research projects and scholarly debates, this concluding chapter takes a different, more speculative direction. It will build on the structural analysis of the previous chapters by stripping the main political ideologies to their core political and territorial claims and by sketching their likely consequences. It will thus assist the reader to imagine the various possibilities emerging out of fifty-five years of Israeli ethnocratic rule and the prospects for transformation and reform.

Given the political, geographical emphasis of this book, it appears appropriate to present, in this concluding chapter, a short discussion of the various configurations of creating a future demos (or demoses) for Israel/Palestine. As discussed in Chapters 2 and 5, the demos represents an important logic of communal and political organization. Democracy (the rule of the demos) therefore depends on the existence of a demos—a relatively stable and inclusive group of equal citizens residing in a given territory over which equal law and political procedure prevail.

Despite the recent powerful processes of globalization, economic liberalization, and growing migration, it appears that in the foreseeable future, the modern state will continue to form the main allocator of power and resources, especially in the non-Western world. Hence, the concept of the demos appears as important as ever, especially as many of these states are grappling with processes of democratization. In many respects, the demos is a competing organizational principle to the ethnos, from which ethnocratic regimes draw their main political and moral authority.

The creation of a demos forms a necessary step to transform regime and society from ethnocracy to democracy. The political geography of a democratic state depends on the demarcation of clear boundaries for the political territory in question, where the law of the land can be applied equally to all members. As shown by numerous studies and theories, the creation of a relatively stable community of equal resident-citizens is also a necessary condition for the establishment of civil society, which operates in the space between state, capital, and household and creates webs of organizations, institutions, parties, and networks as a foundation for democratic rule.

The assertions above require two important qualifications. First, the political geography of the demos is a necessary, but by no means sufficient, foundation for democracy, which requires an additional set of legal, political, and material conditions. Second, I do not wish to advocate fixity with territorial political communities. Obviously, in today's network society, and within the context of a globalizing economic and political world, the state is no longer a tight political container or a supreme controller of resources. Yet, it is still a main shaper of most people's lives and a major determinant of the distribution of resources and power. The logic of the state system and the promise of democratic governance are thus still major mobilizing forces in today's politics, especially in regard to marginalized minorities.

Moving to Israel/Palestine, the book has shown how powerful ethnocratic processes have undermined the making of a demos. These have included, first and foremost, the rupturing of Israel's borders through long-term occupation and settlement of the occupied territories and through the empowerment of Jewish diasporas in key policy arenas. The inferior citizenship of Palestinian Arabs in Israel and the lack of a legal and cultural foundation for an inclusive polity have also worked to diminish the perception and empowerment of Israeli (as distinct from Jewish) and Palestinian demoses. Israel/Palestine also has a painful legacy of ethnic cleansing, violence, terror, Arab rejectionism, ethnoclass stratification, and ethnic political polarization—all working against the reinforcement of a demos as a foundation for an inclusive and active civil society.

It may be appropriate at this point, to ask two questions. Who should be the members of the Israeli and Palestinian demoses? Who are the main claim makers for political power in Israel/Palestine? On a basic level, it is possible to list six major ethnopolitical groups, marked by their different histories and geographies, that possess the main claims to political power in Israel/Palestine:

- Jewish citizen-residents of Israel;
- Palestinian Arab citizen-residents of Israel;
- Jewish settlers in the occupied territories;
- Palestinian residents of the occupied territories;
- Jewish diasporas; and
- Palestinian diasporas.

On this basis, Figure 12.1 depicts the various political-geographical configurations advocated at present as possible futures for Jews and Palestinians by these groups. These are articulated here as six scenarios and are described below.

REPRESSIVE CONSOLIDATION

In the near future, repressive consolidation is the most likely scenario. It assumes that present policies (with necessary adjustments) will persist due to the dominance of nationalist politics in Israel and in the United States of America. Palestinian weakness, both locally and internationally,

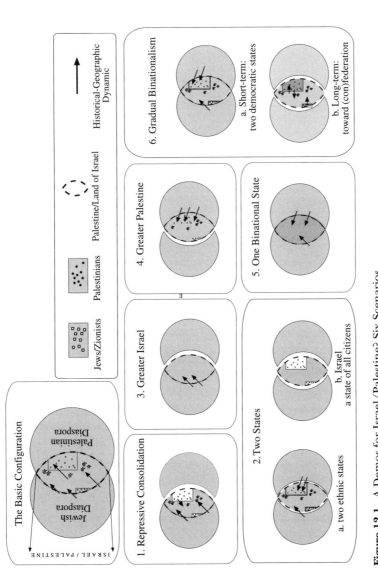

Figure 12.1. A Demos for Israel/Palestine? Six Scenarios

would remain a main factor in the lack of movement toward structural change. At the same time, Israel would avoid annexing the occupied territories (except the de facto annexation of Jewish settlements). This would enable the state to deal with the Palestinians often unilaterally as a neighboring nation, thereby bypassing the need to share power and resources. This approach may include several future Israeli "disengagements," such as the 2005 withdrawal from Gaza in order to improve Israel's ability to control the main concentrations of Palestinians. The Palestinian Authority may turn into a provisional state but would exercise only limited autonomy in fragmented parts of the territories, over which Israel would retain control. Most areas of Israel/Palestine would remain open to Jewish immigration and settlement but closed to Arabs, who would remain confined in their traditional, residential enclaves with the aid of military power, planning law, and the new separation barrier. This combination of policies and regulation would likely continue the process of "quiet transfer" whereby Palestinians residing in isolated pockets, where it is impossible to conduct normal life, would move to larger Palestinian towns and cities. In other words, the situation would result in *neither two independent states nor one* in Israel/Palestine. As shown in the book, such dynamics create an unsustainable process of creeping apartheid and a further retreat from democracy, accompanied by persistent ethnic conflict, deepening economic crisis, and internal fragmentation.

Two Ethnic States

This scenario of two ethnic states entails the repartitioning of Israel/Palestine and Jerusalem, most likely along the Green Line, and the creation of two states for two peoples—a Palestinian Arab state and an Israeli Jewish state. Jewish and Palestinian diasporas would have free access (only) to their respective states, meaning that returning Palestinian refugees would settle only in the Palestinian state. It is the most common prescription for the settlement of the conflict among both peoples and in international circles.

This scenario does present a reasonable possibility for the creation of legitimate Israeli and Palestinian demoses, although it leaves several key issues unresolved. These include the evacuation of (most) Jewish settlements in the occupied territories; the viability of a fragmented and weak Palestinian state, likely to remain largely dependent on Israel; and the status, rights, and capabilities of Palestinian citizens in the (self-declared) Jewish state. These are not mere technical details but major stumbling blocks, which may cause ongoing instability and undermine the establishment of stable and legitimate political communities. Further problems may result from the likely ethnocratic nature of both states, which may see the persistence of anti-Jewish or anti-Arab policies and rhetoric and lead to a precarious and conflict-riddled type of Israeli-Palestinian coexistence.

GREATER ISRAEL

The scenario of a greater Israel resembles the existing situation, where Israel controls most of historic Palestine, between Jordan and the sea. The main difference is that unlike the post-Oslo situation, the Palestinians in the West Bank and Gaza would enjoy neither a status of state in the making nor provisional statehood. This agenda is held by Israel's ruling Likud Party, which passed a resolution during its 2002 conference that "there shall be no second state in Eretz Yisrael."[1] Under this scenario, the land would be open to Jewish immigration and settlement but closed to Arabs, who would remain constrained in their residential enclaves, exercising only municipal and cultural autonomy.[2]

This scenario would see the abandonment of the Oslo framework and the disbandment of the Palestinian Authority. As the platform of most rightist Zionist parties suggests, Palestinians would hold Jordanian citizenship and participate in Jordanian electoral politics. The scenario may also lead to the implementation of the goal of population transfer, prevalent among Jewish right-wing parties, that is, the encouragement or coercion of Arabs to leave Israel/Palestine and settle in other countries. In whichever version, the greater Israel agenda, which has dominated Israeli politics since the 1970s, will continue to transform the state into an apartheid society, with a near certainty of escalating ethnonational conflict and economic decline. No legitimate demos or stable regime can eventuate under this scenario.

GREATER PALESTINE

The greater Palestine scenario entails the regaining of Palestinian (and/or Islamic) control over historic Palestine, with free return of refugees to the West Bank and Gaza as well as Israel proper. Jews would be allowed to stay as a minority, exercising cultural autonomy, but free Jewish immigration to the land would cease. This was the consensus vision during the rise of the Palestinian national movement, but following the acceptance of a two-state solution by the PLO in 1988, it has remained the platform of most rejectionist Palestinian organizations, including the increasingly popular Hamas and Islamic Jihad. It has also gained popularity during the al-Aqsa *intifada* in the Gaza Strip and among the Palestinian diasporas. Radical versions of this scenario, mainly held by Islamic organizations, call for the transfer of most, or some, Jews from the land, where their existence is perceived as illegal and illegitimate.

A subversion of this scenario is the PLO's historic demand for a secular and democratic state over historic Palestine, a scenario that is still held by several nationalist Palestinian organizations, such as the Democratic and Popular Fronts for the Liberation of Palestine, and the Sons of the Village in Israel. Despite the democratic potential of a secular state, the material expression of this scenario, in terms of ethnonational relations, may not be substantially different from the vision of Arab-Islamic Palestine. The mass return of Palestinian refugees (and, perhaps, the ongoing presence of Jews in West Bank settlements) would be sure to sharpen ethnic conflict. The demographic advantage of Palestinians in a one-state situation, coupled with a lack of a constitutional guarantee of Jewish self-determination and other key collective rights, would make the chance of creating a legitimate demos, and hence democratic rule, improbable.

One Binational (and Multicultural) State

A binational and multicultural state calls for establishing a consociational state over the entire historic Palestine, with political parity between Jews and Palestinians. Each nation would exercise full self-determination and autonomy in most aspects of communal life. Within Jewish and Palestinian nations, the existence of ethnic and religious minorities would be respected and protected. Following the settlement of the Palestinian refugees, future immigration of Jews and Palestinians would be determined jointly and evenly between the two national communities. Most resources, including land, would be distributed according to the principles of proportionality and need, while respecting the validity of current property arrangements.

The state would be decentralized both geographically (into administrative regions) and ethnically. Freedom of movement, residence, and employment would be protected. Local authorities (Arab or Jewish) would have the autonomy to shape the public space. Jerusalem/al-Quds would be an open, joint, and shared capital.

This scenario has its roots in the Jewish thinkers of the 1920s, and later among both Jewish and Palestinian groups. Lately, it has received renewed attention among Palestinians, mainly in Israel and the diaspora. It possesses a good potential to create a legitimate demos in Israel/Palestine, although, in the short term, it appears highly unlikely that any major Jewish body would accept this scenario, which amounts to a major loss of power— the end to Jewish sovereignty and a sharp decline in Jewish control over territory and resources. Because a democratic binational state can only be established by mutual agreement, the sweeping Jewish opposition renders this option, at this point in time, highly unlikely.

Gradual Binationalism

Gradual binationalism envisages a gradual resolution of the conflict, beginning with a two-state-like arrangement, but simultaneously moving to create binational frameworks to manage the joint and small Israeli/Palestinian territory. For a set period (perhaps for a generation; that is, twenty-five to thirty-five years), immigration would be mainly restricted to a mother state, that is, Palestinians would have free access to Palestine and Jews to Israel (with some exceptions regarding Palestinian refugees, as detailed below). In parallel to the establishment of two states, arrangements enabling increasing Israeli-Palestinian integration would be put in train in many spheres of state governance. These would gradually increase the accessibility of the two political spaces to one another and establish joint processes, agreements, and institutions for managing the economy, employment, trade, environment, and security. After such a period, with cessation of violence between the two peoples, and the new consciousness of coexistence, the most logical and efficient next move, for both states, would be the establishment of a confederation or highly decentralized federation. This would preserve their national self-determination while improving the management, security, prosperity, and openness of their joint land.[3]

In such a scenario, the joint metropolitan region of Jerusalem/al-Quds would have a pivotal role in establishing a ground-breaking example for binational management of space, first on an urban level and later on regional and statewide scales. In addition, such a phased framework would give legitimacy to multicultural arrangements vis-à-vis minorities inside Israel and Palestine, most notably autonomy of the Arab and ultra-Orthodox groups in Israel, and special arrangements with the Christians, Bedouins, Armenians, and other minorities in Palestine.

These are the six most prevalent options for the future political geography of Israel/Palestine. Several other scenarios no doubt exist, but probably not with the same level of acceptability to large constituencies. The main point here is not to recite a well-known list of political agendas but rather to open up the question of the deliberate redesign of the demos as a path to transform ethnocracy to democracy. In that vein we can ask: Which configuration is best suited for the creation of inclusive and stable political communities? Which will create the best conditions of reconciliation and development for Jews and Palestinians?

It is clear that the first, third, and fourth options (namely, repressive consolidation, greater Israel, and greater Palestine) harbor severe difficulties. The latter two would be driven by goals of ethnicization (either Judaization or Arabization) and hence would be likely to exacerbate the conflict. The second option (two ethnic states) is held internationally as the best scenario for peace and indeed has the potential to enhance reconciliation. Yet it is likely to create two ethnocracies between Jordan and the sea. This is no doubt preferable to the existing situation of one-sided occupation, oppression, and reciprocal violence, but it is not the best platform to achieve a stable demos. This scenario would be especially difficult to implement inside Israel, with an increasingly assertive Arab minority and deepening conflict between secular and orthodox Jews on the meaning and geography of the Jewish state. A stark illustration of this difficulty (and by no means the only one) was the 1995 assassination of Prime Minister Rabin by an Orthodox Jew who opposed both Rabin's willingness to retreat from the Land of Israel territories and to form a political partnership with Israel's Palestinian citizens.

We are then left with the fifth and sixth options, both accepting, at a deep level, the binational structure of the land and attempting to reconfigure political frameworks to reflect and to legitimize this structural reality. As already noted, the fifth option (one binational state) also appears problematic, as the immediate creation of a binational state may be fraught with severe conflicts owing to the disruptions associated with rapid redistribution of major resources (especially land, housing, and employment) and to the fierce opposition likely to arise from most Jews. It should be remembered that the collective Jewish psyche is still driven by the memory of genocide, dislocation, and fear, and that communal security and self-determination of the Jewish nation is a goal that will not be relinquished by the vast majority of Jews. Hence, the theoretical democratic design of a joint state may result not in the creation of a legitimate demos but in additional rounds of communal violence.

Therefore, the most promising and politically sustainable scenario, based on the analyses presented in this book, is the sixth option, namely phased binationalism. It is based on the long-term creation of new frameworks and consciousness of coexistence, premised on the legitimacy of both Jewish and Palestinian bonds to their common, relished homeland. It is also premised on dealing with the denied root causes of the conflict, such as the return of Palestinian refugees and the Jewish right of self-determination, and on the creation of new spaces for shared management of Israel/Palestine, with a potential to gradually blunt Jewish-Palestinian dichotomies.

This scenario challenges the very logic of the ethnocratic state, by—first and foremost—granting equal status to the Palestinian and the Jewish Israeli nations. As explained below, it also attempts to create a long-term framework of an open homeland for both peoples, a position that is diametrically opposed to the ethnocratic endeavor to impose an endless set of ethnic boundaries, barriers, and obstacles concerning the development and mobility of weakened groups. It also endeavors to envisage a new Israeli demos, which would empower a range of ethnicities and individuals in a new democratic and multicultural Israeli polity.

The first stage under this scenario is the ending of Israeli occupation, the evacuation of most Jewish settlement in the occupied territories, and the creation of two sovereign political entities—Israel and Palestine, based on the Green Line.[4] One of the most urgent tasks of the two states would be to settle the complex refugee question, especially concerning issues of property and citizenship, while not undermining the self-determination and security of the two nations. This requires open negotiation between conflicting rights and conflicting decisions of international bodies. Under the gradual binationalism scenario, the arrangement would be based on acknowledgment of Israel's historic responsibility for the plight of the refugees, as well as Arab and Israeli responsibility for mutual violence and terror.[5] This would be accompanied by statements of public apology and recognition of the right of the two nations to exist securely in Israel/ Palestine.

Under this scenario the Palestinian right/claim of return would be acknowledged by Israel as manifestation of the collective and unbroken bond of the Palestinians to all parts of historic Palestine. However, the individual implementation of Palestinian return to Israel proper would be constrained—by agreement—by two major factors: (a) recognition of the full set of relevant international decisions (including UN General Assembly 181, 194, and UN Security Council 242) that acknowledge the right of Jewish self-determination (based on the arrival of most Jews in Palestine/Israel as refugees or coerced migrants during the twentieth century), with its territorial manifestations, including Israeli control of immigration within its sovereign boundaries; and (b) the likely problematic consequences of large-scale Palestinian immigration into Israel proper, namely the danger of chronic and violent instability, born of ethnic conflicts over history, property, resources, and political rights.

Given these constraints, a system of gradual refugee return would be initiated, based primarily on criteria of individual needs. Under such a setting, it is likely that two to three hundred thousand refugees—chiefly stateless communities from Lebanon—would gradually return to Israel. The majority of refugees, however, would either resettle in the Palestinian state or remain in their current locations, gaining full compensation for their lost property and sufferings. The right of Jewish settlers to remain in a Palestinian state as citizens without collective territorial claims would also be recognized. It is further envisaged that the majority of Jewish settlements and their elaborate infrastructures would be used for the settlement and development of Palestinian refugees, thereby providing (indirect) Israeli assistance for resolving the refugee question. In order to stabilize the population, the two states would also declare a particular period—possibly a decade—after which the Palestinian and Jewish right of automatic immigration into their homeland states (the Right of Return and the Law of Return, respectively) would cease to exist.

Under gradual binationalism the Jerusalem/al-Quds Capital Region would form a model for creating binational (and bistate) frameworks to manage the multiplicity of joint civil and urban affairs with which the two intertwined states would have to deal. In a later phase, perhaps after two to three decades, as security, mobility, and accessibility improve, both states would become increasingly open to one another regarding employment, investment, tourism, marriage, leisure, study, and even residence. As noted earlier, the arrangements between the two states would then move toward a confederation or decentralized federation—two sovereign entities jointly managing many areas of life, while ensuring freedom of movement and the self-determination of each national community. At that time, with the increasing impact of globalization and interstate cooperation in the Middle East, the emotional power attached to ethnonational sovereignty would subside, enabling the new confederational arrangements to be accepted by most Jews and Palestinians.

One of the main features of the binational framework is the legitimacy, and hence security, it would endow to the existence of a Jewish Hebrew nation in the Middle East. Given the tragic history of Jews, and the persisting rejection of Israel and Jewish nationalism in parts of the Middle East, this would be a major step toward allaying the existential fears of many Jews, thereby quelling most Jewish aggression. We should not lose sight that one of the most profound long-term issues related to the Zionist-Palestinian conflict is the acceptance and of Jews in the Middle East as a legitimate national and political collectivity. This legitimacy would also allow Jewish public discourse to move away from its recent preoccupation with demographic danger and the need for separation (manifest in the brutal and internationally condemned separation barrier constructed in the West Bank). Notably, Jewish voices—many from the Zionist left—have often used the demographic danger and the need for separation as possible reasons for retreating from some Palestinian territory in order to improve security and advance toward peace. But ironically, the steps taken by Israel have fed the conflict with new waves of anxiety following ever harsher security measures imposed on Palestinian movement and political freedom in the name of security and peace. This has had the effect of destroying trust, thereby making Jews even less secure.

The gradual binational framework would address this concern by granting historical and moral recognition to Jewish nationalism by its most belligerent nemesis—the Palestinian national movement. This would open the way for broader and deeper acceptance and legitimacy in the Middle East, provided of course that Israel ends the occupation of Palestinian territories, stops the massive use of violence, and assists in settling the refugee problem. This would also depend on Palestinian society finding ways to restrain most of its anti-Israeli and anti-Jewish public rhetoric and especially to suppress Palestinian terror against Jewish civilians.

The phased binationalism approach is, at present, a distant, almost utopian, scenario, likely to be constantly undermined by state aggression and ethnic violence. Movement toward such a scenario will probably be slow and require deep transformation in a multitude of societal spheres, including education, mass culture, land policies, the impact of militarist and religious elements on politics, and patterns of economic development and resource distribution. It will also require the leadership among Jews and Palestinians to firmly adopt a strategy of peace, as well as direct intervention of international bodies (ending Israel's exceptionalism in defying the legitimate decisions of the international community on Palestine, while ensuring its security in the Middle East).

Yet, despite its remoteness at present, the articulation of such a normative scenario is vital for the construction of resistance to the current oppressive order and for the formation of new social, economic, cultural, and political agendas. For the short term, the repressive consolidation approach will dominate the political geography of Israel/Palestine, exacerbating the process of creeping apartheid and ethnic conflict. However, these conflicts may be tempered by several short-term measures, such as security fences and tightening surveillance, or, at times, by selective easing of the grip over Palestinians, or even the declaration of a provisional Palestinian state. Yet none of these measures can get to the root of the Jewish-Palestinian conflict and thereby address the conditions for long-term coexistence, as does the gradual binationalism approach.

To sum up, I argue that lasting Jewish-Palestinian reconciliation is impossible without a long-term vision that includes the creation of a legitimate, inclusive political community (a demos). This would entail the introduction of political arrangements, which would end Israeli occupation, enfranchise all permanent residents of Israel/Palestine, and ensure the security and legitimacy of both Palestinian and Jewish nations on that land. The most promising possibility of progressing toward such a future, I contend, lies in imagining, planning, and implementing the vision of phased binationalism, wherein two demoses are initially created along with parallel, joint Israel-Palestinian institutions and frameworks that would progress toward establishing a thin confederation over the entire land.

Phased Binationalism and the Israeli Demos

Beyond this broad Israeli-Palestinian framework, the normative ending of this book requires further comment on the nature of the Israeli demos. The geography, demography, and power arrangements of the demos, on which we focused above, are necessary but not sufficient conditions to create a democratic polity with legitimacy. Three additional factors—the place of the Palestinian minority, the impact of resource distribution, and the making of a multicultural polity—are all critical for the making of the Israeli demos.

Within two decades, the population of the Palestinian-Arab national minority will grow to one-quarter of the size of the Israeli citizenry, creating in effect a binational situation inside Israel proper. This reality is not likely to receive official recognition or political legitimacy quickly among Jewish elites. Yet, within the framework of an Israeli-Palestinian agreement, and as part of the legitimacy to the binational reality of Israel/Palestine, the democratization of Israeli society should be enhanced significantly, especially as regards the rights and capabilities of Arab citizens. The new political framework and improved security for both Jews and Palestinians would allow a variety of aspects to be reformed from below and reshape the Israeli polity.

As discussed in several of the book's chapters, the Arabs have been creating what can be described as a fractured region within Israel. This process is likely to continue with piecemeal moves toward cultural autonomy and devolution of certain regime functions to the Arab communal, economic, and political leadership. These measures may resemble some of the arrangements enjoyed by the ultra-Orthodox sector, which protects its cultural and material autonomy within Israel.

Under this scenario, and as depicted in Figure 12.2, it is likely that Israel will be reshaped as a multicultural (plural) state, with the Palestinian-Arab and ultra-Orthodox sectors forming two important largely nonassimilating, and relatively autonomous communities of citizens. The recognition of these sectors, and the allocation of collective rights and capabilities, by their very nature, would devolve the highly centralized nature of the Israeli state. At the same time, however, they may be compatible with the desire of most non-Orthodox Israeli Jews to maintain a Jewish-Hebrew public sphere in many of the state's arenas, within which the identities of other subgroups could be molded through the forces of assimilation, solidarity, and conflict. Whichever arrangement is achieved, the existence of a prominent and autonomous Palestinian community in Israel, which should receive a constitutional status as a national minority, is sure to strengthen the binational framework for the entire Israel/Palestine and the transformation of the Israeli state into a more devolved and democratic regime.

A QUESTION OF RESOURCES

The deep materiality of ethnic, social, and political relations should never be ignored. Discussions of rights, identities, cultures, and political configurations must be constantly framed within the concrete reality in which they are enmeshed. Hence, the re-creation of a legitimate Israeli demos profoundly depends on the nature of allocating scarce material resources between the state's ethnoclasses.

As we have seen in several of the book's chapters, one of the main characteristics of the Israeli ethnocracy has been the uneven allocation of resources, most notably land, development, municipal areas, employment, services, and facilities. This has created long-term patterns of conspicuous ethnoclass stratification. It is clear that part of the ethnic divergence and polarization of Israeli society relates to this long-term stratification, and any future reform must seriously address these issues.

Moreover, the dominant processes at present lead in the opposite direction, with the gradual but profound liberalization of the Israeli economy. This process began in the mid-1980s and has accelerated during the last five years. The state has attempted to reduce its welfare safety net by shrinking public allowances and expenses and by selling off government assets and companies. At the same time, it has increased the incentives for capital

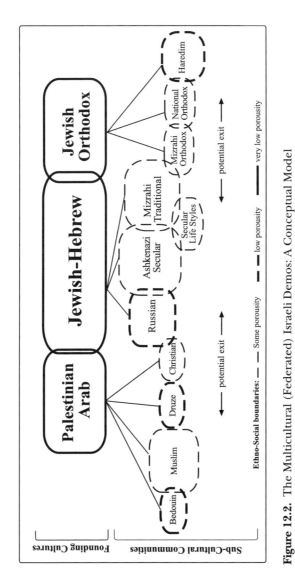

Figure 12.2. The Multicultural (Federated) Israeli Demos: A Conceptual Model

investment and reduced taxes. The state has also weakened organized labor, deregulated money markets, reduced tariffs, and allowed the mass importation of foreign labor.

The retreat of the state from the market and the opening up of the economy may have a positive potential for individual members of peripheral groups. On a structural level, however, they reinforce the gaps between ethnoclasses, as a result of what was termed earlier in the book the ethnic logic of capital. This is particularly true in times of economic crisis, as experienced in Israel since the year 2000.

While the liberalization of the Israeli economy may (or may not) improve several economic arenas, such as gross domestic product, inflation, and average income, repeated analyses show that this liberalization will have little effect on the critical gap between groups and on the welfare of the lower socioeconomic rungs. In terms of the Israeli demos, it is clear that existing processes will further undermine the creation of a political community with a high degree of legitimacy. Therefore, it is imperative that the state remains a strong actor in the market, that it regulates the distribution and use of public lands according to transparent and just criteria, that labor remains organized, and that public policies work to equalize the material existence of all Israelis.

Several Forms of Israeliness?

The creation of an Israeli demos is further complicated by the multiplicity of groups whose cultures, ideology, and goals diverge greatly. (Several of these are nonassimilating groups that have rigid ethnic, religious, or geographical boundaries.) The multiplicity of cultures, ethnic groups, and sectors seriously impedes the crystallization of an overarching Israeliness and the construction of solidarity and tolerance. The development of a sense of Israeliness, as shown throughout the book, is particularly hampered by the Judaization project, which promotes Jewishness in the public sphere at the expense of peripheral minorities. The sense of Israeliness is also undermined by the growing disengagement of Israel's Palestinian citizens, whose aversion to state symbols, duties, and identity is strengthening.

Given this setting, the Israeli demos can no longer be perceived—descriptively or normatively—as a melting pot into which all immigrants and minorities could assimilate. This was the dominant approach among Jewish Ashkenazi policy makers until the 1990s, which caused much tension among ethnic and religious groups who were expected to adopt Israeli Ashkenazi culture. A similar approach attempted to turn the Palestinian citizens into Israeli Arabs devoid of their history, nationality, and collective aspirations.

By the same token, the Israeli demos, and the promise of full and equal citizenship, cannot ignore the connections that need to be fostered between groups. Citizenship cannot rest solely on legal equality and group identity. It has to rest on the making of a common political space and a degree of mutual solidarity and trust. This stands in contrast to the conspicuous politics of identity recently advocated by several minority leaders, mainly between Arab and ultra-Orthodox groups. Such an approach is often enhanced by a deliberate process of othering, whereby identity is shaped by emphasizing the tension with the other groups. Given the very different, and often conflicting, definitions of the collective good by these groups, an overemphasis on identity is likely to generate separatism and result in protracted conflicts and oppression of minorities.

Therefore, the Israeli demos—if it is genuinely to emerge—needs to balance ethnic identity and citizenship. The new Israeliness must respect group identities, histories, and visions while creating institutions and processes that promote a degree of common citizenry, as well as joint societal goals, ideologies, and interests. It can possibly be promoted through the introduction of a new language of coexistence to the official public discourse, through revised education curriculum, more accessible forums of resource allocation, and restructured sites of communal representation.

This transformation may be assisted by the devolution of the Israeli state in two main directions. First, geographically, the management of many aspects of life should be devolved to regions. This would encourage groups to cooperate and form regional (multiethnic) institutions, parties, and interests; it would also encourage them to come into closer contact, not as rivals, but rather as partners in common struggles. Israel should decentralize its highly centralized administrative, legal, economic, and electoral structure, and it should promote the development of regional, crosscultural, and multiethnic identities. Past experiences in deeply divided societies, such as Malaysia and Canada, show that geographic (nonethnic) regionalism assists in the management of protracted conflicts.

Second, Israel should recognize several *founding communities* as forming the cultural bases for its multicultural society. At present, there appear several obvious candidates: (a) mainstream secular Jews (who hold a Hebrew culture); (b) ultra-Orthodox Jews (Jewish culture); and (c) Palestinian citizens (Palestinian-Arab culture). These groups are large, relatively stable, and would serve as durable communal foundations. The state should be restructured to reflect the depth and aspirations of these founding cultures, which would be protected and resourced under a new constitution. This could be achieved by the sanctioning of a communal (ethnic) education system, electronic and printed media, housing development, and local government areas. It is therefore possible to imagine a future Israel as having several autonomous communities in partnership, simultaneously promoting their respective Hebrew, Jewish, and Arab cultures yet held together by a common Israeli layer of civil and political activity and identity.

The state's recognition of these founding cultures, however, should not be premised on their incorporation as separatist but rather as groups integrating into the Israeli polity. The Israeli polity should be designed as an expression of collective needs and identities within the realms of Israeli citizenship, resembling the asymmetric federalism established in recent years in post-Franco Spain, in which autonomous ethnic communities, such as the Catalans, Galicians, and Basques enter into specific tailor-made constitutional arrangements with the central state. Under such settings, the fierce debate about the nature of the Jewish state would lose much of its venom, since the point of contention would focus less on the state's formal definition and more on the collective rights and capabilities it endows to each community. From the perspective of the scenario sketched here, the best option would be to define Israel as an *Israeli* or to a lesser extent a *Hebrew* (but not Jewish) state. The Israeli definition would maintain a special link to Jewish and Hebrew history through the special meaning attached to the word "Israel." But such a state would also allow a path of entry for non-Jewish minorities, currently denied under the state's official Jewish definition. But even if the state continues to be defined as Jewish, the *federal-type* regime structure suggested here would allow each community to secure its own identity and culture and to possess formal involvement in state decision making. Crucially, the state would then cease to be a Judaizing state, thereby losing many of its conflict-inducing ethnocratic characteristics.

Beyond the founding communities, whose autonomy and sustainability should be enhanced, the state should also enable the articulation and protection of other (sub)cultures and communal lifestyles. These will depend on the mobilization of sufficient demand and will entail softer forms of cultural autonomy, not constitutionally guaranteed but enabling the initiation of education programs, media outlets, residential communities, and communal institutions. As illustrated in Figure 12.2, candidates for such collective arrangements are Russian, Mizrahi, religious (Jewish, Muslim), Druze, *kibbutz*, and gay communities, to name but a few.

It should be stressed, however, that these arrangements, regarding both founding and other cultures, must be premised on voluntary association. Members of all groups should maintain at all times an exit option; that is, they should be able to exist as individual Israelis and enjoy full civil rights without institutionally belonging to any specific substate cultural community. In terms of regime principles, the proposed scenario is close to the recent ideas of the philosopher Iris Mirian Young, who articulated a vision of "nondominating self-determination" as a fundamental collective right and "differentiated solidarity" as a normative vision of group coexistence within a deeply divided political system (Young 2005).

Clearly, the above is but a rough and brief sketch designed to provoke thought and promote debate. What is clear, however, is that without serious thinking of the possibilities of creating a legitimate and sustainable demos, the Israeli polity itself will be under severe stress, constantly struggling against disgruntled minorities. The current repressive consolidation approach, which dominates Israeli policy making, is amplifying the current situation and grievances. It is never too early to start thinking about a moral, effective, and workable design for the troubled Land of Israel/Palestine. As I have shown above, gradual binationalism and a new perception of the Israeli demos have the potential to establish legitimate political communities, which are the prerequisite for the different, democratic, and peaceful future both Israelis and Palestinians deserve.

Finally, I chose to illustrate the new sprit required (and desired) for the future of Israel/Palestine by drawing on Palestinian and Israeli poetic skills. First, Shobhi al-Zobaidi advances a new version of Palestinian love of the homeland, not based solely on ethnically pure territory, history, earth, and holiness but rather on a simple attachment to one's place.

Love (Dance of the Resistance)[6]
Greetings . . . to love,
To the homeland,
To my beloved sun.

. . . Tomorrow they'll draw a melody
with notes embroidered upon the cheek
Like a beauty mark.
The melody will say
The homeland is a tear,
Not a hill or a spring.
The homeland is human.

The homeland is human,
With eyes gazing
At those that say
That the homeland is just
A handful of earth.
(al-Zobaidi 1987)

In a similar vein, the Mizrahi poet-singer Etti Ankri offers a critical interpretation of the Israeli homeland discourse. Ankri unpacks the holiness of the land, the quest for total (national and male) control, and the unquenchable thirst for territorial expansion. She makes an exceptional break from the typically inward-looking Israeli Jewish writing by giving voice to the local Arab who reminds the settling Jew that the land remains just land, "before and after" being sanctified by settlers and conquerors. By unpersonifying the land, Ankri rehumanizes its inhabitants and allows a new, equalizing perspective to paint the injuring encounter between Palestinian and Jew. Holding on to the land, we are told, involves human "nourishment" (symbolized by the "watering" metaphor), as opposed to the brutal, hollow force so commonly used. Al-Sobhi's and Ankri's lyrics then open the door to new thinking, where Jews and Palestinians—both members of traumatized national communities—can dialogue equally about their joint homeland. In that quest they may genuinely initiate the complex, painful, but necessary journey towards recognition, decolonization and coexistence.

Land Before, Land After

She was wild, you came and touched
You sang to her songs at night
She was sand dunes, you wore khaki
And fertilized inaccessible sites

You grip her desperately
But under your arm she slips
You planted in her hopes
But didn't give her water to sip

She doesn't know about you and me
Because your voice has been faint
Land before, land after
That you made her into a human saint

She was honey, you squeezed the milk
You put guards on her walls
Roads you paved through the desert
Gathered into lines on her soul

Then you wanted another
One that looks like a picture
The one at home is already old
A jaded, faded creature

She will stay here, when you are gone
She is a whore with a fleshy past
She lies prostrate under all powers
If they continue to feed her with blood

Above her nations fall
But she has no ears or lips
She buries her own children
When she has no water to sip

She doesn't know about you and me
Because your voice has been faint
Land before, land after
That you made her into a human saint
(Ankri 1990)[7]

Ethnocracy: A Conceptual Tour

This appendix provides a brief tour through the terms, concepts, and language of the ethnocratic approach. The following is, in essence, an annotated glossary of terms, abstractions, and ideas that combine to create the conceptual architecture of the ethnocratic theory. The appendix summarizes most of the original concepts, meanings, and ideas I have coined or developed in my work since the early 1990s. This may prove to be a useful guide for the reader to the various chapters in this book.

Some of the terms are explained in more depth within specific chapters. However, the definition of these terms in sequence, as outlined here, will enable the reader to appreciate the linkages between the concepts and their role in forming a cohesive ethnocratic framework. This combined appreciation may be more difficult to achieve by reading the individual chapters separately.

The concepts defined below are methodologically designed to function as ideal types; that is, pure articulations of a state of affairs that are rarely realized in full. But critically, unlike the somewhat rigid Weberian approach usually associated with ideal types, the ethnocracy model is inherently dynamic, focusing on the process of ethnicization. The main goal of this appendix, hence, is to offer signposts that help dissect and fathom the main forces and processes in a complex and changing reality.

Ethnocracy

Ethnocracy denotes a type of regime that facilitates and promotes the process of *ethnicization*, that is, expansion and control. It surfaces in disputed territories, where one ethnonational group is able to appropriate the state apparatus and mobilize its legal, economic, and military resources to further its territorial, economic, cultural, and political interests. The struggles over the process of ethnic expansion become the central axis along which social and political relations evolve.

The term "ethnocracy" harbors an additional meaning: not only does it denote the dominance of a specific ethnic group, it also denotes *the prominence of ethnicity* in all aspects of communal life. This is due to the elevation of the ethnos over the demos as a principle of political organization. Ethnocracy legitimizes the use of ethnicity (that is, cultural identity based on belief in a common past at a specific place) as a tool for intranational group stratification and marginalization.

Examples of ethnocratic regimes include the past regimes in settler societies such as nineteenth-century Australia, Canada, South Africa, the United States, and New Zealand, and more contemporary states such as Latvia, Estonia, Serbia, pre-1997 Northern Ireland, pre-1974 Cyprus, Sri Lanka, Malaysia, Israel/Palestine, pre-1975 Lebanon, and Uganda.

Most ethnocracies are neither democratic nor authoritarian or totalitarian. They possess deep ethnic and racial hierarchies, expressed in most aspects of the public domain. Ethnocracies may range in their levels of oppression and freedoms, but invariably they are chronically unstable and replete with ethnic conflicts and tensions. During the last three decades, several ethnocratic regimes have democratized, most notably Canada, Belgium, and New Zealand.

Ethnos and Demos

These are two competing principles of political organization and collective identities. The ethnos determines group membership by common origin, promoting kin relations as the main (often mythical) principle of delineating group boundaries. As such, it tends to racialize and essentialize group identities, thereby minimizing boundary crossing and the making of new identities. The demos determines group membership by residence in a common territory (regardless of ethnic origins). It promotes the institutions of citizenship, law, and patriotism as the main tools in creating a territorial political community.

Ruptured Demos

A central characteristic of ethnocratic regimes is their diminution of the political concept of the demos, which requires equal citizenship in a bounded territory over which the law of the land is equally applied. Ethnocratic regimes tend to "rupture" the demos in two chief manners: (a) they often disregard political borders by capturing and/or settling regions beyond their recognized territory and by empowering co-ethnic diasporas; and (b) they establish unequal citizenship based on ethnic hierarchy.

Settling Ethnocracy

A special type of ethnocratic regime can be found in settler societies. These are typically colonial states that settle populations in a project that aims to diminish the control of local, indigenous, or rival groups. Settling ethnocracies may be internal or external. The latter relates mainly to European colonial states, which seized and settled vast lands in the Americas, southern Africa, and Asia. The former includes states that manipulate their internal ethnic geography in order to expand the territorial holding of the dominant ethnos.

Ethnicization

Ethnicization is the key engine driving ethnocratic societies. It is a process by which a dominant ethnonational group expands the bounds and depth of its control over competing groups. It may involve military, geographical, immigration, economic, political, legal, or cultural means that advance the goals, interests, and will of the dominant groups. Ethnicization also works within the national community, where one version of culture and identity (usually belonging to the most powerful group within the nation), assumes the position of prominence. This creates the diminution of competing cultural constructions within the nation, leading to the marginalization or assimilation of peripheral ethnoclasses.

Two Levels of Ethnicity

Ethnic relations and identities are formed in ethnocratic states along two main levels: ethnonations and ethnoclasses. The former denotes the most dominant and essentialist level of identity discourse, which ascribes a rigid ethnonational identity to each resident and constructs the main apparatus of mobilization according to ethnonational narratives. The latter is a more subtle, yet pervasive form of differentiation and segregation, which is formed in parallel with and as a result of the ethnonational conflict.

Ethnoclasses

In ethnocratic societies, the dynamics of ethnonational expansion largely determine the internal distribution of scarce public resources, especially land, capital, and political power. Hence, territorial expansion is often accompanied by a parallel process of socioeconomic stratification, whereby the social logic of ethnicity reinforces the logic of capital accumulation. This creates ethnoclasses, which are broad social strata characterized and positioned by a combination of ethnicity and class. In general, the more distant an ethnic group is from the founding charter group, the lower it is on the ethnoclass hierarchy. However, despite the persistence of stratification, the level of porosity between ethnoclasses is considerably higher than between the highly segregated ethnic nations.

Internal Frontiers

Ethnocratic regimes are driven by the goal of ethnonational expansion. To accomplish this aim the dominant group often delineates "frontiers," into which it applies the project of ethnicization. These may be geographical frontiers, as in outlying regions, particularly those dominated by minorities, or metaphorical frontiers, such as the modernization of the economy, the education of the ignorant, or the militarization of the young.

Trapped Minority

The expansionist drive of ethnocratic regimes works to trap minorities in a position from which they can neither fully integrate into the state's dominant ethnos nor secede from the political system. Any competing political or identity projects advanced by minorities are marginalized and delegitimized. Minorities can be trapped within the ethnocratic project (and expected to assimilate) or trapped outside the project (and thus remain excluded from the main loci of power and resources).

Fractured Region

Settler ethnocracies (defined above) attempt to reshape the state's human geography by facilitating, planning, and/or coercing an ethnic spatial mix. This phenomenon is most conspicuous in peripheral regions, where the state seeks to break the territorial contiguity of the minority and weaken its ability to mobilize on a geographical basis. The settlers in such regions are often economically deprived members of the dominant ethnos. The result is a fractured region, characterized by an uneven mix of ethnoclasses, by a multitude of intraregional conflicts, and by a lack of ability to mobilize a regional political or economic agenda able to challenge the centers of state power.

The Dark Side of Planning

Ethnocratic regimes use spatial planning as a key arm of their ethnic policies. But rather than using the light side of planning, which has traditionally sought to create a more equitable and prosperous society, the state uses the dark side of planning, which seeks to impose territorial, economic, and political control over minorities. This is achieved through identifying the public with the dominant ethnic group and gearing most planning policies to assist that public good. Because control over space is at the heart of most ethnic conflicts, public planning is used by the majority to enforce ethnic

control through policies of settlement, land control, economic development, and undemocratic decision-making processes.

Ethnic Religion

In most ethnocracies, the identity of the dominant group is concurrently
ethnic and religious. In such cases, religion becomes a border marker for
the expanding ethnic identity vis-à-vis neighboring groups. The exclusion
of other groups is greatly assisted by the religious narrative, which adds historical and spiritual depth to the protection of ethnic boundaries.

Ungendered Ethnicity

Ethnocratic societies are typified by the relative absence of gender issues in
the public arena and by conspicuous gender inequalities. This derives
from the overarching ethnocratic outlook, which constructs the world as
battlefields of ethnicities, stressing values such as territory, militarism, and
fertility. In such a setting, men and women are expected to collaborate in
the great ethnic command of group reproduction and to maintain a powerful, united group. Gender differences are thus underplayed, and femi-
nist voices are routinely silenced or ridiculed.

Urban Ethnocracy

Certain urban areas develop regimes with ethnocratic goals of expanding
ethnic spatial and political control. High levels of ethnic segregation and
wide disparities among ethnoclasses typify these areas. However, urban
regimes are also driven by strong economic forces and are relatively open,
having less control than states over issues such as immigration, land control, and development. Tensions typically rise between the goals of urban
ethnocratic regimes to ethnicize their cities and the relative openness of
the urban housing and labor markets.

The Shadow City

Urban ethnocratic regimes often create implicit citizenship, which endows
its powerful social circles with full rights to the city and its resources, while
denying these rights to other groups of urban dwellers. As a result, informal
shantytowns are often created near the ethnocratic city, while at the same
time large numbers of "illegal" residents settle in existing housing. These
are the shadows necessary for fueling the urban system (mainly with cheap
labor), but the regime does not grant the newcomers equal rights and access to resources. This disparity tends to create unstable social relations.

Asymmetrical Dialectics

The very oppressive nature of the ethnocratic regime indicates the existence of resistance to regime goals and practices. The tension between the forces enhancing the dominance of the leading ethnos and those opposing it often creates a historical dialectic, which polarizes ethnic groups while reshaping their political geography. However, power differentials also shape this process as asymmetrical, often resulting in the deepening of group segregation and inequality.

Notes

Chapter 1. Introduction

1. The term ethnocracy has appeared previously in the literature (see: Linz and Stephan 1996; Linz 1975; Mazrui 1975; Little 1993). However, as far as I am aware, it was generally used as a derogatory term and not developed into a model or concept as formulated in this book. For an earlier formulation of my ethnocratic theory, see Yiftachel 1997b.

2. *Maariv*, April 14 and 15, 2002.

3. *Haaretz*, April 11, 2003.

4. Author's notes from a meeting with Avraham Burg, chairman of the Jewish Agency, in Umbatin, near Beer-Sheva, November 19, 1997.

5. Throughout the book I refer to a range of group identities. Notably, however, I don't regard those identities as given but rather as dynamic products of ceaseless social (re)constructions around material and discursive conflicts.

Chapter 2. The Ethnocratic Regime

1. For important work on the link between social domination and space, see Massey 1993; Paasi 2000; for further comprehensive critiques of nationalism theories along similar lines, see Chatterjee 1993, 1996; Bishara 1999a.

2. Notably, Anderson (1996, 8) reflects critically at his own previous interpretation on this point, and anticipates "an impending crisis of the hyphen that for two hundred years yoked together state and nation." My claim, however, is that in many cases—especially ethnocratic states—state and nation were never "yoked" together.

3. See, for example, a theme issue of the journal *Geopolitics* (7 [2]: 2002) devoted to the question "when is the nation?"

4. This typology corresponds to a large extent to Yuval-Davis's typology of nationalisms (Yuval-Davis 1997), which identified three main types—civic (liberal), cultural, and ethnic.

5. Clearly, exclusion and marginalization do occur also under the civic and cultural types, although minorities still retain the formal possibility of equality and inclusion, which is denied under ethnocratic conditions.

Chapter 3. Zionist and Palestinian Nationalism

1. http://www.israel.org/mfa/go.asp?MFAH00hb0. All translations from He-brew are by the author.

2. http://208.55.122.96/politics/indep.html. All translations from Arabic are by the author.

3. This does not imply, of course, that the Shoah and the Naqbah are comparable historical tragedies; clearly, the Jewish Holocaust is a disaster of unmatched dimensions.

4. A *nasrin* is a bush typical of Palestine.

5. Knesset Protocols, June 17, 1991.

6. The night Muhammad soared from al-Quds (Jerusalem) to heaven, according to Islam.

7. The value has remained powerful to date; in 1998, for example, Yasser Arafat publically stated that those selling Palestinian land deserve death.

8. A local thorny cactus, adopted as a national symbol by Zionists.

9. *Maariv*, November 10, 1995.

10. *Jerusalem Post*, February 5, 2001.

11. *Haaretz*, December 29, 2002.

12. *The Middle Eastern Times*, February 16, 2001.

13. *Maariv*, April 6, 2001.

14. *Maariv*, September 30, 2000.

15. See http://www.b'tselem.org. These statistics range slightly between the various sources. To compare see http://www.miftah.org/ or http://www.alhaq.org.

16. See http://www.arij.org/. The Israeli government has also investigated this pattern of "semi-illegal" settlement and issued the Sasson Report detailing the involvement of several ministries, most notably housing, security, and infrastructure, as well as the Jewish Agency, with the funding, construction, and protection of these outposts; parts of the report have been leaked to the press; see *Yedio't Ahronot*, January 30, 2005.

17. Uzi Keren, the prime minister's advisor for settlement; see *Haaretz*, July 20, 2003.

18. See extensive reports and special sections throughout 2003 and 2004 in most newspapers, including *Maariv* (http://www.maarivintl.com/), *Haaretz* (www.haaretz.com), *al-Ayyam* (www.al-ayyam.com/); *al-Quds* (http://www.alquds.com/), and the *Jerusalem Times* (http://www.jerusalemtimes.com/).

19. Including the eastern fence, see: http://www.ynet.co.il/articles/1,7340,L-2847306,00.html.

20. See http://www.court.gov.il/heb/index.htm for the Israeli decision and http://www.icj-cij.org/icjwww/idocket/imwp/imwpframe.htm for the ICJ decision.

21. For a comprehensive analysis of the destructive impact of the barrier, see *UN Report on West Bank Security Barrier*, in www.palestinemonitor.org/Reports/UNRWA_special_report_on_wall_July_2003.htm; see also *Haaretz*, August 1, 2003.

22. The government's February of 2005 decision freezes the construction (but not the planning) of the Ariel-Kedumim "fingers," while the Ma'ale Edumim "finger" is to be constructed in the near future.

23. Jewish settlements were removed as part of the Israel-Egypt Peace Treaty during the early 1980s; however, these had not been built within the accepted boundaries of the "Jewish homeland," which according to Israeli public discourse overlaps the borders of British Palestine.

24. See http://www.miftah.org/Index.cfm; http://www.peacenow.org.il/site/en/peace.asp?pi=51.

Chapter 4. Debating Israeli Democracy

1. It should also be mentioned that despite my critique, I still see Israel as relatively democratic in comparison with most Arab regimes, whose norms of freedom and equality are commonly inferior to Israeli standards.

2. This has to be qualified with the fact that Bishara was eventually allowed by the High Court to run for the Israeli elections, following his disqualification by the Knesset electoral committee. Bishara continued to promote the non-Zionist political agenda of the Tajamu'a movement. However, Bishara and a second Arab MK who was disqualified by the Knesset committee (Ahmad Tibbi) stated publicly their acceptance of the Jewish character of the state.

Chapter 5. The Making of Ethnocracy in Israel/Palestine

1. *Qa'adan vs. Israel Land Authority et al.*, Bagatz 6698/95.

2. See http://www.haaretz.co.il/hasite/pages/ShArtPE.jhtml?itemNo=425663& contrassID=2&subContrassID=21&sbSubContrassID=0.

3. *Globes*, January 16, 2003; *Haaretz*, January 23, 2003. In May of 2004, as elaborated in the next chapter, the responsible minister appointed the Gadish Committee to reform the Israel Land Authority, stressing the need for liberalization and the guarding of national interests (see http://www.ynet.co.il/articles/0,7340, L-2944148,00.html).

4. About 4 percent of the Jews, mainly from the former Soviet Union, were not recognized by the religious authorities as Jews but have integrated into the Jewish cultural and ethnic community.

5. Owing to some assimilation and intermarriage, 28 percent of Jewish children born in Israel during the 1990s were of mixed Ashkenazi-Mizrahi origins. The calculation here is based on the father's origins, as determined by the Israeli Bureau of Statistics.

6. Here I follow the popular meaning of secular in Israel as non-Orthodox.

7. The situation was not similar among Jewish communities abroad, where open tensions about the Zionist question have created deep communal rifts since the late nineteenth century (Liebman 1995).

8. Interview with Rabbi Azran, *Globes*, September 28, 1998.

9. Election campaign advertisement, Israeli TV (Channel 1, 10), Broadcast January 26, 2003.

10. Two famous cases were Shalit and Brother Daniel (Kimmerling 2001; Lahav 1997). Neither resolved the ambiguity of becoming Jewish, which has become very different in Israel and among world Jewry. Conversions in Israel have remained under total control of Orthodox Judaism.

11. Here I take issue with Lustick's commentary, following the new wave of Russian immigration, that Israel is turning from a Jewish to a non-Arab state (Lustick 1999). Lustick overlooks the integrative desire of the immigrants as a major force in shaping the boundaries of Israeli Jewish nationalism. Hence, Israel remains well and truly a Jewish state, but the nature of its Jewishness is undergoing considerable change.

12. The majority of conversions are performed among Israel's recent, and much smaller, community of Ethiopian immigrants, averaging 2,092 of an annual total of 3,209 conversions from 1999 to 2002 (Management of Religious Tribunals, quoted in *Haaretz*, March 18, 2003).

13. Orthodox parties hold twenty-seven seats and the rest are held by Orthodox members of other parties.

14. In their rhetoric, religious parties simply attempt to defend the status quo agreement. However, their political discourse and actions are clearly more aggressive than in the past, mirroring the intensifying antireligious secular discourses.

15. In the West Bank and Gaza a full (and not creeping) apartheid is well in place. But given the persistence of democratic practices in large parts of Israeli society and yet the slow slide toward apartheid in Israel proper, I have deemed the term "creeping apartheid" more appropriate to account for the entire Israel/Palestine.

Chapter 6. The Spatial Foundation

1. H.C. 244/00, the Mizrahi Democratic Rainbow (Amutat Siach Hadash).

2. For information on the Mizrahi Democratic Rainbow see: www.hakeshet.org.

3. *Kibbutz* and *moshav* (plural: *kibbutzim* and *moshavim*) are types of Jewish rural collective settlements, established mainly between the 1910s and the 1950s; they received the lion's share of state lands.

4. *Hakibbutz,* January 24, 2001; also, dozens of large, black road signs hung between Jerusalem, Tel Aviv, and Haifa on the first weekend of February of 2002 and stated: "The Rainbow supports the (Palestinian) Right of Return."

5. Yaakov Bachar, a leading figure in the agricultural lobby, Channel 2, February 5, 2002, 11:30 P.M.

6. G. Bargil (chairman of the agricultural lobby), *Ynet News*, February 5, 2002.

7. Granot's (umbrella *kibbutz* organization) response to the High Court (copy with authors).

8. Quoted in Ofer Pittersberg, *Ynet News*, February 12, 2002.

9. Reshet Beit (Israeli Second Radio Channel), Hakkol Dibburim, February 6, 2002.

10. The history of U.S. law, from the beginning of the nation to the present, is premised on the use of sovereign power to allocate property rights in ways that discriminate—and continue to discriminate—against the original inhabitants of the land (Singer 1992). "The failure of the United States courts to protect tribal property rights adequately is based partly on a perceived need to legitimate the current distribution of wealth and power by reference to a mythological picture of the origins and current shape of property rights" (Singer 1992).

11. One dunam equals 0.247 acres, one thousand dunams equals one square kilometer.

12. This number includes about 940,000 dunams of Jewish National Fund land, about 130,000 dunams belonging to the PICA organization, and about 500,000 dunams in private Jewish ownership. For a detailed analysis with different estimates, see Kedar 1998; Kark 1995.

13. The uncertainty as to the exact amount relates to the different ownership categories used by previous (Ottoman and British) land regimes; these have conflicting interpretations (see Kedar 1998).

14. A safety valve regulation allowed the state to sell up to an accumulating total of one hundred thousand dunams of urban land; this amounts to 0.6 percent of its land holdings.

15. Likewise, about 52 percent of the West Bank shifted into Jewish control by the pervasive proclamation of state lands on the basis of *mawat* classification as described above (see B'tselem 2002). Other means of Judaization of the occupied territories were employed as well, such as the establishment of military encampments,

local and regional municipalities, Jewish industrial areas, and recently even Jewish roads (see Benvenisti 1988, 2001; Shehadeh 1998).

16. In *kibbutzim* and community localities there exists a vast Ashkenazi majority, while in *moshavim* there is a small Mizrahi majority, although most of the powerful *moshavim*, established before 1948, are predominantly Ashkenazi.

17. The JNF establishes the Judaization of land at the ownership level, while the Jewish Agency operates at the allocation level. Importantly, both organizations are registered as Israeli companies in order to be represented in the Israeli decision-making bodies. Yet, their financial backing and policy agendas are governed largely by world-Jewry organizations.

18. That is, the agent for Mekarkei Israel (the state, the Development Authority, or the JNF).

19. This includes the area under the jurisdiction of regional councils. The jurisdiction of these councils covers 84 percent of Israel's land area. As a rule, *kibbutzim*, *moshavim*, and community settlements control these councils. Large areas under their jurisdiction are used for agriculture or military purposes and hence are closed to Jewish purchase as well. However, the hundreds of nonurban settlements that are under the jurisdiction of these councils are open for Jews (at least theoretically) but usually not for Arabs.

20. Based on the sources cited in the chapter.

21. The Black Panthers was a group of young Mizrahim who mobilized popular protest against the Israeli elites during the early 1970s. The protest emerged from Jerusalem's poor neighborhoods and spread to other parts of Israel (Bernstein 1984).

22. The most relevant resolutions on this subject include 533, 611, 612, 666, 667, 717, and 737.

23. Arab citizens of Israel too have been excluded from the benefits of this policy change, but unlike the Bedouins they rarely cultivate state lands.

24. On a related matter, Ariel Sharon was recently accused by the state comptroller of a blatant conflict of interest in his direct involvement in the new land regulation. This is because he was at the time both a minister responsible for land and a major landholder. The comptroller's report is a nonlegal document, but it may lead the way to the prosecution of the prime minister (*Haaretz*, August 6, 2003).

25. *Karka*, October 1998: back cover (Hebrew).

26. See framed story in *Karka*, May of 1998.

27. *Haaretz*, real estate supplement, March 16, 1999.

28. See the positions of Adva, Adalah, and the Center for Alternative Planning in Kedar and Yiftachel 1999.

29. The *Mizrahi Democratic Rainbow vs. The Israel Land Authority* (2000-244).

30. Government press release, February 12, 2000.

31. S. Gveretz, letter to the government, reported in *Globes*, January 21, 2001.

32. *Haaretz*, August 6, 2003 (Economics).

33. In recent interviews, Vitkon highly recommended this line of reform (see http://www.ynet.co.il/articles/0,7340,L-2944148,00.html).

34. See the front pages of *Globes*, January 27, 2005; *Haaretz*, January 27, 2005.

35. See the appeal by Adalah: http://www.adalah.org/eng/index.php.

Chapter 7. Fractured Regionalism among Palestinian Arabs in Israel

1. The terms "Arabs" and "Palestinian Arabs" are used interchangeably to describe the Arab citizens of Israel. The addition of "Arabs" is used to prevent confusion with the Palestinian national movement outside Israel, to be consistent with

the terms used by the minority itself, and to make clear the inclusion of the Druze and other communities not identified as Palestinians.

2. See Chapter 6 for details. Given the different land ownership system prior to 1948, it is impossible to classify the ownership of every piece of possessed land and hence the precise extent of state expropriation.

3. See 2002 Report of the Knesset Committee to Investigate Socioeconomic Gaps, headed by MK Ran Cohen: *Review and Report on the Making of Social Gaps in Israel*, Israeli Knesset, Jerusalem, http://www.knesset.gov.il/committees/heb/docs/gap15-4.htm.

4. This section summarizes a detailed study of protest among Israeli peripheries, 1975–98 (see Yiftachel 2006). Overall we documented 726 protest events, 381 among the Arabs and 345 among peripheral Mizrahim. Data were collected from all events reported by any of four leading Israeli newspapers. Events were coded according to their intensity using a composite adapted from Gurr (1993).

5. Givaat Haviva archives, Land Day file.

6. *Kol Yisrael*, October 5, 1999.

7. *Al-Sinnara*, November 4, 2000.

8. Election rally, April 19, 1999, Nazareth, personal recording.

9. Personal account, January of 2001.

10. For details of the Or Commission Report, see http://www.adalah.org/eng/commission.php and http://www.sikkuy.org.il/2003/english03/or03.html.

11. For details of the Lapid Report, see http://www.justice.gov.il/MOJHeb/-Subjects/vaadatLapid.htm.

12. See the full speech at www.adalah.org/bishara/speeches.htm.

13. *Haaretz*, September 22, 2001.

14. See *Maariv*, July 12, 2001 for the first quotation. Rabbi Yosef actually used the Arabic term, *ala keif keifak* to denote a combination of thoroughness and glee with the recommended missile attack. The second statement appeared in *The Jewish Journal of Greater Los Angeles* (August 11, 2000). In his case, the attorney general opened an investigation but concluded there were no grounds for prosecution.

15. Y-Net, November 22, 2002; see internet sites for full testimonies: http://www.idi.org.il/hebrew/catalog.php; http://www.adalah.org/.

16. *Al-Quds al-Arabi*, December 24, 2001 (Arabic).

17. Quoted in *Between the Lines* (2003) 22: 23–24 (English).

18. See the report in the *Washington Post* on the binational idea—http://www.washingtonpost.com/wp-dyn/articles/A36478-2004Jul8_2.html.

19. See *Haaretz*, August 8, 2003.

20. See *Maariv*, August 26, 27, 2002.

21. See http://www.hamoked.org.il/items/5720.htm for the debate in the Knesset. In August of 2003, Adalah—the legal center for Arab minority rights in Israel—appealed to the High Court to strike down the new law as racist and unconstitutional (see www.adala.org).

22. *Al-Ittihad*, December 20, 2002; *Maariv*, December 20, 2002.

23. *Haaretz*, January 16, 2003; *al-Ittihad*, January 16, 2003; the judges were split seven to four.

24. www.jafi.org.il/education/actual/elections/2003

25. See a plan by the government minister Rabbi Benni Elon for voluntary transfer, in an interview with Nadav Shragai, *Haaretz*, February 7, 2002.

26. In several opinion polls in early 2002, 25–46 percent of Jews supported the idea that "Arabs will be asked to move outside the Land of Israel." See *Maariv*, April 5, 2002.

27. *Haaretz*, April 19, 2002, interview with L. Galilee.

28. *Haaretz*, March 22, 2002, interview with A. Shavit.

29. *Haaretz*, December 18, 2003.

30. Not all of the people mentioned agree with the details of Sneh's plan but all support the principles. See articles by R. Gavison, *Yediot Ahronot*, March 25, 2001; A. Oz, *Ynet*, April 1, 2002; A. B. Yehushua, *Maariv*, March 27, 2002.

31. See, for example, *Maariv*, April 12, 2002.

32. *Haaretz*, article by T. Rinat, November 6, 2001. This is in addition to the dozens of small new settlements built in the West Bank since 2000 (known as *ma'ahazim* or outposts, and often described as illegal settlements). These are added to the 941 Jewish settlements already existing in Israel/Palestine and to the ongoing expansion of Jewish settlements in Palestinian territories.

Chapter 8. Bedouin Arabs and Urban Ethnocracy in the Beer-Sheva Region

1. Radio Dorom (Local Radio), Morning Show, May 21, 1998.

2. Arie Sharon is no relation to Israel's current prime minister, Ariel Sharon.

3. Such as *Al Hawashla vs. State of Israel* (1983) and *al-Qaleb vs. Ben-Gurion University* (1984).

4. *Kol Hanegev*, July 11, 2000.

5. *Haaretz*, September 2, 1997.

6. *Akhbar al-Naqab*, July 18, 2003 (Arabic).

7. Stage One Report, p. 4, copy with author.

8. As noted above, this bleak outlook is likely to change somewhat with the release of the new plan for the Beer-Sheva metropolitan area by the team headed by Shamay Assif, and with the 2004 recognition of the rural village of Darijat. Several other rural villages are in the approval pipeline, creating important precedents.

Chapter 9. Mizrahi Identities in the Development Towns

1. In Hebrew, the band's name symbolically means a white-out substance.

Chapter 10. Between Local and National

1. Another option is to bypass the existing political system, as attempted in Israel by ultra-Orthodox groups such as the Jewish Mizrahi Shas and the Islamic movements (see Peled 1998). This will be discussed later in the chapter.

2. In this chapter I do not discuss Tilly's theory of resource mobilization (1978), which assumes that activists in this form of organizing are not marginalized socially or politically, nor subject to social-economic-political discrimination, since this does not, in my opinion, reflect the situation of Mizrahi residents of development towns in Israel.

3. The distinction between immigrant and homeland groups is sharpened for analytical purposes; however this distinction is often blurred in real life and is itself constructed through a multitude of political mobilizations.

4. The analysis included all events expressing dissatisfaction in the public sphere, especially against the state. Data were collected for the years 1960–98 from the reports of two national newspapers (*Haaretz* and *Maariv*) and two local papers (*Kol Hatzafon* and *Sheva*). Data about each act of protest were translated into a numerical

index based on the number of participants, duration, and intensity. Owing to limitation of space, the presentation of results will be quite brief.

5. Data for this comparison were collected from a special series of publications issued by the Central Bureau of Statistics (CBS 1990, 1994, 1999).

6. Data for this analysis were taken from local newspapers published before and after the elections. Several in-depth interviews were also conducted with key figures in the elections in Ofakim and Kiryat Gat.

7. The Labor Party is currently one of the two largest parties in Israel. Until the mid-1970s, Labor was consistently the party in power and dominated all the state institutions. In 1977, Labor lost the national election to the Likud Party, and ever since there has been rivalry between the two for dominance.

8. Likud is currently the party in power in Israel, but it was the main opposition party to the Labor-led government until 1977. Mizrahi candidates had appeared on Likud lists, and therefore the Likud's rise to power was attributed to increased support from Mizrahim, as well as their protest of Labor's attitude toward them in the 1950s and 1960s.

9. Local parties denote electoral groupings organized locally, with no direct association to a known statewide political party. At the same time, branches of statewide parties in the development towns are also led by local people.

10. An Ashkenazi ultra-Orthodox party.

11. *Our Kiryat Gat*, no. 953, November 20, 1998.

12. *Our Kiryat Gat*, no. 953, November 20, 1998, p. 29.

13. *Our Kiryat Gat*, no. 953, November 20, 1998, p. 26.

14. The development town of Bet-Shemesh was established in the 1950s, thirty kilometers southwest of Jerusalem. At the end of 2001, 22 percent of its 50,883 residents were new immigrants (Ministry of Immigrant Absorption 2002).

15. *Maariv*, November 22, 1999.

Chapter 11. A Way Forward?

1. Said 1994, 6. The chapter is based on the discussion of an Israeli-Palestinian workshop on the future of Jerusalem that took place in Bilagio, Italy in 1999. An earlier, shorter, version was published in Yiftachel and Yacobi 2002.

2. The al-Aqsa Mosque is the holiest place for Muslims in al-Quds and in Palestine, and the third holiest place for Muslims worldwide.

3. The wall may change its route according to the ruling of the Israeli High Court, which ruled in May of 2004 that several parts of the separation barrier around Jerusalem should be rerouted to minimize damage for the Palestinians.

4. *Maariv*, May 27, 1997.

5. For details of Israeli Judaizing policies in the city, see, among many, Bollen 2000; Dumper 1996; Khamaissi 1997; Klein 1999.

6. For details and data see Amnesty International Report 1999; B'tselem 1999, 2004.

7. As explained later, following the 1967 war, most Palestinian residents within the Jerusalem municipal area were not offered Israeli citizenship and have refused to apply for such a status, which would legitimize the Israeli occupation.

8. Teddy Kollek from a protocol of the city council, December 17, 1987, cited in B'tselem 1995, 7.

9. Another aspect of the ongoing drive for (Jewish) development has been the increasingly adverse impact of international capital on the city's landscape, often without long-term planning or environmental controls, and with little participation of the city's communities.

10. As recently as the 1980s, close to twenty thousand people lost their lives during the Sikh uprising and its aftermath (Samaddar 2000). This figure is about three times higher than the casualty count in Israel/Palestine since the 1940s.

11. In 2002 Israel closed the Orient House, claiming it conducted illegal diplomatic activities.

12. This approach has already appeared in previous proposals for solving the conflict over the future of Jerusalem (see Hirch and Housen-Couriel 1994).

Chapter 12. Epilogue

1. In a similar vein, a Likud member led a Knesset resolution in July of 2003, following the launch of the international road-map peace initiative, claiming that "the territories liberated by Israel in 1967 do not constitute, and shall never constitute, occupied territories" (*Haaretz* July 18, 2003).

2. Yet it should also be noted, however, that the Likud leader, Prime Minister Ariel Sharon, has repeatedly advocated the establishment of a Palestinian state west of the Jordan River. He has held this position against his party's stance, including during the 2003 elections when he achieved a landslide victory. Notably, though, Sharon has remained vague on the geographical extent of such a state and continues to support Jewish settlement in most parts of the occupied territories.

3. The inclusion of Jordan in this confederational agreement is also a long-term possibility.

4. Here it may be possible to think of small modifications to the Green Line so as to incorporate some Jewish settlements into Israel proper in exchange for land of equal size and quality.

5. This does not imply that the responsibility is equally shared. Israeli expansion and occupation has been the main source of the conflict, but Arab violence and aggression has also played a critical part.

6. The poem was performed by the East Jerusalem Sabreen band and was translated by Fatteh Azzam.

7. Translation by the author.

References

Abu al-Haj, N. 2001. *Facts on the Ground: Archaeological Practice and Territorial Self-Fashioning in Israeli Society*. Chicago: University of Chicago Press.

Abu Manneh, B. 1978. The Rise of the Sanjak of Jerusalem in the Late Nineteenth Century. In D. Ben-Dor, ed., *The Palestinians and the Middle East Conflict: Studies in Their History, Sociology, and Politics* (Arabic). Ramat Gan: Turtledove, 25–43.

Abu Odeh, A. 1992. Two Capitals in an Undivided Jerusalem. *Foreign Affairs* 17: 183–88.

Abu Rabia, A. 2001. *A Bedouin Century: Education and Development among the Negev Tribes in the Twentieth Century*. New York: Berghahn Books.

Abu Saad, I. 1998. Minority Higher Education in an Ethnic Periphery: The Bedouin Arabs. In O. Yiftachel and A. Meir, eds., *Ethnic Frontiers and Peripheries*. Boulder, Colo.: Westview Press, 269–86.

———. 2001. Education as a Tool for Control vs. Development Among Indigenous Peoples: The Case of Bedouin Arabs in Israel. *Hagar: International Social Science Review* 2(2): 241–60.

———. 2003. Bedouin Towns in the Beginning of the Twentieth Century: Negev Bedouin Following the Failure of Urbanization Policy (Hebrew and Arabic). In *Sikkuy Report, 2002–2003*. Jerusalem and Tamra: Sikkuy, 49–59.

Abu Saad, I., Y. Yonah, and A. Kaplan. 2000. Identity and Political Stability in an Ethnically Diverse State: A Study of Bedouin Arab Youth in Israel. *Social Identities* 6(1): 49–61.

Adalah (Legal Center for Arab Minority Rights in Israel). 1998. *Legal Violations of Arab Minority Rights in Israel* (Arabic, English, and Hebrew). Shefaamer: Adalah.

———. 2003. *October 2000: Law and Politics at the Or Commission* (Arabic, English, and Hebrew). Coordinated by Marwan Dalal. Shefaamer: Adalah.

Adva (Center for Social Equality and Justice). 2002. *Social Profile, 2001*. Tel-Aviv: Adva Center.

———. 2003, 2004. *Social Profile*. Tel Aviv: Adva Center.

Agnew, A. J. 1987. *Place and Politics*. Boston: Allen & Unwin.

———. 1999. Mapping Political Power Beyond State Boundaries: Territory, Identity, and Movement in World Politics. *Millennium: Journal of International Studies* 28(3): 499–521.

Akenson, D. 1992. *God's Peoples: Covenant and Land in South Africa, Israel, and Ulster*. Ithaca, N.Y.: Cornell University Press.

Almog, O. 1997. *The Tzabbar: A Profile* (Hebrew). Tel Aviv: Am Oved.

AlSayyad, N. 1994. Squatting and Culture: A Comparative Analysis of Informal Development in Latin America and the Middle East. *Habitat International* 17(1): 33–44.
———. 1996. Culture, Identity, and Urbanism in a Changing World: A Historical Perspective on Colonialism, Nationalism, and Globalization. In M. Cohen, B. Ruble, J. Tulchin, and A. Garland, eds., *Preparing for the Urban Future: Global Pressures and Local Forces*. Baltimore: Woodrow Wilson Center Press.
———. 2001. *Hybrid Urbanism: On the Identity Discourse and the Built Environment*. Westport, Conn.: Greenwood.
AlSayyad, N., and A. Roy, eds. 2003. *Urban Informality in the Era of Globalization: A Transnational Perspective*. Boulder, Colo.: Lexington.
Alterman, R. 1995. Can Planning Help in Crisis? Responses to Israel's Recent Wave of Immigration. *Journal of the American Planning Association* 61(2): 156–77.
———. 2001. Creeping Privatization and Land Lease Is Good for the Economy, but Should Not Continue (Hebrew). *Karka* 52: 48–54.
———. 2002. *Planning in the Face of Crisis: Land Use, Housing, and Mass Immigration in Israel*. New York: Routledge.
Amnesty International. 1999. *Israel and the Occupied Territories—Demolition and Dispossession: The Destruction of Palestinian Homes*. London: Amnesty International.
Andersen, E. 1999. *An Ethnic Perspective on Economic Reform: The Case of Estonia*. Aldershot: Ashgate.
Anderson, B. 1991. *Imagined Communities: Reflections on the Origin and Spread of Nationalism*. 2d ed. London: Verso.
———. 1996. Introduction. In G. Balakrishnan, ed., *Mapping the Nation*. New York: Verso, 1–16.
———. 2001. Eastern and Western Nationalisms. *Arena Journal* 16(1): 121–32.
Ankri, E. 1990. Land Before, Land After. In her album *I see it in Your Eyes* (Roa'h Lecha Ba'enayim). Tel-Aviv: Hed Artzi.
Applebaum, L., and D. Newman. 1991. *The Private Enterprise Settlements* (Hebrew). Jerusalem: Center for Development Studies.
Arian, A. 1997. *The Second Republic: Politics in Israel*. Tel Aviv: Zmora-Bitan.
Avineri, S. 1998. National Minorities in Democratic Nation-States. In E. Rekhess, ed., *The Arabs in Israeli Politics: Dilemmas of Identity*. Tel Aviv: Dayan Center for Middle East and African Studies, 17–31.
Avnon, D. 1998. The Israeli Basic Laws. *The Israeli Law Review* 32(4): 535–66.
Avraham, A. 2000. *The Media in Israel, Center and Periphery: Surveying Development Towns*. 2d ed. Jerusalem: Akademon.
Babai, A. 1997. The State of the Bedouin in Israel. *Karka* 23: 83–74.
Barak, A. 1998. Fifty Years of Israeli Jurisprudence. *Israel Studies* 3(2): 144–51.
Barkan, E. R. 1986. Vigilance versus Vigilantism: Race and Ethnicity and the Politics of Housing, 1940–1960. *Journal of Urban History* 12: 181–94.
Barlow, K. 1996. *Metropolitan Government*. London: Routledge.
Beilin, Y. 2001. *Guide for a Wounded Dove* (Hebrew). Tel Aviv: Keter.
Ben-Ari, E., and Bilu, Y. 1987. Saints' Sanctuaries in Israeli Development Towns: On a Mechanism of Urban Transformation. *Urban Anthropology* 16(2): 243–71.
Ben Artzi, Y. 1996. Normalization Under Conflict? Spatial and Demographic Changes of Arabs in Haifa, 1948–92. *Middle Eastern Studies* 32(4): 281–95.
Ben-David, I. 1995. *Feud in the Negev: The Land-Conflict Between the Bedouin and the State*. Beit Berel: Center for the Research of Arab Society.
———. 1997. The Negev Bedouins: Land Conflict and Proposal for Solution (Hebrew). *Karka* 61: 45–54.
Ben-Eliezer, U. 1995. *The Emergence of Israeli Militarism: 1936–1956* (Hebrew). Tel Aviv: Dvir.

———. 1998. Is Military Coup Possible in Israel? *Theory and Society* 27: 314–49.

———. 2003. New Associations or New Politics? The Significance of Israeli-Style Post-Materialism. *Hagar: International Social Science Review* 4(1): 6–24.

Ben-Eliyahu, S., and G. Vitkon. 2003. *Israel Land Authority: Proposals for Reducing Public Intervention.* Hertzeliyya: The Multidisciplinary Center.

Benhabib, S., ed. 1996. *Democracy and Difference: Contesting the Boundaries of the Political.* Princeton, N.J.: Princeton University Press.

Benski, T. 1993. Testing Melting-Pot Theories in the Jewish Israeli Context. *Sociological Papers* 2(2): 1–46.

Benvenisti, M. 1988. *The West Bank Data Project.* Washington, D.C.: American Enterprise Institute.

———. 1996. *City of Stone: The Hidden History of Jerusalem.* Berkeley: University of California Press.

———. 2001. *Sacred Landscapes.* Los Angeles: University of California Press.

Ben Zadok, E. 1993. Oriental Jews in the Development Towns: Ethnicity, Economic Development, Budgets, and Politics. In E. Ben-Zadok, ed., *Local Communities and the Israeli Polity.* Albany, N.Y.: State University of New York Press, 91–123.

Berg, E. 2002. Local Resistance, National Identity, and Global Swings in Post-Soviet Estonia. *Europe-Asia Studies* 54(1): 109–22.

Bernstein, D. 1984. Political Participation: New Immigrants and Veteran Parties in Israeli Society. *Plural Societies* 5: 13–32.

Bernstein, Deborah, and Shlomo Swirsky. 1982. The Rapid Economic Development of Israel and the Emergence of Ethnic Division of Labor. *British Journal of Sociology* 33: 64–85.

Bhabha, H. 1994. *The Location of Culture.* London: Routledge.

Billig, M. 1995. *Banal Nationalism.* London: Sage.

Biran, S. 2002. *Brief (Answers of Respondents 9–15) in HC 244/00.* Not published. Submitted to the Israeli High Court of Justice in January of 2002. Copy with the author.

Bishara, A. 1993. On the Question of the Palestinian Minority in Israel (Hebrew). *Teorya Uvikkoret* (Theory and critique) 3: 7–20.

———. 1999a. One Hundred Years of Zionism. In A. Ophir, ed., *Fifty to Forty Eight: Critical Moments in the History of the State of Israel.* Jerusalem: Van Leer Institute, 507–22.

———. 2000. The Sovereignty Process Has Not Been Completed (Hebrew). In Y. David, ed., *State of Israel: Between Jewishness and Democracy.* Jerusalem: Israel Center for Democracy, 325–29.

———. 2001. New Forms of Apartheid. *Between the Lines* (November): 13–16.

———, ed. 1999b. *Between Me and Us: The Construction of Israeli Identities* (Hebrew). Jerusalem: Van Leer Institute, 129–52.

Bishara, M. 2002. *Palestine/Israel: Peace of Apartheid.* London: Zed Books.

Blomley, N. 1994. *Law, Space, and the Geographies of Power.* New York: Guilford Press.

———. 2001. Acts, Deeds, and the Violence of Property. *Historical Geography* 28: 86–107.

Blomely, N., D. Delaney, and R. T. Ford, eds. 2001. *Legal Geographies Reader.* Oxford: Blackwell.

Bloom, M. 2003. Ethnic Conflict, State Terror and Suicide Bombing in Sri Lanka. *Civil Wars* 6(1): 54–84.

Blumer, M., and J. Solomon 2001. Conceptualizing Multiethnic Societies. *Ethnic and Racial Studies* 24(1): 889–91.

Bollen, S. 1999. *Urban Peace-Building in Divided Societies.* Boulder, Colo.: Westview Press.

────. 2000. *On Narrow Ground: Urban Policy and Ethnic Conflict in Jerusalem and Belfast.* Albany, N.Y.: State University of New York Press.

Bonacich, E. 1972. A Theory of Ethnic Antagonism: The Split Labor Market. *American Sociological Review* 37: 547–59.

Boullata, K. and M. Ghossein. 1979. *A Palestinian Poet in Exile.* Detroit: Association of Arab-American University Graduates.

Boymel, Y. 2000. Israel's Policy towards the Arab Minority, 1958–1968. Ph.D. thesis, Haifa University.

Brawer, M. 1988. *Israel's Borders: Past, Present, and Future* (Hebrew). Tel Aviv: Yavne.

Brenner, N. 2003. Metropolitan Institutional Reform and the Rescaling of State Space in Contemporary Western Europe. *European Urban and Regional Studies* 10: 297–325.

────. 2004. *New State Spaces: Urban Governance and the Rescaling of Statehood.* New York: Oxford University Press.

Brubaker, R. 1996. *Nationalism Reframed: Nationhood and the National Question in the New Europe.* New York: Cambridge University Press.

B'tselem. 1995. *A Policy of Discrimination: Land Expropriation, Planning, and Construction in East Jerusalem.* Jerusalem: B'tselem

────. 1999. *On the Way to Annexation: Human Rights Violation Resulting from the Establishment and Expansion of the Ma 'aleh Adumim Settlement.* Jerusalem: B'tselem.

────. 2002–3. *Report on Casualties in Israeli-Palestinian Hostilities, September 2000–December 2002.* Jerusalem: B'tselem.

────. 2004. *Forbidden Families: Family Unification and Child Registration in East Jerusalem.* Jerusalem: B'tselem.

al-Budeiri, M. 1998. Reflections on al-Nakba. *Journal of Palestine Studies* 109 (autumn 1998): 39–49.

Carmon, N., D. Czamanski, S. Amir, H. Law Yone, B. Kipnis, and G. Lipshitz. 1991. *The New Jewish Settlement in the Galilee: An Evaluation.* Haifa: Center for Urban and Regional Research.

Castells, M. 1984. *The City and the Grassroots: A Cross-Cultural Theory of Urban Social Movements.* Berkeley: University of California Press.

────. 1997. The Information Age: Economy, Society, and Culture. Vol. 2, *The Power of Identity.* Oxford: Blackwell.

CBS-a (Central Bureau of Statistics). Select years, 1950–2004. *Israel Statistical Yearbook.* Jerusalem: Central Bureau of Statistics.

────. CBS-c 1990–2003. *Results of Elections to the Local Authorities.* Jerusalem: Central Bureau of Statistics.

────. CBS-b 1999. *Results of Elections to the Local Authorities, 10.11.1998.* Special Series No. 1112. Jerusalem: State of Israel, Ministry of the Interior.

Chatterjee, P. 1993. *The Nation and Its Fragments.* Princeton, N.J.: Princeton University Press.

────. 1996. Who's Imagined Community? In G. Balakrishnan, ed., *Mapping the Nation.* London: Verso, 214–25.

Cohen, E. 1970. Development Towns: The Social Dynamics of Planted Urban Communities in Israel. In S. N. Eisenstadt, R. Bar Yosef, and C. Adler, eds., *Integration and Development in Israel.* Jerusalem: Israel University Press, 587–617.

Cohen, Y., and Y. Haberfeld. 1998. Second Generation Jewish Immigrants in Israel: Have the Ethnic Gaps in Schooling and Earnings Declined? *Ethnic and Racial Studies* 21(3): 507–28.

Collier, D., and S. Levitski. 1997. Democracy with Adjectives: Conceptual Innovation in Comparative Research. *World Politics* 49(April): 430–51.

Comaroff, J., and J. Comaroff. 2000. Naturing the Nation: Aliens, Apocalypse, and Postcolonial State. *Hagar: International Social Science Review* 1(1): 7–40.

Connor, W. 1994. *Ethnonationalism: The Quest for Understanding.* Princeton, N.J.: Princeton University Press.

———. 2002. Nationalism and Political Illegitimacy. In D. Conversi, ed., *Walker Connor and the Study of Nationalism.* London: Routledge, 19–36.

Daes, E. A. 1996. *Standard-Setting Activities: Evolution of Standards Concerning the Rights of Indigenous Peoples.* New York: UN Commission on Human Rights, Sub-Commission on Prevention of Discrimination and Protection of Minorities.

———. 1999. *Special Rapporteur, Human Right of Indigenous Peoples: Indigenous People and Their Relationship to Land* (Second Progress Report). Electronic reference format. Retrieved June 3, 1999 from http://www.un.org.

Dahan-Kalev, H. 2000. Feminism and Ethnicity in Education: An Israeli Case Study (Hebrew). *Schools and Society* 14: 193–210.

Dahl, R. 1989. *Democracy.* New Haven, Conn.: Yale University Press.

———. 1995. *Democracy and Its Critics.* New Haven, Conn.: Yale University Press.

Davies, W. K. D., and D. T. Herbert. 1993. *Communities within Cities.* London: Belhaven Press.

Davis, U. 2003. *Apartheid Israel: Possibilities for the Struggle Within.* London: Zed Books.

Delaney, D. 2000. Of Minds and Bodies and the Legal-Spatial Constitution of Sanctuary. *Historical Geography* 28: 25–40.

———. 2001. The Boundaries of Responsibility: Interpretation of Geography in School Desegregation Cases. In D. Blomely, R. Delaney, and Ford, T. eds., *Legal Geographies Reader.* Oxford: Blackwell, 54–68.

Dellapergola, S. 1992. Major Demographic Trends of World Jewry: The Last Hundred Years. In B. Bonne-Tamir and A. Adam, eds., *Genetic Diversity among the Jews.* New York: Columbia University Press, 3–30.

———. 2001. *Some Fundamentals of Jewish Demographic History.* Jerusalem: Harman Institute of Contemporary Jewry.

De-Ridder, M. 1996. The Brussels Issue in Belgian Politics. *Western European Politics* 9: 376–92.

Dery, D. 1994. *Who Governs Local Government?* (Hebrew). Jerusalem: Institute for Democracy.

De Silva, K. M. 1986. *Managing Ethnic Tensions in Multi-Ethnic Societies: Sri Lanka 1880–1985.* Lanham, Md.: University Press of America.

DIMA (Australian Department of Immigration and Multicultural and Indigenous Affairs). 2000. Annual Report. Canberra: Government Printers.

Doumani, B. 1995. *Rediscovering Palestine: Merchants and Peasants in Jabal Nablus, 1700–1900.* Berkeley: University of California Press.

Dowty, A. 1998. *The Jewish State: One Hundred Years Later.* Berkeley: University of California Press.

———., ed. 2004. *Critical Issues in Israeli Society.* Westport, Conn.: Praeger.

Dumper, M. 1996. *The Politics of Jerusalem since 1967.* New York: Columbia University Press.

Efrat, E. 1989. *The New Town of Israel: A Reappraisal.* Munich: Minerva.

EHDR (Estonian Human Development Report) 1999–2000. Electronic reference format. Retrieved July 24, 2001 from http://www.undp.ee/nhdr98/en/2/3/html.

Eisenstadt, S. N. 1969. *Israeli Society.* London: Weidenfeld & Nicolson.

Elmelech, Y., and N. Lewin-Epstein. 1998. Immigration and Housing in Israel: Another Look at Inequality (Hebrew). *Megamot* 39: 243–69.

Esses, V. M., J. F. Dovidio, L. M. Jackson, and T. L. Armstrong. 2001. The Immigration Dilemma: The Role of Perceived Group Competition, Ethnic Prejudice, and National Identity. *Journal of Social Issues* 57(3): 389–412.

Etkin, A. 2002. *Wage Levels in Different Localities in Israel, 1993–1999* (Hebrew). Tel Aviv: Adva Center.

Ezrahi, Y. 1996. *Rubber Bullets*. Princeton, N.J.: Princeton University Press.

Ezrahi, Y., and M. Kremitzer. 2001. *Israel Towards Constitutional Democracy* (Hebrew). Jerusalem: Israeli Institute of Democracy.

Fainstein, S. 1995. Politics, Economics, and Planning: Why Urban Regimes Matter. *Planning Theory* 14: 34–43.

Fairuz and Rahbani. 1968. Draw your Swords! http://almashrig.hiof.no/lebanon/ 700/780/fairuz/index.html.

Falah, G. 1983. The Development of Planned Bedouin Resettlement in Israel, 1964–82: Evaluation and Characteristics. *Geoforum* 14: 311–23.

———. 1989. Israelization of Palestine Human Geography. *Progress in Human Geography* 13: 535–50.

———. 1996. Living Together Apart: Residential Segregation in Mixed Arab-Jewish Cities in Israel. *Urban Studies* 33(6): 823–57.

———. 2003. Dynamics and Patterns of the Shrinking of Arab Lands in Palestine. *Political Geography* 22(2): 179–209.

Falah, G., and Newman, D. 1995. The Spatial Manifestation of Threat: Israelis and Palestinians Seek a Good Border. *Political Geography* 14(4): 689–706.

Feitelson, E. 1999. Social Norms, Rationales, and Policies: Reframing Farmland Protection in Israel. *Journal of Rural Studies* 15: 431–46.

Fenster, T. 1996. Ethnicity and Citizen Identity in Planning and Development for Minority Groups. *Political Geography* 15(5): 405–18.

———. 1998. Gender, Space and Planning. *Research of the Geography of Eretz Yisrael* 15: 229–94 (Hebrew).

Ferguson, K. 1993. *Kibbutz Journal: Reflections on Gender, Race, and Militarism in Israel*. Pasadena, Calif.: Trilogy Books.

Fernandes, E., and A. Varley. 1998. Law, the City, and Citizenship in Developing Countries: An Introduction. In D. Fernandes and A. Varley, eds., *Illegal Cities: Law and Urban Change in Developing Countries*. London: Zed Books, 3–17.

Fincher, R., and J. M. Jacobs, eds., 1998. *Cities of Difference*. New York: Guilford.

Flyvbjerg, B. 1996. The Dark Side of Planning: Rationality and Realrationalitat. In S. Mandelbaum, L. Mazza, and R. Burchell, eds., *Explorations in Planning Theory*. New Brunswick, N.J.: Center for Urban Policy Research, 383–96.

Forest, B. 2000. Legal Geographies: Placing the Law in Geography. *Historical Geography* 28: 5–12.

Foundation for Middle East Peace. 1997. *Report on Israeli Settlement in the Occupied Territories*. Washington, D.C.: Foundation for Middle East Peace.

Fredrickson, G. 1988. Colonialism and Racism: United States and South Africa in Comparative Perspective. In G. Fredrickson, ed., *The Arrogance of Racism*. Middletown, Conn.: Wesleyan University Press, 112–31.

Friedmann, J. 1996. Two Centuries of Planning Theory: An Overview. In S. Mandelbaum, L. Mazza, and R. Burchell, eds., *Explorations in Planning Theory*. New Brunswick, N.J.: Center for Urban Policy Research, 10–30.

———. 2002. *Prospects for Cities*. Minneapolis: University of Minnesota Press.

Frisch, H. 2003. Debating Palestinian Strategy in the al-Aqsa Intifada. *Terrorism and Political Violence* 15(2): 61–80.

———. 2004. *Palestinian Strategy and Attitudes*. Ramat-Gan: BESA (The Begin-Sadat Center for Strategic Studies), Bar-Ilan University.

Gale, F. 1990. Aboriginal Australia: Survival by Separation. In M. Chisholm and D. M. Smith, *Shared Space, Divided Space: Essays on Conflict and Territorial Organization*. Boston: Unwin Hyman, 217–34.

Gans, H. 1973. The Possibilities of Class and Racial Integration in American New Towns: A Policy-Oriented Analysis. In H. S. Perloff and N. C. Sandberg, eds., *New Towns: Why and for Whom*. New York: Praeger, 137–58.

————. 2003. *The Limits of Nationalism*. Cambridge: Cambridge University Press.

Gavison, R. 1998. A Jewish and Democratic State? In E. Rekhess, ed., *The Arabs in Israeli Politics: Dilemmas of Identity*. Tel Aviv: Dayan Center for Middle East and African Studies, 125–37.

————. 1999. Jewish and Democratic? A Rejoinder to the Ethnic Democracy Debate. *Israel Studies* 4(1): 44–72.

————. 2002. The Jews' Right to Statehood: A Defense. *Azure* 14: 50–88.

Gellner, E. 1983. *Nations and Nationalism*. Oxford: Blackwell.

————. 1996. Do Nations Have Navels? *Nations and Nationalism* 2(3): 366–71.

Ghanem, A. 1998. State and Minority in Israel: The Case of Ethnic State and the Predicament of Its Minority. *Ethnic and Racial Studies* 21(3): 428–47.

————. 2000. *The Palestinian-Arab Minority in Israel, 1948–2000*. Albany: State University of New York Press.

Ghanem, A., and S. Ozacky-Lazar. 2001. *A Year after the October Events: What Has Changed?* (Hebrew). Givaat Haviva: The Institute for Peace Research.

————. 2003. The Status of the Palestinians in Israel in the Era of Peace: Part of the Problem but Not Part of the Solution. *Israel Affairs* 9(1–2): 263–89.

Ghanem, A., and N. Rouhana. 2001. Citizenship and the Parliamentary Politics of Minorities in Ethnic States: The Palestinian Citizens of Israel. *Nationalism and Ethnic Politics* 7: 66–86.

Ghanem, A., N. Rouhana, and O. Yiftachel. 1998. Questioning Ethnic Democracy. *Israel Studies* 3(2): 252–67.

Golan, A. 2001. *Spatial Change—the Result of War: Ex-Arab Areas in the State of Israel 1948–1950*. Sde-Bokker: Center for Ben-Gurion Heritage.

Golani, G. 1976. *New Town Planning: Principles and Practice*. New York: John Wiley and Sons.

Goldberg, G. 2001. Changes in Israeli Voting Behavior in the Municipal Elections. In D. J. Elazar and C. Kalchheim, eds., *Local Government in Israel* (Hebrew). Jerusalem: Jerusalem Center for Public Affairs, 249–76.

Gonen, A. 1995. *From City to Suburb*. Aldershot: Avebury.

Gradus, Y. 1984. The Emergence of Regionalism in a Centralized System: The Case of Israel. *Environment and Planning D: Society and Space* 2: 87–100.

————. 1993. Beer-Sheva: Capital of the Negev Desert. In Y. Golani, S. Eldor, and M. Garon, eds., *Planning and Housing in Israel in the Wake of Rapid Changes*. Jerusalem: Ministry of the Interior, 251–65.

Gradus, Y., and R. Blustein. 2001. *Globalization and Multiculturalism in the Beer-Sheva Region* (Hebrew). Beer-Sheva: Negev Center for Regional Development.

Gradus, Y., and Y. Einy. 1984. Trends in Core-Periphery Industrialization Gaps in Israel. *Geography Research Forum* 2–6: 71–83.

Gradus, Y., and S. Krakover. 1977. The Effect of Government Policy on the Spatial Structure of Manufacturing in Israel. *Journal of Developing Areas* 11(3): 393–409.

Gradus, Y., and R. Livnon-Blushtein. 2001. *The Urban Ecology of Beer-Sheva in the Era of Globalization: A Socio-Political Atlas* (Hebrew). Beer-Sheva: Negev Center for Regional Development.

Gradus, Y., and E. Stern. 1980. Changing Strategies of Development: Toward a Regiopolis in the Negev Desert. *Journal of the American Planning Association* 46: 410–23.

Gradus, Y., O. Yiftachel, and R. Livnon. 1998. *Industry in the Negev: Processes, Structure, and Location*. Beer-Sheva: Negev Development Authority.

Gramsci, A. 1971. *Selections from the Prison Notebook*. Edited and translated by H. Quintin and N. Geoffrey. London: Lawrence & Wishart.

Greenfeld, L. 1992. *Nationalism: Five Roads to Modernity*. Cambridge, Mass.: Harvard University Press.

———. 2001. *The Spirit of Capitalism: Nationalism and Economic Growth*. Cambridge, Mass. Harvard University Press.

Gregory, D. 1994. *Geographical Imaginations*. Cambridge, Mass.: Blackwell.

Grinberg, L. 1991. *Split Corporatism in Israel*. Albany: State University of New York Press.

———. 2001. Social and Political Economy (Hebrew). In E. Yaar and Z. Shavit, eds., *Trends in Israeli Society*. Vol. 1. Tel Aviv: Open University, 585–704.

Gross, E. 2000. Democracy: Ethnicity and Legality in Israel (Hebrew). *Israeli Sociology* 2(2): 647–74.

Gunasekara, S. L. 1996. *Tigers, "Moderates," and Pandora's Package*. Colombo: Multi Packs (Ceylon) Limited.

Gurr, T. 1970. *Why Men Rebel*. Princeton, N.J.: Princeton University Press.

———. 1993. *Minorities at Risk*. Washington, D.C.: U.S. Institute of Peace.

———. 2000. *Peoples Versus States: Minorities at Risk in the New Century*. Washington, D.C.: U.S. Institute of Peace.

Gurr, T., and B. Harff. 1994. *Ethnic Conflict in World Politics*. Boulder, Colo.: Westview Press.

Guttman Institute. 2000. *Israeli Jews: A Profile*. Jerusalem: Institute of Democracy.

Habermas, J. 1996. The European Nation-State—Its Achievements and Its Limits. On the Past and Future of Sovereignty and Citizenship. In G. Balakrishnan, *Mapping the Nation*. London: Verso, 281-94.

Habermas, J., ed. 2001. *The Postnational Constellation: Political Essays*. Cambridge, Mass.: MIT Press.

Haidar, A. 1991. *Social Welfare Services for Israel's Arab Population*. Boulder, Colo.: Westview Press.

al-Haj, M. 1993. The Impact of the Intifada on Arabs in Israel: The Case of a Double Periphery. In A. Cohen and G. Wolsfeld, eds., *Framing the Intifada: People and Media*. Norwood, N.J.: Albex, 64–75.

al-Haj, M. 2002. Ethnic Mobilization in an Ethno-National State: The Case of Immigrants from the Former Soviet Union in Israel. *Ethnic and Racial Studies* 25(2): 238–57.

al-Haj, M., and E. Leshem. 2000. *Immigrants from the Former Soviet Union in Israel: Ten Years Later*. Haifa: Center for Multicultural and Education Research, University of Haifa.

al-Haj, M., and U. Ben-Eliezer, eds. 2003. *In the Name of Security: Sociology of Peace and War in Israel in a Changing Era* (Hebrew). Haifa: University of Haifa Press.

Hajjar, L. 2005. *Courting Conflict: The Israeli Military Court System in the West Bank and Gaza*. Los Angeles: University of California Press.

Hakli, J. 2001. In the Territory of Knowledge: State-Centred Discourses and the Construction of Society. *Progress in Human Geography* 25(3): 403–22.

Hall, S. 1992. Cultural Identity in Question. In S. Hall, D. Held, and T. McGrew, eds., *Modernity and Its Futures*. Cambridge: Polity.

———. 1997. Introduction: Who Needs Identity? In S. Hall and P. du Gay, eds., *Questions of Cultural Identity*. London: Sage, 1–18.

Hallik, K. 1998. Non-Estonians: Historic and Demographic Background (Estonian). In M. Heidmets, ed., *Russian Minority and Challenges for Estonia*. Tallinn: TPÜ, 13–28.

Harvey, D. 1989. *The Condition of Postmodernity*. Oxford: Blackwell.

———. 1990. *The Urban Experience*. Oxford: Blackwell.

———. 1993. Class Relations, Social Justice, and the Politics of Difference. In M. Keith and S. Pile, eds., *Place and the Politics of Identity*. London: Routledge, 41–66.

———. 2001. *Spaces of Capital: Towards a Critical Geography*. New York: Routledge.

Hasson, S. 1981. Social and Spatial Conflicts: The Settlement Process in Israel During the 1950s and the 1960s. *L'Espace Geographique* 10(3): 169–79.

———. 1992. How Are the Immigrants? Where and How Are They Living? Where Will They Live in the Future? *Israel Studies* 5: 19–24.

———. 1998. From Frontier to Periphery. In O. Yiftachel and A. Meir, eds., *Ethnic Frontiers and Peripheries: Landscapes of Development and Inequality in Israel.* Boulder, Colo.: Westview Press, 217–29.

Hasson, S. 2001. Spaces of Resistance in Jerusalem. In O. Yiftachel, J. Little, D. Hedgcock and I. Alexander, *The Power of Planning: Spaces of Control and Transformations.* Dordrecht: Kluwer Academic, 33–44.

Hasson, S., and K. Abu Asba, eds. 2004. *Jews and Arabs in Israel Facing a Changing Reality.* Jerusalem: Floresheimer Institute.

Head, L. 2000. *Second Nature: The History and Implications of Australia and Aboriginal Landscape.* Syracuse, N.Y.: Syracuse University Press.

Hechter, M. 2000. *Containing Nationalism.* Oxford: Oxford University Press.

Hechter, M., and M. Levi. 1979. The Comparative Analysis of Ethnoregional Movements. *Ethnic and Racial Studies* 2(2): 260–74.

Held, D. 1990. *Models of Democracy.* London: Polity Press.

Helman, S. 1999. War and Resistance: Israeli Civil Militarism and Its Emergent Crisis. *Constellations* 6(3): 391–410.

Hennayake, S. K. 2004. Is LTTE the Sole Representative of Tamils? Electronic reference format. Retrieved May 20, 2004 from *SPUR—Society for Peace, Unity, and Human Rights in Sri-Lanka,* http://www.spur.asn.au/SH_Is_LTTE.htm.

Herb, G., and D. Kaplan, eds. 1999. *Nested Identities: Nationalism, Territory, and Scale.* Boulder, Colo.: Rowman & Littlefield.

Herman, T. 1996. Do They Have a Chance? Protest and Political Structure of Opportunity in Israel. *Israel Studies* 1(1): 144–70.

Hertzeliyya Forum. 2001. *The Balance of National Strength and Security: Policy Directions* (Hebrew). Hertzeliyya: Hertzeliyya Multidisciplinary Center.

Herzog, H. 1994. Penetrating the System: The Politics of Collective Identity. In A. Arian and M. Shamir, eds., *The Elections in Israel 1992.* Albany: State University of New York Press, 81–102.

Hever, H., Y. Shenhav, and P. Motzafi-Hallar, eds. 2002. *Mizrahim in Israel: A Critical Observation into Israel's Ethnicity.* Jerusalem: Van Leer Institute.

Hirch, M., and D. Housen-Curiel. 1994. *The Jerusalem Question: Proposals for Its Resolution* (Hebrew). Jerusalem: Jerusalem Institute for Israel Studies.

Hobsbawm, E. 1990. *Nations and Nationalism since 1780.* Cambridge: Cambridge University Press.

Holtzman-Gazit, Y. 2002. Trial and Status Symbol: The Israel National Fund Law 1953 (Hebrew). *Iyyunei Mishpat* 27: 601–44.

Horowitz, T. 2003. The Increasing Political Power of Immigrants from the Former Soviet Union in Israel: From Passive to Active Citizenship. *International Migration* 41(1): 47–71.

al-Hout, B. N. 1991. *Palestine: The Cause, the People, the Civilizations* (Arabic). Beirut: Dar al-Istiqlal al-Nashar.

Howitt, R. 2001. A Nation in Dialogue: Recognition, Reconciliation, and Indigenous Rights in Australia. *Hagar: International Social Science Review* 2(2): 277–94.

Hussain, R. 1965. My Palestine. In K. Boullata and M. Ghossein, *A Plaestinian Poet in Exile.* Detroit: Association of Arab-American University Graduates, 1979.

Hutchinson, J. 2000. Ethnicity and the Modern Nation. *Ethnic and Racial Studies* 23(3): 651–69.

Human Rights Watch. 2000. *Estonia.* www.hrw.org.

Jackson, P. 2000. Rematerializing Social and Cultural Geography. *Social and Cultural Geography* 1(1): 9–14.

Jackson, P., and J. Penrose. 1993. Introduction: Placing Race and Nation. In P. Jackson and J. Penrose, eds., *Constructions of Race, Place, and Nation.* Minneapolis: University of Minnesota Press, 1–23.

Jacobs, J. 1993. Shake'm This Country: The Mapping of the Aboriginal Sacred in Australia. In P. Jackson and J. Penrose, eds., *Construction of Race, Place, and Nation.* Minneapolis: University of Minnesota Press, 100–120.

Jiryis, S. 1976. *The Arabs in Israel* (Hebrew). Haifa: Al-Ittihad.

Johnston, R. J. 1982. Voice as Strategy in Locational Conflict: The Fourteenth Amendment and Residential Separation in the United States. In K. R. Cox and R. J. Johnston, eds., *Conflict, Politics, and the Urban Scene.* London: Longman, 111–26.

Kaiser, R. 2002. Homeland Making and the Territorialization of National Identity. In D. Conversi, ed., *Ethnonationalism in the Contemporary World: Walker Connor and the Study of Nationalism.* London: Routledge, 229–47.

Kalia, R. 1999. *Chandigarh: The Making of an Indian City.* New Delhi: India Oxford Press.

Kallus, R. 2004. The Political Construction of the "Everyday": The Role of Housing in Making Place and Identity. In H. Yacobi, ed., *Constructing a Sense of Place: Architecture and the Zionist Discourse.* Aldershot: Ashgate, 136–64.

Kark, R. 1995. *Land and Settlement in Eretz Israel 1830–1990* (Hebrew). Jerusalem: Sivan.

———., ed. 1990. *Redemption of the Land of Israel: Ideology and Practice* (Hebrew). Jerusalem: Yad Izhak Ben-Zvi.

Karka (Journal of the Institute for Land Policy). 2001. *Proceedings of the First Jerusalem Conference for National Land Policy* (Hebrew). Jerusalem: Jewish National Fund.

Kaufman, E., ed. 2004. *Rethinking Ethnicity: Majority Groups and Dominant Minorities.* London: Routledge.

Keating, M. 1988. *State and Regional Nationalism.* New York: Harvester & Wheatsheaf.

———. 1996. *Nations against the State: The New Politics of Nationalism in Quebec, Catalonia, and Scotland.* Basingstoke: Macmillan.

Kedar, A. 1996. Israeli Law and the Redemption of Arab Land, 1948–1969. Ph.D. diss., Harvard University Law School.

———. 1998. Minority Time, Majority Time: Land, Nation, and the Law of Adverse Possession in Israel (Hebrew). *Iyyunei Mishpat* 21(3): 665–746.

———. 2000. A First Step in a Difficult and Sensitive Road. *Bulletin of Israel Studies* 16: 3–11.

———. 2001. The Legal Transformation of Ethnic Geography: Israeli Law and the Palestinian Landholder 1948–1967. *NYU Journal of International Law and Politics* 33(4): 997–1044.

———. 2003. On the Legal Geography of Ethnocratic Settler States: Notes Towards a Research Agenda. In J. Holder and C. Harrison, eds., *Law and Geography: Current Legal Issues 2002.* Vol. 5. Oxford: Oxford University Press, 401–42.

Kedar, A., and O. Yiftachel. 1999. *Agricultural Lands Toward the Next Millennium* (Hebrew). Haifa: Faculty of Law, Haifa University.

Keith, M., and S. Pile, eds. 1993. *Place and the Politics of Identity.* London: Routledge.

Kemp, A. 1997. Talking Boundaries: The Making of Political Territory in Israel 1949–1957 (Hebrew). Ph.D. diss., Tel Aviv University.

———. 2002. "Wandering Peoples" or the "Great Fire": State Control and Resistance in the Israeli Frontier (Hebrew). In H. Hever, Y. Shenhav, and P. Mutzafi-Hellas, eds., *Mizrahim in Israel: A Critical Observation into Israel's Ethnicity.* Jerusalem: Van Leer Institute, 36–52.

Kemp, A., D. Newman, U. Ram, and O. Yiftachel, eds. 2004. *Israelis in Conflict: Hegemonies, Identities, and Challenges.* London: Sussex Academic.

Kennedy, D. 1997. *A Critique of Adjudication: Fin de Siecle.* Cambridge, Mass.: Harvard University Press.

Khalidi, R. 1988. *The Arab Economy in Israel.* London: Croom Helm.

———. 1997. *Palestinian Identity: The Construction of Modern National Consciousness.* New York: Columbia University Press.

Khalidi, W. 1992. The Future of Arab Jerusalem. *British Journal of Middle Eastern Studies* 19: 133–44.

Khamaissi, R. 1992. *Planning, Housing, and the Arab Minority in Israel.* Boulder, Colo.: Westview Press.

———. 1997. Israeli Use of the British Mandate Planning Legacy as a Tool for the Control of Palestinians in the West Bank. *Planning Perspectives* 12: 321–40.

———. 2001. *Toward Strengthening Arab Local Government in Israel* (Hebrew). Jerusalem: Floresheimer Institute.

———. 2002. *Towards Expansion of Arab Municipal Areas* (Hebrew). Jerusalem: Floresheimer Institute.

Kimmerling, B. 1983. *Zionism and Territory.* Berkeley: Institute of International Studies, University of California.

———. 1995. Religion, Nationalism and Democracy in Israel (Hebrew). *Zmanim.* (56): 116–31.

———. 1989. Boundaries and Frontiers in the Israeli Control System: Analytical Conclusions. In B. Kimmerling, *The Israeli State and Society: Boundaries and Frontiers.* Albany: State University of New York Press, 267–88.

———. 1999. Religion, Nationalism, and Democracy in Israel. *Constellations* 6(3): 339–65.

———. 2001. *The Invention and Decline of Israeliness: State, Society, and the Military.* Los Angeles: University of California Press.

———. 2003. *Politicide: Ariel Sharon's War against the Palestinians.* London: Verso.

Kimmerling, B., and J. Migdal. 1999. *The Palestinians: The Making of a People* (Hebrew). Tel Aviv: Keter. Updated version of 1993 English publication, New York: Free Press.

Klein, M. 1999. *Doves over Jerusalem's Sky: The Peace Process and the City, 1977–1999* (Hebrew). Jerusalem: Jerusalem Institute for Israel Studies.

———. 2003. The Origins of Intifada and Rescuing Peace for Israelis and Palestinians. Lecture delivered at the Israel Studies Conference, April, Boulder, Colo. (notes with author).

Knox, P. L. 1982. Residential Structure, Facility Location, and Patterns of Accessibility. In K. R. Cox and R. J. Johnston, eds., *Conflict, Politics, and the Urban Scene.* London: Longman, 62–87.

Kretzmer, D. 1990. *The Legal Status of the Arabs in Israel.* Boulder, Colo.: Westview Press.

———. 2002. *The Occupation of Justice: The Supreme Court of Israel and the Occupied Territories.* Albany: State University of New York Press.

Kymlicka, W. 1992. *Contemporary Political Philosophy: An Introduction.* Oxford: Clarendon Press.

———. 1995. *Multicultural Citizenship: A Liberal Theory of Minority Rights.* Oxford: Clarendon Press.

———. 2001. *Politics in the Vernacular: Nationalism, Multiculturalism, and Citizenship.* Oxford: Oxford University Press.

Laclau, E. 1994. Introduction. In E. Laclau, ed., *The Making of Political Identities*. London: Verso, 1–8.

Laclau, E., and C. Mouffe. 1985. *Hegemony and Socialist Strategy: Towards a Radical Democratic Politics*. New York: Verso.

Lahav, P. 1997. *Judgment in Jerusalem: Chief Justice Simon Agranat and the Zionist Century*. Berkeley: University of California Press.

Landa, J., M. Copelano, and B. Grofman. 1995. Ethnic Voting Patterns: A Case Study of Metropolitan Toronto. *Political Geography* 14(5): 434–49.

Landau, Y. 1993. *The Arab Minority in Israel: Political Aspects, 1967–1991*. Jerusalem: Am Oved.

Lane, J. E., and S. O. Ersson. 1991. *Politics and Society in Western Europe*. 2d ed. London: Sage.

Lauria, M. 1997. *Restructuring Urban Regime Theory*. London: Sage.

Law Yone, H., and R. Kalus. 1995. *Housing Inequalities in Israel* (Hebrew). Tel Aviv: Adva Center.

Lefebvre, E. 1991. *The Production of Space*. Oxford: Blackwell.

Lefebvre, H. 1996. Philosophy of the City and Planning Ideology. In H. Lefebvre, ed., *Writings on Cities*. Oxford: Blackwell, 97–101.

Lehman-Wilzig, S. 1990. *Stiff-Necked People in a Bottled-Necked System: The Evolution and Roots of Israeli Public Protest, 1949–86*. Bloomington: University of Indiana Press.

———. 1993. Copying the Master? Patterns of Israeli Protest, 1950–1990. *Asian and African Studies* 27(1–2): 129–47.

Lewin-Epstein, N., Y. Elmelech, and M. Semyonov. 1997. Ethnic Inequality in Home-Ownership and the Value of Housing: The Case of Immigrants to Israel. *Social Forces* 75(4): 1439–62.

Lewin-Epstein, N., and M. Semyonov. 1993. *The Arab Minority in Israel's Economy: Patterns of Ethnic Inequality*. Boulder, Colo.: Westview Press.

Lewin-Epstein, N., M. Semyonov, and J. W. Wright. 1988. The Israeli Dilemma over Economic Discrimination and Labor Market Competition. In J. W. Wright, ed., *The Political Economy of the Middle East Peace Process: The Impact of Competing Trade Agendas*. New York: Routledge.

Liebman, C. 1995. Religion and Democracy in Israel (Hebrew). *Zmanim*, no. 5:134–44.

Lijphart, A. 1984. *Democracies*. New Haven, Conn.: Yale University Press.

Linz, J. 1975. Totalitarian vs Authoritarian Regimes. In F. Greenstein and N. Polsby, *Handbook of Political Science*. Reading: Addison Wesley, 3: 175–411.

———. 1978. *The Breakdown of Democratic Regimes: Crisis, Breakdown, and Reequilibration*. Baltimore: Johns Hopkins University Press.

Linz, J., and A. Stepan. 1996. *Problems of Democratic Transition and Consolidation*. Baltimore: John Hopkins University Press.

Lipshitz, G. 1991. Immigration and Internal Migration as a Mechanism of Polarization and Dispersion of Population and Development: The Israeli Case. *Economic Development and Cultural Change* 39(2): 391–408.

———. 1992. *Immigrant Absorption in a Development Town: The Case of Qiryat-Gat*. Jerusalem: Jerusalem Institute for Israel Studies.

Lissak, M., and E. Leshem. 2001. *From Russia to Israel: Identity and Culture in Transition* (Hebrew). Tel Aviv: Hakibbutz Hameuchad.

Lithwick, H. 2000. *An Urban Development Strategy for the Negev's Bedouin Community*. Beer-Sheva: Negev Center for Regional Development and the Center for Bedouin Culture.

Little, D. 1993. *Sri Lanka: The Invention of Enmity*. Washington, D.C.: U.S. Institute of Peace.

Lofland, J. 1985. *Protest: Studies of Collective Behavior and Social Movements.* New Brunswick, N.J.: Transaction Books.

Lustick, I. 1979. Stability in Deeply Divided Societies: Consociationalism vs. Control. *World Politics* 31: 325–44.

———. 1980. *Arabs in the Jewish State: Israel's Control over a National Minority.* Austin: University of Texas Press.

———. 1988. *For the Land and the Lord: Jewish Fundamentalism in Israel.* New York: Council of Foreign Relations.

———. 1989. The Political Road to Binationalism: Arabs in Jewish Politics. In I. Peleg and O. Seliktar, eds., *The Emergence of a Binational Israel.* Boulder, Colo.: Westview Press, 97–124.

———. 1993. *Unsettled States, Disputed Lands.* Ithaca, N.Y.: Cornell University Press.

———. 1996. The Fetish of Jerusalem: A Hegemonic Analysis. In M. Barnett, ed., *Israel in Comparative Perspective.* Albany: State University of New York Press, 143–72.

———. 1999. Israel as a Non-Arab State: The Political Implications of Mass Immigration of Non-Jews. *Middle East Journal* 53(3): 417–33.

———. 2002. In Search of Hegemony: Nationalism and Religion in the Middle East. *Hagar: International Social Science Review* 3(2): 171–202.

Mann, M. 1999. The Dark Side of Democracy: The Modern Tradition of Ethnic and Political Cleansing. *New Left Review* 235: 18–45.

Mann, M. 2004. *The Dark Side of Democracy: Explaining Ethnic Cleansing.* Cambridge, Cambridge University Press.

Marcuse, P. 1995. Not Chaos, but Walls: Postmodernism and the Partitioned City. In S. Watson and K. Gibson, eds., *Postmodern Cities and Spaces.* Oxford: Blackwell, 187–98.

Marcuse, P., and M. Van Kempen, eds. 2000. *Globalising Cities: A New Spatial Order?* Oxford: Blackwell.

Markusen, A. 1987. *Regions: The Economics and Politics of Territory.* Towata, N.J.: Rowman & Littlefield.

Masalha, N. 2000. *Imperial Israel and the Palestinians.* London: Pluto.

Massey, D. 1993. Questions of Locality. *Geography* 78 (339): 142–49.

———. 1994. *Space, Place, and Gender.* Oxford: Blackwell.

———. 1996. Space/Power, Identity/Difference: Tensions in the City. In A. Merrifield and E. Swyngedouw, eds., *The Urbanization of Injustice.* London: Lawrence & Wishart, 100–116.

Massey, D., and P. Jess, eds. 1995. *A Place in the World?* New York: Oxford University Press, 1–4.

Mautner, M., ed. 2000. *Distributive Justice in Israel* (Hebrew). Tel Aviv: Ramot.

Mazrui, A. 1975. *Soldiers and Kinsmen in Uganda: The Making of a Military Ethnocracy.* Beverly Hills: Sage.

McCrone, D. 1993. Regionalism and Constitutional Change in Scotland. *Regional Studies* 27: 507–12.

McGarry, J. 1998. Demographic Engineering: The State-Directed Movement of Ethnic Groups as a Technique of Conflict Regulation. *Ethnic and Racial Studies* 21(4): 613–38.

McGarry, J., and B. O'Leary. 1995. *Explaining Northern Ireland: Broken Images.* Cambridge: Basil Blackwell.

———. 2000. *Policing Northern Ireland: Proposals for a New Start.* London: Blackstaff.

———, eds. 1993. *The Politics of Ethnic Conflict Regulation.* London: Routledge.

Mena Committee. 1997. *Mena Committee Report on Bedouin in Israel* (Hebrew). Jerusalem: Israeli Knesset.

Meir, A. 1988. Nomads and the State: The Spatial Dynamics of Centrifugal and Centripetal Forces among the Israeli Negev Bedouin. *Political Geography Quarterly* 6: 251–70.

———. 1997. *When Nomadism Ends: The Israeli Bedouin of the Negev*. Boulder, Colo.: Westview Press.

Mercer, D. 1993. Terra Nullius, Aboriginal Sovereignty and Land Rights in Australia. *Political Geography* 12(4): 299–318.

Migdal, J. S. 1996. Integration and Disintegration: An Approach to Society-Formation. In L. van de Goor, K. Rupesingheand, and P. Sciarone, eds., *Between Development and Destruction: An Enquiry into the Causes of Conflict in Post-Colonial States*. London: Macmillan, 91–106.

Mikesell, M., and A. Murphy. 1991. A Framework for Comparative Study of Minority Aspirations. *Annals of the Association of American Geographers* 81: 581–604.

Minda, G. 1995. *Postmodern Legal Movements*. New York: New York University Press.

Ministry of Immigrant Absorption. 2002. *Immigrant by Place of Residence*. Internal report (copy with the author). Jerusalem: Ministry of Immigrant Absorption.

Mitchell, D. 2003. *The Right of the City: Social Justice and the Fight for Public Space*. New York: Guilford.

Morris, B. 1987. *The Birth of the Palestinian Refugee Problem, 1947–1949*. Cambridge: Cambridge University Press.

———. 1990. *The Birth of the Palestinian Refugee Problem, 1947–1949* (Hebrew). Tel Aviv: Am Oved.

———. 1993. *Israel's Border Wars, 1949–1956*. Oxford: Oxford University Press.

———. 1999. *Righteous Victims: A History of the Zionist-Arab Conflict, 1881–1999*. New York: Knopf.

Mouffe, C. 1995. Post-Marxism: Democracy and Identity. *Environment and Planning D: Society and Space* 13: 259–65.

Murphy, A. 1988. *The Regional Dynamics of Language Differentiation in Belgium: A Study in Cultural-Political Geography*. Chicago: University of Chicago.

———. 1991. Regions as Social Constructs: The Gap between Theory and Practice. *Progress in Human Geography* 15(1): 22–35.

———. 1996. The Sovereign State System as a Political-Territorial Ideal: Historical and Contemporary Considerations. In T. Biersteker and S. Weber, eds., *State Sovereignty as Social Construct*. Cambridge: Cambridge University Press, 81–120.

———. 2002. The Territorial Underpinnings of National Identity. *Geopolitics* 7(2): 193–214.

Nagel, J. 1986. The Political Construction of Ethnicity. In S. Olzak and J. Nagle, eds., *Competitive Ethnic Relations*. Orlando: Academic Press, 93–112.

Naor, A. 2001. *Greater Israel: Ideas and Debates* (Hebrew). Haifa: University of Haifa and Zmora Bittan.

Nazri, Y., ed. 2004. *Eastern Appearance: Mother Tongue*. Tel Aviv: Babel.

Nazzal, N. A. 1974. The Zionist Occupation of Western Galilee, 1948. *Journal of Palestine Studies* 4 (spring): 58–72.

Negev Center for Regional Development. 1993–2003. *Statistical Yearbook for the Negev, No. 1–5*. Beer-Sheva: Negev Center for Regional Development and the Negev Development Authority.

———. 1999. *Statistical Yearbook of the Negev, Negev Center for Regional Development*, Beer-Sheva: Negev Center for Regional Development and the Negev Development Authority.

Neuberger, B. 1998. *Democracy in Israel: Origins and Development*. Tel Aviv: Open University.

Nevo, Y. 2000. From Ethnocracy to Theocracy: The Trajectory of Israeli Political Development. Paper delivered at the international conference "Challenges to

Democracy," Humphrey Center for Social Research, Ben-Gurion University, May.

———. 2003. The Politics of Un-Recognition: Bedouin Villages in the Israeli Negev. *Hagar: International Social Science Review* 4(1–2): 203–13.

Newman, D. 1989. Civilian Presence as Strategies of Territorial Control: The Arab-Israeli Conflict. *Political Geography Quarterly* 8: 215–27.

———. 1996. The Territorial Politics of Ex-urbanisation: Reflections on 25 Years of Jewish Settlement in the West Bank. *Israel Affairs* 3(1): 61–85.

———. 2000. Citizenship, Identity, and Location: The Changing Discourse of Israeli Geopolitics. In K. Dodds and D. Atkinson, eds., *Geopolitical Traditions: A Century of Geopolitical Thought*. London: Routledge, 207–31.

———. 2001. From National to Post-National Territorial Identities in Israel-Palestine. *Geoforum* 53: 235–46.

———. 2003. Boundaries. In J. Agnew, K. Mitchell, and G. Toal, eds., *Companion to Political Geography*. Oxford: Blackwell, 123–37.

———. 2004. On Borders and Power: A Theoretical Framework. *Journal of Borderlands Studies* 18(1): 13–25.

Newman, D., and T. Herman. 1992. A Comparative Study of Gush Emunim and Peace Now. *Middle Eastern Studies* 28(3): 509–30.

Newman, D., and A. Paasi. 1998. Fences and Neighbours in the Post-Modern World: Boundary Narratives in Political Geography. *Progress in Human Geography* 22(2): 186–207.

Newman, S. 1996. *Ethnoregional Conflict in Democracies*. London: Greenwood Press.

Nissan, E. 1984. *Sri Lanka: In Change and Crisis*. New York: St. Martin's Press.

———. 1996. Sri Lanka: A Bitter Harvest. *Minority Rights Group International Report*.

Nitzan-Shiftan, A. 2004. Seizing Locality in Jerusalem. In N. alSayyad, ed., *The End of Tradition?* New York: Routledge, 231–55.

Offe, C. 2002. Political Liberalism, Group Rights, and the Politics of Fear and Trust. *Hagar: International Social Science Review* 3(1): 5–18.

Oliel, H. 1992. Land of Milk and Honey. In Sfatayim, *From Morocco to Zion*. Tel Aviv: Pomkol.

Olzak, S. 1992. *The Dynamics of Ethnic Competition and Conflict*. Stanford, Calif.: Stanford University Press.

Omi, M., and H. Winant. 1994. *Racial Formation in the United States: From the 1960s to the 1990s*. New York: Routledge.

Oz, K. 1995. Dust Heights.

———. 1995. Ma'ale Avi. In the album *Achaia Balafa*. Tel Aviv: Hed Artzi.

Paasi, A. 1991. Deconstructing Regions: Notes on the Scale of Spatial Life. *Environment and Planning A* 23: 239–56.

———. 2000. Territorial Identities as Social Constructs. *Hagar: International Social Science Review* 1(2): 91–114.

Palestine Liberation Organization, Department of Refugee Affairs. 2001. *The Palestinian Refugees 1948–2000*. Ramallah and Jerusalem: Factfile.

Palestinian Central Bureau of Statistics (PCBS). 2002. *Palestinians at the End of the Year*, publication no. 854. Ramallah: Palestinian Authority.

Paramenter, B. 1994. *Giving Voice to Stones: Place and Identity in Palestinian Literature*. Austin: University of Texas Press.

Peach, C. 1996. The Meaning of Segregation. *Planning Practice and Research* 11(2): 137–50.

Pearson, D. 2000. The Ties That Unwind: Civic and Ethnic Imaginings in New Zealand. *Nations and Nationalism* 6(1): 91–110.

Pedahzur, A. 2001. The Transformation of Israel's Extreme Right. *Studies in Conflict and Terrorism* 24: 25–42.

Peiris, G. H. 1996. *Development and Change in Contemporary Sri Lanka: Geographical Perspectives.* Colombo: Lake House.

Peled, Y. 1990. Ethnic Exclusionism in the Periphery: The Case of Oriental Jews in Israel's Development Towns. *Ethnic and Racial Studies* 13(3): 345–66.

———. 1992. Ethnic Democracy and the Legal Construction of Citizenship: Arab Citizens of the Jewish State. *The American Political Science Review* 86(2): 432–43.

———. 1998. Toward a Redefinition of Jewish Nationalism in Israel: The Enigma of Shas. *Ethnic and Racial Studies* 21(4): 703–27.

———. 2002. Theories of Nationalism: A Critical Introduction. *Ethnic and Racial Studies* 25(2): 337–38.

———., ed. 2001. *Shas: The Challenge of Israeliness* (Hebrew). Tel Aviv: Yediot Ahronot.

Peled, Y., and A. Ophir, eds. 2001. *Israel: From Mobilized to Civil Society?* Jerusalem: Van Leer Institute and Kibbutz Meuhad.

Peled, Y., and G. Shafir. 1996. The Roots of Peacemaking: The Dynamics of Citizenship in Israel, 1948–93. *International Journal of Middle East Studies* 28 (August): 391–413.

Peleg, I. 2004. Jewish-Palestinian Relations in Israel: From Hegemony to Equality? *International Journal of Politics, Culture, and Society* 17(3): 415–37.

Penrose, J. 2000. The Limitation of Nationalist Democracy: The Treatment of Marginal Groups as a Measure of State Legitimacy. *Hagar: International Social Science Review* 1(2): 33–62.

Perera, J. 1990. Sri-Lanka: History of Ethnic Relations, Formation of the Tamil National Identity and the Demand of Separate State. *Scandinavian Journal of Development Alternatives* 2–3: 67–82.

Peres, Y., and S. Smooha. 1981. Israel's Tenth Knesset Elections: Ethnic Insurgence and Decline of Ideology. *The Middle East Journal* 35: 506–26.

Peres, Y., and E. Yuchtman-Yaar. 1998. *Between Consent and Dissent: Democracy and Peace in the Israeli Mind* (Hebrew). Jerusalem: The Israeli Democracy Institute.

Pettai, V., and K. Hallik. 2002. Understanding Processes of Ethnic Control: Segmentation, Dependency, and Cooptation in Post-Communist Estonia. *Nations and Nationalism* 8(4): 505–29.

Pettman, J. J. 1988. Learning about Power and Powerlessness: Aborigines and White Australia's Bicentenary. *Race and Class* 39(3): 69–85.

Phillips, D. R., and A. G. O. Yeh. 1987. *New Town in East and South East Asia.* Hong Kong: Oxford University Press.

Portugali, J. 1993. *Implicate Relations: Society and Space in Israel.* Dordrecht: Kluwer Academic Publishers.

Pugh, C. 1997. International Urban and Housing Policy: A Review of the Cambridge Studies, 1989–1995. *Environment and Planning A* 29: 149–67.

Rabinowitz, D. 1994. The Common Memory of Loss: Political Mobilization among Palestinian Citizens of Israel. *Journal of Anthropological Research* 50: 27–49.

———. 1997. *Overlooking Nazareth: The Ethnography of Exclusion in Galilee.* Cambridge: Cambridge University Press.

———. 2001. The Palestinian Citizens of Israel, the Concept of Trapped Minority, and the Discourse of Transnationalism in Anthropology. *Ethnic and Racial Studies* 24(1): 64–85.

Rabinowitz, D., and C. Abu Bakker. 2002. *The Stand-Tall Generation* (Hebrew). Jerusalem: Keter.

Ram, U. 1996. In Those Days and These Times: Zionist Historiography and the Invention of a Jewish National Narrative (Hebrew). *Iyyunim Betkumat Yisrael* (Ben-Gurion University) 6: 116–25.

————. 1999. The State of the Nation: Contemporary Challenges to Zionism in Israel. *Constellations* 6(3): 325–38.

————. 2001. The Promised Land of Business Opportunities: Liberal Post-Zionism in the Global Age. In G. Shafir and Y. Peled, eds., *The New Israel.* Boulder, Colo.: Westview, 217–40.

————. 2003. From Nation-State to Nation–State: Nation, History, and Identity Struggles in Jewish Israel. In E. Nimni, ed., *The Challenge of Post-Zionism: Alternatives to Israeli Fundamentalist Politics.* London: Zed Books, 20–41.

————. 2004. The State of the Nation: Contemporary Challenges to Zionism in Israel. In A. Kemp, D. Newman, U. Ram, and O. Yiftachel *Israelis in Conflict: Hegemonies, Identities, and Challenges.* London: Sussex Academic, 305–20.

Rawls, J. 1999. *The Law of Peoples.* Cambridge, Mass.: Harvard University Press.

Razin, A. 1991. The Policy of Dispersing Industry in Israel. In H. Surkis, A. Rapp, and T. Shahar, eds., *Changes in the Geography of Eretz Israel: Center and Margins.* Jerusalem: Ma'alot.

Razin, E. 1996. Shifts in Israel's Industrial Geography. In Y. Gradus and G. Lipshitz, eds., *The Mosaic of Israel Geography.* Beer-Sheva: Ben-Gurion University, 205–16.

Raz-Krakotzkin, A. 1993. Exile within Sovereignty: Critique of Negation of Exile in Israeli Culture (Hebrew). *Teorya Uvikkoret* (Theory and critique) 4: 23–55.

————. 1994. Diaspora within Sovereignty: Critique of "Negation of the Diaspora" in Israeli Culture (Part Two) (Hebrew). *Teorya Uvikkoret* (Theory and critique) 5: 113–32.

Regev, M., and E. Seroussi. 2004. *Popular Music and National Culture in Israel.* Los Angeles: University of California Press.

Rekhess, E. 1998. Israelis After All (Hebrew). *Panim* 5: 60–67.

Reynolds, H. 1987. *Frontier, Aboriginals, Settlers, and Land.* Sydney: Allen & Unwin.

————. 1989. *Dispossession.* Sydney: Allen & Unwin.

————. 1993. Native Title and Pastoral Leases. In M. A. Stephenson and S. Ratnapala, eds., *Mabo: A Judicial Revolution.* Queensland: University of Queensland Press, 119–31.

Roded, B. 1999. Settlers and Frontiers: The Israeli Negev and Sri Lankan Mahaweli. M.A. thesis, Ben-Gurion University.

Ronen, B., ed. 1997. *Report of the Committee Reforming Israel Land Policy.* Jerusalem: Government Printers. Electronic reference format. http://www.justice.gov.il/ MOJHeb/Sifria/Dochot/ (Hebrew).

Rouhana, N. 1997. *Palestinian Citizens in an Ethnic Jewish State: Identities and Conflict.* New Haven, Conn.: Yale University Press.

————., ed. 2004. *Citizenship without Voice: The Palestinians in Israel* (Arabic). Haifa: Mada al-Karmel Center.

Rouhana, N., and A. Ghanem. 1998. The Crisis of Minorities in Ethnic States: The Case of Palestinian Citizens in Israel. *International Journal of Middle East Studies* 30: 321–46.

Rouhana, N., and N. Soultani. 2003. Redrawing the Boundaries of Citizenship: Israel's New Hegemony. *Journal of Palestine Studies* 33(1): 5–22.

Rubinstein, E. 2000. *Legal Aspects of National Land Policy: Comments of the Government's Attorney General* (Hebrew). Jerusalem: The Institute for Land Use Research.

Rumley, D. 1999. *The Geopolitics of Australia's Regional Relations.* London: Kluwer Academic.

Russell, P. 1998. High Courts and the Rights of Aboriginal Peoples: The Limits of Judicial Independence. *Saskatchewan Law Review* 61: 247–68.

Ruutsoo, R. 1998. Estonian Citizenship Policy in a Context of Emerging Nation-State. In M. Heidmets, ed. *Russian Minority and Challenges for Estonia* (Estonian). Tallinn: TPÜ, 139–202.

Saban, I. 2000. *The Legal Status of Minorities in Democratic Deeply Divided Countries: The Arab Minority in Israel and the Francophone Minority in Canada.* LL.D. thesis, Hebrew University.

Sack, R. 1986. *Human Territoriality: Its Theory and History.* Cambridge: Cambridge University Press.

Said, E. 1992. *The Question of Palestine.* London: Vintage.

———. 1993. *Culture and Imperialism.* London: Vintage

———. 1994. *The Politics of Dispossession: The Struggle for Palestinian Self-Determination.* London: Catto & Windus.

———. 1996. *Peace and Its Discontents: Essays on Palestine in the Middle East Peace Process.* New York: Vintage Books.

Salih, M. 1988. *The Origins of Palestinian Nationalism.* New York: Columbia University Press.

Samaddar, R. 2000. Governing Through Peace Accords. *Hagar: International Social Science Review* 1(2): 5–32.

Sandercock, L. 1998. *Toward Cosmopolis: Planning for Multicultural Cities and Regions.* London: Wiley & Sons.

Sartori, G. 1987. *The Theory of Democracy Revisited.* Chatham, N.J.: Chatham House.

Sassen, S. 1999. A New Emergent Hegemonic Structure? *Political Power and Social Theory* 13: 277–89.

———. 2001. *The Global City: New York, London, Tokyo.* Princeton, N.J.: Princeton University Press.

Sassoon, A. S. 1987. *Gramsci's Politics.* Minneapolis: University of Minnesota Press.

Sayigh, Y. 1997. *Armed Struggle and the Search for State: The Palestinian National Movement, 1949–1993.* New York: Oxford University Press.

Sayigh, Y. 2001. Arafat and the Anatomy of a Revolt. *Survival* 43(3): 243–53.

———. 2002. The Palestinian Strategic Impasse. *Survival* 44(4): 7–21.

———. 2002. War as Leveler, War as Midwife: Palestinian Political Institutions, Nationalism, and Society since 1948. In Steven Heydeman, ed., *War, Institutions, and Social Change in the Middle East.* Los Angeles and Berkeley: University of California Press, 200–234.

Schnell, Y. 1994. *Perceptions of Israeli Arabs: Territoriality and Identity.* Aldershot: Avebury.

Schnell, Y., and M. Sofer. 2000. The Restructuring Stages of Israeli Arab Industrial Entrepreneurship. *Environment and Planning A* 32(12): 2231–50.

Segal, J., S. Levy, N. Said, and N. Katz. 2001. *Negotiating Jerusalem.* Albany: State University of New York Press.

Segal, R., and E. Weizman, eds. 2003. *A Civilian Occupation: The Politics of Israeli Architecture.* London: Verso.

Segev, T. 1999. *The New Zionists* (Hebrew). Jerusalem: Keter.

Seliktar, O. 1984. Ethnic Stratification and Foreign Policy in Israel: The Attitudes of Oriental Jews Towards the Arabs and the Arab-Israeli Conflict. *International Journal of Middle-Eastern Studies* 28: 34–49.

Semyonov, M., and N. Lewin-Epstein. 1987. *Hewers of Wood and Drawers of Water.* Ithaca, N.Y.: CLR Press.

Shachar, A. 1971. Israeli Development Towns: Evaluation of a National Urbanisation Policy. *Journal of American Planning Association* 32(3): 362–72.

———. 2000. A Country of Four Metropolises (Hebrew). *Panim* 13: 3–11.

Shafir, G. 1989. *Land, Labor, and the Origins of the Israeli-Palestinian Conflict 1882–1914.* Cambridge: Cambridge University Press.

———. 1995. *Immigrants and Nationalists: Ethnic Conflict and Accommodation in Catalonia, the Basque Country, Latvia, and Estonia.* Albany: State University of New York Press.

Shafir, G., and Y. Peled. 1998. Citizenship and Stratification in an Ethnic Democracy. *Ethnic and Racial Studies* 21(3): 408–27.

———. 2002. *Being Israeli: The Dynamics of Israeli Citizenship.* Cambridge: Cambridge University Press.

Shalev, M. 1992. *Labour and the Political Economy of Israel.* Oxford: Oxford University Press.

Shalom-Chetrit, S. 1999. *The Ashkenazi Revolution Is Dead* (Hebrew). Tel Aviv: Bimat Kedem.

———. 2000. Mizrahi Politics in Israel: Between Integration and Alternative. *Journal of Palestine Studies* 34 (summer): 52–65.

———. 2004. *The Mizrahi Struggle in Israel: Between Oppression and Liberation, Identification and Alternative, 1948–2003* (Hebrew). Tel Aviv: Am Oved.

Shamir, M., and A. Arian. 1997. *Collective Identity and Electoral Competition in Israel.* Tel Aviv: The Pinhas Sapir Center for Development, Tel Aviv University.

———. 1999. Elections in Israel 1996. In A. Arian and M. Shamir, eds., *Collective Identity in the 1996 Election.* Albany, N.Y.: Westview Press, 45–65.

Shamir, M. and A. Shamir. 1982. The Ethnic Vote in Israel's 1981 Elections. *Electoral Studies* 1(3): 315–31.

Shamir, R. 1990. "Landmark Cases" and the Reproduction of Legitimacy: The Case of Israel's High Court of Justice. *Law and Society Review* 24(3): 781–805.

———. 1996. Suspended in Space: Bedouins under the Law of Israel. *Law and History* 30(2): 231–59.

———. 2000a. Zionism: Past, Future, and the Qaadan Family (Arabic, English, and Hebrew). *Adalah Notebooks* 2: 24–27.

———. 2000b. *The Colonies of Law: Colonialism, Zionism, and Law in Early Mandate Palestine.* Cambridge: Cambridge University Press.

Sharkansky, I. 1997. *Policy Making in Israel: Routines for Simple Problems and Coping with the Complex.* Pittsburgh: University of Pittsburgh Press.

Sharon, A. 1951. *Physical Planning in Israel* (Hebrew). Jerusalem: Government Press.

Shehadeh, R. 1997. Land and Occupation: A Legal Review. *Palestine-Israel Journal* 4(2): 25–31.

Shekaki, K. 2001. *Old Guard, Young Guard: The Palestinian Authority and the Peace Process at Cross Roads.* Ramalla: Palestinian Center for Policy and Survey Research.

Shelly-Neuman, A. 1996. Nocturnal Voyage: Meetings between Immigrants and Their New Place. In D. Ofer, ed., *Between Immigrants and Veterans: Israel in the Great Aliyah 1948–1953.* Jerusalem: Yithak Ben Tzvi Memorial, 285–98.

Shenhav, Y., ed. 2003. *Space, Land, Home.* Jerusalem: Van Leer Institute.

———. 2004. *Coloniality and Postcolonial Condition: Implications for Israeli Society* (Hebrew). Jerusalem: Van Leer Institute.

Shiblak, A. 1986. *The Lure of Zion: The Case of the Iraqi Jews.* London: Al Saqi Books.

Shields, R. 1991. *Places on the Margin: Alternative Geographies of Modernity.* New York: Routledge.

Shiftan, D. 2002. The New Identity of Arab Knesset Members. *Tchelet* 13: 11–22.

Shohat, E. 1997. The Narrative of the Nation and the Discourse of Modernization: The Case of the Mizrahim. *Critique* (spring): 3–19.

———. 2001. *Forbidden Reminiscence: Toward Multi-Cultural Thought* (Hebrew). Tel Aviv: Bimat Kedem.

Shor, N. 1998. *History of the Holy Land* (Hebrew). Tel Aviv: Dvir.

Shuval, J. T., and E. Leshem. 1998. The Sociology of Migration in Israel: A Critical View. In E. Leshem and J. T. Shuval, eds., *Immigration to Israel: Sociological Perspectives*. New Brunswick, N.J.: Transaction Publishers, 3–50.

Sibley, D. 1995. *Geographies of Exclusion*. London: Routledge.

Sikkuy. 1995. *Report on the Achievement of the Government in Promoting Jewish-Arab Equality in Israel, 1992–5*. Jerusalem: Sikkuy.

———. 1996. *Arabs and Jews in Israel: Comparative Data over Time* (Hebrew). Jerusalem: Sikkuy.

Silberstein, L. 2000. Mapping, Not Tracing: Opening Reflection. In L. J. Silberstein, ed., *Mapping Jewish Identities*. New York: New York University Press, 1–36.

———. 2002. Postzionism: A Critique of Zionist Discourse (Part A). *Palestine-Israel Journal* 9(3): 307–15.

Singer, J. 1992. Re-reading Property. *New England Law Review* 26: 711.

Singh, G., ed. 1994. *Punjab: Past, Present, and Future*. Delhi: Ajanta.

Smith, A. D. 1995. *Nations and Nationalism in a Global Era*. Cambridge: Polity.

———. 1996. Memory and Modernity: Reflections on Ernest Gellner's Theory of Nationalism. *Nations and Nationalism* 2(3): 371–88.

———. 1996. Nationalism and the Historians. In G. Balakrishnan, ed., *Mapping the Nation*. London: Verso, 175–97.

———. 2002. When Is the Nation? *Geopolitics* 7(2): 5–33.

Smith, M. D. 1990. Introduction: The Sharing and Dividing of Geographical Space. In M. Chisholm and D. M. Smith, eds., *Shared Space, Divided Space*. London: Unwin Hyman, 1–21.

Smooha, S. 1982. Existing and Alternative Policy Towards the Arab in Israel. *Ethnic and Racial Studies* 5(1): 71–98.

———. 1990. Minority Status in an Ethnic Democracy: The Status of the Arab Minority in Israel. *Ethnic and Racial Studies* 13(3): 389–412.

———. 1992. *Arabs and Jews in Israel: Change and Continuity in Mutual Intolerance*. Boulder, Colo.: Westview Press.

———. 1993. Class, Ethnic, and National Cleavages in Israel (Hebrew). In U. Ram, ed., *Israeli Society: Critical Perspectives*. Tel Aviv: Brerot, 134–55.

———. 1997. Ethnic Democracy: Israel as an Archetype. *Israel Studies* 2(2): 198–241.

———. 1998. The Model of Ethnic Democracy: Characterization, Cases, and Comparisons. Paper delivered at the Multiculturalism and Democracy in Divided Societies conference, Haifa University, Haifa.

———. 2002. Types of Democracy and Modes of Conflict Management in Ethnically Divided Societies. *Nations and Nationalism* 8(4): 423–31.

Social Security Institute. 1996. *Annual Report on Poverty in Israel*. Jerusalem: Social Security Institute.

Soffer, A. 1991. Israel's Arabs Towards Autonomy: The Case of the Galilee Sub-System (Hebrew). *Mechkarim Begeografia Shel Eretz Yisrael* (Studies in the geography of the Land of Israel) 12: 198–209.

———. 2001. The Peace Accord: Territorial Apocalypse Now (Hebrew). *Karka*: 110–18.

Soysal, Y. 1994. *Limits of Citizenship: Migrants and Postnational Membership in Europe*. Chicago: University of Chicago Press.

———. 2000. Citizenship and Identity: Living in Diasporas in Post-War Europe? *Ethnic and Racial Studies* 23(1): 1–15.

Spilerman, S., and J. Habib. 1976. Development Towns in Israel: The Role of Community in Creating Ethnic Disparities in Labor Force Characteristics. *American Journal of Sociology* 81(4): 781–812.

Stasiulis, D., and N. Yuval-Davis. 1995. Introduction: Beyond Dichotomies—Gender, Race, Ethnicity, and Class in Settler Societies. In D. Stasiulis and N. Yuval-Davis, eds., *Unsettling Settler Societies*. London: Sage, 1–38.

State Comptroller. 2000 *Annual Report 50B of the State Comptroller for the Year 1999 and for Accounts for the Financial Year 1998.* Jerusalem: State of Israel.

Statistical Office of Estonia. 2000–2002. Electronic reference format. Retrieved May 20, 2003 from http://www.stat.vil.ee/.

Swirski, S. 1989. *Israel: The Oriental Majority.* London: Zed Books.

———. 1995. *Seeds of Inequality* (Hebrew). Tel Aviv: Brerot.

———. 2005. *The Cost of Arrogance: The Price Israel Pays for the Occupation* (Hebrew). Tel Aviv: Mappa.

Swirski, S., and B. Shoshani. 1985. *Development Towns: Toward a Different Tomorrow.* Tel Aviv: Brerot.

Tehar-Lev, Y. 1980. Arise and Walk Through the Land. http://www.e-mago.co.il/e-magazine/teharlev.html.

Tamari, S. 1991. Historical Reversals and the Uprising. In R. Brynen, ed., *Echoes of the Intifada: Regional Repercussions of the Israeli-Palestinian Conflict.* Boulder, Colo.: Westview Press, 112–27.

Tamari, S., and R. Hammami. 2000. The Second Intifada: Anatomy of an Uprising. *Middle East Research and Information (MERIP)* 30(4): 4–10.

Taylor, P. J. 1993. *Political Geography: World-Economy, Nation-State, and Locality.* 3d ed. London: Longman.

———. 1994. The State as a Container: Territoriality in the Modern World-System. *Progress in Human Geography* 18(2): 151–62.

———. 1995. Beyond Containers: Internationality, Interstateness, Interterritoriality. *Progress in Human Geography* 19(1): 1–15.

Taylor, P. J. 1999. Places, Spaces, and Macys: Place-Space Tensions in the Political Geography of Modernities. *Progress in Human Geography* 23(1): 7–26.

———. 2000. World Cities and Territorial States under Conditions of Contemporary Globalisation. *Political Geography* 19(1): 5–32.

———. 2001. Specification of the World City Network. *Geographical Analysis* 33: 181–94.

Tehar-Lev, Y. 1980. Arise and Walk through the Land. http://www.e-mago.co.il/e-magazine/teharlev.html.

Theile, C. 1999. The Criterion of Citizenship for Minorities: The Example of Estonia. *ECMI Working Paper #5.* Electronic reference format. Retrieved April 5, 2003 from http://www.ecmi.de/doc/public_papers.html.

Tilly, C. 1978. *From Mobilization to Revolution.* Reading: Addison-Wesley.

———. 1996. The Emergence of Citizenship in France and Elsewhere. In C. Tilly, ed., *Citizenship, Identity, and Social History.* London: Cambridge University Press, 223–36.

Troen, I. 1994. New Departures in Zionist Planning: The Development Town. In I. Troen and K. Bade, eds., *Returning Home.* Beer-Sheva: Humphrey Institute for Social Ecology, Ben-Gurion University, 441–59.

Tuan, Y. F. 1977. *Space and Place: The Perspective of Experience.* Minneapolis: University of Minnesota Press.

Tzfadia, E. 2000. Immigrant Dispersal in Settler Societies: Mizrahim and Russians in Israel. *Geography Research Forum* 20: 52–69.

———. 2001. Competition on Political Resources: The Development Towns' Municipal Elections (Hebrew). *Horizons in Geography* 53: 59–70.

———. 2002a. Between Nation and Place: Localism in the Israeli Development Towns Opposes Russian Immigration (Hebrew). *Studies in the Geography of the Land of Israel* 16: 97–122.

———. 2002b. Israeli Space in the Era of Peace: Between National and Economic Forces (Hebrew). In M. Benvenisti, ed., *The Morning After: The Era of Peace—No Utopia.* Jerusalem: Truman Institute, 257–322.

Tzfadia, E., and O. Yiftachel. 2004. Between Urban and National: Political Mobilization among Mizrahim in Israel's "Development Towns." *Cities* 21(1): 41–55.

UNESCO. 2002. *The Impact on the Palestinian Economy of Confrontation, Border Closure, and Mobility Restrictions.* New York: United Nations.

Uyangoda, J. 1994. The State and the Process of Devolution in Sri-Lanka. In S. Bastian, ed., *Devolution and Development in Sri Lanka.* Colombo: International Centre for Ethnic Studies, 83–121.

———. 1998. Biographies of a Decaying Nation-State. In M. Tiruchelvam and C. S. Dattathreya, eds., *Culture and Politics of Identity in Sri-Lanka.* Colombo: International Centre for Ethnic Studies, 168–86.

Viroli, M. 1995. *For Love of Country: An Essay on Patriotism and Nationalism.* Oxford: Oxford University Press.

Vitkon, G. 2001. The Privatization in Collective Agricultural Lands: Potential and Risks (Hebrew). *Karka* 51: 27–37.

Vitkon, G., and S. Ben-Eliyahu. 2003. Israel Land Administration: Proposal for Reducing Public Intervention (Hebrew). Hertzeliyya: The Multidisciplinary Center.

Weingrod, A. 1995. Styles of Ethnic Adaptation: Interpreting Iraqi and Moroccan Settlement in Israel. In S. I. Troen and N. Lucas, eds., *Israel: The First Decade of Independence.* Albany: State University of New York Press, 523–42.

Weitz, Y. 1950. *The Struggle for the Land* (Hebrew). Tel Aviv: Tabersky.

Wilmsen, E. N. 1996. Premises of Power in Ethnic Politics. In E. N. Wilmsen and P. McLlister, eds., *The Politics of Difference.* Chicago: University of Chicago, 1–24.

Winichakul, T. 1994. *Siam Mapped: A History of a Geo-Body of a Nation.* Bangkok: University of Hawaii Press.

Yacobi, H. 2003. The Architecture of Ethnic Logic: Exploring the Making of the Built Environment in the Mixed City of Lod, Israel. *Geografiska Annaler* 84(3–4): 171–87.

Yiftachel, O. 1992a. The Ethnic Democracy Model and Its Applicability to the Case of Israel. *Ethnic and Racial Studies* 15(1): 125–36.

———. 1992b. *Planning a Mixed Region in Israel: The Political Geography of Arab-Jewish Relations in the Galilee.* Aldershot: Avebury.

———. 1994. The Dark Side of Modernism: Planning as Control of an Ethnic Minority. In S. Watson and K. Gibson, eds., *Postmodern Cities and Spaces.* Oxford: Blackwell, 216–42.

———. 1995a. Planning as Control: Policy and Resistance in a Deeply Divided Society. Progress in Planning 44: 116–87.

———. 1995b. Arab-Jewish Relations Reflected in Research: Public Policy and Political Implications (Hebrew). *State, Governance, and International Relations* 40: 185–218.

———. 1996. The Internal Frontier: Territorial Control and Ethnic Relations in Israel. *Regional Studies* 30(5): 493–508.

———. 1997a. *Guarding the Grove: Majd al-Krum as Example* (Hebrew). Jerusalem: Van Leer Institute, Center for Research on Arab Society.

Yiftachel, O. 1997b. Israeli Society and Jewish-Palestinian Reconciliation: "Ethnocracy" and Its Territorial Contradictions. *Middle East Journal* 51(4): 505–19.

———. 1997b. Israeli Society and Jewish-Palestinian Reconciliation: Ethnocracy and Its Territorial Contradictions. *Middle East Journal* 51(4): 1–16.

———. 1997c. The Political Geography of Ethnic Protest: Nationalism, Deprivation, and Regionalism among Arabs in Israel. *Transactions: Institute of British Geographers* 22(1): 91–110.

———. 1998a. Democracy or Ethnocracy? Territory and Settler Politics in Israel/Palestine. *Middle Eastern Research and Information (MERIP)* 28(2): 8–14.

———. 1998b. Nation-Building and the Social Division of Space: Ashkenazi Dominance in the Israeli Ethnocracy (Hebrew). *Nationalism and Ethnic Politics* 4(3): 33–58.

———. 1998c. Planning and Social Control: Exploring the Dark Side. *Journal of Planning Literature* 12: 395–406.

———. 1999a. Between Nation and State: Fractured Regionalism among Palestinian-Arabs in Israel. *Political Geography* 18(2): 285–307.

———. 1999b. Ethnocracy: The Politics of Judaizing Israel/Palestine. *Constellations* 6(3): 364–90.

———. 2000a. Ethnocracy, Geography, and Democracy: Notes on the Judaization of the Land (Hebrew). *Alpayim* 19: 78–105.

———. 2000b. Ethnocracy and Its Discontents: Minorities, Protest, and the Israeli Policy. *Critical Inquiry* 26(4): 725–56.

———. 2000c. Social Control, Urban Planning, and Ethno-Class Relations: Mizrahi Jews in Israel's Development Towns. *International Journal of Urban and Regional Research* 24(2): 417–34.

———. 2001a. Centralized Power and Divided Space: Fractured Regions in the Israeli Ethnocracy. *GeoJournal* 53: 283–93.

———. 2001b. From Fragile Peace to Creeping Apartheid: Political Trajectories in Israel/Palestine. *Arena Journal* 16(1): 13–24.

———. 2001c. The Homeland and Nationalism. *Encyclopedia of Nationalism* 1: 359–83.

———. 2002. Territory as the Kernel of the Nation: Space, Time, and Nationalism in Israel/Palestine. *Geopolitics* 7(3): 215–48.

———. 2004. Contradictions and Dialectics: Reshaping Political Space in Israel/Palestine. *Antipode* 36: 607–13.

Yiftachel, O., and N. Carmon. 1997. Ethnic Mix and Social Attitudes: Jewish Newcomers and Arab-Jewish Issues in the Galilee. *European Planning Studies* 5(2): 219–38.

Yiftachel, O., and A. Kedar. 2000. Landed Power: The Making of the Israeli Land Regime (Hebrew). *Teorya Uvikkoret* (Theory and critique) 16: 91–110.

Yiftachel, O., and E. Tzfadia. 1999. *Policy and Identity in Development Towns: The Case of North African Immigrants, 1952–1998* (Hebrew). Beer-Sheva: Negev Center for Regional Development.

Yiftachel, O., and H. Yacobi. 2002. Planning a Bi-National Capital: Should Jerusalem Remain United? *Geoforum* 33: 137–45.

Yonah, Y. 2001. Israel's "Constitutional Revolution": The Liberal-Communitarian Debate and Legitimate Stability. *Philosophy and Social Criticism* 27: 41–74.

Yonah, Y., and Y. Saporta. 2000. Land and Housing Policy in Israel: The Discourse of Citizenship and Its Limits (Hebrew). *Teorya Uvikkoret* (Theory and critique) 18: 129–52.

Yonah, Y., and Y. Shenhav. 2002. The Multicultural Condition (Hebrew). *Teorya Uvikkoret* (Theory and critique) 17: 163–87.

Young, E. 1995. *Third World in the First: Development and Indigenous Peoples.* New York: Routledge.

Young, I. M. 2002. *Inclusion and Democracy.* Oxford: Oxford University Press.

———. 2003. Activist Challenges to Deliberative Democracy. In J. S. Fishkin and P. Laslett, eds., *Debating Deliberative Democracy.* Philosophy, Politics, and Society 7. Oxford: Blackwell, 102–20.

———. 2005. Self-determination as Non-domination: Ideals Applied to Palestine/Israel. *Ethnicities* 5: 139–59.

Yuval-Davis, N. 1997. *Gender and Nation.* London: Sage.

———. 2000. Multi-layered Citizenship and the Boundaries of the Nation-State. *Hagar: International Social Science Review* 1(1): 112–27.

Zakaria, F. 1997. The Rise of Illiberal Democracy. *Foreign Affairs* 76(6): 22–43.

Zalzberger, E., and A. Kedar. 1998. The Quiet Revolutioni. More on Judicial Review According to the New Basic Laws. *Mishpat Umimshal* 4(2): 489–520.

Zayad, T. 1978. We Are Staying Here. http://ping-palestine.org/poetry/poetry.html.

———. 1983. *Hunna Bakoon.* http://ping-palestine.org/poetry/poetry/html.

Zerubavel, Y. 1995. *Recovered Roots: Collective Memory and the Making of Israeli National Tradition.* Chicago: University of Chicago Press.

———. 2002. The Mythological Sabra and Jewish Past: Trauma, Memory, and Contested Identities. *Israel Studies* 7(2): 115–44.

al-Zobaidi, S. Homeland. In *Palestine, a People's Record* (Filastin, Siji Sha'b), 110'. Documentary Film (Palestine/Syria).

Zreik, R. 2000. On Law, Planning, and the Shaping of Space. *Hagar: International Social Science Review* 1(1): 167–75.

———. 2003. The Palestinian Question: Themes of Justice and Power. Part II: The Palestinians in Israel. *Journal of Palestine Studies* 33(1) (2003): 42–54.

Zureik, E. T. 2001. Constructing Palestine through Surveillance Practices. *British Journal of Middle Eastern Studies* 28(2): 205–27.

Zureik, E. T. 1979. *Palestinians in Israel: A Study of Internal Colonialism.* London: Routledge & Kegan Paul.

———. 1993. Perception of Legal Inequality in Deeply Divided Societies: The Case of Israel. *International Journal of Middle East Studies* 25(3): 423–42.

Index

Page references in italics refer to illustrations.

283–84. *See also* Jerusalem/al-Quds, binational proposal for

Biran, Shraga, 132, 150–51

Bishara, Azmi, 94, 164, 175, 176, 180, 181, 183, 297n.2 (ch. 4)

Bitton, Erez, 232

Black Panthers, 143, 242, 305n.21

Bnei Shimon, 206

Bokker, Eli, 188

Bosnia, 161

boundaries, 96–97

Brazil, 134

British Mandate, 51, 55, 75, 107, 137, 139

Brubaker, R., 21

Brussels, 264–65

Buddhist culture, 23

building, unauthorized, 204–5

Bukharian Party, 251

Bund, 54

Burg, Avraham, 4, 173

Bush, George W., 82

Byzantine Empire, 53

Camp David Summit (2000), 73, 75–76, 184

Canaanites, 53

Canada, 40–41, 136, 291, 296

capital: and cities, 189, 191; and ethnocratic regimes, 12, 14–15, 17, 37, 106, 115, 168

Capital Region, *266–67, 269–73, 271,* 285. *See also* Jerusalem/al-Quds, binational proposal for

Carmiel, 144, 154

Carmon, N., 111, 142

Castells, M., 227, 249

Catalans (Spain), 161, 292

Center for Alternative Planning, 150

Chandigarh (India), 264–65

charter groups, 38. *See also* ethnoclasses

Chinese (Malaysia), 161

Christians, 162

cities. *See* urban ethnocracy

citizenship: and democracy, 16, 91, 93; and ethnic affiliation/registration, 126; and Israeli democracy, 85–86, 88–90, 93–94; and liberalism, 89–90; of Palestinian Arabs, 182–83, 184, 291–92, 308n.7; and republicanism, 89–90; of Soviet immigrants, 119; universal, 21. *See also* creeping apartheid; demos

Citizenship Law (Estonia, 1992), 29

Clinton, Bill, 73, 75, 261

Cohen, David, 207

Cohen, Moshe, 208

collective memory of loss, 167

Collier, David, 92

colonialism. *See* settler societies

Committee for the Preservation of Agricultural Land, 144–45

Communism, 245

Communist Party, 63

computing industry, 195

conceptual stretching, 89–90, 91–93

consent to inequality, 95

consolidation, repressive, 278, 279

constitutional law as a foundation of ethnocracy, 37

constitutional patriotism, 89

Coronation Hill (Northern Territory, Australia), 28

creeping apartheid, 276; citizenships constructed/institutionalized by, 126, 127 (table); economic-development component of, 126; effects of, 128; ethnic-affiliation component of, 126; ethnocracy created via, 102, 113, 115, 121, 125–28, 127 (table); vs. full apartheid, 303–4n.15; as Judaizing of Israel/Palestine, 7, 8–9, 85, 129; and political geography, 82–83; spatiality component of, 126, 127–28

Crusaders, 53

culture: Arab Islamic, negative images of, 230; Ashkenazim, dominance of, 216, 230, 232; founding cultures, 291–92; immigrants, transformation of, 233; Mizrahi preferences, 227, 228, 230, *231,* 232–35; popular/public, and ethnocracy, 37, 106, 108; and power relations/oppression, 233

Dahamsheh, Abed al-Malik, 181

Dahari, Aviram, 254

Damari, Shoshana, 233

Darijat, 206, 208, 307n.8

Darwish, Mahmud, 164

Dayan, Ilana, 232

Dayan, Moshe, 200

decolonization, 9, 82, 109

Dellapergola, S., 184–85

democracy: and civil rights/minorities, protection of, 91, 98; conceptions of, 91; and demos, 16, 91, 93, 277; and elections/universal suffrage, 90, 91; and equality, 34; vs. ethnocracy, 5, 12, 16, 21,